Protecting the Empire's Frontier

WAR AND SOCIETY IN NORTH AMERICA

Series Editors: Ingo Trauschweizer and David J. Ulbrich

Editorial Board:

Janet Bednarek
Andrew Cayton
Michael W. Doyle
Nicole Etcheson
Joseph Fitzharris
John Grenier
John Hall
Paul Herbert
James Westheider
Lee Windsor

Hero of the Angry Sky: The World War I Diary and Letters of David S. Ingalls, America's First Naval Ace, edited by Geoffrey L. Rossano

Protecting the Empire's Frontier: Officers of the 18th (Royal Irish) Regiment of Foot during Its North American Service, 1767–1776, by Steven M. Baule

PROTECTING THE EMPIRE'S FRONTIER

Officers of the 18th (Royal Irish) Regiment of Foot during Its North American Service, 1767–1776

Steven M. Baule

OHIO UNIVERSITY PRESS
ATHENS

Ohio University Press, Athens, Ohio 45701
ohioswallow.com
© 2014 by Ohio University Press
All rights reserved

To obtain permission to quote, reprint, or otherwise reproduce or distribute material from Ohio University Press publications, please contact our rights and permissions department at (740) 593–1154 or (740) 593–4536 (fax).

Printed in the United States of America

Ohio University Press books are printed on acid-free paper ♾ ™

24 23 22 21 20 19 18 17 16 15 14   5 4 3 2 1

Library of Congress Cataloging-in-Publication Data
Baule, Steven M., [date]–
 Protecting the empire's frontier : officers of the 18th (Royal Irish) Regiment of Foot during its North American service, 1767–1776 / Steven M. Baule.
    pages cm. — (War and society in North America)
 Includes bibliographical references and index.
 ISBN 978-0-8214-2054-6 (hc : acid-free paper) — ISBN 978-0-8214-2055-3 (pb : acid-free paper) — ISBN 978-0-8214-4464-1 (electronic)
 1. Great Britain. Army. Regiment of Foot, 18th (Royal Irish)—History—18th century. 2. Great Britain. Army. Regiment of Foot, 18th (Royal Irish)—Officers—Biography. 3. Great Britain. Army—History—Revolution, 1775–1783. 4. United States—History—Revolution, 1775–1783—British forces. I. Title.
 UA65118th .B38 2014
 356'.1092241—dc23
                                      2013042983

Contents

List of Illustrations	ix
Acknowledgments	xi
Introduction	1
The Early History of the Regiment	2
North American Service	10
Captain Hugh Lord's Detachment in Illinois	19
Atlantic Seaboard Service	21
1 The Officer Corps of the 18th (Royal Irish) Regiment	27
The Makeup of the Officer Corps	38
Officer Careers	53
Courts-Martial and Discipline	66
Wives and Children	70
The Officers' Biographies	75
2 Field Officers	77
Henry Folliott	79
Isaac Hamilton	81
John Saunders Sebright	85
John Shee	88
John Wilkins	92
Adam Williamson	99
3 Captains and Captain Lieutenants	102
Hugh Antrobus	103
Thomas Batt	104

	William Blackwood	108	
	Benjamin Chapman	110	
	Charles Edmonstone	113	
	John Evans	117	
	Henry Fermor	118	
	Robert Hamilton	119	
	Matthew Lane	121	
	Hugh Lord	122	
	Benjamin Charnock Payne	128	
	William Richardson	135	
	George Stainforth	138	
	John Stewart	141	
	Lewis Wynne	142	

4 Lieutenants — 144

George Bewes	144	
George Bruere	146	
William Conolly	149	
Edward Crosby	152	
John de Birniere	153	
John Peter DeLancey	156	
John Joyner Ellis	160	
Alexander Fowler	162	
Francis John Kelly	169	
John Mawby Jr.	170	
Marcus Paterson	172	
William Perkins	172	
Edmund Prideaux	173	
William Raymond	175	
William Smith	176	
Nicholas Trist	176	

5 Ensigns and Volunteers — 182

James Aldcroft	182	
Charles Hoar	183	
Francis Howard	185	
George Mawby	186	
Sebright Mawby	188	
John Piercy	191	
Thomas Serle	192	
Henry Shaw	193	
William Henry Slator	194	

Godfrey Tracey	195	
Samuel Twentyman	196	
John Wilcocks	197	

6 Staff Officers — 199

George Buttricke	201
Edward Hand	204
John Handamede	207
Stanley Leathes	208
John L. Lynn	208
John Mawby Sr.	210
Robert Jocelyn Newburgh	213
William Smith	217
Daniel Thomas	219
Thomas Thomasson	220
Samuel Turner	222

7 Absentee Officers — 224

Horace Churchill	224
Caesar Colclough	225
John Cope	226
Thomas Cuming	227
William Greaves	228
Claudius Hamilton	228
John Hamilton	229
Benjamin Johnson	229
John Wilmot Prideaux	231
James Taylor Trevor	232
Francis Wadman	234

8 Other Officers Associated with the Royal Irish in America — 237

John Bailey	237
Thomas Bruce	238
Robert Douglas	239
George Gordon	241
Francis Seymour Hearst	241
Thomas Hutchins	242
John MacKay	244
Henry Miller	245
John Pexton	245
James Rumsey	246
George Sinclair	248

	John Smith	249
	Jonas Watson	250
Epilogue		252
Notes on Sources		263
Notes		271
Bibliography		311
Index		325

Illustrations

Figures

I.1	King's colour, 18th (Royal Irish) Regiment, 1751–1801	4
I.2	Postings of the Royal Irish Regiment, 1767–1776	16
I.3	Map of North America, 1775	21
1.1	Officer's button, 18th (Royal Irish) Regiment, ca. 1775	76
2.1	John Sebright's coat of arms	85
2.2	John Shee's coat of arms	88
3.1	George Stainforth's coat of arms	138
4.1	George Bewes's coat of arms	144
4.2	George Bruere's coat of arms	146
4.3	John Joyner Ellis's coat of arms	160
5.1	Charles Hoar Harland's coat of arms	183
6.1	Stanley Leathes's coat of arms	208
7.1	John Wilmot Prideaux's coat of arms	231
8.1	Jonas Watson's coat of arms	250

Graphs

1.1	Establishment of the Royal Irish Regiment, April 1767	29
1.2	Establishment of the Royal Irish Regiment, July 1767	30
1.3	Establishment of the Royal Irish Regiment, April 1771	31
1.4	Establishment of the Royal Irish Regiment, November 1778	32

Tables

1.1	Establishment of the officer corps in regiments of foot stationed in America, 1767–1775	28
1.2	Commission prices in 1766	37

Illustrations

	1.3	Nationalities of the officers assigned to the Royal Irish	42
	1.4	Nationalities of the officers who actually served with the Royal Irish	43
	1.5	Soldiers who received commissions	49
	1.6	Officers commissioned from the ranks	52
	1.7	Ages of officers of the Royal Irish when first commissioned	55
	1.8	Average ages of officers serving in the Royal Irish Regiment by rank	58
	1.9	Highest rank achieved by officers of the Royal Irish	60
	1.10	Officers' reasons for end of service	62
	1.11	Number of regiments served in by Royal Irish officers	64

Acknowledgments

I had a great deal of help in completing this compendium. One of the most rewarding aspects of this project was learning what a giving and supportive community of researchers exists regarding the British Army during the period of the American Revolution. Todd Braisted provided information about those men who served as provincial officers, as well as other links and leads. John Houlding was extremely gracious in responding to a variety of inquiries and pleas for assistance. Paul Pace provided a great deal of information about the officers who had also served in the 42nd (Royal Highland) Regiment of Foot. Eric Schnitzer was helpful in providing details about some of the officers who served in General John Burgoyne's campaign. Don Hagist provided a great deal of assistance and support throughout. Ryan Gale and John Nietz assisted with the coats of arms. T. J. Wendel helped me to search for materials at the University of Virginia. Bernie Kazwick provided several excellent leads. Michael Barrett was instrumental in digging up records for me at the National Archives in Kew, England; without his assistance, this book would never have been completed. This is a better and more complete piece of scholarship because of the assistance of these individuals.

Thank you also to the staffs of the Archives of the Lloyds of London, the William Clements Library at the University of Michigan, the Newberry Library of Chicago, the Illinois State Historical Society, and the Latter-Day Saints Family History Center in Wilmette, Illinois. Special mention must be made of Ellen McCallister Clark and Elizabeth Frengel of the Society of the Cincinnati Library; they were not only helpful but welcoming and gracious as well. Frengel was gracious enough to help

Acknowledgments

me double-check a number of items in my final review. In addition, Judy Goveia of the New Trier High School Library in Winnetka, Illinois, and Jeannine Plath of the North Boone High School Library in Poplar Grove, Illinois, searched for interlibrary loan materials for me.

Finally, a special thanks to my wife and children for putting up with me while I worked on this project.

Introduction

Britain's redcoated soldier is often portrayed as one of the greatest villains in American history. However, just as the years have worn away the edges of the few buildings and monuments that the British left in America, time has ravaged the memory of the individuals who served with King George III's army. A few examples remain notable, such as Earl Cornwallis, who is remembered for surrendering at Yorktown (Virginia) but not for his later successes in India; one of the Howe brothers, Admiral Richard or General William; or even Banastre Tarleton, the dashing but ruthless cavalry commander.

However, unlike soldiers from wars both earlier and later, few if any individual soldiers or regimental officers from the American Revolution have made it into the flow of history. Unfortunately, the caricature that results from obscurity and the fog of time is not favorable, to either the British regular soldier or his American opponent. To appreciate the hurdles that the founders of the United States faced, it is important to view the British Army in terms of the professional career officers and solid brave soldiers of which it was mainly composed. On the whole, the officers were neither the blindly dogmatic martinets nor the foppish wastrels popularly portrayed in American literature and film. These individual officers and men deserve to be more fully included in the annals of history.

In this study, we will look at the officer corps of the British Army through the example of the 18th (Royal Irish) Regiment of Foot. Historian Richard Kohn argued in 1981 that in order to make progress in military history, historians need to do three things. First, they have to seek the "true identity of soldiers" by grounding them in the communities and times from which they came. Second, they have to reconstruct military life at a "greater level of depth and detail." Third, they should pay more attention to the interaction between the military and the rest of society.[1] This book will follow Kohn's directives for social historians by providing biographies of each of the officers of the 18th (Royal Irish) Regiment of Foot, including not only their military service but also their lives before and after their military service.

In conducting a review of the officers of the British Army of the period, one must consider the effect of the emerging regimental system. The eighteenth-century British Army was based on the regimental system, which had been established in the 1680s and was further solidified by the numbering of the regiments in 1751. After 1751, a marching regiment (which is what a regular regiment was called) was no longer known only by its colonel's name; instead, it had an identity that transcended its commanding officer. By the end of the French and Indian War (1755–1763), the regiments were almost uniformly known by their numbers and addressed as such in correspondence, both official and unofficial.

I have chosen the 18th (Royal Irish) Regiment of Foot for a number of reasons. First, elements of the regiment served throughout more of British North America than most other regiments did before the start of hostilities in 1775. Second, most of the surviving common soldiers of the regiment were drafted (i.e., transferred to other regiments) in December 1775, whereas the cadre of officers, noncommissioned officers (NCOs), and drummers went home; thus the stories of the men who had served in the Royal Irish help tell the stories of many other regiments that continued to serve in America. Third, the records of the regiment are remarkably intact. Unlike many of the regiments that served in America before and during the American Revolution, nearly all of the regimental muster returns and many other documents are extant. The large number of general courts-martial involving the regiment provide additional primary source materials that provide insight into the officers and men of the regiment. Fourth, the regiment has been virtually ignored by historians since 1922, when the regiment was disbanded upon the establishment of the Irish Free State.

The Early History of the Regiment

The 18th (Royal Irish) Regiment of Foot was among the oldest regiments in the British Army when it embarked for America in May 1767 from

Cork Harbor, Ireland. The title "Royal Regiment of Ireland" dates back to 1660, when King Charles II formed it as a regiment of foot guards. The 18th (Royal Irish) Regiment of Foot traced its history to the regiment raised in Ireland on 1 April 1684 under the command of Arthur Earl of Granard. The regiment was initially formed from existing Irish independent companies of pikemen and musketeers. The regiment, at that time called the Earl of Granard's Regiment, arrived in England in June 1685 and participated in the overthrow of the rebel army at the Battle of Sedgemoor on 6 July 1685. This period in English history was filled with tension between the Protestant English and the primarily Catholic Irish.

The regiment soon returned to Ireland, where in 1686 the Earl of Granard was replaced by his son, Arthur Lord Forbes, as colonel. In 1687, the regiment was encamped on the Curragh at Kildare, where the men were inspected in detail. Any men in the regiment who had relatives who had served in Oliver Cromwell's forces were discharged at this time. The large majority of Protestant officers and soldiers were also dismissed, and the regiment was brought up to strength with Roman Catholics.

In 1688, the regiment was ordered back to England to protect the Stuart monarchy against the Prince of Orange; it landed at Chester and marched to London. At the direction of Lord Forbes, and in a reverse of the orders of 1687, the Roman Catholics of the regiment were disbanded while the Protestants remained in service. The Roman Catholic soldiers of the regiment were sent to the Isle of Wight as prisoners. Afterward they were transferred to the service of the German emperor. The remaining Protestants, numbering 150, were nearly attacked by a mob until they amazed a local vicar with the perfection of their responses to the Church of England liturgy.[2]

In May 1689, the regiment marched into Wales and returned to Ireland in the same year as part of the mission to drive King James II from that island. At Boyne, Ireland, on 1 July 1690, the regiment had the honor of serving under the eye of King William III. The Royal Irish continued to fight against the insurgents through the spring of 1692.

In 1692, with Protestant succession to the throne ensured, the regiment was ordered to Flanders (present-day Belgium). Landing at Ostend, the Royal Irish participated in the capture of Furnes and Dixmunde in present-day Belgium. At the end of the year, the Royal Irish reembarked for England. In 1693, the regiment saw action as marines in the fleet. In 1694, the regiment was back in Flanders; it was present at the Siege of Huy and then wintered at Ghent.

The regiment was present at the Siege of Namur (present-day Belgium) in 1695, where the soldiers stormed the walls of the Castle of Namur in the presence of King William III. Since this was the only regiment to reach the top of the castle walls, King William conferred on the regiment the title of "Royal Regiment of Foot of Ireland." Before that point, the regiment had been known by the name of its colonel. The king also gave it the privilege of bearing his own arms, the Lion of Nassau, upon its colors with the motto *Virtutis Namurcensis Premium* ("the Reward for Valor at Namur").[3] These badges replaced the Cross of St. Patrick that had been previously displayed.[4]

Historian Charles Messenger recounts the participation of the Irish at Namur as follows:

> Then, the Irishmen of the later 18th Foot hurled themselves on the defenses with a wild yell. Their king, watching the action through his spyglass, could see little red dots forever going upwards through the gaps in the smoke until at last they gained

FIGURE I.1 King's colour, 18th (Royal Irish) Regiment, 1751–1801.
Courtesy of Ryan Gale

the summit, only to be knocked off it. Two further days of fierce fighting ensued before the Citadel was finally secured. It was a notable triumph, the first gained by the new British Army in the Cockpit of Europe, and a stark signal to the French that no longer could they take little account of the novices from across the English Channel.[5]

The regiment returned again to Cork, Ireland, in 1697. In 1701, with the outbreak of the War of the Spanish Succession, the Royal Irish was sent to Holland. In 1702, the Royal Irish stole the limelight in storming the fortress guarding Venlo (modern Venlo, the Netherlands) and driving the defenders over a drawbridge and up a sheer rampart that could only be scaled by clutching onto pieces of grass sticking out of its surface. The French were so amazed by the actions of the Royal Irish that they promptly surrendered.[6] The Royal Irish fought on the Continent for the next several years, participating in the 1703 Sieges at Huy and Limburg and the battles of Schellenberg (in modern Germany) in 1704, Blenheim (in modern Germany) in 1704, and Ramilies (in modern Belgium) in 1706), among others. In 1709 at Malplaquet (France), the Royal Irish faced a regiment in French service that was also called the Royal Regiment of Ireland. The Royal Irish bested its French rival in extremely heavy and close fighting.[7]

In 1713, the rank of the Royal Irish among the marching regiments of foot was set at 18, taken from the date of its arrival in England in 1688. Though ranked eighteenth, the regiment was truly senior to all but the first six regiments. The regiment's 1685 service in England and its service in Ireland were ignored when setting the ranks of the regiments in order to give preference to English regiments.

In 1718 the regiment embarked for the island of Minorca. The Royal Irish remained there until it was called to help lift the Siege of Gibraltar in 1727 under the leadership of Colonel Sir William Cosby. The Royal Irish returned to Minorca after the siege was lifted and remained there for an additional fifteen years, until 1742.[8]

The Royal Irish returned to England and disembarked at Portsmouth and Southhampton in September 1742. The regiment marched to Taunton, and it spent the winter of 1742–1743 dispersed between Taunton and the surrounding towns. In the spring of 1743, the regiment was sent to Exeter and Plymouth. In the spring of 1744, the regiment marched to Richmond and its surrounds. The Royal Irish was reviewed that year by the Duke of

Cumberland. Later that year, it was moved to Fareham, where it was responsible for guarding French and Spanish prisoners at Portchester Castle.

Historian John Houlding shows the Royal Irish as marching or being dispersed for 94 percent of the time from 1742 to 1743 and being in four or more grand divisions for 6 percent of the time. Of the twenty-four examples in Houlding's sample, only three regiments—the 21st, 28th, and 36th Regiments of Foot—were dispersed more often.[9]

After the Battle of Fontenoy (in modern Belgium) in May 1745, the regiment was ordered to Flanders along with the 14th Regiment of Foot and a detachment of foot guards. The Royal Irish embarked from Gravesend (England) and disembarked at Ostend. It joined the army under the Duke of Cumberland at Lessines in May. The Royal Irish was then sent to reinforce the fortress at Ostend via Antwerp. Ostend was surrendered, but the garrison was returned to the Allied Army as one of the terms of capitulation. The Royal Irish, along with the rest of the garrison, marched to Mons, where it remained for several weeks opposite a large body of French troops. The French retired upon the arrival of additional allied troops, and the Royal Irish shortly removed to Brussels.

In the fall of 1745, the return of the Jacobite pretender to the throne caused the Royal Irish to be ordered to Williamstadt (modern Willemstad, the Netherlands), where it then embarked for England. The Royal Irish arrived at Gravesend on 5 November 1745 and marched to the main camp at Dartford. The conditions of the camp at Dartford cost the Royal Irish the lives of its surgeon and several other men from disease and exposure.

The Royal Irish embarked at Gravesend again in March 1746, along with the 12th, 16th, and 24th Regiments of Foot. The regiments arrived in Scotland, at Leith, on 19 April 1746, as news of the victory at Culloden reached them. The length of the trip was extended out of a concern about French warships being in the area. The transports were diverted into the Humber, a tidal estuary on the east coast of northern England, until it was determined the report of French warships had been in error. The Royal Irish remained at Leith only briefly before being ordered to Nairn. The regiment landed at Nairn on 1 May 1746 and remained there for three weeks, until it moved to Inverness. It remained with the army at Inverness until ordered to winter quarters around Nairn and Elgin. In the summer of 1747, the regiment marched to Fort Augustus and encamped in the mountains around the fort. It marched to Edinburgh Castle and Stirling for winter quarters in October 1747. During its time in the Scottish

Highlands, the Royal Irish spent its summers building military roads for the movement of troops.

In the spring of 1748, the Royal Irish marched south into England and was stationed at Berwick, Carlisle, and Newcastle. When news of the peace treaty of Aix-la-Chapelle reached England, the Royal Irish was ordered to march to Glasgow, where it embarked for Ireland on 18 February 1749.[10]

Upon arriving in Ireland, the Royal Irish were posted to Enniskillen and Ballyshannon for twelve months. Besides the change of location, peace caused a reduction in the Royal Irish's strength to 2 sergeants, 2 corporals, 1 drummer, and 29 private men (the eighteenth-century term for privates) in each of the ten companies. This was a significant reduction of 2 NCOs, 1 drummer, and 41 private men per company. Overall, the Royal Irish was reduced from a strength of 780 other ranks to 340 men, but keeping regiments in Ireland on a lower establishment saved the Crown money.

In the eighteenth-century British Army, *establishment* could mean a couple of different things. Each regiment was assigned to either the British Establishment (troops in England, Scotland, or Wales) or the Irish Establishment (troops in Ireland). Rates of pay differed slightly, and the number of men in a regiment varied depending upon the establishment, with Irish strengths generally lower. The Irish government in Dublin paid for those troops on the Irish Establishment. Those troops on the British Establishment and overseas were paid for by the English, Scots, and Welsh government in London.

The other meaning of *establishment* was the authorized strength of a regiment. Each regiment was made up of a designated number of companies and specific numbers of officers, NCOs, and private men per company. It was not uncommon for two regiments on the British Establishment, for instance, to each have a different authorized strength or establishment that varied from the de facto standard. Briefly around 1770, troops in America were given a unique organizational structure, which reverted to the British Establishment's troop strength in 1771.

In 1750, the regiment was removed to Kinsale, and all ten companies were listed as being quartered at Charles Fort. In 1751, the regiment was removed to Cork. Six companies remained in Cork, and two each were posted to Rosscommon and Inchageela. The regiment marched to Waterford in 1752 and to Dublin in 1753. While part of the Dublin garrison, the Royal Irish received new colours. This would have been the first time that the Royal Irish was part of a large force since it reached Scotland in 1746. The other regiments in the Dublin garrison of 1753 consisted of the 1st Horse and the 16th, 25th, and 28th Regiments of Foot. In 1754, the regiment was back at Ballyshannon, with a portion of the regiment at Londonderry.[11]

In 1755, the war with France began in North America, and the Royal Irish was shipped to England. It landed at Liverpool on 3 April 1755, which was Easter Sunday that year. The regiment was ordered to march to Berwick and to recruit up to the wartime British Establishment of 70 private men per company. Two additional companies were added to the Royal Irish that summer, and the officers' commissions were dated from 12 October 1755.

This huge increase took a toll on the effectiveness of the Royal Irish. The regiment did receive all new drums, firelocks, bayonets, and cartridge boxes in 1755, but it was short 450 swords, 20 waistbelts, and 33 match cases when the regiment was inspected in mid-October while posted near Newcastle, Berwick, and Carlisle. Major General James Stuart inspected the regiment and wrote the following:

> Evolutions not so well ~ March and Wheel pretty well ~ Carry their Arms well but are not quite Steady ~ which I apprehend is owning to the great number of new Men, and the few Officers left at Quarters to discipline them ~ the Regiment having had sixteen Parties constantly out Recruiting, And the Companies being separated in different Garrisons.

The Royal Irish listed 2 captains, 1 captain lieutenant, 5 lieutenants, and 7 ensigns as absent recruiting. Captain Robert Walsh and 4 ensigns had been gone on recruiting service for at least a year;[12] 15 sergeants, 15 corporals, 2 drummers, and 22 private men were listed as on recruiting service when the Royal Irish was inspected in October 1755. The regiment had gathered 232 new men but was still 129 men wanting to complete the British Establishment.[13] (When a regiment was either missing equipment or short of manpower, the number of items or men needed was included on returns as the number wanting.)

Sometime between April and November 1755, the Royal Irish was ordered to assist the civil power, according to historian John Houlding. The nature of the assignment is not clear, but it was most likely to suppress a potential riot or strike. The regiment was ordered to Edinburgh in late 1755, arrived in November, and remained throughout the winter. In February 1756, the two additional companies were incorporated into the newly raised 56th Regiment of Foot along with two extra companies from the 36th Foot.[14] In May 1756, the Royal Irish was reviewed by

Lieutenant General Humphrey Bland and then sent to Fort William with detachments at various highland posts. The regiment was ordered to proceed to Ireland in February 1757. According to *The Quarters of the Army in Ireland*, all ten companies were stationed at Galway in western Ireland, along with three companies of the 26th Foot by August 1757.[15]

The Royal Irish remained in Ireland until called to North America in 1767. It was stationed in Dublin by 1766. During its service in Ireland, the Royal Irish was involved in the normal peacetime activities of marching regiments in the British Isles. The regular army was charged with supporting the civil powers in putting down civil unrest and supporting antismuggling efforts along the Irish coasts. However, much of that work was done by dragoon and horse regiments. The Royal Irish's experience in Ireland was most likely similar to its experience in England, where it spent the vast majority of its time dispersed in small detachments. However, the Royal Irish seems to have been situated in larger posts in Ireland than it was in England. While the Royal Irish was stationed in Dublin, it would have had the rare chance to drill as a battalion and in larger formations at Phoenix Park.[16]

After the hostilities of the French and Indian War concluded and the Indian uprisings in America were at least calmed to some extent, the British government began to rotate fresh regiments to North America to protect its hard-won colonial gains from France and Spain. Before the French and Indian War, only a few independent companies of soldiers had been stationed in New York and South Carolina. Because of the huge territories gained by the British, including all of Canada and the Ohio Valley, such a small token force would no longer be sufficient to protect the colonists from either foreign invasion or the Indians, who were not content to simply move west and make way for colonial settlement.

General Thomas Gage was appointed to remain in America as the Crown's commander in chief in 1764. His command spanned an immense area, from northern Canada to Florida (recently ceded by the Spanish) and from the Atlantic coast to the Mississippi River. To garrison this area, support the civil authorities, protect settlers from Indian attacks, and prohibit unlawful settlement in the lands west of the Appalachians, Gage had approximately five thousand men at his disposal, in the form of ten regiments of foot and a battalion of the Royal Artillery. In late 1766, the War Office determined that the regiments worn out by American service would be replaced by fresh regiments from Ireland, including the Royal Irish, which was then stationed in Dublin.

In January 1767, the Lord Lieutenant of Ireland was instructed that the Royal Irish was one of five regiments to be sent to America. The other four were the 10th, 14th, 16th, and 26th Regiments of Foot. The 17th, 27th (Inniskilling), 28th, 42nd (Royal Highland), and 46th Regiments of Foot were rotated home in 1767. The *Pennsylvania Gazette* of 4 June 1767 listed the 16th and 26th Regiments as being sent to New York, the 10th to Canada, and the Royal Irish to Philadelphia.[17]

This was part of a broad rotation of forces to bring home the regiments that had fought in America during the French and Indian War and Pontiac's Rebellion and replace them with fresh regiments to garrison the British Crown's expanded North American empire. Four regiments—the 29th, 31st, 52nd, and 59th—had been sent to America in 1766. The 8th (King's), 64th, and 65th Regiments of Foot would be sent to America in 1768. Specifically, in 1767, the Royal Irish was to relieve the 42nd (Royal Highland) Regiment, whereas the 10th, 16th, and 26th Regiments were to relieve the 27th, 28th, and 46th, respectively.[18]

The rotation of regiments was introduced in 1749 by the Duke of Cumberland with a focus on the Mediterranean garrisons at Gibraltar and Minorca. His system functioned until the advent of the Seven Years' War (1755–1763) caused it to break down. Part of the reason for the rotation was the negative effect on both officers and men of being left for decades on overseas stations. An extreme example was the 38th Foot, which was posted to the West Indies in 1716 and did not return to Ireland until 1765. Because of the lack of a rotation system, the Royal Irish spent nearly twenty-four years at Minorca before returning to England in 1742. According to military historian John Houlding, regiments serving abroad for long periods suffered from a variety of maladies, including mismanagement, disease, privation, and a dearth of recruits. The Duke of Cumberland's system of rotation was meant to ameliorate these concerns.[19]

In 1764, Secretary of War Welbore Ellis outlined a plan for a general fixed rotation between the British Isles and North America. A similar plan was put in place for the Caribbean Islands as well. The rotation plan for America was to replace thirteen regiments from 1765 through 1768. This would leave only two of the wartime regiments still in American after the rotations were complete.

For example, in 1773, two regiments of foot were moved from North America to the West Indies along with a regiment from Ireland. Then a regiment from Scotland was sent to Ireland, and another regiment was sent from Ireland to America. A regiment from England was also sent to America, and two from America returned to England. Scotland had two regiments of horse and two of foot go to England in exchange for four regiments of horse and two of foot. Gibraltar and Minorca's garrisons saw no transition in 1773, but Gibraltar had rotated a regiment back to England in 1772. Minorca would send two regiments back to England in 1775.

However, the rotation system broke down again by 1775 as a result of the hostilities in America. In 1774, four more regiments of foot were sent to America, but because of the looming crisis, the four regiments originally planned to be rotated home remained in America. In 1775, an additional ten regiments of foot and one of light dragoons were sent from Ireland to North America. In 1776, fourteen more regiments of foot were sent from Ireland to America, three regiments of foot embarked from Scotland, and three of foot and one of light dragoons embarked for America from England.[20]

As early as the mid-1760s, when a regiment was rotated home, its men were allowed to volunteer to remain in America or were sometimes transferred to regiments that remained in America. Many of the men in the regiments sent home from America in 1775 were drafted to other regiments rather than being sent home. This process of transferring men from one regiment to another was known as *drafting*, and the individuals transferred were referred to as *draughts*. Although officers, NCOs, and drummers benefited from the rotation system, private men generally did not; those still fit for active service were transferred into regiments remaining in America. This process was decidedly unpopular with the private men, so the established strength of the regiments on the British and Irish Establishments was standardized in 1770, which helped to somewhat decrease the need to draft. The Royal Irish received a large group of draughts in this fashion from the 9th Regiment of Foot in 1773 when that regiment stopped in Philadelphia on its way home from being rotated out of the West Indies.[21]

When the 8th (King's) Regiment of Foot was rotated to England from Canada in 1786, the men still fit for service were drafted into the 31st Foot, which was to remain in Canada. Several of those men, including one named Richard McDead, had originally come to America with the Royal Irish in 1767. They were then drafted into the 8th Foot at Detroit when the Royal Irish's Illinois detachment was rotated to England in July 1776. Some of the same men were drafted into the 31st Foot in 1785, when the 8th (King's) Foot was rotated to Britain from Canada. McDead was finally returned home by the 31st Regiment of Foot and discharged in May 1788 at Portsmouth. McDead had served overseas for just over twenty-one years.[22]

An annual rotation plan was put back in place in 1787 for Britain, Gibraltar, Ireland, the West Indies, and Canada. Despite the rotation plan, however, the Royal Irish was left at Gibraltar for ten years, from 1783 through 1793, when it embarked for Toulon, France.

While in Ireland, regiments were placed on the Irish Establishment rather than the British Establishment, which consisted of troops in England and Scotland. As a cost-saving measure, regiments on the Irish Establishment were smaller in the number of private men per company. This allowed the Crown to keep more regiments available for service while still moderating the cost. In Ireland in the 1760s, regiments of foot were limited to twenty-eight private men per company. When a regiment was ordered on foreign service or returned to Britain, the number of private men per company was increased to forty-five.

In 1767, this meant that the Royal Irish needed to find another 153 private men. To bring the Royal Irish up to full strength on the American Establishment, it used two methods: transfers from regiments not ordered overseas, and the recruitment of new men. The Royal Irish and the other three regiments bound for America received transfers of men from other regiments, including forty-nine private men from the 50th Regiment of Foot. Drafting from regiments in this manner caused many problems for the drafted regiments. The major of the 93rd Foot, which was raised in 1760 and disbanded in 1763, experienced drafting several times as the regiment was "turned out into the Barrack Yard, and all the Best men picked out of it."[23] The Royal Irish also sent out recruiting parties across Ireland to help fill up the regiment. The regiment marched from Dublin to Cork Harbor. In addition to the officers and men of the regiment, an unrecorded number of women and children also embarked with it.

The regiment, consisting of nine companies, left Irish soil on 19 May 1767 aboard the transports *AmityBenediction*, *AmityAdmonition*, and *Liberty*.[24] The Royal Irish arrived in Philadelphia on 10 July 1767 and disembarked at five o'clock in the evening on 11 July after the men had been examined by the harbormaster for signs of ill health. The regiment was temporarily quartered in the Second Street Barracks upon its arrival.[25]

The barracks, also known as the North Liberties Barracks, were completed in approximately 1756, a short distance north of Philadelphia proper. The barracks occupied a large block from Second to Third Streets and from St. Tamany Street to Green Street. The barracks were two stories high and were made of brick, with a portico on the inside of the square. The barracks themselves formed a C shape, with the opening on the Second Street side, which was closed off by a palisade fence. The middle of the C was occupied by a large three-story brick officers' quarters that faced Third Street, on the west side of the property, and had a cellar underneath. A large parade ground filled the center of the grounds.

According to secondary sources, the barracks were designed to be occupied by three thousand men. Historian John Jackson was uncertain that the barracks could hold that many soldiers. He identified St. Tamany Street as Tammany Street. The St. Tamany Street side is also identified as Noble Street or Bloody Lane by other secondary sources. Some portion of the Royal Irish remained posted in these barracks from July 1767 until the regiment left Philadelphia in September 1774. After the American Revolution began, the barracks were often referred to as the British Barracks. The barracks were torn down in 1789, but the officers' quarters remained until 1869. That building was used as a police station and mayor's office before becoming the Commissioners Hall for the Northern Liberties. It was torn down in approximately 1869 to make way for the Northern Liberties Grammar School.[26]

In July 1774, Major Isaac Hamilton wrote to the Pennsylvania Assembly about the need for inspection and repairs to the barracks:

> Sirs:
>
> I take the liberty to inform you that his Majesty's troops under my command stand much in need of the aid of the Legislature of this Province; their bedding, utensils, and apartments require inspection and repairs. I have had the pleasure of knowing this Barrack these seven years, and shall always be happy in declaring that no troops have been better supplied, nor any applications from commanding officers more politely attended to that here; from which I am encouraged to hope, that the House of Assemble will, during this sitting, order the necessary inspection, and afford such a supply as their generosity and judgment shall dictate. I have the honour to be, with great respect,
>
> Your most obedient humble servant,
>
> Isaac Hamilton[27]

In October 1767, the regiment was inspected by General Thomas Gage, and, among other tactics, the regiment "represented a Bush Fight, which gave great Satisfaction to some Thousands of Spectators," foreshadowing of the regiment's assignment to the western frontier. According to George Buttricke, the regiment's quartermaster, while in Philadelphia, the officers spent their evenings in the company of Madeira and women. The regimental band played at the commencement ceremonies of Philadelphia College in 1767, and the officers mingled with colonial society.[28]

The splendid days at Philadelphia were soon at an end. Gage wrote the following to Lieutenant Colonel John Wilkins of the Royal Irish on 5 May 1768:

> Great Regulations are wanted to be made at the Illinois, nothing seems to be on a proper footing, and some sensible and discreet Officer is absolutely necessary for that Post to put the King's Affairs in order.
>
> Your Regiment will be divided between Ft. Pitt and Fort Chartres, Which would you choose for yourself? The Illinois was one of the Governments talked of, tho' I find the Affair on some account on those was postponed. If you like it, your friends may have time to solicit such a thing for you. I shall recommend very strongly that the Officer Commanding may be appointed Governor, with some Judiciary power. Let me know your sentiments If you determine on that post for your command I shall have a great deal to communicate to you on the Subject.[29]

The Royal Irish were given formal orders to relieve the 34th Regiment of Foot in the far western garrisons at Fort Pitt in western Pennsylvania and in Illinois on 21 May 1768.

Seven companies, approximately 371 officers and men, of the Royal Irish began a journey from Philadelphia to Fort Chartres. Hostile frontiersmen hid their horses and carts from the soldiers in need of cartage on the first leg of the journey that took the Royal Irish to Fort Pitt. Some of the teamsters who did hire out to the Royal Irish were still appealing to the Pennsylvania Colonial Assembly several years later to receive the wages they were owed.[30]

When the regiment reached Fort Pitt, it prepared for the trip down the Ohio River to Illinois and stopped there long enough to hold several courts-martial for desertion and theft. Several soldiers of the 34th Foot, the regiment then stationed in the Illinois Country and at Fort Pitt, were found guilty, as was Patrick Brannon of General John Sebright's Company of the Royal Irish. Because of the serious nature of Brannon's crimes, he was sentenced to death. General Gage endorsed the sentence and ordered a platoon of the Royal Irish to carry out the sentence.[31]

In late 1767, a cadre of officers, NCOs, and soldiers had been sent to Fort Pitt under Captain Charles Edmonstone, the Royal Irish's senior captain, with a company of recruits for the 34th Foot.[32] Edmonstone's detachment of the Royal Irish at Fort Pitt numbered approximately 40 before July 1768 and 103 after Lieutenant Colonel Wilkins passed through in late July 1768.[33] Ensign Thomas Batt, along with Sergeant Edmond Sutton and Corporal Charles Insley, moved a squad of recruits for the 34th Regiment to Fort Pitt in the late summer of 1767, leaving Philadelphia on August 26. They also appear to have escorted a cache of provincial arms that were to remain in store at the post. Additional soldiers of the Royal Irish served at Fort Pitt before the arrival of the main body of the regiment under Lieutenant Colonel Wilkins.[34]

Upon arrival at Fort Pitt, five companies, including the grenadier company of the Royal Irish, prepared to descend the Ohio River for the thousand-mile trip to Fort Chartres. The five companies departed on 20 July 1768, leaving two companies in garrison at Fort Pitt under the command of Captain Edmonstone. Major Hamilton remained in garrison at Philadelphia with the remaining two companies.

The five companies traveled down the Ohio River to its junction with the Mississippi River. They fought nature, inexperience, and hostile Indians before arriving at Fort Chartres. The British Army had experienced some difficulties in trying to enforce its sovereignty over the Illinois Country. The Illinois Country was gained by victory over the French and Spanish in the French and Indian War, but it took several attempts to reach the French settlements in Illinois and take actual control of Fort Chartres and the surrounding villages. The 22nd Foot had attempted to reach the Illinois Country by going upriver from Louisiana, but it was turned back by Indians near Natchez. Troops were not sent down the Ohio River until the Indian agents of the British were able to negotiate safe passage in 1765. The primary reasons for establishing a British troop presence in the Illinois Country were to control the fur trade and ensure that the furs reached London and not a French or a Spanish port, maintain favor with the Indian tribes in the Illinois Country who were protecting their hunting lands, and deter the French or the Spanish from trying to retake the Illinois Country.[35]

The strong current of the Mississippi River forced Wilkins to send to Fort Chartres for empty bateaus (shallow draft canoes like the vessels favored by French traders in the Illinois Country) to help lighten the load of the boats going upstream. The companies arrived at the once-French fort on 5 September 1768. The 34th Regiment of Foot had renamed the French fort

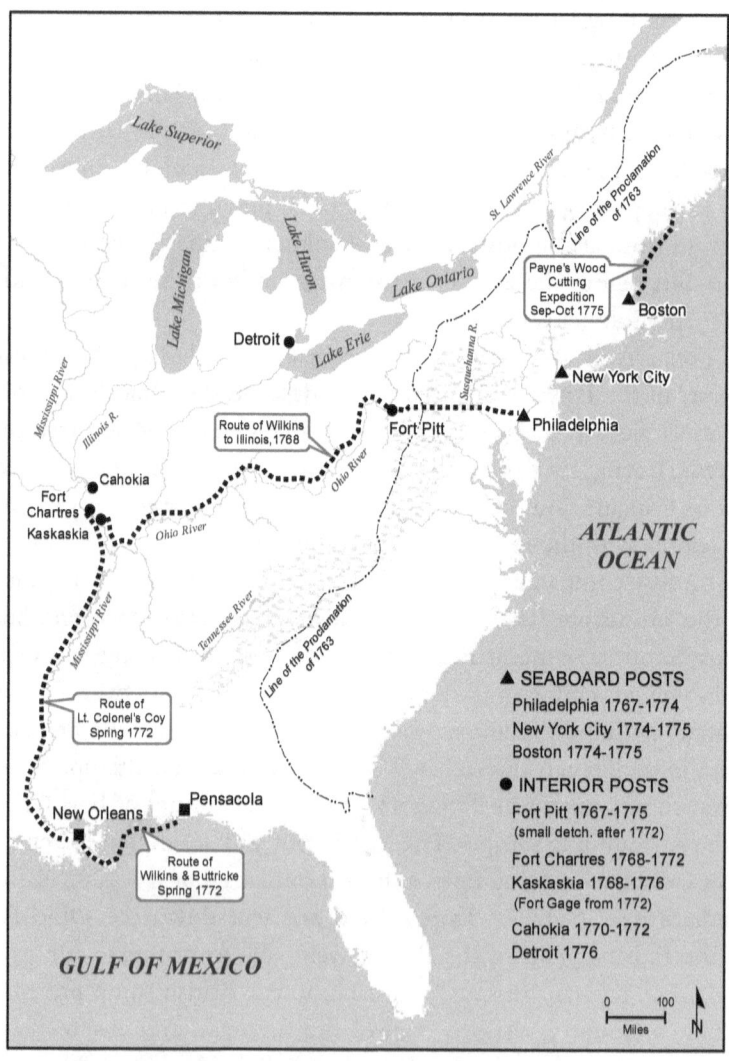

FIGURE I.2 Postings of the Royal Irish Regiment, 1767–1776.
Map prepared by Brian Edward Balsley, GISP

Fort Cavendish after its colonel, but throughout the time it was garrisoned by the Royal Irish, it was known as Fort Chartres. The Royal Irish formally relieved the 34th Foot on 7 September 1768.[36]

Immediately, the Royal Irish began fighting the unforgiving enemy of disease. Fever struck the garrison at Fort Chartres in late September 1768. By the end of October, three officers, twenty-five private men, twelve women, and fifteen children had died. At one point, the garrison, over 250 strong, had only a corporal and six private men for guard duty. According to Quartermaster Buttricke, by February 1769, fifteen more men and "almost all of the Women and thirty Seven Children" were buried in Illinois.[37]

In January 1770, Gage wrote to the Earl of Hillsborough, secretary of state for the colonies, that the troops at Fort Chartres were again sick, although only one officer had died that year. The weakened garrison gave Indians the opportunity to cross to the eastern bank of the Mississippi and alarm the English settlers.[38]

The Royal Irish faced a growing hostility from the Indians. A band of warriors killed three whites near Cahokia, requiring Wilkins to dispatch a detachment from Fort Chartres to that village.[39] Incursions by the Indians continued. The Kickapoos killed three or four more whites in Illinois, and that was followed by the destruction of a plantation within six miles of Fort Chartres in which two men, one white and one black, were murdered. Another white man was taken prisoner.[40] A grenadier, John Knight, was killed in March 1772 within sight of the detachment at Cahokia while tending fields.[41]

Besides being threatened by the Indians, the remote garrison at Fort Chartres had to contend with the Spanish. Gage wrote to Hillsborough that another company of the Royal Irish arrived safely at Fort Chartres in August 1770. This company was sent to reinforce the garrison against a potential Spanish threat. The British command ordered the Royal Irish in Illinois to train to fight in the woods in anticipation of a Spanish attack. The Spanish commander at St. Louis was rumored to be bringing three hundred Spanish soldiers upriver from New Orleans in 1770; although the Spanish soldiers never arrived, the Royal Irish continued to anticipate their arrival throughout its posting at Fort Chartres.[42]

The Royal Irish regiment was augmented in 1770 by an additional battalion company when the regiments in America were asked to increase their recruiting efforts because of the anticipation of hostilities with Spain as a result of the Falkland Island Crisis. The Royal Irish appears to have taken this direction to form an additional company simply as a means of managing the recruits or as a misunderstanding of orders. At least a portion of the recruits for the Royal Irish were gathered from Maryland. The 26th, 29th, and 31st regiments and the 1st and 2nd battalions of the 60th regiment also increased their recruiting efforts in North America at the time. According to Gage, both the Royal Irish and the 26th Foot were able to recruit quite a few Americas at the time.[43]

By 1771, some of the tension between the Spanish and the British had dissipated. Don Piernas, the Spanish commander at St. Louis, visited Fort Chartres on 5 June 1771 as Lieutenant Colonel Wilkins's guest. He was received with a cannon salute that used twenty-eight pounds of powder.[44] The Spanish garrison at St. Louis appears to have numbered around fifty soldiers throughout the period.[45]

In the spring of 1771, the ad hoc 10th company became the light infantry company when light companies were added to all the marching regiments. According to historian Tony Hayter, the reestablishment of the light companies was done partially in response to the Falkland Island Crisis with Spain. The light company was to consist of one captain, two lieutenants, two sergeants, one drummer, three corporals, and thirty-eight private men in common with the other companies of the regiment. In order to cover the cost of the light infantry company, the other companies of the regiment were reduced from forty-five to thirty-eight private men each.[46] The regimental agent paid the War Office one pound and one shilling on 31 May 1771 for the warrant to raise the light company. This company spent the winter of 1771 at Fort Pitt. In the spring of 1772, the light infantry company, along with Major Hamilton, who had been ordered to take command at Fort Chartres the previous year, went down the Ohio River to Illinois. The company arrived at Fort Chartres in April.[47]

It is unclear why Major Hamilton marched the newly formed light company to Fort Pitt instead of taking his own more seasoned company. According to Captain Benjamin Chapman's letter to General Gage, Major Hamilton took the light company, which was made up nearly entirely of new recruits, and marched them west without arms. Major Hamilton planned to arm the company with the stores that were at Fort Pitt for potential provincial use. However, Gage had ordered that the weapons stored for provincial use were not to be used by the Royal Irish. Captain Chapman explained the arms situation to Gage in the following report from his post at Philadelphia:

With respect to your Excellency's remarks on Major Hamilton's marching from this place with your Arms, & c. I am to observe that he could not muster more than 11 stand without disarming his own company here, he therefore proposed furnishing himself if possible at Ft. Pitt. This I am since informed he has done out of the store at that place, but that those Arms are much out of Order & want Bayonets. They are I presume the Provincial Arms that were brought there by Lieut. Batt in March 1768 for I know of none other at least belonging to the 18th Regt.[48]

Sensing the need for more seasoned soldiers in Illinois, Hamilton orchestrated a wholesale transfer of men between the companies at Fort Pitt and the new light company before he went down the Ohio River. The recruits were for the most part left at Fort Pitt, and men from Edmonstone's and Johnson's companies became light infantry.

Captain Hugh Lord's Detachment in Illinois

On 1 December 1771, the British cabinet concluded that Fort Chartres should be abandoned. General Gage, the British commander in chief in North America, received this news in New York in February 1772.[49] This information was sent by General Gage to Fort Pitt to be forwarded to Lieutenant Colonel Wilkins, the commander of the Royal Irish in Illinois. It did not arrive in time to stop Major Hamilton's embarking for Illinois via the Ohio River on 28 February 1772.[50] Major Hamilton and Captain Hugh Lord arrived at Fort Chartres only in time to see its abandonment by British authorities.

Gage ordered Wilkins to "raise Ft. Chartres without delay in the cheapest and most effectual manner."[51] A small temporary garrison was to be left at Kaskaskia, the largest village in the Illinois Country, consisting of a captain, three subalterns (ensigns and lieutenants), two sergeants, and fifty rank and file. The surgeon or his mate was to be left with the detachment, along with the artillery and stores absolutely necessary for the defense of Kaskaskia, while the rest of the troops, artillery, and stores were to be sent away. The troops would receive orders when they arrived at Fort Pitt.

Lieutenant Colonel Wilkins left for New York via New Orleans, leaving Major Hamilton to carry out these orders. Hamilton left Captain Lord in command of the Kaskaskia garrison, where he had under his command the Royal Irish's light company, which had only recently arrived in Illinois, and half of the lieutenant colonel's company, which had been in Illinois since September 1768. The other half of Wilkins's company went downriver with Wilkins and Quartermaster Buttricke as an escort. The regiment's surgeon, Thomas Thomasson, remained with the Illinois garrison.

Lord's Indian problems began before the rest of the regiment had even departed, so when the remainder of Wilkins's company returned to Kaskaskia from New Orleans, it was added to the garrison instead of continuing on to Fort Pitt.

While Major Hamilton was preparing the majority of the Royal Irish to return to Fort Pitt, unfriendly Indians engaged Lord's men. Lord's detachment killed one of the chiefs and wounded two braves.[52] A band of Chickasaw attacked the house of James Rumsey, a Kaskaskia trader, in May 1772. Rumsey, a British subject and former army officer, called upon Lord for assistance. Lord sent an officer with a platoon of men to chase the Indians away, but the Indians soon returned and killed the trader's slave. At that point, the Royal Irish returned fire, killing several of the braves and taking a prisoner. A corporal and six men were left to guard the store.[53]

One of Captain Lord's immediate problems was inadequate defensive works. Before Hamilton had started back to Fort Pitt, Lord had utilized soldier labor to start to repair the defenses at Kaskaskia. Although Kaskaskia had been garrisoned by the British since the 34th Foot had been in Illinois, the fort was in a state of disrepair. The defenses, in Lord's words, were "no better than those of every other house in the Village."[54] When he reported this to Major Hamilton, he was ordered to build a picketed fort, which he began immediately. As late as June 1774, Lord still had a sizable portion of his men involved in the "King's Work at Fort Gage," as the Kaskaskia garrison was sometimes known.[55]

The troops remained at Fort Gage through 1775. Gage's return of forces in North America on 19 July 1775 listed two companies at "Kaskaskias Illinois Country" with seventy-six men.[56]

In April 1776, the troops were ordered to Detroit to enlarge the garrison at that post in anticipation of a rebel attack. The troops left Kaskaskia in May 1776. When the detachment arrived at Detroit, Lord took temporary command of that post, since he was senior to the other officers present.[57] Lord appointed a former French officer, Philippe de Rocheblave, to

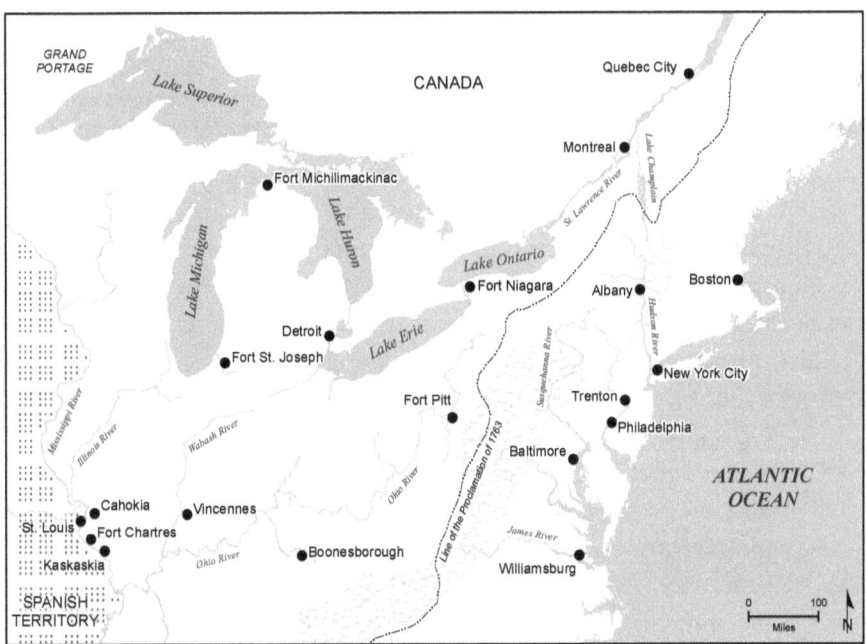

FIGURE I.3 Map of North America, 1775.
Map prepared by Brian Edward Balsley, GISP

command the Kaskaskia militia and serve as commander in Illinois in his absence. Rocheblave surrendered Kaskaskia to George Rogers Clark in 1778 and was taken as a prisoner to Williamsburg, Virginia.[58]

Atlantic Seaboard Service

The grenadier and four battalion companies had returned to Philadelphia via Fort Pitt in the fall of 1772 under the direction of Major Hamilton.[59] Major Edmonstone, commanding the Royal Irish's companies at Fort Pitt, was ordered to withdraw from Fort Pitt as well.[60] Major Edmonstone's companies arrived in Philadelphia in December 1772 after selling off most of the king's supplies and leaving a corporal's guard to protect the remaining material and assist in communicating with Captain Lord's garrison in Illinois. The detachment at Fort Pitt, approximately five men, appears to have remained there well into 1775.[61] This left eight companies of the Royal Irish in garrison in Philadelphia together with a company of the Royal Artillery in December 1772. A detachment of the 47th Regiment of Foot arrived in Philadelphia in the middle of 1773.

The officers of the Royal Irish moved easily back into Philadelphia society. The regimental band was again a key piece of the commencement ceremonies for Philadelphia College in July 1773. In late October or early November 1773, General Gage again reviewed the Royal Irish at Philadelphia. This time, however, the regiment was only eight companies strong and under the command of Major Hamilton.[62]

It would have been at this time that James Wilkinson, later the commanding general of the U.S. Army, encountered a soldier for the first time in his life. It happened that the soldier was a member of the Royal Irish. Wilkinson wrote the following:

> On approaching the gate, for the first time in my life, I beheld a man under arms, in complete uniform; he was a centinel on post, whose appearance riveted my attention; after surveying him attentively from head to foot, I passed without obstruction and entered the barrack yard, where the first, and I may say only, object that struck my eyes was the troops on parade at open order, which exhibited a more impressive spectacle than I had ever seen.[63]

According to Wilkinson, four of the companies of the Royal Irish were quartered at Philadelphia's North Liberty Barracks at that time. The fall of 1774 saw the Royal Irish marching from Philadelphia to Elizabethtown, Perth, and Amboy, New Jersey. On 1 December 1774, the regiment was posted with five companies under Major Hamilton in New York, with three companies under Captain John Shee in Boston, and with two companies under Captain Lord at Kaskaskia.[64]

In Boston, the three companies under Captain Shee were ordered into the 3rd Brigade under General Valentine Jones. Shee's command was joined with two companies of the 65th Foot, and the resulting ad hoc battalion was commanded by Lieutenant Colonel Thomas Bruce of the 65th Foot on 15 November 1774. This battalion grew to nine companies in May 1775 after four additional companies of the 65th Foot were ordered to Boston in April 1775. They embarked from Halifax by 30 April 1775. The original two companies of the 65th Foot were Captain George Sinclair's light infantry company and Captain Jonathan MacKay's battalion company. The companies of Captains Molby Brabazon, William Compton, Archibald K. Gordon, and William Hudson were the four that were added in May 1775. Of the additional four company commanders, only Captain Compton appears to have been present at Boston.⁶⁵

Because it was present in Boston, the grenadier company participated in the march to Lexington and Concord. During this engagement, the grenadiers had one man killed, four wounded, and one captured. John Russell, the man who was killed, had been in the grenadier company since arriving in America in July 1767. He was present at every muster. He was never reported sick, and no discipline problems were recorded. He was a great loss to the Royal Irish.

The Royal Irish recorded the following equipment lost or damaged as a result of the fighting of 19 April 1775: 4 firelocks lost, 1 firelock broken, 3 bayonets lost, 2 pouches with shoulder belts lost, 2 water bottles lost, and 2 slings lost.⁶⁶

It was recorded in a letter between officers that Captain Shee had been wounded severely enough in action that Lieutenant Bruere had to take command of the grenadier company sometime during the retreat from Concord. Shee, however, was not listed as wounded in any official returns.

The man who was captured was Samuel Lee, the Royal Irish's master tailor. The reports on Lee's capture vary greatly. He was alternatively wounded, sick of fighting, or simply a deserter. The evidence does not shed any light on the specifics of his capture. The report that a rebel snuck up on him is plausible, because he was hard of hearing, if not nearly deaf. He remained in the area, opened a tailoring business, married, and raised a family. Either Lee himself or time and Victorian romanticism portray him as an officer of the 10th Foot in some secondary accounts of his capture or desertion.⁶⁷

The grenadiers also fought at the costly Battle of Bunker Hill. The Royal Irish left three private men dead on the field: James Flynn, William Serles, and Thomas Smith. Flynn and Serles were also long-serving soldiers who had been with the Royal Irish since before the regiment embarked for America. However, neither had been in the grenadier company for more than a year. Smith was a soldier who joined the Royal Irish in May 1773 from the 31st Foot. He may have been a deserter who turned himself in during an amnesty period. Lieutenant William Richardson was shot in the leg while mounting the rebel earthworks, which ended his participation in the battle that day. Seven rank and file were reported as wounded. Several of these men died in early July, making

Bunker Hill more deadly to the Royal Irish than was reported in the casualty returns.[68]

Meanwhile, the companies in New York City evacuated the town and sought safety on HMS *Asia* on 6 June 1775. During the evacuation, the troops were confronted by a mob of rebellious colonists. Some offered the men up to fifty pounds to desert on the spot, whereas others threatened the Royal Irish with violence. The regiment's baggage was taken along with the regiment's spare arms. The locks of the spare arms had been removed the night before and buried in the barracks floor, so the mob got nothing more than musket barrels and stocks.

After the events of 6 June, Lieutenant Alexander Fowler accused Captain Benjamin C. Payne, who commanded the five companies that day, of cowardice before the enemy. Payne was found not guilty, but the trial exacerbated a rift between the two factions of officers within the Royal Irish that had begun while the regiment was in Illinois and that was further complicated by the arrival of Chaplain Newburgh, who was a polarizing figure within the regiment. This rift had previously caused Newburgh to be the subject of a court-martial. Fowler was charged with bringing false charges against Payne. Lieut. Fowler was found guilty and sentenced to be cashiered. General Gage showed leniency and allowed Fowler to sell his commission.[69] (When an officer was cashiered, he was not simply discharged from the army, but was unable to sell his commission, effectively fining him the cost of his commission. Fowler is not the only example of a cashiered officer to be allowed by a compassionate commander in chief to sell out.)

At this point, Surgeon's Mate John Linn tendered his resignation. Major Hamilton viewed it as tantamount to desertion, which indeed it was, since Linn was commissioned as the surgeon of the 1st New York Regiment, a regiment of the American Congressional Army, within the month.

Many of the soldiers who had families with them disembarked on Governor's Island, in the harbor of New York City, while most of the single men remained on HMS *Asia* until the arrival of a transport to remove them to Boston.

The companies from New York arrived in Boston without further incident, making eight companies in Boston by July 1775. These eight companies numbered only 209 officers and men instead of the 398 authorized.[70] Sometime in late June or early July, the Royal Irish separated from the 65th Foot and operated again as an independent unit. Major Hamilton, who was not held in high esteem by either General Gage or Lord William Barrington, the secretary at war, retired at the end of July; thus Captain Shee was the commander of the Royal Irish during its final months in Boston. Captain Chapman took over temporary command of the grenadier company.

The only significant service the Royal Irish saw after Bunker Hill was as part of a woodcutting expedition under Captain Payne to Penobscot, Maine. Payne's command included detachments of the Royal Irish under John Peter DeLancey and of the newly formed Royal Fencible American Regiment. The expedition left Boston in October and returned in early November 1775.

The Royal Irish's service in North America was all but over when General Gage was given orders to draft the regiment to the 59th Foot in August 1775.[71] The officers, sergeants, drummers, and the private men who were not drafted returned to England to begin the process of recruiting anew. Officers' servants, bandsmen, and private men to be discharged as worn out or disabled were not transferred to other regiments.

The eight companies of the Royal Irish in Boston were drafted on 5 December 1775, leaving only the two companies in Illinois on American soil.[72] The officers, sergeants, drummers, and remaining men of the regiment returned to England and were posted at Dover Castle, Kent, in February 1776, where they began recruiting a new body of men. A number of men were also discharged in the early months of 1776.

Fifty-eight men of Captain Lord's detachment of the Royal Irish were drafted into the 8th (King's) Regiment of Foot on 8 July 1776 at Detroit. Those men served in that regiment until it was relieved from the northern Great Lake posts in 1786. Buttons from the Royal Irish have been found at Fort Michilimackinac in Michigan. This indicates that at least some of the former Royal Irish were sent to that post. Others most likely remained at Detroit, and some may have been sent to Fort Niagara. Several men from the Royal Irish were captured at Vincennes, while serving in the 8th (King's) Regiment of Foot in the battles against George Roger Clark's Illinois Regiment in 1779.

The men in the eight companies of the Royal Irish drafted at Boston were the first draughts of the war. By the end of the American Revolution, twelve regiments would be wholly drafted. A week later, in December 1775, the 59th Foot was drafted. In 1776, the 6th, 50th, and

65th Regiments were drafted, along with the two remaining companies of the Royal Irish. In 1777, the 14th Regiment was drafted, and in 1778, the 10th, 45th and 52nd Regiments of Foot and the 16th Light Dragoons were drafted after Howe's army returned to New York City from Philadelphia. The 26th Foot was drafted in 1779, and the 16th Foot was drafted in 1782.[73]

1

The Officer Corps of the 18th (Royal Irish) Regiment

The officer corps of the Royal Irish was neither distinctive nor unique in 1767, when the regiment arrived in Philadelphia. Before arriving in America, the regiment had been on garrison duty in Ireland for the previous decade and had not seen large-scale combat in that time. This chapter will give an overview of the officers, and the subsequent chapters will present the individual biographies of those who served with the regiment from 1767 through 1776.

The establishment of the officer corps of each of the British marching regiments of foot was similar in 1767. Military historian John Houlding notes in his work *Fit for Service* that the term *officer corps* should be used advisedly. The eighteenth century had more of an officer *class* than a true officer corps, and as Houlding articulates, the officer class of the British Army was much more fluid than the contemporary Austrian, French, or Prussian officer corps.[1] According to historian Alan Guy, in the British Army of the eighteenth century, peers and commoners shared the officers' mess without the snobbery or friction of later periods: "For the time being, if a man was not already a member of polite society, his commission gave him entry, and the contemporary definition of the title of gentleman left ample latitude as to how social acceptability could be achieved."[2]

A regiment in Britain or America was made up of twenty-seven commissioned line officers and four commissioned staff officers, whereas regiments in Ireland had but three staff officers in 1767. Quartermasters were not allowed on the Irish Establishment until January 1770. All regiments had a single warrant officer, the surgeon's mate. It was usual practice for one or two of the company officers to also hold a staff position, so a regiment would have fewer than thirty-two men filling those thirty-two positions. When light infantry companies were authorized in 1771, an additional three officers were added to each regiment. Further augmentation of the regiments' officer corps would not occur until after hostilities began in 1775. Regiments of horse, dragoons, dragoon guards, and foot guards as well as the Royal Artillery Regiment had establishments that differed from the seventy marching regiments of foot. A few infantry regiments had different structures, but the Royal Irish shared the same basic structure as most of the army's seventy marching regiments of foot.

TABLE 1.1 ESTABLISHMENT OF THE OFFICER CORPS IN REGIMENTS OF FOOT STATIONED IN AMERICA, 1767–1775

	American establishment for a regiment of foot to April 1770	American establishment for a regiment of foot from April 1770 to May 1772	American establishment for a regiment of from August 1775 through 1778, excepting the 18th and 59th Regiments
Colonel & captain	1	1	1
Lieutenant colonel & captain	1	1	1
Major & captain	1	1	1
Captain	6	7	9
Captain lieutenant[1]	1	1	1
Lieutenant	9	11	13
Ensign	8	8	10
Chaplain	1	1	1
Adjutant	1	1	1
Quartermaster	1	1	1
Surgeon	1	1	1
Mate	1	1	1
Total	32	35	41

[1] After 25 May 1772, this officer would rank as a captain, and his commission would read "captain lieutenant & captain."

Table 1.1 shows the number of officers of each rank that the Royal Irish was authorized to have while in America. The colonel, lieutenant colonel, and major were the field officers of the regiment. Each commanded a company as well. The regiment was authorized to have a captain to command each of the other six companies (seven companies, as of 1770). Two subalterns were allowed for each company besides its commander. The grenadier company (and after 1770, the light infantry company) was authorized two lieutenants. Each of the other companies had a lieutenant and an ensign. This allowed for eighteen such officers from 1767 through 1770 and twenty after that point. The exception was the colonel's company, in which the regiment's sole captain lieutenant replaced the lieutenant.

GRAPH 1.1 18TH (ROYAL IRISH) REGIMENT OF FOOT
(IRISH ESTABLISHMENT — 9 COMPANIES), APRIL 1767

31 officers, 18 sergeants, 9 drummers, 2 fifers, 270 rank and file

GENERAL JOHN SEBRIGHT'S COMPANY
1 colonel
1 captain lieutenant
1 ensign
1 adjutant
1 chaplain
1 surgeon
1 mate
2 sergeants
2 corporals
1 drummer
28 privates

LIEUTENANT COLONEL JOHN WILKINS'S COMPANY
1 lieutenant colonel
1 lieutenant
1 ensign
2 sergeants
2 corporals
1 drummer
28 privates

MAJOR HENRY FOLLIOTT'S COMPANY
1 major
1 lieutenant
1 ensign
2 sergeants
2 corporals
1 drummer
28 privates

CAPTAIN CHARLES EDMONSTONE'S GRENADIER COMPANY
1 captain
2 lieutenants
2 sergeants
2 corporals
1 drummer
2 fifers
28 privates

CAPTAIN ISAAC HAMILTON'S BATTALION COMPANY
1 captain
1 lieutenant
1 ensign
2 sergeants
2 corporals
1 drummer
28 privates

CAPTAIN HUGH ANTROBUS'S BATTALION COMPANY
1 captain
1 lieutenant
1 ensign
2 sergeants
2 corporals
1 drummer
28 privates

CAPTAIN GEORGE STAINFORTH'S BATTALION COMPANY
1 captain
1 lieutenant
1 ensign
2 sergeants
2 corporals
1 drummer
28 privates

CAPTAIN JOHN STEWART'S BATTALION COMPANY
1 captain
1 lieutenant
1 ensign
2 sergeants
2 corporals
1 drummer
28 privates

CAPTAIN JOHN SHEE'S BATTALION COMPANY
1 captain
1 lieutenant
1 ensign
2 sergeants
2 corporals
1 drummer
28 privates

Besides the line officers, the Royal Irish had four staff officers, one chaplain, one surgeon, one adjutant, and one quartermaster. These positions were theoretically not to be purchased, since the board of general officers in the 1760s who set the prices of commissions did not include the staff positions in their recommendations.

GRAPH 1.2 18TH (ROYAL IRISH) REGIMENT OF FOOT
(AMERICAN ESTABLISHMENT—9 COMPANIES), JULY 1767

32 officers, 18 sergeants, 9 drummers, 2 fifers, 423 rank and file

GENERAL JOHN SEBRIGHT'S COMPANY
1 colonel
1 captain-lieutenant
1 ensign
1 adjutant
1 quartermaster
1 chaplain
1 surgeon
1 mate
2 sergeants
2 corporals
1 drummer
45 privates

LIEUTENANT COLONEL JOHN WILKINS'S COMPANY
1 lieutenant colonel
1 lieutenant
1 ensign
2 sergeants
2 corporals
1 drummer
45 privates

MAJOR HENRY FOLLIOTT'S COMPANY
1 major
1 lieutenant
1 ensign
2 sergeants
2 corporals
1 drummer
45 privates

CAPTAIN CHARLES EDMONSTONE'S GRENADIER COMPANY
1 captain
2 lieutenants
2 sergeants
2 corporals
1 drummer
2 fifers
45 privates

CAPTAIN ISAAC HAMILTON'S BATTALION COMPANY
1 captain
1 lieutenant
1 ensign
2 sergeants
2 corporals
1 drummer
45 privates

CAPTAIN BENJAMIN JOHNSON'S BATTALION COMPANY
1 captain
1 lieutenant
1 ensign
2 sergeants
2 corporals
1 drummer
45 privates

CAPTAIN JOHN STEWART'S BATTALION COMPANY
1 captain
1 lieutenant
1 ensign
2 sergeants
2 corporals
1 drummer
45 privates

CAPTAIN GEORGE STAINFORTH'S BATTALION COMPANY
1 captain
1 lieutenant
1 ensign
2 sergeants
2 corporals
1 drummer
45 privates

CAPTAIN JOHN SHEE'S BATTALION COMPANY
1 captain
1 lieutenant
1 ensign
2 sergeants
2 corporals
1 drummer
45 privates

However, some staff officer positions were purchased in some regiments, including the Royal Irish. The chaplain and the surgeon were nearly always "professionals," at least in the eighteenth-century meaning of the term: the chaplains had to be ordained ministers of the Church of England, and the surgeons had to be trained in medicine. A chaplain often acted through a deputy, who was often a more junior cleric and to whom the chaplain paid a portion of his salary. Surgeons were, by the nature of their responsibilities, normally required to be present with the regiment, and those in the Royal Irish were always present with the regiment unless they were detached on other military duties.

GRAPH 1.3 18TH (ROYAL IRISH) REGIMENT OF FOOT
(AMERICAN ESTABLISHMENT—10 COMPANIES), APRIL 1771
35 officers, 18 sergeants, 10 drummers, 2 fifers, 420 rank and file

GENERAL JOHN SEBRIGHT'S COMPANY

1 colonel
1 captain lieutenant
1 ensign
1 adjutant
1 quartermaster
1 chaplain
1 surgeon
1 mate
2 sergeants
3 corporals
1 drummer
39 privates

LIEUTENANT COLONEL JOHN WILKINS'S COMPANY

1 lieutenant colonel
1 lieutenant
1 ensign
2 sergeants
3 corporals
1 drummer
39 privates

MAJOR ISAAC HAMILTON'S COMPANY

1 major
1 lieutenant
1 ensign
2 sergeants
3 corporals
1 drummer
39 privates

CAPTAIN JOHN SHEE'S GRENADIER COMPANY

1 captain
2 lieutenants
2 sergeants
3 corporals
1 drummer
2 fifers
39 privates

CAPTAIN HUGH LORD'S LIGHT INFANTRY COMPANY

1 captain
2 lieutenants
2 sergeants
3 corporals
1 drummer
39 privates

CAPTAIN CHARLES EDMONSTONE'S BATTALION COMPANY

1 captain
1 lieutenant
1 ensign
2 sergeants
3 corporals
1 drummer
39 privates

CAPTAIN BENJAMIN JOHNSON'S BATTALION COMPANY

1 captain
1 lieutenant
1 ensign
2 sergeants
3 corporals
1 drummer
39 privates

CAPTAIN GEORGE STAINFORTH'S BATTALION COMPANY

1 captain
1 lieutenant
1 ensign
2 sergeants
3 corporals
1 drummer
39 privates

CAPTAIIN JOHN EVANS'S BATTALION COMPANY

1 captain
1 lieutenant
1 ensign
2 sergeants
3 corporals
1 drummer
39 privates

CAPTAIN JOHN COPE'S BATTALION COMPANY

1 captain
1 lieutenant
1 ensign
2 sergeants
3 corporals
1 drummer
39 privates

The adjutant and the quartermaster were the other two commissioned staff positions in the regiment. The final staff officer was the surgeon's mate, who held a warrant from the colonel in place of a commission from the king.

GRAPH 1.4 18TH (ROYAL IRISH) REGIMENT OF FOOT
(BRITISH ESTABLISHMENT – 10 COMPANIES), NOVEMBER 1778
35 officers, 30 sergeants, 20 drummers, 2 fifers, 740 rank and file

GENERAL JOHN SEBRIGHT'S COMPANY

1 colonel
1 captain-lieutenant
1 ensign
1 adjutant
1 quartermaster
1 chaplain
1 surgeon
1 mate
3 sergeants
4 corporals
2 drummers
70 privates

LIEUTENANT COLONEL ADAM WILLIAMSON'S COMPANY

1 lieutenant colonel
1 lieutenant
1 ensign
3 sergeants
4 corporals
2 drummers
70 privates

MAJOR JOHN SHEE'S COMPANY

1 major
1 lieutenant
1 ensign
3 sergeants
4 corporals
2 drummers
70 privates

CAPTAIN BENJAMIN CHAPMAN'S GRENADIER COMPANY

1 captain
2 lieutenants
3 sergeants
4 corporals
2 drummers
2 fifers
70 privates

CAPTAIN WILLIAM BLACKWOOD'S LIGHT INFANTRY COMPANY

1 captain
2 lieutenants
3 sergeants
4 corporals
2 drummers
70 privates

CAPTAIN BENJAMIN CHARNOCK PAYNE'S BATTALION COMPANY

1 captain
1 lieutenant
1 ensign
3 sergeants
4 corporals
2 drummers
70 privates

CAPTAIN ROBERT HAMILTON'S BATTALION COMPANY

1 captain
1 lieutenant
1 ensign
3 sergeants
4 corporals
2 drummers
70 privates

CAPTAIN WILLIAM RICHARDSON'S BATTALION COMPANY

1 captain
1 lieutenant
1 ensign
3 sergeants
4 corporals
2 drummers
70 privates

CAPTAIN HENRY FERMOR'S BATTALION COMPANY

1 captain
1 lieutenant
1 ensign
3 sergeants
4 corporals
2 drummers
70 privates

CAPTAIN GEORGE BEWES'S BATTALION COMPANY

1 captain
1 lieutenant
1 ensign
3 sergeants
4 corporals
2 drummers
70 privates

Each regimental colonel appointed a regimental agent, who in theory assisted the colonel in managing the accounts of the regiment; he thus served as both accountant and banker to the officers of the regiment. According to Edward Curtis, the agent worked effectively under a power of attorney to manage the financial affairs of the regiment with the War Office and the Treasury.[3]

The agent was generally either in London or Dublin, depending on whether the regiment was currently on the British or Irish Establishment. The name of the agent for each regiment was at the bottom of the regiment's listing in the annual army lists. John Calcraft of Channel Row, Westminster, was the Royal Irish's agent from 1755 to 1757, while it was in England and Scotland. When the regiment returned to Ireland in 1757, Captain Theophilus Desbrisay of Cork Hill, Dublin, was appointed as the Royal Irish's agent. He remained the Royal Irish's agent until William Chaigneau of Dublin was appointed in 1763.

In 1767, William Montgomery of Dublin served as the Royal Irish's agent until the regiment embarked for America. William Cox and Henry Drummond were appointed in 1767, when the Royal Irish arrived in America. Cox was located in Craig's Court, London, and his firm remained the agent for the Royal Irish until the end of this period.[4] Agents generally served multiple regiments. Desbrisay was agent for the 2nd Horse, the 5th and 8th Dragoons, and six regiments of foot in 1763. Chaigneau served the 1st Horse, the 9th and 13th Dragoons, and four regiments of foot in the same year.

The practice of officers' purchasing their commissions is often a source of confusion for modern readers, but the system was put in place as a response to the harsh and arbitrary government of Oliver Cromwell's military dictatorship of the 1650s. Since many of Cromwell's generals had been professional soldiers of fortune, the purchase system was specifically designed to eliminate an officer corps, which had generally been made up of professional soldiers dependent on their pay. The purchase system ensured that the majority of the officer corps was not dependent on the army for either its status or its livelihood. A military uprising was therefore not practical, because the men who led the army would be among those with the most to lose under a military dictatorship. The purchase system created an army with a strong stake in the political and religious status quo.

Charles M. Clode wrote in 1869, two years before the purchase system was eliminated in the British Army: "Parliament has never desired to attract to the Command of the Army, men depended upon their pay either to hold their place in Society as gentlemen or the higher social status assumed by Military Officers over the Civil Community."[5] He went on to explain that foreigners (and, in the period in question, Catholics) were prohibited in the British Army but not in the Royal Navy because the navy could not be used to usurp civil authority in the way that the army could.

Purchase was not unique to the British Army, but the French abolished their purchase system in the reforms instituted after their defeat in the Seven Years' War. According to historian Anthony Bruce, the French Revolutionary Constituent Assembly ended purchase in 1790 without any compensation for the officers who had purchased.

The purchase system was based on promotion by seniority, not only on ability to pay. Once an ensign became the senior ensign in his regiment, he effectively had the right of first refusal for any vacant lieutenancies in his regiment. Similarly, the captain lieutenant had the right of first refusal for a vacant captaincy within his regiment. The senior lieutenant had the option to purchase the captain lieutenancy. If no suitable officer within the regiment was willing or able to purchase, the commission would be made more widely available. In such situations, commission brokers worked to match officers with vacant commissions.

Several times while the Royal Irish was in America, orders were given for officers interested in purchasing to have their agents post the appropriate sums so that their purchases might be quickly confirmed. Occasionally, an officer promoted by the commander in chief would be unable to come up with the purchase price. This slowed the promotion process, and another officer, who was able to purchase, would be found to take his place. The following letter from Isaac Hamilton to Thomas Gage in July 1775 regarding the replacements for Charles Edmonstone and himself is illustrative of the process:

> Agreeable to his Excellencies desire I herewith send you the names of the Officers who can purchase:
>
> Cpt. John Shee; [Lt.] Wm. Blackwood, Ensign Thos Thomasson. The Ensign to be found by the colonel.
>
> I also have Honor to send you the names of Officers who are to Serve to Major Edmonstone's Co. Vtz. Lt. William Conolly or in case of his Money not being valid, Lt. William Fermor, whose money is lodged. For the lieutenancy Ens. John Delancey, The

Ensign also to be found by the Colonel. These Officers are the first for purchase, and Whom I recommend in the strongest Manner for the Succession.[6]

In reality, William Conolly was unable to purchase at that time, and Henry Fermor obtained the captaincy. The other officers were all promoted.

Field-grade purchases were handled in much the same way, but the commander often looked beyond the regiment to other senior captains and majors. It seemed to some extent to be up to the colonel whether the senior captain of the regiment was offered the majority or the vacancy was offered outside the regiment.

In other cases, including at least three in the Royal Irish, officers who were able to purchase were turned down as being unworthy or undesirable by the regiment's colonel, the commander in chief, or the King. Simply having enough money to purchase a given commission was not enough to obtain it. Influence and other political dynamics also played a part, particularly at field rank (i.e., major, lieutenant colonel, and colonel). When Lieutenant Colonel John Wilkins tried to exchange positions with Lieutenant Colonel Thomas Oswald of the former 103rd Foot in 1774, General John Sebright blocked that exchange, saying, "No stranger shall come into the Regiment."[7] It may have been that Sebright did not know Oswald, but the eventual sale went to Adam Williamson of the 61st Foot, who had no history with the Royal Irish, either. However, Williamson did seem to have favor at court, so Sebright either knew him or chose not to stand in the way of an officer with clear influence.

Even with the purchase system, many officers were originally appointed through political patronage or influence with the regiment's colonel. Nicholas Trist was appointed to his ensigncy in the Royal Irish without purchase, possibly because his father was a Whig member of Parliament. Similarly, vacancies created through the death of an officer were generally filled without purchase, providing a lucky officer with a free promotion. Guy stated that as many as one-third of all vacancies were filled without purchase.[8]

One of the complications with the purchase system in the 1760s and early 1770s was the large number of officers relegated to half pay by the reductions in the army after 1763. Half pay was a system that provided an officer with a source of income if his regiment was disbanded at the end of a war. Men who either directly purchased a commission or expended their own funds to recruit soldiers in order to obtain a commission wanted a guarantee that their investment would not be lost when the war in which they were commissioned ended. Half pay was the Crown's guarantee of their original investment. Historian Hew Strachan's research dates the establishment of half pay to the Treaty of Ryswick in 1697. Officers who disbanded at the end of the conflict were eligible for half pay for life. In balance, the Crown was given a ready source of trained officers available to be called back for further service. An officer who was recalled from half pay to active service but who refused the call lost his right to further half pay. Strachan wrote that the 1702 recall of officers on half pay established a precedent for the rest of the eighteenth century.[9]

The Crown had a financial interest in getting as many of those officers as possible back into serving regiments so it no longer had to pay those officers for sitting at home. A number of half-pay officers were promoted into the Royal Irish during this period. A number of half-pay captains were given captaincies in the Royal Irish, and a vacant lieutenancy, which spawned a duel between two ensigns (apparently over who should have been allowed to purchase it), also ended up going to a half-pay officer. When the light companies were authorized in 1770, the newly created captaincy and both lieutenancies were to go to half-pay officers in order to lower the overall cost of adding the light infantry company. John Ellis wrote to General Gage early in the latter's career as commander in chief in North America to inform him that because of the large number of half-pay officers, Gage should not expect the king to confirm commissions offered to gentlemen: "His Majesty's strictly confines himself to taking officers from the half-pay list to fill vacancies. Therefore you must not be surprised that your recommendations of young gentlemen who have not already served, do not nor probably for some time will succeed."[10]

The king's pleasure certainly showed in the Royal Irish after it was in America. Vacant captaincies and lieutenancies were all filled with half-pay officers from 1767 through 1770. In several instances, Gage and Wilkins recommended men for promotion who were not appointed, and officers from half pay were appointed instead. In September 1774, Edward Crosby was the last officer to join the Royal Irish in America from half pay. He was an American who had previously served in Gorham's Rangers.

Prices for commissions varied by rank and the type of regiment in which the officer would serve (see table 1.2). Generally, Guards commissions were the most expensive. Commissions in mounted regiments cost more than those in regiments of foot. In the mid-1760s, a board of general officers set standardized prices for commissions, although in practice the commissions in some regiments still commanded a premium, and market prices varied. The most expensive commission was a lieutenant colonelcy in a regiment of foot guards at £6,700. Ensigncies in the foot guards cost £900. Captaincies ranged from £3,500 for a company of foot guards to £1,500 for a company in a marching regiment such as the Royal Irish. In general, commissions in a "Royal" marching regiment were no more costly than those in the numbered marching regiments that did not possess such a title.

TABLE 1.2 COMMISSION PRICES IN 1766

Commission prices in regiments of foot		Prices of captaincies[1]	
Lieutenant colonel	£3,500	Foot guards	£3,500
Major	£2,600	Horse	£3,100
Captain	£1,500	Horse grenadier guards	£3,000
Captain lieutenant	£800	Horse guards	£2,700
Lieutenant	£550	Dragoon guards & dragoons	£2,500
Ensign	£400	Foot	£1,500

[1] For a more complete list of regulated commission prices, see Curtis, 159–60.

When promoted, an officer paid the difference between his existing commission and the new commission. Thus, an ensign purchasing a lieutenancy would sell his ensigncy, but he would need £150 in addition to the sum he received for the sale. Most extant records show officers of the Royal Irish paying the approved prices for their commissions. For instance, when Lieutenant Lewis Wynne purchased the captain lieutenancy from Francis Wadman, the purchase was completed for the regulated price of £250. Wilkins was a rare example of a Royal Irish officer paying a premium for his commission when paid a £500 premium for his commission as lieutenant colonel.

Unlike most officer commissions, commissions for colonels were no longer sold by 1767. Both King George I and King George II had worked to eliminate the purchase of colonelcies and replace the purchase system with straightforward royal appointments. According to Guy, the kings did not confront the existing officeholders directly, they simply took the opportunity to dispose of each regimental colonelcy without purchase until they had control over the appointment of all the regimental colonels. The 1720 regulations priced colonelcies of regiments of horse between £7,500 and £9,000. Regiments of dragoons were priced at £7,000 and regiments of foot at £6,000. The last colonelcy was purchased in 1762, that of the 1st Dragoon Guards for £6,000. King George I's 1720 regulations obligated the officer wishing to sell to do so at the regulated price to the officer with the most regimental seniority in the rank below him.

Strachan supports Guy's conclusion that George I and George II strove to reduce the proprietary nature of both company and regimental commands. However, Strachan believed they were less successful at the regimental level, since raising for rank continued through the Indian Mutiny in 1857 and colonels were allowed to profit from the cost of regimental clothing until 1854. The purchase system was abolished in 1871. Officers of the Royal Artillery and the Marines did not purchase their commissions and were generally promoted by seniority alone.[11]

The Makeup of the Officer Corps

Understanding the purchase system is important, but more important for this study is answering the question of who purchased or otherwise received a commission. Considering the regiment's title, one might assume that the men, and especially the officers, of the Royal Irish Regiment would be mostly (if not all) Irish, but that was not the case. In fact, the makeup of the officer corps fluctuated depending on where the regiment was stationed. The nationality of the men of the regiment was determined more by where the regiment sent its recruiting parties than by any other factor. The men of the Royal Irish Regiment were predominantly English throughout the period of this study. The Irish soldiers varied from being one-quarter to more than one-third of the whole regiment. English soldiers were always the majority.

In general, the officer corps of King George III's army was a mixture of the nationalities present in the British Isles: English, Scottish, Irish, and Welsh. A few foreign officers served in the army as well, along with some of the King's American and West Indian subjects. The number of foreign officers was small, generally ranging from 2 to 3 percent of the total establishment. Some regiments, like the multiple battalions of the 60th (Royal American) Regiment, historically had larger numbers of foreign, particularly German, officers. The Royal Irish included no foreign officers during its North American service.

The army's annual inspection returns reported the birthplace of each officer, so it is possible to identify the makeup of the Royal Irish's officer corps and the birthplace of nearly every officer who served in the Royal

Irish, with some caveats. Welsh officers were nearly always reported as English, so it is not possible to determine what percentage of English officers were actually Welsh. Americans were also listed in a variety of ways. In the Royal Irish, they were identified as English, but some regiments identified them separately from the English officers.

The Royal Irish Regiment's officer corps was often more Irish in name than in fact. This fluctuated over time based on where the regiment was stationed. The regiment's officer corps was predominantly Irish in 1767, after a decade in Ireland, largely as a result of the Dublin administration's and the Irish parliament's exercise of political patronage. In April 1767, the regiment was inspected at Dublin Castle. Since most young men joined a regiment near their homes, the subalterns of the Royal Irish were mostly Irish. All the regiment's ensigns and six of the nine lieutenants were listed as Irish. The other three lieutenants were English. The colonel, the lieutenant colonel, and one of the captains were English. The major and the other five captains were all listed as Irish. The staff officers, however, were English, except for the mate, who was Irish. So in 1767, three-quarters of the officers were Irish and the rest were English. In comparison, the Royal Irish's enlisted men in 1767 were 61 percent English, 5 percent Scottish, 31 percent Irish, and 1 percent foreign.

The proportion of Irish officers began to decline as soon as the Royal Irish reached America. Quartermaster George Buttricke was English, and Benjamin Johnson, an Englishman from half pay, replaced the late Irish captain Hugh Antrobus. As new officers joined the Royal Irish in America, many came from half pay, and nearly all the new subalterns who joined the regiment in America were English. Of the half-pay officers who joined the Royal Irish in America and whose nationality is definitively known, only one was Irish, John de Birniere.

Several Irish officers who succumbed to disease in 1767 and 1768 were replaced by English officers from half pay, and this started a process in which the national makeup of the officer corps changed entirely. When the regiment was inspected for the first time after returning from America in May 1777, the officer corps had a strong English majority. Of the thirty-two officers who returned with the Royal Irish in May 1777, only nine, or 28 percent, were Irish. The other twenty-three, or 72 percent, were listed as English, including the Americans.

This set the Royal Irish apart with a very small group of regiments. Only six regiments in 1776 had officer corps in which one nationality made up more than two-thirds of the officer corps. The Royal Irish officer corps retained its English majority for some time. In March 1787, the officer corps was still nearly 60 percent English. Of the twelve Irish officers in the regiment, five were veterans of American service who had been with the regiment since before 1767. Another was the son of one of those veteran officers. Five of the other six Irish officers were subalterns. Two Americans remained with the regiment: Grenadier Captain John Peter DeLancey and his nephew, Lieutenant John DeLancey.

The Royal Irish was somewhat unusual in not having Scots in its officer corps. Scots made up 25 percent of the British Army's officers in 1774, but none actually served with the Royal Irish. Englishmen were 41 percent of the entire officer corps that year, and Irishmen made up 32 percent of the officers. It is possible that two of the half-pay officers briefly assigned to the Royal Irish were Scottish: William Greaves and John Hamilton, who were assigned to the regiment but who never served in America. The next Scottish officer to serve with the Royal Irish was Surgeon's Mate William Gilfillan, a warrant officer who was appointed on 8 October 1779. John Hope, a Scot, joined as an ensign in July 1782. He was the first commissioned Scottish officer to actually serve in the Royal Irish in at least fifteen years.[12]

Regarding the English officers, there was no specific geographic area from which they were drawn. For example, Hugh Lord appears to have been from Hampshire in the south,; George Buttricke was from Nottinghamshire in central England, Thomas Thomasson was from York in north-central England, and Nicholas Trist was from Devonshire in the far southwest. None appear to have been Welsh. Unfortunately, it is more difficult to determine the places from which the Irish officers originated, but they were also from throughout the kingdom. John Shee was from Kilkenny County. Edward Hand was from Kings County near Dublin, and Henry Folliott was probably from Sligo County.

A few officers were Americans. John Peter DeLancey was from an established New York family. Edward Crosby, who joined the Royal Irish from half pay in 1774, had served in Gorham's Rangers in the French and Indian War and was certainly American. John Lynn was an American, and when hostiles broke out in America, he left the Royal Irish to practice medicine among the Continental troops. Alexander Fowler was originally commissioned in an independent company in Jamaica and may have been from the West Indies. Brumwell's study of the officers in America in 1757 shows that 6.5 percent of the officers were identified as American. A similar percentage was listed as foreign.[13]

The other regiments with kingdom titles in the period also had officer corps that did not necessarily follow the expected national composition. For example, the 23rd (Royal Welch Fusiliers) Regiment of Foot was not predominantly Welsh. In the 23rd Foot, there were thirteen Irish officers and only eleven English and Welsh officers. Three others were Scots, in 1769. However, the 42nd (Royal Highland) Regiment's officer corps was almost entirely Scottish in character. In 1775, the 42nd had one English and one Irish officer; the others were all Scottish. The 1784 inspection returns for the 42nd Foot still listed only two non-Scottish officers: one English and one Irish.

In comparison, consider the 55th Foot, which was stationed in southeastern Ireland after its return from the French and Indian War in America. It had originally been raised at Stirling, Scotland, in 1755. In 1775, after serving in Ireland for more than a decade, the regiment was nearly 60 percent Irish, 20 percent English, and 20 percent Scottish. Five of the seven Scottish officers had at least nineteen years of service. The 2nd Horse, which had been in Ireland for a considerable time, had four English officers and fifteen Irish officers.

The 6th (Inniskilling) Regiment of Dragoons might be assumed to have a strong Irish representation in its officer corps, but many years of service in England changed that. When it was reviewed at Blackheath in May 1775, its officer corps included fourteen Englishmen, two Scots, and only five Irishmen. The 10th Dragoons, which rarely ventured from England, was entirely officered by Englishmen. Even its enlisted ranks were predominantly English, with 160 of its 186 troopers being of English origin. Among the regiments of foot in England, the 32nd Foot, reviewed at Guilford in 1775, included a strong majority of English officers, at 67 percent. Another 12 percent were Irish, and 19 percent were Scottish. One of the most mixed regiments was the 36th Foot, with thirteen English, six Irish, eleven Scottish, and four foreign officers when it was reviewed at Winchester in 1775.[14]

The officer corps of the Royal Irish therefore followed a somewhat typical pattern throughout its American service and the periods immediately before and after that service. It tended to draw subalterns from the area in which it was serving. While in America, it gathered officers from a wider range of backgrounds than it did when in either Ireland or England. When it was posted to the Channel Islands in 1781 and then to Gibraltar in 1783, it again began to attract officers from a wider range of backgrounds.

Of the 66 officers identified as part of the regiment's officer corps while in service in North America, the nationalities of 56 are definitely known (see table 1.3). Of those 56, 32 were listed as English, including 3–5 Americans, and 25 were Irish. Of the 10 officers whose nationality was not definitely identified, 2 were probably Scottish, and another 2 were most likely English. One officer was listed as both English and Irish on various lists. He is included in the English officers in this study.

TABLE 1.3 NATIONALITIES OF THE OFFICERS ASSIGNED TO THE ROYAL IRISH

Nationality	Total no. of officers assigned to the Royal Irish Regiment			
	Identified	Probable	Total	Percentage of corps (rounded)
English[1]	27 (32)		27 (32)	40% (48%)
Americans[2]	3	2	5	7.5%
Irish	25		25	37%
Scottish		2	2	3%
Foreign	0		0	0%
Unknown			8	12%
Total			67	

1 The parenthetical number includes the known and probable Americans, listed separately.
2 Americans were listed as English by the Royal Irish and so are included in the number of English officers.

It was somewhat unique that the Royal Irish did not include any Scottish officers who actually served with the regiment in America even though nearly 25 percent of the British Army's officer corps was Scottish by 1775. Guy estimated the Scottish segment of the officer corps to be as high as one-third of the total commissioned men by the mid-1760s. Unfortunately, the reason the Royal Irish did not have any Scottish officers in its ranks is not clear. It could simply be that Colonel John Sebright was not fond of Scots, but there is no evidence to support that theory. Strachan's research found that Scots were overrepresented in the officer ranks, and he stated that Scots embraced the opportunities opened to them through the army and the creation of Britain.[15]

Simply finding officers from all three countries and the colonies was only the first step. Those officers then had to embark with their troops and be convinced to remain there. Officer absenteeism was a significant problem for the British Army for much of the eighteenth century. At least within the Royal Irish during its North American service, it appears that

Irish officers were much more likely to actually actively serve with the regiment than English officers were (see table 1.4). Three of the English officers who did not serve with the regiment included Colonel Sebright and two of the regiment's chaplains. It was rare for the regiment's colonel to actively serve with the regiment regardless of the posting, and the same was true of the chaplains. A chaplain usually appointed a deputy, a (usually young) cleric to accompany the regiment for part of the pay.

TABLE 1.4 NATIONALITIES OF THE OFFICERS WHO ACTUALLY SERVED WITH THE ROYAL IRISH

Nationality	Total no. of officers who served with the Royal Irish Regiment in America			
	Identified	Probable	Total	Percentage of officers (rounded)
English	22 (27)		22 (27)[1]	42% (52%)
Americans[2]	3	2	5	10%
Irish	23		23	44%
Scottish			0	0%
Foreign			0	0%
Unknown	2		2	4%
Total	50		52	

1 The number in parentheses includes the known and probable Americans, listed separately.
2 Americans were listed as English by the Royal Irish and so are included in the number of English officers.

Chaplain Leathes was an extreme example: he does not appear to have served at all with the Royal Irish during the twenty-two years he drew pay as the regiment's chaplain. In fact, when Chaplain Daniel Thomas asked Sebright for permission to sell his commission, Sebright insisted it be sold to a clergyman willing to actively serve with the regiment in America. Leathes's absenteeism is not the worst example. Chaplain Peter Vatass of the 14th Regiment of Dragoons is listed in the 1772 inspection returns of his regiment as "not yet joined," and he had been appointed on 24 December 1745. He had not served even one day with the regiment in twenty-seven years, but he was still listed as the regiment's chaplain in 1780. By then, he had drawn thirty-five years of pay without ever giving a single sermon to the regiment. When the four chaplains of the Royal Artillery were ordered to attend a royal review in 1785, one begged leave because he was eighty-six. Among the regiments of General John Burgoyne's expedition from Canada in 1777, no chaplain was present—only a deputy, a Reverend Brudenell.[16]

In terms of the number of officers actually present with the Royal Irish, of the thirty men who held commissions before the regiment embarked for America, all but three served in America. Those three included the colonel, the chaplain, and a one lieutenant. The absentee lieutenant, Francis Wadman, would technically remain with the regiment until 1771, and he was promoted to captain lieutenant while absent. Only Sebright would remain commissioned in the regiment throughout its American service even though he never served in America.

Absenteeism was not the only way to avoid American service; several officers chose to sell their commissions before embarking. After the 1 January 1767 order to embark for America was given to the Royal Irish, three ensigns and the surgeon resigned. Samuel Scott, the regiment's surgeon since 1752, simply might not have wanted to bother traveling to America. Ensign James Taylor Trevor was approximately eleven years old when the regiment was ordered to embark, so his parents may have played a role in selling his commission. He purchased a commission in the 55th Foot before the Royal Irish embarked. However, the 55th had just returned from America in 1763 and would remain in Ireland for more than a decade. It was a safe choice for Trevor in his teenage years.

Ensigns Claudius Hamilton and Caesar Colclough also left the Royal Irish. Neither continued a military career. The Royal Irish would see another set of officers retire or resign in April to June 1775, when Gage ordered all absentee officers to join their regiments in America and the Royal Irish was faced with active campaigning in New England. In other regiments, a similar pattern emerged as older officers, mostly veterans of the French and Indian War, sold their commissions before their regiments embarked for America in 1775. For example, the 55th Foot, stationed in Ireland in 1774 and 1775, lost a couple of veteran officers who had served in America during the previous war. Captain William Winepress had served as the regiment's adjutant during the previous war but sold his commission in July 1774. Henry Gudgeon had been a lieutenant in the 55th since 1760 and sold his commission in 1775.[17]

Of the thirty-five officers who were commissioned in the Royal Irish after it arrived in America, ten, or 29 percent, do not appear to have ever served with the Royal Irish, including Chaplain Daniel Thomas. He appears to have officiated through a deputy until he sold his commission in 1772. Of the other nine officers who did not serve in America, four had been appointed to the regiment from half pay. Three of those officers resigned, and the fourth went back on half pay. Two of the others were appointed late in the regiment's North American service and were simply not able to join the regiment before its American service ended, but both of those officers, Adam Williamson and James Aldercroft, actively served in the Royal Irish and other regiments during their careers. Two others purchased ensigncies in the Royal Irish and then waited to find "better" commissions in mounted regiments. The last of the nine officers, John Wilmot Prideaux, appears to have purchased a commission simply to be able to say he was in the military. It is also possible that he purchased it with the intention of giving it to his younger brother Edmund, who did eventually serve with the regiment in America.

Historian Stephen Conway did a study of the absenteeism rates among the British regiments of foot from 1760 to 1780. His study found high levels of absenteeism, with an average of slightly more than 41 percent of the officers absent during both the Seven Years' War and the American War of Independence. During the interwar period, 1765–1775, he found an absentee rate of 47.4 percent among the regiments studied. The lowest absenteeism rate was 22.6 percent for the 44th Foot in Ireland in January 1772.

Given that backdrop, the absenteeism of the Royal Irish appears minimal. According to Guy, attendance regulations allowed for one-third to one-half of captains to be absent in time of peace, and at least one of the field officers was supposed to be present, which allowed the other to be absent. Lord Barrington sent Gage a request from the Duke of Northumberland to allow Major Henry Pulleine of the 16th Foot to return to Britain for his health in May 1768. The duke's request noted that "there is another field officer on the spot to have the charge of the regiment in his absence," which supports Guy's assertion that only one field officer had to be present in peacetime.[18] It was so common for at least one of the field officers to be absent from a regiment, even during active campaigning, that Lieutenant Colonel Eyre Massey of the 27th Foot bragged in a memorial to Lord Jeffery Amherst that he was the only field officer in America who had not been absent from his regiment at some point during the French and Indian War. Similarly, the 55th Foot was commanded by a captain at Princeton, New Jersey, in January 1777 because all the field officers were absent on other duties.[19]

When the regiment was inspected in April 1767 at Dublin, all but four officers were present. Three of those four did not serve in America. The number of officers present was higher than any regiment reported by Stephen Conway. When the Royal Irish was reviewed in April 1767, 87 percent of the officers were present. The rate of officers absent with leave from the regiment remained at 13 percent through October 1767, when the regiment was mustered in Philadelphia.

In April 1768, as the regiment prepared to set out for the western posts in Pennsylvania and Illinois, 17 percent of the officers were absent. The increase in absenteeism was directly related to the death of Hugh Antrobus, who was replaced by an absentee from half pay, Benjamin Johnson. Ensign Henry Shaw died in November 1767 but was not replaced in time for the April muster. His commission went to absentee Sir John Wilmot Prideaux.

The next few years saw the absentee rate increase as the officers who died at the western posts were replaced by a number of officers from half pay, several of whom never joined the regiment. Others needed time to make their way to their new assignments. Alexander Fowler was appointed to a lieutenancy from half pay in August 1768. He finally reached his company in Illinois in the spring of 1770. John Ellis was either less able or less inclined to reach his new assignment in Illinois after he purchased a commission in the Royal Irish in April 1770. The adopted son of a former Georgia governor, Ellis waited in Philadelphia for his company to come to him. He was given permission in December 1771 to serve with the company, which remained in Philadelphia, while he worked out his western travel arrangements. Before he could embark for the Ohio River, his assigned company was one the five ordered to return to the East Coast.

When eight companies of the Royal Irish were again mustered at Philadelphia in November 1772, nine officers were absent out of twenty-seven assigned. Excluding the four officers in Illinois, the absentee rate among officers had risen to 33 percent. However, the spring of 1773 would see more officers absent; many were on leave after having been at the western posts for more than four years. Only 50 percent of the officers were serving with the Royal Irish in July 1773. By July 1774, the officers were returning to the regiment from leave, and 69 percent of the officers were on duty, including one officer on recruiting service. Only one muster was recorded after the fighting began at Boston, but Gage's order to the absentee officers to rejoin their regiments had had its effect on the Royal Irish: less than 10 percent of the officers were absent from their companies in either Boston or Illinois. It was the lowest rate of absenteeism the regiment experienced during its North American service.

The Royal Irish was next mustered at Dover, England, in August 1776, and the absenteeism rate of the officers still remained low. Sixteen (50 percent) of the officers were at Dover Castle. Seven (21 percent) were on recruiting service throughout the British Isles. Another six (18 percent) were in America, either with Hugh Lord's detachment at Detroit or with provincial regiments. Only four officers were absent, including William Richardson, who was recovering from wounds received at Bunker Hill.

The trend continued in the Royal Irish, and only four officers were listed as absent when the regiment was inspected in May 1777. This included Lieutenant John DeLancey, but he was in fact on his way to America to serve with Ferguson's Rifle Corps. Excluding the colonel, the other two absent officers were young, recently appointed ensigns. So 91 percent of the officer corps were performing their duties. Included in that group were five officers on recruiting duty and one officer, Benjamin Charnock Payne, serving in America. At Warley Camp, outside London, in August 1779, the Royal Irish was still missing only a few of its officers at inspection. The colonel and the lieutenant colonel were both absent, and four commissions were vacant because of recent promotions in newly raised regiments. Twenty-four of the regiment's twenty-nine assigned officers were present, and DeLancey was serving in America. So the Royal Irish's absentee rate among its officer corps was only 12 percent.[20]

Overall, the Royal Irish maintained a particularly low rate of absenteeism among its officer corps throughout the majority of its North American service—significantly lower than many regiments and less than half of the lowest rate identified in Conway's study.

Although there is no clear explanation for the Royal Irish's officers to have been more attentive to duty than officers in similar regiments, Colonel Sebright seems to have taken a strong interest in only bringing officers into the regiment who would actually serve. Sebright's oversight of and interest in the Royal Irish regiment was probably responsible for the high level of service shown by the officers.[21]

Sebright's concern for and influence on the Royal Irish played out in other ways as well. One of the most extreme forms of influence a colonel could exert was to raise a man out of the ranks. Sebright's patronage was potentially felt the strongest by John Mawby Sr., whom he raised from the ranks. Few officers in the eighteenth-century British Army could trace their origins back to enlisted service. At best, the purchase system severely limited access to a commission for men born without money or influence. The few men who did are now often referred to as *rankers*, for having served in the ranks of the battalion, but the term does not appear to have been commonly used in the late eighteenth century. Less than 5 percent of the officers in the army came from the ranks. Bruce stated that the purchase system itself effectively limited candidates from the ranks and that large-scale promotion from the ranks did not occur until World War I.

A comprehensive review of British Army officers who served in America, however, identified at least thirty-seven officers who were promoted from the ranks during the Revolutionary War period, out of more than three thousand officers studied. A review of four regiments showed only five men who had been promoted from the ranks, out of nearly four hundred officers included in the study. Alfred Temple Patterson noted that the sergeants promoted into new regiments in 1778 and 1779 were given those roles because of a shortage of officers and not necessarily because of any systematized plan to promote men of such backgrounds. Houlding identified approximately two hundred former sergeants who were commissioned in the 1730s and 1740s and potentially up to seven hundred men who were commissioned in total from the ranks during the eighteenth century. Most of those promotions were made during periods of extreme expansion of the army when shortages of officers existed.[22]

The Royal Irish had at least two officers who had served in the ranks: George Buttricke and John Mawby Sr. Mawby held dual commissions in the Royal Irish and was the regiment's adjutant for the majority of its American service. Buttricke was the regiment's quartermaster from 1767 until 1778. He received his ensigncy in 1773. Buttricke served as an enlisted soldier in the 1st and 2nd Battalions of the 60th (Royal American) Regiment of Foot, and Mawby almost certainly served in the Royal Irish as an enlisted soldier. The significance to Mawby of his promotion can be seen in the fact he named his youngest son Sebright in honor of the colonel who had recommended his commissioning from the ranks.

The specific circumstances of Mawby's ascension from the ranks have not been determined. Buttricke, however, struggled for years to become an officer. His story starts with his enlistment in the 2nd Battalion of the 60th (Royal American) Regiment, most likely in 1756. He was promoted quickly through the ranks, becoming the sergeant major of the 1st Battalion of the 60th by 1760.

Buttricke then set his sights on a commission. For an enlisted soldier to desire a commission was at best an unrealistic goal. In the three regiments for which relatively complete returns exist, the number of men promoted from the ranks was extremely low, as shown in table 1.5.

TABLE 1.5 SOLDIERS WHO RECEIVED COMMISSIONS

Regiment	Total no. of enlisted soldiers	No. of soldiers who received commissions	Percentage of total
18th (Royal Irish) Regiment of Foot	763	4	0.5%
22nd Regiment of Foot	1,005	4	0.4%
33rd Regiment of Foot	1,000	2	0.2%

Not even one man in two hundred could expect to be promoted from the ranks, and of those, extremely few reached beyond the staff ranks of adjutant or quartermaster. Of the ten men listed in the table, five became ensigns—two in the Royal Irish and three in the 22nd Foot. The others never advanced beyond a staff commission. The nature of the chaplain and the surgeon, as men with a trade (a profession, in modern parlance) and not simply gentlemen, seems to have also influenced some officers to view the roles of adjutant and quartermaster to be beneath the dignity of gentlemen. Some contemporary accounts show that line officers did not see the role of quartermaster in particular as a gentleman's assignment. Lieutenant Colonel John Beckwith of the 44th Foot told its quartermaster in 1764, "A quartermaster is no gentleman." Lord Amherst similarly affirmed he would be willing to commission a deserving sergeant as a quartermaster, "but I cannot approve of making him an Ensign."[23]

Buttricke was faced with objections from the regiment's colonel, Henry Bouquet, who thought it was inappropriate for a man who had served as a tailor in the regiment to hold a commissioned rank. Although Buttricke was first recommended for a commission in November 1760 by a major in the 60th Foot, Bouquet's opposition effectively ended his chances of obtaining one in the 60th Foot.

Finally, in 1764, Buttricke was able to obtain a commission as the quartermaster of the 46th Foot. He joined the Royal Irish in the same capacity in 1767, when the 46th Foot left America. Lieutenant Colonel Wilkins, according to Buttricke's letters, often held out the potential for him to receive an ensigncy in the Royal Irish when there were several openings in 1768 and 1769. However, Buttricke did not obtain his first commission as a line officer until 1773, after having worked toward that goal for more than twelve years.

Buttricke was not alone is struggling to obtain a commission, but even obtaining a commission did not end the problems for many men from the ranks. An example is Thomas Gilfillan, who had served as the sergeant major of the 55th Foot for more than a decade before purchasing the adjutancy of that regiment. In April 1776, he wrote to James Grant, the 55th's colonel, asking for a recommendation for an ensigncy. Gilfillan never received that promotion in the 55th Foot, but he purchased a commission in the 64th Foot as a lieutenant in March 1777. It is not clear why Grant did not help a fellow Scot, but it might have been because Grant did not believe that officers from the ranks were deserving of line commissions.[24]

Lieutenant Thomas Grant faced a similar struggle after obtaining a commission in the 51st Foot in October 1755 from having been a sergeant in an independent company in America. He was placed on half pay when that regiment was disbanded but returned to active service with the 23rd Foot in 1757. However, the colonel of the 23rd Foot, John Huske, would not allow Grant to remain with the 23rd Foot because he had been "Made from a Serjeant."[25] Grant was ultimately allowed to transfer to the 68th Foot, which had been the 2nd Battalion of the 23rd Regiment before the regiment was split in 1758.

These examples show that a field officer's views on whether men should be promoted from the ranks had a great influence on the career path of men from the ranks.

After Buttricke's resignation as quartermaster in 1778, the Royal Irish promoted its own sergeant major, Thomas Holland, to quartermaster. Sergeant Major William Musgrave replaced Holland in 1781 upon Holland's promotion to an ensigncy in an invalid company. Musgrave remained as the quartermaster of the Royal Irish until 1794. During the Royal Irish's American service, the regiment generally filled the adjutancy with a traditional line officer, although both Mawby and Buttricke served in that role—Mawby formally, Buttricke informally while in Illinois.

During the American Revolution, the rules seem to have changed somewhat, making the appointment of deserving sergeants to the staff roles more acceptable, if not standard. A directive to commission former rankers as quartermasters may have come from the king. In July 1779, Lord Jeffery Amherst provided the king's direction in a letter to Lord North, articulating that by the king's rules, "the commission of Quartermaster is not [to be] given to an Officer, but Lord North may name any Serjeant or Person who has served to execute that Duty."[26] In that case, North had been hoping to provide the new captain lieutenant of Lord North's Cinque Port Fencibles with a dual commission, making him quartermaster as well. The king rejected that idea.

A review of regiments raised from 1778 to 1780 shows a pattern of promoting rankers to the staff as adjutant and quartermaster.

The 75th Foot was organized by Hugh Lord, who had served in the Royal Irish; he was appointed major and oversaw the raising of the regiment. He was later joined by John Shee, who had also served in the Royal Irish. The 75th Foot's original quartermaster, Thomas Dixon, had been a sergeant in the 12th Foot.[27] Two sergeants from the Royal Irish, Walter Elliot and Martin Bell, served as the quartermasters of the 75th Foot beginning in 1780.

Other newly raised regiments show a similar pattern. The 86th (Rutland) Regiment's initial officer corps included two sergeant majors as the adjutant and quartermaster. The adjutant also received an ensign's commission. The 90th Foot included both the sergeant major and a sergeant from the 52nd Foot, recently returned from America, as the adjutant and quartermaster. The 91st Foot, raised under Dudley Ackland, included no rankers in its initial officer corps. The 95th, 96th, and 97th Regiments, raised in 1780, each included a single ranker. In the 96th Foot, he was to be the quartermaster. In the 95th and 97th, the former sergeant was to be the adjutant.

An extreme example is that of the 79th Regiment of Foot, raised in June 1778 under Thomas Calcraft. At least five rankers were among the twenty men appointed to lieutenancies in the 79th Foot:

    4 lieutenants who had previously left the service

    1 lieutenant from half pay

    1 militia lieutenant

    6 ensigns currently serving in regiments of foot

    1 ensign who had previously left the service

    1 former adjutant of the 122nd Foot

    1 quartermaster of the 59th Foot

    1 troop quartermaster from the 1st Dragoon Guards[28]

    3 serving sergeant majors from regiments of foot

    1 serving sergeant from a regiment of foot

Thus, of the 79th's new lieutenants, at least five and perhaps as many as seven were rankers—a higher percentage than in any of the other regiments reviewed when it is considered that the 79th began with a total of only forty-two officers. None of the 79th's ensigns came from the ranks. The adjutant was to be the quartermaster from the 1st Dragoon Guards, Timothy Russell, who was awarded a dual commission. The 79th's quartermaster was one of the lieutenants who had previously left the service.[29]

Besides receiving the appointments in the Royal Irish mentioned above, rankers were appointed to the staff roles of adjutant and quartermaster in marching regiments that existed before the war. For example, the 10th Regiment of Foot appointed former sergeants to the roles of adjutant and quartermaster during the war. A grenadier sergeant of the 10th Foot, Arthur Leversuch, was promoted to quartermaster on 28 June 1775 and held that position at least twenty years. William Hamill, the sergeant major of the 10th Foot, was promoted to adjutant in that regiment in 1778. He obtained an ensign's commission in 1779 and was promoted to lieutenant in 1784 while still serving as adjutant.[30]

The regiments of Foot Guards, considered elite units with high commission prices, were among the least likely to promote a soldier from the ranks. In fact, no one was ever promoted from the ranks into the 3rd (Scots) Regiment of Foot Guards until after 1780.[31]

Table 1.6 shows the number of officers appointed from the ranks from a number of marching regiments.

TABLE 1.6 OFFICERS COMMISSIONED FROM THE RANKS

Regiment	Total officers[1]	Rankers	Percentage of total
8th (King's) Regiment of Foot	79	0	0.0%
12th Regiment of Foot	85	3	3.5%
18th (Royal Irish) Regiment of Foot	65	2	3.0%
17th Regiment of Foot	121	1	0.8%
22nd Regiment of Foot	88	4	4.5%
33rd Regiment of Foot	81	2	2.4%
35th Regiment of Foot	111	1	0.9%
42nd (Royal Highland) Regiment of Foot	100	8	8.0%
55th Regiment of Foot	69	2	2.8%
62nd Regiment of Foot	50	3	6.0%
79th Regiment of Foot	42	5	12.0%

[1]The time span covered for each regiment is different. The data for this table come from Odnitz, 182, for the 8th, 12th, 17th, and 35th Regiments. The data for the 22nd and 33rd Regiments come from WO 12/3872 and WO 12/4802/2. The data from the 42nd Regiment come from Pace, n.p. The data for the 55th Foot come from WO 12/3501. The data for the 62nd Foot come from WO 12/7164. WO 65 was used for all the regiments except those from Odnitz.

Unlike most regiments, the highland regiments were remarkably homogeneous in the birthplaces of their officers. The relatively high number of rankers produced by the 42nd (Royal Highland) Foot may have been the result of the need for experienced highland officers in the multitude of highland regiments raised during the war, which put a strain on the 42nd's existing officer corps. Nearly every one of the newly raised highland regiments included at least one officer from the 42nd Foot, so those regiments caused a drain on the officer corps that was felt by the 42nd Regiment more than by the other existing regiments.[32]

Rarely did a ranker reach beyond the subaltern ranks. Mawby was a rare example, becoming the Royal Irish's major in 1790, twenty-eight years after obtaining his initial commission. Sergeant James Stirling of the 42nd (Royal Highland) Regiment of Foot was an extreme example: He enlisted in the 42nd Foot in 1774 and was promoted to sergeant by 1776. He became the quartermaster of the ad hoc 2nd Battalion of the 42nd Foot in America and was promoted to ensign in 1777 and lieutenant in 1778. He obtained a captaincy in 1795, became a major in 1796, and retired as a major general in 1822.[33]

Officer Careers

The British Army's officer corps was diverse in age. The purchase of an officer's first commission set his place in the regiment's seniority and allowed him to seize the earliest opportunity to purchase, which was, at least in theory, dictated by seniority. At the extremes, preteens purchased commissions as ensigns in order to start accruing seniority, and septuagenarians served alongside them in independent companies and sometimes in the embodied militia, unable to purchase a lieutenancy and make ends meet without the meager pay an ensigncy provided.

The ages of the officers in the Royal Irish appear to have been fairly typical of the period. Of the fifty-six officers whose birth years can be established, the mean age at their first commission was 18.6 years, and the median age was 18. The youngest officers received their initial commissions at approximately 10 or 11. The oldest was 37.

The Royal Irish has two examples of extremely young officers: John de Birniere and James Taylor Trevor. De Birniere obtained his initial commission in 1755 in the 55th Regiment of Foot when it was first raised. He served with the regiment in America, at some point, because he was promoted to lieutenant in the 44th Foot during the war and was in America at the war's end.

Trevor sold his first commission at age twelve, within a year after purchasing it in 1766, because he chose not to accompany the Royal Irish to America. He then purchased an ensigncy in the 55th Foot, which had just rotated to Ireland from America. As an absentee officer, he slowly gained seniority and was able to obtain a lieutenancy in the 55th Foot in 1770. He began to serve with the 55th Foot sometime after that. He purchased the captain lieutenancy in 1774 and was promoted to captain without purchase in August 1775, when the regiment was expanded before embarking for America.[34]

Other regiments also provide examples of very young officers. Gonville Bromhead was only ten when he was commissioned into the 62nd Foot as its quartermaster. He was not present at the regiment's 1772 inspection because he was on recruiting service with Lieutenant Thomas Reynall. Bromhead eventually reached the rank of lieutenant general in 1813, but his grandson, who fought at Rouke's Drift in South Africa in 1879, obtained more lasting military fame. Charles Graham of Drainie, Scotland, was first commissioned into the 42nd Foot at age ten and was the major of the 1st Battalion of the 42nd Foot by the end of the American Revolution.

Among the youngest officers was Cornet John Brown of the 14th Regiment of Dragoons. He was commissioned at age nine in 1769 but by 1772 had still not joined the regiment. However, he had accrued three years' seniority. Possibly the youngest subaltern was Henry Walton Ellis, the infant son of John Ellis. The elder Ellis had served in the Royal Irish until promoted into the newly raised 89th Foot. Ellis secured his infant son an ensigncy in the 89th Foot before it was reduced to half pay in 1783. Henry was promoted to lieutenant at age four, when his father became the major of the reorganized 41st Regiment of Foot in 1787. Shortly after the elder Ellis became the lieutenant colonel of the 23rd (Royal Welch Fusiliers) Regiment of Foot, Henry received a company. He was thirteen years old at the time.

By any modern standard, a thirteen-year-old infantry company commander would seem ridiculous. However, the 23rd Foot seems to have accepted the Ellis family.[35] A memorial in honor of Henry Ellis lists fifteen years of active service with the 23rd beginning in 1799, when he would have been approximately seventeen years old. He served in the 23rd Foot throughout the Napoleonic period in Egypt, Holland, and the Americas. Ultimately, he obtained a lieutenant colonelcy in the regiment and commanded it on the Iberian Peninsula beginning in 1807.

Henry Ellis was wounded several times and eventually killed. He was shot through the right hand at the Battle of Albuera (Spain) in 1811, he was wounded the following year at the Siege of Badajoz, he was severely wounded at the Battle of Salamanca, and he was mortally wounded at Waterloo after forming his regiment into square. He is mentioned in the Duke of Wellington's dispatch to the king after the battle, and is buried on the field at Waterloo. The officers and other ranks of the 23rd Foot took up a subscription to erect a monument in his honor, and the prince regent awarded an augmentation to the family coat of arms in recognition for his service. Henry Ellis was named a knight commander of the Order of the Bath in January 1815.[36] Ellis was clearly not an incapable fop with a silver spoon in his mouth. However, he began his career at an incredibly early age and was surely more ornamental than functional during the early years of his career.

Odnitz's study lists twenty-eight officers who obtained commissions at age twelve or thirteen. This is 8 percent, lower than the 12 percent of officers in the Royal Irish who received their first commissions before they were fourteen years old. However, only James Trevor, Henry Folliott, and Matthew Lane received their initial commissions in the Royal Irish.[37]

As shown in table 1.7, two out of three officers began their military careers between the ages sixteen and twenty-three. However, the Royal Irish had a higher percentage of officers at each extreme than other samples.

TABLE 1.7 AGES OF OFFICERS OF THE ROYAL IRISH WHEN FIRST COMMISSIONED

Age	No. of officers	Percentage of total
10–11	2	3.57%
12–13	5	8.93%
14–15	6	10.71%
16–17	9	16.07%
18–19	11	19.64%
20–21	8	14.29%
22–23	8	14.29%
24–25	1	1.79%
26–27	2	3.57%
28+	4	7.14%
Total	56	

The officers who received their initial commissions after age twenty-four can generally be identified as rankers or staff officers. The exceptions were absentee officer Francis Wadman and Nicholas Trist. Wadman apparently decided to join the army at age twenty-eight, particularly late in life for a man who must have had some influence at court. Princess Amelia Sophia, to whom he was a gentleman usher (an usher at various ceremonial functions), might have decided that he needed a uniform for some occasion, or Wadman himself, who was active in politics and at court, might have decided that he needed at least minimal military credentials. Trist joined the Royal Irish in 1770 at age twenty-seven. He joined without purchase, and the late start to his military career may indicate a lack of direction in his earlier life. His commission might have been given as a favor to his father, who was not sure what to do with him in England.

John Mawby Sr. was the oldest to receive his first commission; he did so at age thirty-seven and had had twenty years of enlisted service beforehand. John Lynn, who served the regiment briefly as the surgeon's mate, was the next oldest, at thirty-six. Chaplain Stanley Leathes was thirty-two years old when first commissioned.

Excepting colonels, the oldest officers in the British Army in the mid-eighteenth century tended to be in the independent companies of invalids throughout Great Britain and Ireland. These were often officers who had served in active regiments but were no longer fit for active service. However, they could still be of use in the less demanding invalid companies, which generally served as castle or fort garrisons and were not expected to actively participate in the field. Ensign Archibald McCorkell of the independent company at Dumbarton Castle may have been the army's oldest subaltern in 1775 at age seventy-two. He was listed as having forty-nine years of service and was present with the company when it was inspected. The ensigns in the independent companies at Edinburgh and Stirling Castles were comparatively young men in their forties. Colonel William Strode of the 62nd Foot was listed as eighty-five in 1772.[38]

Thus, we can see that officers often started in their teens and occasionally in their preteen years, and many officers had long careers. In many cases, officers remained on active service into their forties and even beyond, particularly if they were able to obtain field rank.

The average ages of the officer corps as a whole varied throughout the period. Several factors affected the average age of the corps as a whole.

In 1767, when the regiment arrived in America, the average age of the officers was twenty-seven years old. The oldest was fifty-three-year-old Chaplain Leathes. The youngest were three seventeen-year-old ensigns: William Blackwood, Henry Fermor, and Robert Hamilton. John Shee was the youngest captain, at age twenty-six.

In 1768, the 8th (King's) Regiment was ordered to America after a long stretch of service in England. The age and length of service of its officer corps was similar to that of the Royal Irish's when it embarked for America. The 8th (King's) Regiment's field officers averaged forty-three and a half years of age with twenty-eight years of service. The captains averaged thirty-seven years of age with nineteen years of service. The lieutenants were twenty-eight years old with ten years of service. The ensigns averaged twenty-one years of age with four years of service.[39]

In 1770, the average age of an officer in the Royal Irish Regiment was twenty-nine years old, but the ages of several officers who came from half pay cannot be determined; if these were known, they would most likely skew the average to an older age. The youngest officer was sixteen-year-old Edmund Prideaux, who had not yet joined the regiment. The eldest were John Sebright and John Mawby Sr., both of whom were forty-five. John Wilkins and Isaac Hamilton were both forty-four.

By 1775, the average age of the officers in the Royal Irish had risen to thirty-three years old. Of the twenty-nine officers who served that year and whose ages are known, fifteen were thirty or older. The youngest officer was a twenty-year-old ensign, Charles Hoar. Colonel Sebright and John Mawby Sr. were now fifty. Major Hamilton was a sickly forty-nine and spent most of the winter of 1774–1775 too sick to perform his duties.[40]

The ensigns in April 1775 averaged twenty-five years old. The range was from twenty-year-old Charles Hoar to thirty-seven-year-old George Buttricke. This was not too far from the average age of an ensign in the 1st Battalion of the 42nd Foot in 1784, which was twenty-three years old.[41] The average age of the lieutenants was only twenty-six years old, the range being from twenty-two to twenty-eight years old. The average captain was thirty-five years old, the range being from twenty-five to fifty. The field officers averaged forty-nine years of age in 1775.

Table 1.8 shows the average ages and years of service of the officers by rank.

TABLE 1.8 AVERAGE AGES OF OFFICERS SERVING IN THE ROYAL IRISH REGIMENT BY RANK[1]

Officers	Average age, 1767	Average years of service	Average age, 1775	Average years of service
Field officers	39	23	49	30
Captains	32	14	35	19
Lieutenants	28	9	26	10
Ensigns	21	1.25	25	5
Staff officers	31	8	32	12

Officers	Average age, 1777	Average years of service	Average age, 1779	Average years of service
Field officers	43	26	45	28
Captains	33	17	33	14
Lieutenants	29	11	24	6
Ensigns	22	2	19	0
Staff officers	37	17	34	4

[1] Ages for 1767 based on the 11 April 1767 inspection return completed at Dublin. Ages for 1775 based on regimental assignments of 15 April 1775. Years of service includes time on half pay.

The officer corps of the Royal Irish was fairly similar in its makeup in 1767 and 1775. The biggest difference was the more experienced group of ensigns present in 1775. The effect of the start of hostilities on the regiment was significant for the regiment's experience base. The lieutenant colonel, the major, and two of the captains retired. A third captain retired when he returned to England in 1777. The surgeon's mate resigned rather than fight in America.

Almost all the Royal Irish officers took extended leaves upon their return to England. Those who were not promoted in late 1775 because of retirement in the Royal Irish seem not to have begun looking for greener pastures until the new corps began to be raised as France entered the war.

In the five years after the regiment's American service, the average age and experience of the officers of the regiment plummeted as experienced officers either retired or were promoted into new corps. Eleven officers who served in America with the regiment gained promotions during the expansion of the army between 1776 and 1780.

John Sebright was promoted to lieutenant general in 1770, making him the officer of the Royal Irish to obtain the highest rank. Sebright happens to have also been a close associate of John Ligonier, 1st Earl Ligonier, one of the four field marshals appointed during the Seven Years'

War. Adam Williamson also obtained the rank of lieutenant general in 1797. John Joyner Ellis reached the rank of major general in 1798 while also serving as lieutenant colonel of the 23rd (Royal Welch Fusiliers) Regiment.

As mentioned earlier, nearly all the colonels were already generals when they were appointed to command regiments. That held true for Sebright, Williamson, and Ellis, who all reached the rank of general before being given command of a regiment. Sebright was originally given command of the 83rd Regiment of Invalids in 1758, which later became a traditional marching regiment. He was promoted to the Royal Irish in 1762. Williamson was given command of the 47th Foot in 1790. Ellis did not obtain the command of a regiment but was promoted to colonel in the army in 1793.

Field rank commissions were obtained by a large percentage of the whole, but only about one-third of the men who entered the officer corps would reach field rank. This is also somewhat inflated, since some officers were given army rank beyond that of their regimental rank. For instance, Charles Edmonstone was promoted to major in the army in 1772. He remained a captain in the Royal Irish, receiving the pay and allowances of a captain. However, he was addressed as major, and when serving outside the regiment, he took precedence as a major and not as a captain. Such rank was often awarded for performance or even given locally to ensure that a sufficient number of high-ranking officers were available in a theater of operations.

Several general officers were given the "local rank" of full general in America to ensure they outranked the officers sent by the German states. George Bruere was promoted to the local rank of lieutenant colonel "in the island of Bermudas only" in 1779. In Bruere's case, and a few others, the officer also skipped a step. Bruere was only a captain when he was made a local lieutenant colonel. Tto advance within a regiment, he would still need to purchase a major's commission before being able to purchase a lieutenant colonelcy.

Table 1.9 shows the highest rank achieved by the officers of the Royal Irish. None of the adjutants or quartermasters who served with the Royal Irish during the period failed to obtain a line commission, so to simplify the table, the three chaplains and Surgeon Mate John Linn were excluded.

TABLE 1.9 HIGHEST RANK ACHIEVED BY OFFICERS OF THE ROYAL IRISH

Highest rank reached	No. of officers	Percentage of officers who served	Percentage of officers who obtained this rank
Lieutenant general	2	3.2%	3.2%
Major general	1	1.6%	4.8%
Colonel	0	0%	4.8%
Lieutenant colonel in a regiment	4	6.5%	11.3%
Lieutenant colonel in the army or locally	3	4.8%	16.1%
Major in a regiment	7	22.3%	27.4%
Major in the army[1]	5	8.1%	35.5%
Captain	18	29.0%	64.5%
Captain lieutenant	4	6.5%	70.9%
Lieutenant	11	17.7%	88.7%
Ensign	7	11.3%	100%

[1]Includes two men who achieved the rank of major in provincial regiments.

In general, an officer entering the Royal Irish could expect to serve approximately three to four years as an ensign before being promoted to lieutenant. Lieutenants spent about twice that long before being promoted to captains. At that point, most captains had ten to eleven years of total service. Obtaining the rank of major took a captain nearly nine years, and on average more than eighteen years of total service. Since each regiment had six or seven captains but only one major, this was an important step in obtaining access to future promotions. A major could expect to serve six years in that rank before being able to obtain a lieutenant colonel's commission.

Houlding's armywide study of officers of foot showed that in 1767 it took an average of six years to obtain a lieutenancy, but in 1775 it took only four years. In 1767, all the lieutenants in the Royal Irish had taken less time than Houlding's average to become a lieutenant. Francis Wadman obtained his lieutenancy in only thirteen months. The other seven lieutenants in the Royal Irish in 1767 who had been ensigns had taken between four and five years to obtain that rank.

Captaincies took nine years to obtain in 1767 and ten in 1775. In 1767, the six captains in the Royal Irish took between eight and thirteen years of total service to obtain their companies, which was slower than the army average. The rank of major could be earned in nineteen years in 1767 and in eighteen years in 1775. Shee became a major in 1775 in just over fifteen years. Wilkins took sixteen years to become one in 1762, and Folliott took seventeen years to become one in 1766. Only Isaac Hamilton took longer than the army average to become a major: it took him twenty years.

Obtaining a lieutenant colonelcy in 1767 took only seventeen years. Wilkins took longer than average, nineteen years, to obtain his lieutenant colonelcy. The lieutenant colonelcy took twenty years to earn in 1775. It would take Shee twenty years to obtain his lieutenant colonelcy in 1779, which was right in line with Houlding's average progression. According to Houlding, it was common for the lieutenant colonel to have no more service than the major of the regiment; rather, "birth, wealth, and influence" played a stronger role in helping officers quickly move from major to lieutenant colonel.[42]

The majority of officers reached the rank of captain. Among those who never rose above ensign, three died in the service and a fourth appears to have resigned because of illness. Edward Hand had purchased his ensigncy after serving as the surgeon's mate, and he left the service to marry and set up a medical practice. John Wilmot Prideaux sold his commission before actually serving with the regiment.

William Raymond had the only situation that does not have an obvious explanation. It is possible that he simply did not wish to serve in Illinois. He had served three years with the regiment, then he sold his commission shortly after the Royal Irish was ordered to garrison the western posts.

Among the eleven officers who rose only to the rank of lieutenant before the end of their careers, six died in the service: five apparently succumbed to disease, and the sixth was killed in a duel.

The officers of the Royal Irish ended their careers in one of three ways: they resigned, they died, or they were placed on half pay and continued to receive pay until they died. Among those who lived to see retirement, only William Smith had served more than a decade without spending time on half pay and had failed to obtain promotion. He appears to have quietly served his twelve years, mostly with the grenadier company, and retired after returning from Illinois in 1772.

Death was the most severe way to end one's military service. Luckily for the officers of the Royal Irish, none of them were killed in combat. However, at least two officers were wounded in combat while serving with the Royal Irish in Massachusetts. John Shee was slightly wounded on the march to Concord, but he was not included in the official casualty lists. William Richardson was severely wounded at Bunker Hill.

Several other officers were wounded in battle during their careers. Adam Williamson was wounded near Fort Du Quesne (modern Pittsburgh, Pennsylvania) in 1754 and at Quebec in 1759. John Wilkins survived a head injury at Fort Ticonderoga (New York) in 1758 while serving in the 55th Foot, and he suffered from headaches and blurred vision the rest of his life. George Bruere was probably wounded at Beauford, South Carolina, in 1779.

A large number of officers died during active service from disease or accident. The first officer to die after embarkation in May 1767 was Hugh Antrobus, who died at sea on 1 July 1767. Ten more officers died of disease or accident during the Royal Irish's American service. Godfrey Tracey was killed in a duel near Fort Pitt by Robert Hamilton in late 1768 or early 1769. Six more officers died after returning from America while still actively serving. Two died in England with the Royal Irish, and four others died while serving with other regiments—two of them in the West Indies.

A few officers left the military to take up professions. Edward Hand and Thomas Thomasson both left to practice medicine. There were no formal retirement benefits available to officers in the eighteenth-century British Army except for the profit from the sale of their commissions, so officers simply resigned or sold their commissions when they were ready to leave the army. There is no way to determine with certainty who planned to retire and who was simply leaving the army. Some stayed past their ability to actively serve but retained the commission as a source of income, prestige, or perhaps both. Similarly, some officers died while still holding commissions, but they should be distinguished from those who died in active service. At least three officers died while still holding active commissions, but they were not actively serving.

Table 1.10 shows officers' reasons for ending their service.

TABLE 1.10 OFFICERS' REASONS FOR END OF SERVICE	
Reason	*No. of officers[1]*
Died of disease or accident in active service	18
Retired or sold commission	15
Decided not to serve in America	6
Had ill health or was unfit for active service	5
Got married	5
Died on half pay	4
Settled in America	4
Died while not in active service	3
Killed in a duel	2
Wanted to practice medicine	2
Banned from further service by the king	1
Cashiered but allowed to sell out	1
Joined the U.S. Army	1
Passed over for promotion	1
Wanted to become a wine merchant	1
Unknown	6

[1]Total exceeds 66 because some officers are included in multiple categories. Edward Hand, for instance, left to settle in America and practice medicine and is therefore represented under both categories.

Some "cleansing" of the regiment's officer corps appears to have been common when a regiment was to embark on active service. Officers not fit for active service appear to have resigned rather than accompany a regiment overseas. Several officers of the 55th Foot resigned rather than accompany that regiment to America in 1775.

Three officers of the Royal Irish, all young ensigns, resigned before the regiment embarked to America. James Taylor Trevor was twelve years old at the time of embarkation and later purchased another commission; he died in America in 1777. Caesar Colclough does not appear to have sought further military service. Two more officers resigned shortly after the regiment arrived in America. Henry Folliott resigned in late 1767 due to some apparently "unfortunate" family situation, possibly related to his recent marriage. Thomas Batt, Edward Hand, and Nicholas Trist all left the military after marrying American women. Chaplain Leathes resigned in late 1767, probably due to pressure from Sebright, who seemed to have wanted a chaplain to actually serve with the regiment in America.

Other officers appear to have left the regiment out of a desire to avoid American service or because they had had enough of it. Many of the absentee officers who came from half pay resigned or exchanged back to half pay rather than travel to America to serve.

The actual outbreak of fighting in America in April 1775 also caused a few resignations from the officer corps. This time it was older men who were not ready to undergo the hardships of active campaigning. Isaac Hamilton, Charles Edmonstone, and Benjamin Johnson all retired directly after hostilities commenced. John Linn resigned and took a commission in the Congressional Army. Alexander Fowler and Edward Hand also both served in the U.S. military, but there was a lapse between their leaving the British Army and joining the American military.

Throughout an officer's career it was not be uncommon to serve with several regiments. Although the British regimental system was in place by the 1750s, it was less rigid in the 1760s and 1770s than it would be later in the Victorian era. Although the regiment was the home for the enlisted men and transfers between regiments were uncommon, except when regiments were drafted, a fair amount of movement between regiments did occur among officers.

This movement occurred in four basic ways: (1) to or from half pay; (1) promotion in a new regiment raised for wartime service; (3) exchange of individuals of the same rank between regiments; and (4) transfer to obtain a promotion, a more desirable regiment, or a better geographic location. The first reason for movement was based to some extent on the second. Officers still eager to serve were put on half pay at the end of war as the army reduced both the total number of regiments and the number of companies in those regiments which remained. Officers whose regiments were reduced had no choice but to look to other regiments if they wanted to continue their military careers.

Only a few officers in the Royal Irish took the fourth option. Benjamin Charnock Payne was a notable example. He served in the 27th Foot as a lieutenant and transferred to the 28th Foot to become a captain. He then transferred to the Royal Irish to remain in America. When the Royal Irish left America in 1775, Payne remained behind, serving on the general staff. He was ultimately promoted to major in the 99th (Jamaica) Regiment of Foot when it was raised.

Two young officers who wanted to improve their positions by leaving the Royal Irish were Thomas Cuming, who purchased a commission in the 1st Dragoon Guards, and Horace Churchill, who purchased a commission in the 6th (Inniskilling) Regiment of Dragoons. Neither ever served with the Royal Irish in America.

John Piercy's transfers to and from the Royal Irish seem to be related to his desire to remain in America and take part in active service. He left the 45th Foot to join the Royal Irish in America, then transferred to the 47th Foot, which remained in America in late 1775. He later transferred from the 47th Foot to the 9th Foot to be promoted to lieutenant while a prisoner of war. He served in a total of four regiments, all of which were in America, before he retired from the 9th Foot in 1791.

Overall, half of the officers who served in the Royal Irish during its American service also served in at least one other regiment (see table 1.11). Three served as provincial officers after having resigned their regular commissions before the war. Two more, John Peter DeLancey and Edward

TABLE 1.11 NUMBER OF REGIMENTS SERVED IN BY ROYAL IRISH OFFICERS		
No. of British regiments served in	*No. of Officers*	*Percentage of officers*
18th (Royal Irish) Regiment only	32	48.0%
Two regular regiments	14	21.0%
Two regiments, including provincial units or the general hospital	3	4.5%
Three regiments	10	15.0%
Four regiments	4	9.0%
Five regiments	2	2.9%
Six regiments	3	4.5%
Seven regiments	1	1.5%

Crosby, served in provincial regiments while retaining their regular commissions in the Royal Irish. Crosby had originally served as a provincial officer in Gorham's Rangers in the French and Indian War and came to the Royal Irish from half pay.

Twenty-two of the officers, or 33 percent, appear to have made one or more transfers between regiments to further their careers, including being promoted into newly raised regiments. Captain William Blackwood transferred to the 45th Foot at the very end of his career to allow Thomas Sebright, a son of Colonel Sebright, to return to the Royal Irish. Only five of the officers who served in more than one regiment appear to have been forced to make those transfers entirely because of reductions in force. Adam Williamson served in the most regiments. He served in the Royal Irish and five other marching regiments. He also served in the Royal Engineers and in several staff positions. Three officers from the Royal Irish served in the American Army under George Washington: Alexander Fowler, Edward Hand, and John Linn. Linn later served in the U.S. Navy as well.

Besides serving in other regiments, several officers served the Crown in other military capacities while still holding their commissions in the Royal Irish, which accounts for some of the absenteeism noted earlier. Among these capacities were staff positions detached from the regiment. Such assignments normally affected the regiment more in wartime, but they were necessary at other times for the staff functions of the army to be managed. Captain Payne served as a deputy quartermaster general in America beginning in 1775. He was actively engaged on American service while the regiment was being rebuilt at Dover Castle in England. John Peter DeLancey served as the adjutant of Ferguson's Rifle Corps during the Philadelphia campaign and then as major of a provincial corps until ordered to return to his regiment in 1780. John Mawby Sr. served as the major of a brigade and was therefore removed from daily service with the regiment in 1778 at Coxheath Camp in Kent, England. Three other officers served at some point as majors of brigades—effectively, the adjutants for the brigades. Williamson was appointed as the deputy adjutant general of the forces in south Britain in 1778 and thereafter effectively ceased to serve with the Royal Irish, although he was still actively serving in the army.

John Mawby Jr. served as an acting deputy judge advocate while the regiment was in England. Benjamin Chapman held a staff post in the West Indies in the 1790s. Other officers held civil appointments while retaining their officers' commissions. The prime example is John Sebright, who represented Bath in Parliament during most of the time the regiment was in America. According to Strachan, sixty-eight army officers served in Parliament from 1747 to 1754, and between 1790 and 1820, nearly 20 percent of the members of Parliament were army officers.[43] Lieutenant George Bruere served as lieutenant governor and then as acting governor of Bermuda while holding an active commission. Adam Williamson later served as lieutenant governor of Jamaica while commanding troops in the West Indies. Lieutenant Francis Wadman was a gentleman usher to Princess Amelia of England during his entire tenure with the Royal Irish.

John Wilkins, Isaac Hamilton, and Hugh Lord all exercised at least some form of quasi-civilian governorship while in Illinois. Many officers in the Royal Irish, including these three, were responsible for some level of treaty making with Indians and the enforcement of customs duties in the Illinois Country. In permanent and less remote garrisons, like Fort Pitt or Detroit, separate Indian agents were often appointed, but in the remote Illinois Country, those responsibilities often fell directly on the commanders of small detachments.

Courts-Martial and Discipline

Three of the officers of the Royal Irish were tried by general courts-martial while in America. The most severe sentence went to Alexander Fowler, who was ordered to be cashiered and removed from the service. This carried the penalty of losing his commission and not being able to sell it, which was in fact a nine-hundred pound penalty. Thomas Gage, the commander in chief at the time of Fowler's September 1775 court-martial, overrode the sentence and allowed Fowler to sell his commission before returning to England. Fowler had been charged as follows:

> Lieut. Alexander Fowler of His Majesty's 18th or Royal Irish Regiment of foot, having been put under an Arrest, by Major Hamilton Commanding the said Regiment, by desire of the Officers of the Regt., was accused before the Court of having behaved in a manner unbecoming the Character of an Officer and a Gentleman, by Exhibiting frivolous, malicious, wicked, and ill grounded Charges against Capt. Benjamin Charnock Payne, also of the said Regt. before a General Court Martial.[44]

Benjamin Payne, whose court-martial was held in July and August 1775, was found not guilty of four of the five charges:

> That he had propagated infamous, scandalous, and groundless falsehoods leading not only to affect the good name and reputation of him (the said Lieut. Fowler) as an Officer but impeaching him of High Treason against his Sovereign, as being connected with the most violent Sons of sedition and rebellion in the City of New York and thereby affecting his life and Commission.[45]

Payne was censured by the guilty verdict being read at the head of the regiment. He continued his career, whereas Fowler was forced out of the army. According to Fowler, Payne's patrons were many and in high places, whereas he was without patronage. Gage was apparently one of Payne's patrons and had the testimony from Fowler's court-martial sealed. Only a general summary was included in the court-martial returns.

The third officer court-martialed was Chaplain Robert Newburgh, who desired the court-martial in order to clear his name of scandalous charges raised by other officers in the regiment. Although Fredrick Haldimand, the acting commander in chief, and Major Hamilton both tried to get the issue resolved without resorting to a general court-martial, in the end, Newburgh forced a court-martial by having a soldier charge him with committing an unnatural act. He was formally charged as follows:

> Having been guilty of Vicious and immoral behaviour by committing willful perjury, Prevarication, and falsehood, together with other Scandalous and Indecent Acts, unbecoming a Gentleman and Derogating from the Sacred Character which he is Invested, as also in having treated Major Hamilton his Commanding Officer in a disrespectful manner.[46]

Newburgh was found guilty of some of the charges and suspended from duty for six months in August 1774. Gage, however, commuted the sentence and ended Newburgh's suspension by general order on 20 November 1774.[47] Newburgh then went to civil court to press charges against Thomas Batt, a retired captain, who had allegedly been the one to start the rumors about Newburgh's behavior.

Batt was not the only officer of the Royal Irish to struggle with civilian charges against him. Robert Hamilton was ordered to be tried for the murder of Godfrey Tracy in 1771 by the Colony of Pennsylvania. The reason for a civilian trial more than two years after the duel at Fort Pitt are not clear. No verdict has surfaced, but Hamilton must have been found not guilty if the court actually convened. John Wilkins left Illinois in 1772 (in part, at least) to manage civil litigation in London. Benjamin Chapman was accused of attempted rape by the wife of a soldier when the regiment was still in Ireland in 1767. It does not appear that he was tried for the crime. William Blackwood was accused of taking another man's slave while stationed in Illinois. That issue was taken up by Wilkins's civil court in Illinois. However, no record of the verdict has been found.

A number of officers were charged with military crimes that did not rise to the level of a general court-martial. Many of the officers of the regiment were accused by one another of some type of wrongdoing in 1773–1774 as the officer corps dissolved into a dysfunctional set of opposing camps. This dysfunction, according to Fowler (who in the end lost the most for participating in this feud), started because Chapman, Payne, and Shee were trying to drive Wilkins and Hamilton out of the regiment so that Shee and Chapman could be promoted.

Hamilton and Edmonstone end up being viewed as weak officers unable or unwilling to control their subordinates. Fowler's view of Hamilton was shared by General Gage, the commander in chief in America, and Lord Barrington, the secretary of war. Wilkins seems to have been a strong officer and, rightly or wrongly, perceived as a bully by some of the captains and subalterns. Thus, when Wilkins left for England, Hamilton was unable to control the same men who took advantage of being under the command of a weak officer. Batt and Payne seem to have been the key agitators, and the Newburgh and Fowler were the prime targets of their attacks.

Hamilton and Shee were both charged with a variety of crimes by Nicholas Gaffney, a private in Shee's company. Fowler's explanation of the court proceedings in a letter to Wilkins does not exactly show a model of military judicial excellence:

> Last Month Nicholas Gaffney, formerly a corporal, but now a Private Soldier in the Grenadier Company, Commanded by Cpt. Shee, exhibited several charges against him while Commanding at Caho in the Illinois, three of which were very serious ones.
>
> 1. For issuing stinking Venison & Bears meat as Rations to him & the garrison against their Wills said provisions being Cpt. Shee's own property
>
> 2. That by the Sale of Liquor, sugar, coffie & c to him Cpt. Shee was interested in the sale thereof

3. That by Cpt. Shee's Misconduct when he Commanded at Caho in the Illinois Country, John Knight, a soldier of his Company was murdered by Savages.

A court martial (as it was called tho it was in reality a Court of Enquiry) was Order'd and sat four Weeks on this very perplexing Affair—when we gave our opinion with respect to the Validity of the Charges, on the course of the Enquiry, the Complainant Gaffney complained loudly of the Court's partiality to Captain Shee, he insisted to be heard before a General Court Martial, which the General has granted and he attends with his Evidences which are Numerous at the Court Martial at Brunswick to prosecute his Captain. I sat as a Member of the Court of Enquiry and although I did not write the minutes of the proceedings, I minuted down Reflections thrown on your Conduct and Character.

Fowler's letter is not totally accurate: it was Gaffney, not Shee, who ended up tried by a general court-martial at Amboy. Shee does not appear to have been tried above the regimental level.[48]

Wilkins had to deal with his own set of allegations, made against him by Thomas Hutchins of the 2nd Battalion of the 60th (Royal American) Regiment for the improper use of government funds. The allegations dragged on for more than two years, prohibiting Wilkins from selling his commission during that time, but in the end no charges were formally made.

Edmonstone was the subject of a court of inquiry regarding his role in dealing with the quartermaster and commissary supplies at Fort Pitt. In the end, no negative actions were taken against him, either.

Chapman was investigated for his management of funds as the regimental paymaster and also found not guilty.

The only captains to escape the fray were Benjamin Johnson and Hugh Lord. Johnson does not appear to have ever been present with the regiment, and Lord spent nearly all his service isolated from his peers.

Wilkins appears to have placed several lieutenants under arrest from time to time in Illinois, but no indications of the nature of the charges remain. Some officers seem to have claimed that Wilkins would arrest officers when they did not agree with him and then release them when they came around to his way of thinking. One document, included in a letter from Wilkins to Gage in August 1774, indicates that Wilkins did not always get along with his officers:

From the officers, 1 April 1770

We, Cpt. Shee, Cpt. John Evans, Ens. Thomas Hutchins, & Ens. Wm. Blackwood, Wm Conolly do in Consequence of Lt. Col. Wilkins desire of bringing Matters to an Accommodation which desire he Expressed to Lieut Chapman Most Sincerely & Solemnly forgive and forget every Transaction whether of a private or Publick Nature, that many have ever happen'd either in respect of Duty or Otherwise, betwixt us & the said Lt. Col Wilkins and we hereby exchange a Mutual obligation of Burying every Circumstance in Oblivion & do declare that we shall ever be happy to live upon the best of terms with Col. Wilkins both as an Officer and a Gentleman.[49]

William Conolly was placed under arrest at least twice by Wilkins, and Lieutenant William Perkins was also listed as under arrest at one point. In neither case are the exact charges evident.

The majority of the officers in general, and Shee and Payne specifically, appear to have been fairly harsh disciplinarians with the men. Payne and Mawby Sr, are both mentioned as having beaten men. In court-martial testimony, Payne's servant stated he was beaten only when he deserved it. An extant regimental punishment book for Shee's detachment at Boston in 1774–1775 shows punishments much more severe than those given for similar crimes in other regiments. Lashings were frequent. It appears that Wilkins was a more lenient commander with the men, but there are no specific records that support that.

For example, a soldier of the Royal Irish, Brent Dabbadee, was sentenced to four hundred lashes in May 1774 for "being very drunk and dirty when parading for church." His punishment rendered him unable to travel to testify at a general court-martial. In the 3rd Foot, similar offenders received three weeks of extra duty; another man of the 3rd Foot, Arthur Crawford, received two weeks of fatigue duty for "being drunk when for church." William McKillip of the 36th Foot received two hundred lashes for "behaving in an indecent Manner in the Presence of the Clergyman when going to Church" in October 1776. Dabbadee deserted shortly after being flogged.[50]

Wives and Children

Just as many of the specific circumstances of the informal imprisonment of the subalterns by Wilkins are lost to history, so too are the domestic situations of many of the officers hard to determine. We know that a number of the officers brought their wives with them on their American service. In some cases, other records, including the officers' wills, illuminate their family situations. At least twenty-two of the officers were married; although it is not clear how many were married while serving. The most advantageous marriage among the officers seems to be Charles Hoar's marriage to Ann Harland in 1802. At that time, the king granted Hoar the use of the Harland name and coat of arms. He was appointed a baronet on 24 September 1808 and thereafter called Sir Charles Hoar Harland, 1st Baronet of Sutton Hall.

Several men did not marry until after they left the regiment, but others were married and brought their wives and children with them to America. John Mawby Sr. and George Stainforth brought their entire families with them to America. Lieutenants Fowler and Wynne took their wives to Illinois in 1770. Hugh Lord's family accompanied him to Illinois in 1772, and his wife remained there for some time after the capture of the Illinois Country by George Rogers Clark in 1778.

A young son of Mawby's features in a court-martial in 1774, which shows that he was clearly in and around the regiment on a day-to-day basis in Philadelphia at that time. One of Mawby's daughters married the Russian consul at Gibraltar while the Royal Irish was stationed there. So it appears that the family of Mawby accompanied him on all his postings.

It is unclear whether any other officers' wives traveled to Illinois, but nearly all the women who did accompany the Royal Irish to Illinois in 1768 died of disease within the first year. Thirty-seven children likewise perished that year. Shee's sons apparently were in Illinois, and his first wife might have died there. Fowler's and Trist's wives and young children were with the regiment in the barracks in New York City during the winter of 1774–1775.

Several officers left the service shortly after marrying. Folliott married in 1765 and resigned in 1767. Batt married an American woman and resigned to become a merchant in Philadelphia. Hand and Trist both married American women. DeLancey, a New Yorker by birth, also married an American. The most unusual marital situation was that of Benjamin Charnock Payne, who married Maria Beaufoy, the widow of his friend George Durant. When Payne passed away, Benjamin Chapman then married Beaufoy.

Of the officers whose birth-order positions can be determined, nearly all were younger sons. Only George Bewes and John Wilmot Prideaux appear to have been firstborn sons. Several officers had brothers who also served in the army, and a few also had brothers in the navy. Four of the officers eventually succeeded to titles. Two inherited them after joining the army. Sir John Wilmot Prideaux, who does not appear to have actually served in any active military capacity and retired from the service as an ensign, held his title prior to purchasing a commission. It appears that Prideaux simply wanted to be an officer, for one reason or another. Hoar, mentioned above, was granted his title in 1808, long after he was finished actively serving.

In late eighteenth-century society, anyone who served as an officer in the king's army would have had servants. During the period of this study, officers were allowed to have servants during their service. A number of servants can be identified through court-martial transcripts. Most were soldiers taken from the ranks, which the army allowed. Some might have also had civilian servants, and soldiers' wives certainly served the wives and children of the officers. At least two officers held slaves while in Illinois. One of those officers, John de Birniere, asked that the slave be set free on his eighteenth birthday by Henry Hamilton at Detroit. It appears that de Birniere left the slave in America when he returned to England in 1776. It is likely that Payne was involved in the West Indian slave trade at some level, since George Durant, his associate, made his fortune involved in that trade.

Whereas some officers had ample capital to purchase slaves, not all officers were flush with cash or other financial resources. Young men who aspired to hold commissions but who did not have the money to purchase one or the influence to obtain one without purchase sometimes became volunteers. Others may have simply been waiting for the "right" vacancy, and serving as a volunteer put them in the right place for when the desired vacancy would appear. They accompanied a regiment and served as private men in the ranks, but they socialized with the officers. The exact service expected from these men in the ranks is unclear, but the volunteers from the Royal Irish were enrolled in the regiment and therefore paid as privates before obtaining their commissions.

During the American Revolution, a large number of Scots, in particular, turned to this method of serving in order to obtain a commission. Fraser's Highlanders, the 71st Foot, brought a large number of volunteers to America. In America, service with the light infantry battalions seems to have provided the best opportunities for advancement.

Thomas Gage does not appear to have a high opinion of gentlemen volunteers or their usefulness to the army. He wrote the following to Barrington in June 1775 in a letter marked private:

> I am particularly averse to the encouragement of Volunteers. I have always understood them to be both useless and inconvenient in Armies & giving them Commissions would encourage an abuse of which you complained some months ago & which has been carried to great lengths in the North American Army.[51]

However, volunteers were in America, and more were on their way by the time Gage penned his letter to Barrington. By the end of the war, more than a hundred officers obtained commissions in America by serving as volunteers. In comparison, it was nearly three times as likely for a vacant commission to go to a volunteer than to a sergeant.

Arthur Brooke was one of the volunteers Gage referred to at Boston in 1775. Brooke earned a commission in the 52nd Foot as an ensign on 18 June 1775. He had been wounded the day before, "shot through the body" after attaining the top of the entrenchment on Breed's Hill during the Battle of Bunker Hill, present Charleston, Massachusetts. His gallantry and courage under fire earned him a commission he most likely could not have purchased. Brooke was promoted to lieutenant in the 52nd Foot on 8 May 1777. John Montague Clarke served as a volunteer with the 59th Foot before the breakout of hostiles in America. He obtained a vacant ensigncy in the 43rd Foot on 10 July 1775 and retired on 1 December 1779, unable to advance beyond his ensigncy.[52]

The Royal Irish does not appear to have had any ordinary volunteers. Instead, the Royal Irish had the Mawby family to provide a regular stream of young men interested in obtaining commissions. Samuel Twentyman was listed as a volunteer when he was first commissioned in the Royal Irish; the regiment he previously served with was not specified.[53]

John Mawby Jr. and, later, his brothers George and Sebright were listed as privates in the returns of the Royal Irish, but it is unclear whether they were really volunteers trying to earn a commission without purchase or were simply carried on the rolls as a favor to their father. The latter is more likely. In fact, John Jr. was never present at a muster before he obtained his commission, but he was always listed as "on duty" in the company where his father was a lieutenant until he was appointed as an ensign in November 1768. Since the entire Mawby family came to America with the regiment, John Jr. was probably carried on the rolls to help his father's pocketbook.

John's younger brother George was the next Mawby carried on the muster rolls as a private. The rolls show him as a private in the same company as his father beginning in June 1773, and he remained on the rolls in the general's company through July 1776. He was then given leave and removed to the lieutenant colonel's company, where his brother John was the lieutenant. Like his older brother, George was never present for a muster. He was listed as on duty, on command, or on leave at each muster until he was commissioned as an ensign. He was then listed as "not yet joined" for several months.

Sebright Mawby was only about ten years old when he was first listed as a private, having entered on 25 August 1773 in Captain Payne's company. He was, of course, not present at the muster and was listed as "on duty." In one instance—the 29 July 1774 muster of Payne's company—Sebright was listed as a volunteer. He was most likely several years shy of his tenth birthday at the time. Sebright was then listed on duty or on leave until he was commissioned on 23 July 1787. Sebright Mawby's biography in the *Royal Military Calendar* states that he served with the Royal Irish at Gibraltar as a volunteer before purchasing his ensigncy in the Royal Irish. If that is accurate, he was among the army's longest-serving volunteers, nearly fourteen years.[54]

The Mawby family does not appear to have been alone in posting their young sons as enlisted soldiers before they obtained their initial commissions. Lieutenant Colonel James Cockburne carried his son William on the rolls of the 35th Foot. Captain Henry Ornsby of the 12th Foot did the same with his son. The Morris family served with the 17th Foot for at least four generations. William Darby of the 17th Foot was enrolled as a soldier by his father, the regiment's colonel. He was then sent to school in England while other officers covered his regimental duties. The officers of the 17th complained to the secretary of war only when Colonel Darby tried to obtain a lieutenancy for his son to the detriment of actively serving officers.[55]

Thomas Batt was probably the son of Robert Batt. The Batts would have served together in Ireland before the elder's retirement in 1765. Thomas Batt's son was also given a commission in his provincial regiment during the war. John Sebright's son also served with the Royal Irish after its return to England.

After American service, fathers and sons continued to serve together in the Royal Irish. After the Royal Irish returned to England, Benjamin Chapman and William Conolly both had their sons serve in the Royal Irish with them. It is also possible that William Richardson's son served with the regiment. It was common for the colonel's sons and even extended family members to hold commissions in the same regiment as the colonel. Henry Folliott, the major of the Royal Irish when it embarked from Ireland in 1767, was certainly the son of the former colonel, Lieutenant General John Folliott.

Colonel Bigoe Armstrong served as ensign and lieutenant colonel of the Royal Irish before his promotion to the colonelcy of the 8th Foot. Armstrong was notorious for bringing his extended family into his regiment. He filled every nonpurchase vacancy of the 8th Foot during his tenure as colonel in that regiment with either a family member or a neighbor. Armstrong had originally received his ensigncy in the Royal Irish when his uncle John was the regiment's colonel.[56] He had shown a similar pattern in the Royal Irish, though on a smaller scale.

Such patronage was not limited to field officers; even junior captains occasionally had a share in the patronage opportunities of the regiment. While a captain, John Peter DeLancey worked hard to find a home for his extended family in the Royal Irish. Before DeLancey left the army, he placed two nephews in the Royal Irish in the 1780s.

The Officers' Biographies

The remaining chapters provide individual biographies of each of the officers who held a commission in the Royal Irish either directly before or during its American service. The men are grouped by the highest rank they attained while the Royal Irish was in North America. Two men who served as volunteers with the Royal Irish but who were not commissioned during its American service are included in the same chapter as the ensigns, but they are not included in the statistical analysis of the officer corps.

In chapter 8, a few men who were closely associated with the regiment during its American service are included: Thomas Hutchins, an American who served as an acting engineer officer in Illinois; Robert Douglas, an officer of the Royal Artillery who served at Fort Chartres, Illinois, with the regiment; and James Rumsey, a former highland officer who served as John Wilkins's secretary in Illinois and tried to purchase a commission in the Royal Irish but was denied by Thomas Gage. The officers of the 65th Foot who have been identified as having served with the Royal Irish in a composite battalion in Boston from November 1774 to June 1775 are also included, but the officers of the 65th Foot who served only briefly with the Royal Irish (from mid-May to late June 1775) are not included.

FIGURE 1.1 Officer's button, 18th (Royal Irish) Regiment, ca. 1775.
Courtesy of Ryan Gale

When officers have been listed as subscribers to books, those titles are mentioned. Unfortunately, none of the officers of the Royal Irish left a comprehensive library list for prosperity. A few officers did note specific books in their wills, and those are generally also mentioned.[57]

There are four officers not included in this volume: the four sergeants of the Royal Irish who earned commissions after leaving America. Their names were Martin Bell, Walter Elliott, Thomas Holland, and William Musgrave. They will be included in a future volume, which will provide the biographies of the men of the Royal Irish who served in America.

2
Field Officers

The officers in this chapter reached field rank in the Royal Irish during its North American service. The term *field officer* derived from the fact that these men were designated to command the regiment "in the field." They were titled colonel, lieutenant colonel, and major, in descending order. One might question why Major Charles Edmonstone is not included in this chapter. His rank of major was only an army rank; within the regiment, he in fact ranked as a captain. Officers, particularly at field grade, often held two ranks, a regimental rank and an army-wide rank. If the officer held an army rank above his regimental rank, he was generally referred to by the higher rank. The best examples in the Royal Irish are John Sanders Sebright, who held army rank as a lieutenant general but was also the regimental colonel; and Charles Edmonstone, who ranked as a captain in the Royal Irish but held an army rank as major. Both men were normally referred to by their higher army rank, even within regimental records. Army rank was a way for the king to honor a long-serving officer or an officer on a specific assignment without otherwise interrupting the purchase system.

Generals held only army rank; they retained the regimental rank of colonel as long as they continued to command a regiment. Occasionally, army rank was limited to a specific location and was then called local rank. For instance, in order for Guy Carleton and William Howe not to be outranked by the generals leading the German Auxiliary troops being sent to America, both were given the local rank of full general in America on 1 January 1776. More than a dozen officers were given local promotions in America in 1776 to major general or higher. Army rank rarely exceeded one step above an officer's regimental rank.[1]

The Royal Irish may have been drafted in 1775 because General Thomas Gage and Lord Barrington had little regard for Major Isaac Hamilton, and Lieutenant Colonel John Wilkins had recently been granted leave and was actively trying to sell his commission. When Major Hamilton resigned, it seemed certain that the Royal Irish would be drafted. These men all experienced more than two decades of military service. All these officers, except Hamilton, served in other regiments beyond the Royal Irish at some point in their careers.

A regiment of foot had three field officers. A single colonel commanded each regiment, and the colonel of the Royal Irish was Major General Sir John Sebright. Colonels had originally served with the regiment and commanded it in the field, but this was generally no longer expected in the British Army. Like nearly all of the regimental colonels in the British Army, Sebright was expected to take a paternal interest in the regiment, but he was not necessarily expected to serve with it. Nearly all regimental colonels were already generals before being appointed as colonels of regiments. In 1767, in addition to being a respected member of British court and social circles, Sebright was the member of Parliament for Bath. He was the only man to serve as colonel during the regiment's North American service.

Below the regiment's colonel were the two other field officers, the lieutenant colonel and the major. Unlike the colonel, these men had almost certainly purchased their commissions through a long career of service with one or more regiments. A few particularly well-connected men could reach field rank in a short time, but the process took most officers nearly two decades of service. Historian John Houlding gives the extreme example of Lord George Lennox, who was the second son of the Duke of Richmond. Lennox was initially commissioned in 1751 at age thirteen and was a lieutenant colonel seven years later, at age twenty. He was awarded the colonelcy of a regiment in 1762. However, Lennox had the advantages of significant influence and money. Most officers took twenty-three to thirty years to reach the rank of lieutenant colonel, according to Houlding's research. The exception was in 1759, when the average lieutenant colonel had only fifteen years of service in regiments of foot.

The reduction in years of service was a direct corollary to the expansion of the army during the Seven Years' War. Generally, it took officers in mounted regiments slightly more time to reach field rank before 1773.

After 1773, officers in mounted regiments were generally promoted more quickly, according to Houlding's study. Alan Guy's research showed that in 1740, it took twenty-seven years for an officer to reach the rank of lieutenant colonel and twenty-six years to reach major; in 1759, it took sixteen and thirteen years, respectively.²

Nearly every regiment was under the de facto command of an officer of one of these two ranks during North American service. While in America, the Royal Irish was commanded by Lieutenant Colonel Wilkins (1767–1772), Major Hamilton (1772–1775), and Captain (later Major) John Shee (1775).

One of the structural issues that contributed to the shortage of officers in British regiments was that each of the field officers was also the commander of a battalion company. The companies commanded by the field officers were generally known as the general's company, the lieutenant colonel's company, and the major's company. Formally, the officers were known as colonel & captain, lieutenant colonel & captain, and major & captain. Rarely were such titles used, however, except in formal military reports. Among other things, company command allowed them access to the additional fiscal incentives available to a frugal company commander, but the custom meant that a regiment in the field was short of at least one company commander even if all the officers were present, since someone had to command the regiment itself. According to Guy, such additional fiscal incentives were significantly curtailed during the reigns of George II and his grandson George III. From 1767 to 1787, not a single return shows all the Royal Irish's officers present.³

Henry Folliott

Henry Folliott (ca. 1733–ca. 1804) was probably the son of Lieutenant John Folliott, who served as colonel of the Royal Irish from 1747 until Sebright's appointment in 1762.⁴ Henry Folliott was first commissioned in the army at age eleven as an ensign in the 61st Regiment of Foot, which had become his father's regiment in June 1743. He is listed as Irish in the returns and was appointed as a second lieutenant in the 61st Foot on 31 October 1745.

Folliott was put on Irish half pay when the regiment was disbanded on 5 December 1748 and transferred from half pay to an ensigncy in the 2nd Battalion of the 1st Foot on 22 April 1749. He was promoted to lieutenant in the Royal Irish, while his father was the colonel, on

24 January 1752. Later that year he was assigned to Major Bigoe Armstrong's company at Waterford. He was assigned to the same company in 1754, but it was then under a lieutenant colonel and was stationed at Derry, Ireland.

Folliott was present in October 1755 when the regiment was inspected in northwest England. He was one of the few lieutenants present, since many of the regiment's officers were out on recruiting duty.[5]

Folliott was a captain lieutenant from 3 April 1759 until he became a captain in the Royal Irish on 4 March 1760. He had the same date of rank as Isaac Hamilton but was ranked ahead of him in the War Office's Army Lists. He became the major of the Royal Irish on 1 January 1766 and married Mary Uniacke in 1766 in Cork while the Royal Irish was stationed in Ireland.[6]

The April 1767 inspection listed Folliott as being absent by leave since 30 March 1767. He did, however, join the regiment before it embarked for America, and he arrived with the Royal Irish at Philadelphia.

Folliott left almost no record that he came to America with the Royal Irish. One letter from Wilkins to Gage, dated 27 July 1767, from the Philadelphia barracks, mentions Folliott. The letter was written less than three weeks after the Royal Irish arrived at Philadelphia. Wilkins wrote that Folliott was on his way to New York City to explain his "unhappy situation & request to return home in a Ship then going from this place with part of the 42nd Regt."[7] The exact nature of the unhappy situation was not explained, since Wilkins thought that Folliott would explain it to the commander in chief in person in New York. Gage must have found Folliott's reasoning sound, since the major was listed as being on leave granted by Gage in the October 1767 muster roll. Lieutenant John Mawby Sr. was commanding the company in Folliott's absence. Wilkins applauded Folliott for coming to America as a "punctilio of Honor" before selling his commission.

The exact family situation that required the major to retire has not been uncovered. It is clear that Folliott had already arranged for Isaac Hamilton to purchase his commission as major while the regiment was still in Dublin, but the price of that sale is not shown in the regimental ledgers, which indicates that the money changed hands before the regiment left for America. Wilkins also noted to Gage that Colonel Sebright had already consented to allow Hamilton to purchase the commission of major before the Royal Irish left for America.

Folliott officially left the army in December 1767. He is listed as a subscriber to Captain John Knox's *Historical Journal of the Campaigns in North America, For the Years, 1757, 1758, 1759, and 1760*.⁸

A "Henry Folliott, Esq." is listed in the List of Prerogative Wills of Ireland as residing at Stephen's Green, Dublin, and passing away in 1804.⁹

Folliott was paid £90 17s. for subsistence from 11 July to 15 December 1767 for the Royal Irish's initial 158 days in America, although he was not present with the regiment during most of that time. His pay for the same period amounted to £19 15s. 3d, and he appears to have still been owed £29 9s. 4¾d. from the regimental agents as late as 1 October 1773.¹⁰

Isaac Hamilton

Isaac Hamilton (ca. 1726–?) entered the army on 9 October 1747 as an ensign in the Royal Irish Regiment. He had gotten a relatively late start on his career, having joined the army when he was already twenty-one years old. In 1752, he was assigned as the ensign of Major General John Folliott's company stationed at Waterford, and he was still in the same company two years later, then stationed at Derry.¹¹ He was promoted to lieutenant on 1 October 1755.

Hamilton arrived in America as the Royal Irish's second senior captain and the commander of the senior battalion company. Before leaving Ireland, he arranged to purchase the commission of major in the Royal Irish from Folliott, who was planning to leave the service after traveling to America. Hamilton had held his captaincy since 4 March 1760, and he and Lieutenant Colonel Wilkins were the oldest officers present (at forty-one years old) when the regiment arrived in America.

Hamilton was formally promoted to major in the Royal Irish Regiment on 16 December 1767, but he still retained command of his old battalion company. John Evans, who replaced Hamilton as a captain, received Major Folliott's company. Hamilton was left in command of the two companies of the Royal Irish that remained in Philadelphia when the other seven companies embarked for Fort Pitt and Fort Chartres. In the spring of 1769, his command at Philadelphia was reduced to one company. He was a subscriber to Stephen Payne Adye's *A Treatise on Courts Martial*, published in 1769.

Hamilton moved to Fort Pitt in 1771 and stayed for almost a year before accompanying the newly raised light infantry company under

Captain Hugh Lord to the Illinois Country in the early spring of 1772. Gage had anticipated that Hamilton would reach Illinois in the summer or fall of 1771.[12]

According to his own affidavit during Lieutenant Alexander Fowler's court-martial, Hamilton found the whole regiment up in arms against Lieutenant Colonel Wilkins when he arrived in Illinois. He took the side of the subordinate officers, although he later believed he had done so unjustly. When Wilkins left for England in May 1772, Hamilton took command of Fort Chartres. Within a short time, he oversaw the destruction of Fort Chartres and the detachment of Captain Lord's men to Kaskaskia. He then took the remaining five companies back up the Ohio River to Fort Pitt. From Fort Pitt, the seven companies of the Royal Irish removed to Philadelphia, where they joined with Hamilton's own company.

In James Wilkinson's *Memoirs of My Own Times*, Hamilton is the first of a list of officers with whom Wilkinson spent time while studying in Philadelphia. Wilkinson stated, "My acquaintance with Major Hamilton . . . was not favourable to my professional studies, but it was extremely grateful to me taste."[13] When the regiment was ordered to march from Philadelphia to Perth Amboy, New Jersey, Hamilton accompanied the regiment. Before the march, Hamilton apparently had a disagreement with Nicolas Trist and possibly others, because Trist remarked that when Hamilton invited him to dinner with other officers, he was surprised. Trist wrote the following to his wife:

> The boy of the Inn came to me with [illegible] Gentlemen's Complts (that is the Major & C) to acquaint one that breakfast was ready, since we have messed together as if nothing had ever happened and not a word of former disputes ever mentioned, this I make no doubt will give you great pleasure and satisfaction.[14]

As Hamilton's time at Philadelphia drew to a close, the sentiment against the Crown was having an effect on his ability to perform his duties. He was sued in civil court by a ship's captain for the loss of a sailor who was apprehended as a deserter from the 46th Foot. The man from the 46th deserted again, and the court found Hamilton liable for £29 in damages to the ship's captain on the second occasion. Hamilton wrote to Gage for advice on whether to appeal, and Gage seems to have been of the opinion that any appeal would be won by Hamilton. It was clear that the populace were not interested in allowing the regiment to perform its duties and apprehend deserters without disruption.[15]

When the majority of the regiment was ordered to New York City, Hamilton went with those five companies, and he remained in direct command of the regiment until his retirement. He appears to have been extremely sick during the winter of 1774–1775 and was unable to function as commander. During this time, Captain Benjamin Charnock Payne was in actual command of the detachment at New York City. Dr. John Linn, under whose care Hamilton recovered, testified via letter at Captain Payne's court-martial that Captain Payne had offered him £100 to poison Hamilton. It is unclear whether that testimony had any merit. It appears that the testimony (attributed to Captain Payne by Ensign Trist) that Hamilton "has grown childish, and a disgrace to the Regiment" had some merit. It was clear that Hamilton was no longer fit for service.[16]

Hamilton moved to Boston with the rest of his depleted companies in early June 1775. He wrote the following memorial to General Gage on 20 July 1775, asking for permission to sell his commission:

> That your Memorialist's Health had for Eight Years past been in a very declining State, and that notwithstanding he had had the joint Advice of the most Skillful Physicians, as well as tried a Variety of the Climates of the American Continent, his Disorder has not only baffled every Effort, but gathers strength as your Memorialist advances in Years, insomuch that his Memory is impaired, and his Constitution enfeebled in the most Alarming degree.
>
> Under such Circumstances, your Memorialist thinks it a duty incumbent upon him to represent his Situation, and at the same time to request your Excellency's Permission to Retire from the Service, which he apprehends he cannot longer remain in with Advantage of Propriety. But must at the same time remark that he feels the deepest Anguish at being necessitated to take a Step of this nature, when his Country in involved in a Civil War with the most Unnatural Rebels.
>
> As your Memorialist purchased his Commission and has faithfully Served his King and Country for the space of 28 Years,

he doubts not your Excellencies goodness will indulge him to the Sale of it—And as Captain Shee is next in Seniority to your Memorialist, and is desirous of Succeeding to the Majority, he begs leave in the Strongest manner to recommend him to your Excellency as an Officer who has Served long and is in every respect worthy of such an Appointment.

From a Consideration of the above Circumstances Your Memorialist is induced to hope your Excellency will not refuse this his earnest Request for which Mark of your goodness he will be ever bound to Pray.[17]

Stephen Conway has implied that Barrington and Gage forced Hamilton out because of his incompetence, but it is more likely that Hamilton's health was the actual cause of his retirement. Hamilton was sick to the point of incapacity during at least a portion of the winter of 1774–1775. However, Barrington had surely lost confidence in Hamilton's ability to command. He wrote to Gage in June 1775, "I hear every day more & More of Major Hamilton's Inability & of the necessity there is of a good Field Officer to command the Royal Irish."[18]

Fowler appears to have held similar beliefs about Hamilton's character. However, he found Hamilton to be more intellectually weak and unable to stand up to the scheming of his brother officers. Fowler wrote the following to Wilkins on 24 October 1774 about Hamilton and Edmonstone, the senior captain of the regiment:

No doubt the Two Majors are two very Contemptible things, & are utterly unfitted by Nature for the Rank they hold—for from their not exerting their Authority Springs all our disquiet. The duty of the regiment is at a Stand as the Major "has now submitted himself entirely to the direction of the Associates, who are great & mighty Men." The Poor fellows Lives are made truly Miserable. They are now so docile that the youngest Ens in the Regt. Rides them at Will.[19]

Hamilton retired on 24 July 1775, selling his commission as major to John Shee. It is certain he was worn out from twenty-eight years of service with the Royal Irish.[20]

John Saunders Sebright

FIGURE 2.1 John Sebright's coat of arms. *Courtesy of Ryan Gale*

John Saunders Sebright (19 October 1723–23 February 1794) was born in Flamstead Parish, Hertfordshire, England. He was the second son of Thomas Saunders Sebright, the fourth baronet (the rank above knight and below baron), and Henrietta Dashwood. His middle name came from his paternal grandmother, Ann Saunders.

Sebright was commissioned in the 1st Regiment of Foot Guards as an ensign on 18 April 1741, at age sixteen. He was promoted to lieutenant and captain in the 1st Foot Guards on 20 February 1743 and was made captain and lieutenant colonel on 2 May 1749.

On 14 October 1758, Sebright was named colonel of the 83rd Foot (Sebright's Invalids).[21] The 83rd was converted to a regiment of the line in 1759.[22] Sebright was promoted to major general on 13 March 1761, and the 83rd was part of an expeditionary force that landed in Lisbon on 6 May 1762. The regiment marched to Coimbra, Portugal, took part at Alvito, and ended the campaign at Protalegre. A company of the 83rd under Captain Thomas Browne fought at the defense of Fort Marvao alongside the Portuguese in November 1762. The 83rd remained in Portugal until February 1763 and then was disbanded in England in April. However, Sebright did not serve with that regiment overseas because he was promoted to the colonelcy of the 18th (Royal Irish) Regiment of Foot before its embarkation, and in April 1762, he was given command of the regiment.[23]

Sebright's association with Bath (as a member of Parliament) appears to have been because of John Ligonier, a lieutenant general of ordnance who represented Bath for some time. Sebright took the place of William Pitt in the March 1761 parliamentary election and wrote to Pitt that the electors were only with great difficulty "persuaded to accept the customary treats," because they understood the exceptional nature of electing William Pitt as the member of Parliament from Bath. When Pitt resigned in October 1761, John Ligonier returned to the seat until he was elevated to a viscount (the rank above baron and below earl) in 1763. Then Sebright offered to stand for election for Bath, with the support of Pitt.

On 28 April 1763, Sebright was elected to Parliament for Bath. His opponent was a local, Walter Long of Wraxall, who received only five votes; Sebright received twenty-two. He served in Parliament from 1763 to 1774, returning unopposed in March 1768. Sebright then lost a contested election on 10 October 1774 against two local men. The year was not without a political victory for Sebright, however, because he had supported William Plumer and Thomas Halsey for election to Parliament in his native Hertfordshire. He was also a member of the social group known as "the Gang," along with Henry Drummond, a banker, army agent, and MP for Midhurst, Sussex. Other members of the Gang were William Amherst, Thomas Bradshaw, Lord Fredrick Campbell, Anthony Chamier, and Thomas Harley.[24]

Sebright returned again to Parliament through a special election on 24 November 1775, when John Smith, his opponent the previous October, died. Sebright again took part in a contested election in 1780, but because of his ill health, he withdrew a week before the election.[25]

Sebright seems to have been a quiet politician and does not appear to have spoken in Parliament. He supported Prime Minister George Grenville (1763–1765). He voted against the repeal of the Stamp Act in 1766, against the Land Tax in 1767, and against the Nullum Tempus Bill, which was designed to protect individuals from dormant claims by the Crown, in 1768. He supported the North ministry (1770–1782) until he left Parliament in 1780, and in April 1780 he opposed a resolution that the influence of the Crown was increasing and should be decreased. Sebright was clearly a strong supporter of King George III and conservative in his political views.

Sebright seems not to have served directly in many military capacities during the Royal Irish's time in America. He was promoted to lieutenant general on 30 April 1770 and to general on 20 November 1782.[26] Sebright served on a court-martial board that convened from 5–9 May 1772 under a special warrant from King George III to try Lieutenant General William Strode, colonel of the 62nd Regiment of Foot, for having wronged his men by withholding portions of their 1769 clothing allowance.[27]

In 1765, upon the death of his older brother, Thomas Sebright, the fifth baronet, John Sebright became the sixth baronet.[28] He married Sarah Knight at Wolverley, Worcestershire, on 15 May 1766.[29] Sebright fathered five children: John Saunders, the seventh baronet (b. 23 May 1767); Thomas Saunders (b. 29 July 1768); Henrietta Saunders (b. 6 May 1770); Edward Amherst (b. 3 October 1771); and Anna Maria Saunders (b. 18 January 1775).

Thomas and Edward followed their father into the army. Thomas purchased a commission as ensign in the Royal Irish on 20 March 1783 and was later promoted to lieutenant in the Royal Irish. He received his captaincy in the 45th Regiment of Foot on 15 May 1790 but transferred back into the Royal Irish on 4 June 1790. Thomas was brevetted—given a higher rank than the commission for which he paid—to major in the army on 3 May 1794 while still serving in the Royal Irish.[30]

Edward purchased a commission in the 7th Regiment of Light Dragoons as a cornet on 21 January 1794. He is a wonderful example of how quickly the British purchase system allowed a young man of means to advance. Edward was appointed lieutenant in the 88th Regiment of Foot on 22 July 1794 and advanced to captain lieutenant of the 24th Regiment of Light Dragoons on 5 August 1794.[31]

John Sebright appears to have been active in court life around London. On 1 August 1783, Sebright received the king's permission to travel to Germany, but the specifics of his trip are not known. He purchased a house from Hugh Hume-Campbell, the Third Earl of Marchmont, on Curzon Street in 1786 and bequeathed a number of early Irish books to Trinity College Dublin in the same year, including *The Yellow Book of Lecan* and *The Book of Leinster*.[32] The books were part of a collection his father originally purchased from the estate of an antiquarian, Edward Lhuyd. The British statesman Edmund Burke, understanding the significance of the books, seems to have urged Sebright to donate them. Today they form part of the core of Trinity College Dublin's Irish manuscript collection. Sebright and his wife were mentioned as frequently attending the king's levees (receptions) and drawing room events. Sebright attended the queen's birthday celebration at least as late as 1792.³³ He died at his home on 23 February 1794.³⁴

John Shee

FIGURE 2.2 John Shee's coat of arms. *Courtesy of Ryan Gale*

John Shee (ca. 1741–1812) was born in Kilkenny County, Ireland, at Ballyreddan³⁵ to Marcus Shee and Anna Mutlow. He was most likely their second son. All contemporary military documents support a birth year of 1741 or 1742, but some later documents give his birth year as 1747. His great-grandfather, Marcus Shee of Wassehays, had been outlawed as a Jacobite (a supporter of King James II and the House of Stuart in preference to King George and the House of Hanover) in April 1691, causing the family to move to Ireland.

John Shee joined the army as an ensign in the Royal Irish on 31 December 1759, when Daniel Holroyd was promoted to lieutenant in the 90th Foot. Shee was promoted to lieutenant in the Royal Irish Foot on 13 February 1762 and received his captaincy on 1 January 1766. He appears to have married Elizabeth Walsh and had a son, John Shee Jr., in 1767. Elizabeth probably accompanied her husband to America; it appears that Shee took at least some of his family to Illinois. Both a Walter and a Bartles Shee are mentioned in Wilkins's court records for 1770. However, neither of those names appears in other lists of John Shee's children. He was present in command of the junior battalion company at the 11 April 1767 inspection at Dublin.³⁶

Shee came to America with the regiment in 1767 and traveled to Illinois via Fort Pitt and the Ohio River in the spring of 1768. While at Fort Pitt, he served on a general court-martial board that tried five deserters from the 34th Foot in July 1768.³⁷ Soon after arriving in Illinois, he took command of the grenadier company upon the death of Captain John Stewart. Shee commanded a detachment at Cahokia, made up of his grenadier company, for some time beginning in 1770. In 1771, he is noted giving presents to more than one hundred Indians as payment for scouting for him. His situation at Cahokia was dangerous. His own men were not allowed to travel through the country except in armed groups of six or more. Indians killed one of his grenadiers, John Knight, in March 1772 while Knight was plowing Shee's personal plantation fields in the company of another soldier.[38]

Shee rose in seniority quickly in the Royal Irish because of the number of officers who died during the regiment's first years in America. This quick rise may have contributed to Fowler's conception that Shee actively conspired to get Wilkins to retire so Shee could ultimately obtain the regiment's majority. Both Fowler and Robert Newburgh wrote to warn Wilkins that Shee and Benjamin Chapman were his true enemies.[39]

Shee and Hamilton led the troops back from Illinois up the Ohio River to Fort Pitt and on to Philadelphia in the summer and fall of 1772. He commanded the regimental parade in August 1773 and may have been the de facto commander of the regiment for much of 1773 and 1774, if Hamilton was as sickly as some records indicate.[40] In 1773, Shee was accused of selling poor-quality goods to his own soldiers at a profit while at Cahokia. The accuser was Nicholas Gaffney, a private of his company who had been promoted to and then demoted from corporal by Shee. Gaffney charged Shee with issuing provisions to the men of his company against their will, notably "stinking Venison and Bears meat," and he also accused him of misconduct in allowing John Knight to be killed by Indians at Cahokia. Shee was found not guilty of Gaffney's charges.

In October 1774, Shee was ordered to Boston in command of two battalion companies and his own grenadier company. In February 1775, his dog was lost, and he ran the following advertisement in the *Boston Gazette*:

> Lost, a blue speckled Bitch, of the Pointer kind, not above six Months old, had on when lost, a brass Collar with Captain Shea's Name, of the Royal Irish. She has long brown Ears and a large round brown Spott on the middle of her back, the rest of her marked as above. Whoever will bring her to the Serjeant Major of the royal Irish, at their Barracks, shall receive Five Shillings Sterling Reward, and no Questions ask'd

N. B. As she has been accustomed entirely to Soldiers, it is hoped she has followed some who will secure her and bring her as directed. Boston, Feb. 10th, 1775.[41]

Shee's name appears to have been misspelled in the advertisement, which might have been a printer's error, or perhaps the soldier who was sent to place the advertisement made the mistake.

Shee served on a court-martial board from 22 March through 1 April 1775 for the trial of Ensign Somerville Murray of the 43rd Foot, who was charged with behaving in a manner unbecoming of an officer and a gentleman.[42]

Shee's grenadier company fought at Lexington and Concord and thus took the regiment's first combat losses (excluding those in Indian battles) in America. Lieutenant George Bruere's petition to the king states that Bruere took command after Shee was wounded, possibly on the return trip near Lexington, but Shee is not listed as a casualty in any of the official returns of casualties. It is probable that he was slightly wounded.[43]

At Bunker Hill, the Royal Irish grenadiers had one-quarter of their men killed or wounded. Captain Shee became Major Shee on 26 July 1775 upon the retirement of Isaac Hamilton. However, he was still listed in contemporary documents as Captain Shee in Boston as late as November 1775. It is questionable exactly when his promotion to major was announced, but the October 1775 muster rolls of the Royal Irish indicate that he was in actual command of the regiment in Boston at that time.

Shee served on the court-martial board for the trial of William Beck of the 43rd Foot on 29 August 1775 at the "Heights of Charlestown." He again served on a court-martial board in Boston from 7 to 13 November 1775 and is listed as a captain in those documents. Included in that duty was the court-martial of Lieutenant Edward McGouran, against whom Captain Payne had brought some of the charges.[44]

Shee returned to England with the cadre of the Royal Irish in early 1776. He was ordered to be the president of a general court-martial for two deserters from the Royal Irish, William Green and Henry Knight, in late 1777 at Dover, but he wrote to the judge advocate asking for another officer to be appointed president because he personally planned to prosecute one of the cases. Both men were found guilty, and Green was executed. Shee seems to have been eager to instill a strong respect for the Articles of War in the new recruits of the regiment now that he was its major. Clearly Green was executed as an example to the regiment, and

Shee appears to have been zealous in prosecuting the case against him. In fact, the judge advocate general's office later questioned Mawby to be sure that some of the evidence presented by Shee—which was hearsay (though certainly true), according to the army's lawyers—was not considered by the board in determining Green's guilt or innocence.[45]

Shee was present at Coxheath Camp in Kent in 1778 and was the field officer of the day for the left wing on 6 July and 4 August 1778 at that encampment. He sat on the court-martial board at Coxheath Camp on 31 August 1778 to try Private Bryan Sheridan of the Royal Irish for desertion; Sheridan was found guilty and was sentenced to be shot to death.[46] Shee was present with the regiment at Warley Camp outside of London in the summer of 1779, and he remained with the Royal Irish until 14 October of that year. At that time he was promoted to lieutenant colonel in the 75th (Prince of Wales's) Regiment of Foot, which had been raised the previous year. The major of the 75th was Hugh Lord, who had served briefly with Shee in Illinois.[47] Shee trained the 75th Foot so well that Lieutenant General William Haviland made the following observation in the 75th's inspection return in 1781:

> The general good appearance of this Corps, the neatness of their dress, the excellent of their Appointments, their steadiness & attention in the Field, are all testimonies of the uncommon care of their Commanding Officer, Lieut. Colonel Shee, who has greatly improved the Regiment since last Review, when I have much satisfaction in doing justice to their merit, by marking a very favorable Report of them.[48]

This is possibly a unique example of an individual being cited positively in a regiment's inspection return.

With the end of the war in America, the army was going to be reduced. Shee transferred to the more senior 50th Foot and then to the 35th Foot on 13 June 1783, when James Cockburne was dishonorably discharged from that regiment. The 35th was stationed in the West Indies until 1786, but it is not clear whether Shee was present with the regiment there. He remained with the 35th until his retirement on 4 April 1789. Lord John Strathhaven replaced him as the 35th Foot's lieutenant colonel.

On 26 November 1797, Shee married his second wife, Honoria O'Conor, the daughter of the chief of the O'Conor clan, at St. Mary's Church in Dublin. The couple appears to have had two daughters, Anne

Elizabeth and Honoria Mary. They may have also had two sons, Marcus and Richard, but these sons might have been from Shee's first marriage. His eldest son, John, entered the army as an ensign in the 35th Foot.⁴⁹

Shee was instrumental in constructing the Bennetsbridge Protestant Church in 1795. His eldest son later helped build a Catholic church in the area. Shee may have also had a house at Highgate, London, in the early 1800s.

Shee probably died in November 1812. A grave marker still extant in 2006 stated that his burial at Bennetsbridge Chapel was in November 1822, but this is undoubtedly a mistake.⁵⁰ A second gravestone marked Elizabeth Shee's interment, and a third gravestone inside the ruins of the church marked the graves of his father and an older brother, James.⁵¹ Shee's ancestral home, Sheestown House, was razed in 1833.

John Wilkins

It is unclear where John Wilkins (ca. 1726–1789) was born, but the army lists him as English in its returns. Three reasonable options for his genealogy exist. The most probable is that he was the son of William and Grace Wilkins on Hurstbourne Tarrant, Hampshire, and christened on 24 August 1725. He may have been the son of John and Elizabeth Wilkins, born 13 December 1726; if so, he was born in Westminster, London. He could also have been born to John and Elizabeth Wilkins of Melksham, Wiltshire, on 26 March 1727.⁵²

According to the biography of William Smith, Wilkins and Smith were schoolmates at Aberdeen. So it appears that Wilkins had some formal schooling for a while.⁵³ He served as a subaltern, quartermaster, paymaster, captain, and major of brigade for more than twenty years, according to his 3 March 1773 letter to Gage, and all of his superiors were pleased with his performance. By the time he wrote to General Gage from Fort Chartres in the Illinois Country of North America, he had purchased seven commissions, including his lieutenant colonelcy for £4,000 including a premium.⁵⁴

Wilkins joined the army on 21 May 1746 as a second lieutenant in the 32nd Foot. He was appointed as quartermaster of the 32nd Foot on 19 November 1748 and remained in that role while also an ensign until 18 May 1753. He was appointed adjutant of the 32nd Foot on 16 June 1753 and retained that role until he left the 32nd Foot. He was promoted to lieutenant in the 32nd Foot on 29 October 1754.⁵⁵

Wilkins purchased a captaincy in the newly raised 55th Foot on 30 November 1755, then went to America with the regiment and participated in campaigns against the French. His vision appears to have suffered from a head wound received at Fort Ticonderoga in 1758. Wilkins was transferred to the 1st Battalion of the 60th Foot and promoted to major on 9 June 1762. In his own words, he was "mostly on severe service even in time of peace."[56]

Wilkins took command of Forts Niagara and Schlosser in 1763, immediately before Pontiac's Rebellion began. Major Henry Gladwin, commanding at Detroit, sent word to him in May about the uprising and asked him to warn the other frontier forts about the possibility of Indian attacks. In July 1763, when Captain James Dalyell and Major Robert Rogers arrived at Niagara with troops from eastern New York, including some from the 55th and 60th Regiments, Wilkins reluctantly gave Dalyell two companies of the 80th Regiment from Wilkins's garrison at Fort Niagara to reinforce his command, which was to embark to relieve Detroit. However, Dalyell's troops met heavy resistance, and he was forced back to Fort Schlosser.

A second relief attempt by water resulted in the death of seventy men in severe weather. On 14 September 1763, Wilkins led a relief force to the Devil's Hole from Niagara to avenge the Indian ambush near that site that killed nearly 112 men. In October, he was ordered by General Jeffery Amherst to take the majority of his troops to reinforce Detroit.[57]

Wilkins had already been formally reduced to half pay on 24 August 1763, but he transferred from half pay back to being major of the 1st Battalion of the 60th (Royal American) Regiment of Foot upon the retirement of Herbert Munster of that regiment on 15 August 1764.[58]

Wilkins purchased the lieutenant colonelcy of the Royal Irish in June 1765 for £4,000 and returned to Ireland to command the regiment. It is unclear what circumstances allowed Wilkins to purchase a lieutenant colonelcy so shortly after having become a major. He was present with the Royal Irish at Dublin when it was inspected in April 1767.

Wilkins embarked with the Royal Irish in May 1767 from Cork Harbor and landed with the regiment at Philadelphia on 11 July 1767. While in Philadelphia, he appears to have appointed William Smith, his former childhood acquaintance, as the regiment's deputy chaplain. His trip out to Fort Chartres in the spring of 1768 was a difficult one. The journey from Philadelphia to Fort Pitt was marred by the colonial teamsters demanding high wages, which Wilkins would not pay. They struck, and Wilkins charged them for their provisions, deducting the subsistence costs from their pay. The teamsters eventually sued Wilkins for back pay in the Pennsylvania courts.

Wilkins had left two companies of the Royal Irish under Major Hamilton at Philadelphia and then set off to Fort Pitt with seven companies. While at Fort Pitt, Wilkins served as president of a general court-martial board that tried five soldiers of the 34th Foot for desertion and other crimes in July 1768.[59] At Fort Pitt, Captain Charles Edmonstone was left in command of two companies while Wilkins and the remaining five companies went down the Ohio River to Fort Chartres in the Illinois Country. Wilkins arrived at Fort Chartres on 5 September 1768, and his force relieved four companies of the 34th Foot. The detachment of the 34th Foot left within days of Wilkins's arrival for a long return trip to Philadelphia.

Wilkins issued a proclamation on 21 November 1768, establishing a court of justice in Illinois "for settling all disputes and controversies between man and man, and all claims in relation to property both real and personal." Gage had written to Barrington on 15 May 1768, asking for permission to erect civil courts and to appoint Wilkins as the civil governor. Gage reminded Barrington that Wilkins "is a Discreet and Intelligent Officer of such a one has been long wanted in that Country [Illinois]."[60]

The court consisted of seven justices to provide civil justice in the Illinois Country. The first session was held on 6 December 1768, and sessions were held monthly thereafter. The civilian populace was unhappy with the fact that the court did not allow for a trial by jury, but it was an improvement over martial law and trials by military tribunals, which had been in place until Wilkins's arrival. Wilkins appointed his friend George Morgan as the president of the court. However, as he and Morgan grew estranged, the situation in Illinois became one of two rival camps. George Buttricke wrote that he found it difficult to deal with the antagonism of the two groups, both of which he felt were at fault for the situation.[61] The court was marred by intrigue, and Wilkins appears to have been doing everything but overtly selling civil judgments.

Wilkins extended the court's power to criminal cases on 4 March 1770. In July 1770, when Joseph Chauvin Charleville, a French resident of Kaskaskia, presented a petition of protest against Wilkins's rule to Ensign William Conolly at Kaskaskia, Wilkins had the man confined for attacking his character. Wilkins disbanded the court on 6 June 1771. He does not appear to have handled his role as civil governor particularly well.[62]

Wilkins also used his influence to try to obtain judgments in the favor of Baynton, Wharton, and Morgan, a colonial trading firm. He had concluded an agreement with the firm that promised him 5 percent of its profits from the Illinois trade, which was to be protected and encouraged by the officers and soldiers of the Royal Irish. Wilkins was to receive a bounty that contemporary sources valued between £1,000 to £2,500, but he appears to have been paid only £500 of that amount because of the meager earnings of the firm. According to Theodore Pease, this was because Wharton and Morgan determined that it was unethical to pay Wilkins for doing what was effectively his duty: supporting British traders over French and Spanish traders.

Wilkins retaliated by removing Morgan's friends from his court, and he ultimately imprisoned Morgan at Fort Chartres. Morgan escaped to New York and eventually told both his story and the stories of the frustrated officers serving in Illinois to General Gage. Wilkins's constitution was impaired by the ills of the Illinois Country to the point where he borrowed to insure his life for the greater part of the cost of his lieutenant colonelcy, £4,000.[63]

Wilkins appears to have made land grants on 12 April 1769 to several of his friends for the "better settlement of the colony" in which he was thought to have been a silent partner for a one-sixth interest. Henry Brown commented that many later landholders, including John Edgar and John Murray St. Clair, purchased their large holdings in the region through the titles confirmed by Wilkins while he was military governor.[64] It is possible that Lieutenant Fowler received some of his lands through Wilkins's largess; that would explain Fowler's continued loyalty to Wilkins while nearly all of the rest of the officers of the regiment were unhappy with Wilkins.

On 19 April 1769, Wilkins ordered a premium on the scalp of any Indian seen near Fort Chartres after sunset. This offer was in direct response to the intrusion of Kickapoo from the Wabash region. According to Buttricke, on 16 April the Kickapoo had surprised a soldier and his wife in bed and scalped both of them. On 14 May, the Sauk and Fox raided the area near the fort and killed six Kaskaskia Indians who were living in a fortified village erected with the help of the garrison. Wilkins now had five to six hundred Indians gathered for protection from their enemies; he was obliged not only to protect them but also to provide powder, lead, vermillion, and rum. According to Buttricke,

> [Wilkins] very prudently filled all the stores with provisions and sent an Officer with the arm'd Boat to get in a quantity of Wood

which was happily effected in a very short time and now we have 280 cords piled up under the Walls of the Fort and we can now bid defiance to all the Indians in America.[65]

For the next several years, Wilkins had to contend with the difficult task of Indian negotiations while still trying to maintain British sovereignty despite the intrigues of the French and Spanish. In a cost-saving move at about the same time the Royal Irish arrived at Fort Chartres, the British Crown eliminated the Indian Department staff of a commissary, gunsmith, interpreter, and doctor at the post, leaving the task of maintaining positive Indian relationships to Wilkins and his officers. None of the officers present at Fort Chartres in the fall of 1768 had any experience maintaining relationships with the native peoples. Wilkins became the de facto Indian agent in the Illinois Country. Wilkins kept a journal of his dealings with the Indians while in Illinois, as did at least one of his subordinates, William Conolly. Their journals show that they gave presents to a wide range of Indians. In many cases, Wilkins provides his opinion of the Indian in question, as with the Shawnee Chief Corn Cob, whom he considered a "Man of great Consequence"; or a Kaskaskia chief, of whom he wrote, "I believe like most Savages very deceitfull [sic]." The tribes most frequently listed in his journal are the Kaskaskia, Michigamea, and Peoria. It does appear that Wilkins often conferred directly with Sir William Johnson, Superintendent for Indian Affairs, and not through Gage, when dealing with Indian issues. Included among the documents sent to Johnson were speeches given by Indians to Wilkins, which in the late summer of 1769 appear to show that the Indians were still unhappy that the English had replaced their beloved French in the Illinois Country.[66] It appears that Wilkins became a better Indian agent over time. Presents were key to Indian diplomacy, and the Indians who visited Fort Chartres were given more than £2,000 in gifts and services between April and October 1769. Presents were drastically reduced in the following years to save money. Wilkins spent only about £215 on the Indian Department between February 1771 and February 1772.[67]

Wilkins also had to protect the primarily French inhabitants of the Illinois Country. In May 1770, three white men were killed by "disguised" Indians at Cahokia, a village north of the fort. Wilkins sent Captain Shee and the grenadier company to investigate the murders. In the end, the Spanish commander at St. Louis was able to determine that the murders were the work of Pontiac's brother.⁶⁸ Pontiac (1720–20 April 1769) was a chief of the Ottawa tribe. His struggle against British rule (1763–1766) is known as Pontiac's Rebellion. He lived in the Illinois Country from 1768 until his death.

Wilkins issued a proclamation in December 1771 as a result of the discordant nature of the inhabitants of the Illinois Country and in order to reduce the number of lawsuits coming before the courts. Wilkins ordered that all future agreements between the inhabitants be executed before magistrates that each of the three districts in Illinois would appoint from among "the most respectable Inhabitants." The commander of the militia in each district would serve as the third officer in each district. Agreements were to be in writing, and Wilkins would set an example. He had ordered all Crown accounts to be settled only by written order as early as 3 August 1770.⁶⁹

In Wilkins's 10 January 1772 letter to Gage, he told the general that he wished to resign but that he was concerned about his ability to sell his commission without a premium and at a loss of £500. He found the charges of corruption that Ensign Thomas Hutchins of the 2nd Battalion of the 60th Regiment leveled against him to be fraudulent and ungrounded. Wilkins left Fort Chartres in May 1772 and traveled down the Mississippi River to New Orleans with Quartermaster Buttricke and half of his own company on his way to New York. He and Buttricke continued to Pensacola, Florida, and then to London.

Wilkins's excuse for not returning to New York was that he had given his berth on the ship to a lady in distress who needed to return to New York. He then got on the next ship, which just happened to be bound for London. Most likely Wilkins thought that he would be tried in London at the king's bench and wanted to present his side of the situation before Gage sent the accusations to London. He may have had some personal business in London as well.

Both Gage and Sebright appear to have blocked Wilkins's ability to sell his commission while the accusations by Hutchins and others remained unresolved. Gage did so by holding him liable for more than £1,500 in unpaid commissary notes from Illinois and for some of the expenses for public works that were raised by Hutchins. All the regiment's officers who were present in Philadelphia in April 1773 signed a memorial to Sebright and Gage asking them to bring Wilkins before a general court-martial to face Hutchins's charges and defend the honor of the regiment. Fowler later wrote that he should not have signed the petition and that the majors did so only under severe pressure from Chapman and Shee. Wilkins later sent extracts from several documents that seemed to denote a formal "ending of hostilities" between him and various officers, such as the following one from 1 April 1773:

> We, Cpt. Shee, Cpt. John Evans, Ens. Thomas Hutchins, & Ens. Wm. Blackwood, Wm Conolly do in Consequence of Lt. Col. Wilkins desire of brings Matters to an Accommodation which desire he Expressed to Lieut Chapman Most Sincerely & Solemnly forgive and forget every Transaction whether of a private or Publick Nature, that many have ever happen'd either in respect of Duty or Otherwise, betwixt us & the said Lt. Col Wilkins and we herby exchange a Mutual obligation of Burying every Circumstance in Oblivion & do declare that we shall ever be happy to live upon the best of terms with Col. Wilkins both as an Officer and a Gentleman.[70]

Wilkins appears to have had several fallings-out with his subordinates. Hamilton wrote to Gage on behalf of the officers of the Royal Irish in February 1775 that they no longer felt the need to review Wilkins's conduct, in part because the evidence was so dispersed between Illinois and West Florida, among other places. In December 1774, Gage had pushed the officers to either drop their insistence for a court-martial or level specific charges. In the end, nothing came of the charges except to provide a significant taint on Wilkins's career as an administrator. Barrington authorized Wilkins to begin a six-month leave of absence in February 1775. Gage recommended to Barrington to unbar Wilkins from selling his commission in June 1775.[71]

Wilkins had tried to transfer into half pay with Lieutenant Colonel Thomas Oswald of the 103rd Regiment of Foot in 1774, but Sebright blocked that exchange by saying that "no stranger shall come into the Regiment." Wilkins was involved in a civil suit in July 1774 in London.[72] He finally sold his commission after much difficulty on 7 December 1775, to Adam Williamson of the 61st Regiment.[73]

On 28 February 1776, Wilkins petitioned the Lords of the Treasury to reimburse him for expenses incurred, £112, while serving as governor and chief magistrate in the Illinois Country One of the difficulties in obtaining his money was that Lieutenant Hutchins, the engineer at Fort Chartres, stated that £105 was incurred for Wilkins's private use. Wilkins, however, produced vouchers for the whole amount, many signed by Hutchins, according to a copy of a supportive letter from General Gage dated 11 February 1776. Gage also wrote that Captain Thomas Sowers of the engineers, Hutchins's supervisor in America, had approved all the expenses. This letter seems to entirely absolve Wilkins of Hutchins's charges. The resolution of Wilkins's petition is not clear from existing records. Wilkins addressed his letter from Butlers Gardens in Chelsea.[74]

Wilkins drafted a will that was proved at London on 1 April 1789. It was fairly complicated. He owned thirteen houses on Bull and Mouth Streets in London, which were leased for thirty-nine years in 1787. He also had a house in Chelsea, where he appears to have been living and which he left to his wife, including all the furnishings. The will mentions four children: John, Charles, George, and Sophia. Wilkins left enough money for two of his sons to purchase colours, join the army as ensigns, and be promoted to lieutenancies and companies (captains). Wilkins's copy of the 1776 army list is extant in the Fort Ticonderoga library. Wilkins was also a subscriber to Charles Churchill's *Poems by C. Churchill*, volume 2, published in 1768.[75]

Adam Williamson

Adam Williamson (1736–21 October 1798) was the son of Lieutenant General George Williamson, who commanded the artillery during the siege of Louisburg, Canada.[76] Adam became a cadet gunner on 1 January 1748, and entered the Royal Military Academy at Woolwich in 1750. He was appointed practitioner-engineer on 1 January 1753 and went to North America with Braddock in 1754, where he was the engineer officer on an ill-fated expedition against the French. He was wounded at Du Quesne on 9 July 1754 and was commissioned as an ensign in the 6th Foot on 14 October 1755 while still serving in North America as an engineer. Williamson was promoted to lieutenant in the 5th Foot on 25 September 1757 and to captain lieutenant and engineer extraordinary on 4 January 1758. He served at Montreal and was wounded a second time at the siege of Quebec in 1759. In 1760, he was promoted to captain in the 40th Foot. He accompanied his father back to England the next year.

Williamson returned to North America in 1761 and participated in the capture of Martinique and Guadeloupe in the West Indies in 1762. He went back to England in 1763 and was promoted to major in the 16th Foot on 16 August 1770. Later that year, 4 December, he was promoted to engineer in ordinary. He was transferred to the 61st Foot on 12 September 1775 and purchased the lieutenant colonelcy of the Royal Irish from John Wilkins on 8 December 1775. He appears to have joined his regiment at Dover in 1776. The *Dictionary of National Biography* recalled Williamson's participation in the Battle of Bunker Hill, but primary sources do not support that claim. Valentine stated that Williamson was in America as lieutenant colonel and colonel from 1775 to 1782, but there is no primary source support of that claim, either. The Royal Irish returns from 1776 to 1780 generally show Williamson present with his regiment in southern England.

In 1778, Williamson was present at Coxheath Camp and served as field officer of the day for the left wing on 23 June and 7 July 1778.[77] He was appointed deputy adjutant general of the forces in south Britain later in 1778, and in that role, he was involved in preparing for the threat of a Franco-Spanish invasion of England during 1778 and 1779. He was also involved in organizing the troop dispositions related to the London's Gordon Riots in 1780 but was not directly in command of the Royal Irish during that time. Williamson was promoted to colonel in the army on 15 February 1782, was promoted to major general on 1 May 1790, along with fifteen other colonels, and received the colonelcy of the 47th Foot on 16 July 1790. At that time, he officially left the Royal Irish and Chapman was promoted in his place as lieutenant colonel.

Williamson was given the honor of kissing the king's hand at a levee in July 1790 because of his promotion to colonel of the 47th Foot.[78] He was sent to Jamaica as lieutenant governor and commander in chief and was acting governor by the end of 1791. When the hostilities with France again commenced, a deputation of citizens of Santo Domingo approached him in Jamaica and entreated him to invade their island. Williamson sent the 13th Regiment of Foot and the 49th Foot's flank companies to capture the island, which he established as a British protectorate in September 1793. He was appointed governor of Santo Domingo in October 1794. Williamson had been transferred to the colonelcy of the 72nd Highland Regiment on 19 March 1794 and was made a knight of the Order of the Bath on 18 November 1794. He was promoted to lieutenant general on 26 January 1797.[79]

Williamson appears to have been a supporter of literature and the arts in his final years. He was a member of the Society for the Encouragement of Arts, Manufactures, and Commerce from at least 1790 until his death.[80]

He subscribed to *Woodland Cottage*, an anonymous novel published in London in 1796, as well as to Joseph Wildman's *The Force of Prejudice: A Moral Tale*, which was published in 1799.[81] His niece, Priscilla Belford, married Christopher Carleton, later Lord Dorchester, in August 1791.[82] Williamson returned from the West Indies in 1798 to his home in Wiltshire, his health shattered and his personal fortune spent. He died on 21 October 1798 at his home in Avesbury House, Wiltshire, as the result of a fall.[83]

3
Captains and Captain Lieutenants

From 1767 through 1770, the Royal Irish had six captains commanding companies in addition to the three field officers; one of the six commanded the grenadier company, and the other five commanded battalion companies. A seventh captain was added in 1770 when a tenth company was authorized.

Captain was the rank at which officers started to be able to live on their pay in a manner considered suitable for a gentleman. They received additional income as company commanders and often received even more compensation when commanding a garrison without a field officer.

Because of the limited number of field officers in a regiment, captains often commanded multiple company detachments; this was true in the Royal Irish as well. Captain Charles Edmonstone commanded two companies at Fort Pitt from 1768 to 1772. Captain John Shee commanded three companies at Boston from 1774 to 1775, and Captain Hugh Lord commanded two companies in Illinois from 1772 to 1776 and multiple companies—including some from the 8th (King's) Regiment at Detroit—in 1776. Captain Benjamin Charnock Payne appears to have been in actual command at New York during the winter of 1774–1775 because of the poor health of both Isaac Hamilton and Edmonstone.

The captain lieutenant was really the regiment's senior lieutenant, but beginning on 25 May 1772, that officer ranked as the junior captain. His new title in 1772 was officially captain lieutenant & captain. This officer replaced the lieutenant of the colonel's company, and since the colonel was always absent from the company and nearly always absent from the regiment, the captain lieutenant was the company's de facto commander. John Mawby Sr. was the captain lieutenant of the Royal Irish when that change was made. One of the oddities of this rank was that it could be skipped over in an officer's career advancement, so one could purchase a commission as captain directly from the rank of lieutenant. Thus, since Mawby was unable or unwilling to purchase vacant captaincies, Robert Hamilton and others were able to bypass the captain lieutenancy. Returns show that about one-third of superior officers served in this role at some point in their careers.

Hugh Antrobus

Hugh Antrobus (ca. 1732–1 July 1767)[1] was the second son of Reverend John and Rebecca Leeson Antrobus and one of five children.[2] Reverend Antrobus was the rector of St. Michan's Dublin until his death in 1761. Hugh's older brother, George, followed his father into the ministry. Hugh joined the army as an ensign in the 14th Foot on 27 March 1753, at age nineteen or twenty.[3] However, the 1767 inspection return for the Royal Irish lists him as having fourteen years of military service as of 11 April 1767.

Antrobus obtained his lieutenancy in the Royal Irish on 2 October 1755 while the regiment was quartered at Ballyshannon and Derry in Ireland.[4] The Royal Irish was expanded in late 1755 in response to the Seven Years' War. Antrobus remained a lieutenant for four and a half years before advancing to the rank of captain lieutenant on 6 May 1760, and he was promoted to captain on 13 February 1762.

Antrobus never reached North America. In fact, he was the first casualty of the Royal Irish Regiment's American service. He died at sea on board the transport *Liberty* on 1 July 1767, ten days before the regiment reached Philadelphia. There is no indication of his cause of death. He was the only recorded member of the regiment to die on its voyage to America.

Antrobus was approximately thirty-five years old at his death, and he had commanded one of the regiment's eight battalion companies up to that time. His captaincy went to Benjamin Johnson.[5] The *Gentleman's Magazine* for October 1767 reported his demise and his replacement.

Antrobus left two sons, John and Hugh Jr. His wife may have preceded him in death, because his sister Elizabeth administered his estate in the Prerogative Court of Dublin in 1768. Hugh, his second son, also joined the British Army, rising to the rank of lieutenant colonel in the 26th (Cameronians) Regiment of Foot before his death in 1813.[6]

The only notation in the Cox & Meir papers for Antrobus was an entry to the Irish Treasury for sixty-eight days of subsistence from 11 July to 16 September 1767, at £7 16s. Irish per day. A balance of £17 14s. was left on the ledger.[7]

Thomas Batt (ca. 1743–15 July 1781) is listed as Irish in military records. His surname is also sometimes given as Bat or Batte. He was most likely the son of Captain Robert Batt, who served before him in the Royal Irish.[8] Thomas Batt joined the Royal Irish as an ensign on 26 May 1762, while the regiment was stationed in Ireland. When Batt came to America with the Royal Irish in 1767, he was the regiment's senior ensign. He was assigned along with Captain Edmonstone and Lieutenant William Smith to escort a number of recruits from the 34th Regiment of Foot to Fort Pitt in western Pennsylvania soon after arriving at Philadelphia. The detachment left Philadelphia on 26 August 1767, according to Sergeant Edmond Sutton, who was under Batt's direct command on that detail.[9] Batt was promoted to lieutenant on 16 December 1767.

Batt must have returned to Philadelphia by the early spring of 1768, because he was ordered to command a party of thirty-five men to Fort Pitt from Philadelphia in March 1768. This party was to provide some protection to Colonel George Croghan, an Indian agent, against a group of "lawless men" called the Black Boys, formed by James Smith. Batt was apparently supposed to meet up with Croghan at Lancaster, Pennsylvania. A few years earlier, in March 1765, the Black Boys had destroyed some traders' goods at Fort Loudon, Pennsylvania. They appear to have been menacing Croghan in the spring of 1768, according to a partial letter from Samuel Wharton to Sir William Johnson.[10]

While in the backwoods of Pennsylvania, Batt had some time to search for deserters and sit on courts-martial. He was one of the junior members of the court-martial board that convicted several soldiers of the Royal Irish and the 34th Regiment of desertion and theft in July 1768, immediately before the Royal Irish's journey down the Ohio River to Illinois. Batt remained at Fort Pitt as the lieutenant of Captain Benjamin Johnson's company from July 1768 to June 1771. Since Johnson does not appear to have been present, Batt was in command of the company.[11] Batt was a subscriber to Stephen Payne Adye's *A Treatise on Courts Martial*, published in 1769.

Batt married Catherine McCall of Philadelphia on 10 January 1771 at Christ Church, Philadelphia.[12] On 3 June 1771, he became a captain in the Royal Irish, ranking exactly one day behind Benjamin Chapman. By April 1772, Batt was commanding the 4th Battalion company stationed at Philadelphia. When the majority of the regiment returned to Philadelphia, there was some strife among the officers. Court-martial returns show that a dispute had arisen between Batt and the Robert Newburgh, and it was significant enough that the regiment's enlisted tailors knew of it. As a result of the rising disagreements within the regiment and because of his need to support his growing family, Batt sold his captaincy on 21 January 1773 to Robert Hamilton.[13]

Batt did not return to Ireland but took the proceeds from the sale of his commission, along with Catherine's dowry of £1,600, and entered business as a wine merchant in Philadelphia. When Batt later left for active service, Catherine remained in Philadelphia and managed the wine business until she could no longer collect on her debts. She then moved her children to Trenton, New Jersey, until the British took Philadelphia. She returned to Philadelphia in 1777 but evacuated it with Howe's army in 1778 and moved to New York.

Batt appears to have been quickly embraced by his fellow merchants and was elected a member of the Society of the Friendly Sons of St. Patrick on 17 September 1773. According to the history of the society, he was "for some time vice-president of the society" and a "man of highly respectable character." However, his attachment to the "Tory party" at the commencement of the Revolution caused the society to vote to expel him at Philadelphia's City Tavern on 18 December 1775, for his "active part again the liberties of America." The vote was postponed "in order for more deliberate consideration" until the 11 March 1776 meeting of the society at Smith's Tavern, when Batt was unanimously expelled from the society.[14]

Batt traveled to New York City in August 1774 to testify at the court-martial of Reverend Newburgh. According to letters written by Lieutenant Alexander Fowler, Batt had a significant hatred of Newburgh, and since the court-martial against Newburgh was not successful, Batt began to focus his wrath on Fowler. Fowler wrote the following on the subject:

> He [Batt] views Lieutenant Fowler as the parson's advisor and savior, and transfers his malice from the latter to the former; and as he had missed the wicked blow he aimed at the Rev. Mr. Newburgh, he was determined to make sure work with that of his friend. He whispers at Head Quarters, and swears, when swearing will have effect, that Lieutenant Fowler was as violent a Whig as Adams and as damn'd a rebel as Lee.[15]

When the rebellion began in 1775, Batt was with his family in Philadelphia. Catherine Batt reported the following in her memorial to the Lords of the Treasury:

> That upon the breaking out of the Rebellion he bought a Vessel, loaded it with wine and other kind of Necessaries to the amount of Two Thousand pounds Sterling and went therewith to Boston to the Relief of the Garrison at that time in the Greatest distress under the Command of General GAGE, having had Several Letters from Officers there, requesting him to Come to their Assistance.
>
> That the Greater part of this Cargo together with the Ship were Entirely lost.
>
> That the Rebels were so Exasperated at his Succouring the British Troops that it was unsafe for him to think of returning to his wife and Family and his Attachment to the Royal Cause so Strong that he Chearfully accepted a Company in the Royal American Fencibles, which was given to him by General GAGE as a reward for his Loyalty and Military skill.[16]

Thomas Gage initially appointed Batt as the adjutant of the light infantry battalion on 15 May 1775, but he was replaced within days.[17] Apparently, since Batt was no longer a serving officer, some officers thought that he was not an appropriate choice for adjutant, so he was shortly replaced by an officer holding a current commission.

Fowler gave a different reason for Batt's arrival in Boston. He claimed that Newburgh had a "civil prosecution commenced against him" and that Batt journeyed to Boston to escape the civil jurisdiction and stay in a place under military rule.[18]

Batt was shortly thereafter commissioned as the senior captain of the Royal Fencible Americans upon its raising. It was to be a light infantry corps along the lines of Gage's 80th Light Armed Regiment from the French and Indian War.[19] His captaincy in the Fencibles was dated from 5 June 1775.[20]

Batt traveled to Nova Scotia to recruit, and he raised his company at his own expense, according to his wife's later memorial. He remained in garrison at Halifax for the majority of the war. On 23 May 1776, upon Major Thomas Moncrieff's resignation from the Royal Fencible Americans, Batt was promoted to major in that regiment. However, because of the low number of men in the regiment at the time, his captaincy was not filled and remained open through at least November 1777.[21] He is listed as donating ten shillings for the relief of orphans of British soldiers in 1776 in Major Robert Donkin's text, *Military Collections and Remarks*.[22]

Major General Eyre Massey sent Batt, with approximately two hundred men, to Fort Cumberland (also in Nova Scotia) from Halifax on HMS *Vulture*, which landed in the vicinity on 28 November 1777. The American commander described the sortie to raise the siege under Batt's command in the following words:

> The enemy to the number of 200, came out in the night, by a round about march; got partly within our guards, notwithstanding we had scouts out all night, and about sunrise furiously rushed upon the barracks where our men were quartered, who had but just time enough to escape out of the houses and run into the bushes.[23]

Batt's report to Lieutenant Colonel Joseph Gorham described the actions of his command, which included a detachment of the Royal Fencible Americans and British Marines to sortie out of Fort Cumberland and raise the siege by Jonathan Eddy's colonials on 29 November 1776.[24] The report was reprinted in the *Royal American Gazette* of New York on 16 January 1777.

Catherine then traveled with her two sons to Halifax and remained there until May 1780, when Batt sent them to Ireland for safety.[25] He remained in Nova Scotia in command of Fort Cumberland. There appears to have been at least some consideration of giving Batt command of the Nova Scotia Volunteers. However, Lieutenant Colonel John Bayard of the King's Orange Rangers wrote to Sir Henry Clinton, commander in chief in North America, complaining loudly that such a promotion would be a personal affront to Bayard. Batt was not given the command and remained with the Royal Fencible Americans.[26]

There seems to have been some dispute between Gorham, who commanded the Fencibles, and Batt. It is unclear how it arose, but Gorham pressed the following charges against Batt:

> 1st Article—
>
> For ungentleman and unsoldierlike behaviour in exhibiting several false Groundless, and Scandelous Informations Contained in a

letter, dated 10th July 1777 to Lieut. Col. PATTERSON Adjutant General, against Lieut. Colonel GOREHAM, highly Prejudicial, to his Character and to His Majestys Service.

2d Article—

For renewing, and Publishing, at Fort Cumberland in hand bills and otherwise in the Garrison and among the Inhabitants, some of those Articles of Complaint, which he had before Exhibited, against Lieut. Colonel GOREHAM, and for which he had been tryed, and honorably acquitted, and thereby, disobeying General Orders.

3d Article—

For repeatedly acting unbecoming the Character of an Officer, and a Gentleman, and using Expressions tending to Excite Mutiny, and Sedition in the Garrison.[27]

The exact outcome of the difficulties between the two officers is unclear, but it appears to have resulted from the efforts of Brigadier General Francis McLean.

James Brace replaced Batt as major of the Royal Fencible Americans on 29 June 1781, and Batt died on 15 July at Fort Cumberland, Nova Scotia.[28] Catherine Batt is listed among the refugee Loyalist widows at New York on 25 November 1783.[29] She eventually returned to Philadelphia, where she died, and she was buried at Christ Church on 10 November 1793.[30] Catherine, listed as Kitty in the burial records, most likely died of yellow fever, since her death occurred during a violent outbreak of that disease in Philadelphia.

A son, Thomas Batt Jr., was born on 9 October 1771 and baptized on 26 January 1772 at Christ Church, Philadelphia. The "son of the late major of the regiment" was listed as a "gentleman" born in America, serving as an ensign in the Royal Fencible Americans for two years. He would have been only twelve years old at the end of the war, which means he would have been commissioned an ensign at age ten. No other information is available on Batt's children.[31]

William Blackwood

William Blackwood (ca. 1750–1794) came to America while the ink was still wet on the commission that he had received on 4 March 1767. He was present at Dublin with the regiment when it was inspected on 11 April 1767, and he was listed as being eighteen years old and Irish in the general return of officers included in that inspection.³² He served with Captain John Stewart's battalion company when the regiment arrived in America on 11 July 1767, and he was assigned to Lieutenant Colonel John Wilkins's company by October 1768, shortly after he arrived at Fort Chartres, Illinois.

Blackwood was promoted to lieutenant on 26 December 1770. At that time, Blackwood was assigned to be the lieutenant of Captain George Stainforth's company, still stationed at Fort Chartres. He was transferred to Captain Chapman's company on 24 April 1771 and was assigned to the grenadier company as the junior lieutenant by April 1772.³³

Blackwood returned to Philadelphia with the majority of the regiment in the summer of 1772. He remained in Philadelphia until ordered to Boston in October 1774 with the grenadier company and two battalion companies under the command of Captain Shee.

Fowler seems to have had a low opinion of Blackwood; he referred to him as a "perfect negative." Blackwood was also involved in a dispute with Wilkins, which led to a written appeal to Wilkins in 1770 to put all their disagreements behind them. The nature of the disagreement remains unclear.³⁴

Blackwood remained with the grenadiers until 16 April 1775, when he was ordered to do duty with Captain George Sinclair's light infantry company of the 65th Foot. This seems to have been done because the 65th was short of qualified flank company officers. Blackwood appears to have remained with the light company of the 65th through the Battles of Lexington and Concord, so he would have participated in searching Concord for hidden arms and the destruction of the cannon and ammunition found there. He might have remained attached to the 65th's light company through the Battle of Bunker Hill, but that is not clear from the extant records.

According to the Royal Irish's returns, Blackwood was transferred to Robert Hamilton's company on 21 April 1775. That might have been done retroactively, however. The extant orderly book does not show Blackwood returning to the grenadiers before its ending on 5 June 1775.³⁵ He was officially promoted to captain on 26 July 1775, taking Captain Shee's commission, but he did not seem to have learned of his promotion until at least after November 1775. From 16 to 29 November 1775, Blackwood, still listed as a lieutenant, served on the court-martial board for Thomas Bailey of the Marines, who was charged with insolent and mutinous conduct and striking an officer; for Richard James of the 10th Foot, for breaking and entering and quitting his sentry post; and for Lieutenant William Hamilton of the 63rd Foot for scandalous conduct.[36]

Blackwood returned with the cadre of the regiment to England, arriving in February 1776, and he was given command of one of the battalion companies at that time. He was present with the regiment when it was inspected at Dover Castle on 15 May 1777 by Major General George Lane Park, and he was present on a general court-martial board at Dover in November 1777 that tried William Green and Henry Knight for desertion. Blackwood was in command of (and present with) the light infantry company at Warley Camp near London in the summer of 1779 and at Finchley Camp, also near London, in 1780. In March 1780, he was present with his company at Berkhampstead.[37]

While the Royal Irish was stationed outside London in 1781, Blackwood was given leave in February, and he returned to the regiment between November 1782 and June 1783, when he was again present with his company in the Channel Islands.

Blackwood was present with the regiment during its muster at Gibraltar in June 1784, and he returned to a battalion company sometime before March 1787.[38]

Blackwood was still serving as a company commander in the Royal Irish in 1790. He transferred into the 45th Foot on 4 June 1790, exchanging with Thomas Sebright, who wanted to return to the Royal Irish, which was commanded by Sebright's father.[39] Most likely there was some inducement to Blackwood to exchange before retiring; had he simply retired, the Royal Irish's captain lieutenant would have had the first opportunity to purchase the commission. This would have potentially made it difficult for Sebright to return to his father's regiment.

Blackwood probably never served with the 45th Foot. He retired on 10 July 1790, selling his commission to Lieutenant William Henry Clinton of the 7th Light Dragoons.[40] Blackwood spent slightly more than twenty-three years in the Royal Irish, the last fifteen years as a captain. He drafted his will in 1780, leaving all of his estate to his wife, Susanna. There are no children mentioned in his will. He died in 1794.[41]

Benjamin Chapman

> My knowledge of the Americans is founded on long experience, from their own writings and from my intimacy with many of the first characters amongst them; rely upon it, their aim is independency.
>
> —Benjamin Chapman to an Irish friend, 21 June 1775

Benjamin Chapman (ca. 1744–1829) purchased an ensigncy in the Royal Irish on 8 March 1760 at the tender age of sixteen. He is listed as Irish in army records. He was promoted to lieutenant on 11 September 1765 and was present with the regiment when it was inspected in April 1767. When he came to America with the Royal Irish from Ireland in 1767, he was the lieutenant of the lieutenant colonel's company.[42] He remained in Philadelphia until the spring of 1768, when the regiment moved to Fort Pitt and then embarked for the Illinois Country via the Ohio River.

While at Fort Pitt, Chapman served on a general court-martial board that tried five deserters from the 34th Foot in July 1768.[43] While serving with that company, Chapman handled all its affairs on a day-to-day basis. This left Wilkins free to concern himself with the regiment as a whole. Chapman served as the Kaskaskia garrison commander for part of 1770. He did not think that Wilkins properly supported his initial efforts to obtain a captaincy in 1770. He wrote to Wilkins, "For god sakes, Sir, think of all that I have suffered by having strangers put over me into the regt."[44] This was in response to all of the half-pay officers brought into the regiment and over which Wilkins had no control or influence.

Chapman did finally become a captain on 2 June 1771. Shee had loaned him £350 to assist in the purchase. Chapman also became the regimental paymaster in 1771, which ended his career in Illinois. He headed back to Philadelphia, where he could have easier communication with New York and London. By November 1771, Chapman was listed present in Philadelphia, and deserter ads directed those who would apprehend and secure any of the deserters to give notice to Captain Benjamin Chapman, paymaster. He was still the regimental paymaster as late as 1779. Gage regularly found fault and irregularities with Chapman's accounts.[45]

While in Philadelphia, Chapman ordered Mary Shaw out of the barracks of the Royal Irish in 1772. He was accused of doing this out of spite because her husband, Elijah Reeves, alleged that Chapman had tried to sleep with her while he was still in Ireland, and being rebuffed, he constantly harassed her. Chapman had also barred her from traveling to Illinois with the regiment in 1768.

Throughout the next few years, Fowler, in his letters to Wilkins, blamed Chapman and Shee for causing much of the discord in the regiment and fermenting trouble for Wilkins in order to get him replaced and clear the way for their own promotions.

In May 1774, Chapman wrote to Gage for permission to travel to Canada to conduct some "particular business." DeLancey expressed a desire to accompany him, but it is not clear whether he did. Chapman was back with the regiment by October 1774, when his company was ordered to Boston. Chapman testified against Newburgh at his general court-martial, and afterward, Newburgh charged Chapman with falsely accusing him.[46]

Chapman's company moved to Boston under Captain Shee in late 1774. While there, Chapman disrupted the proceedings of the Boston Massacre Memorial Service in March 1775. He shouted, "Fie! Fie!" to make the crowd believe there was a fire. He also juggled pistol balls in the face of Dr. Warren, who was speaking, until someone dropped a handkerchief over his hand.[47] Chapman served on the court-martial board of Lieutenant Colonel Walcott and Ensign Patrick of the 5th Foot from 27 March to 14 April 1775. Both officers were charged with "quarreling on the Evening of Thursday the 23rd [March] and Consequences that ensued, which are reported to be blows given and a challenge to fight."[48]

Chapman took command of the grenadier company when the regiment returned to England, and he became the senior captain of the Royal Irish in 1777, when Hugh Lord left the regiment. At that point, Chapman was thirty-two years old and had eighteen years of service. He was present on a general court-martial board at Dover in November 1777 that tried William Green and Henry Knight for desertion.[49]

Chapman was present with the regiment at Coxheath Camp in 1778 and Warley Camp in 1779. He sat on the court-martial board at Coxheath Camp on 31 August 1778 to try Private Bryan Sheridan of the Royal Irish Foot for desertion. Sheridan was found guilty and sentenced to be shot to death.[50]

Chapman appears to have journeyed to Bath for his health and was listed as being sick there on 17 March 1779. He was promoted to major in the Royal Irish on 16 November 1781. It appears that a son, Benjamin Chapman Jr., purchased an ensigncy in the regiment on 29 July 1782. Chapman Sr. accompanied the regiment to Gibraltar in 1783 and was in command of it there in 1787. In 1788, he was challenged to a duel by Captain John DeLancey for an unknown reason. When DeLancey stated that he would not fire until his pistol's muzzle touched Chapman's breast, Chapman threw his weapon down and walked off the field, unwilling to fight an "assassin." Chapman was reprimanded for accepting a challenge from a subordinate officer.[51]

The *London Gazette* reported that according to War Office orders dated 1 May 1790, Major Benjamin Chapman was appointed to be deputy quartermaster general to the forces in Jamaica. Chapman ranked as a lieutenant colonel in the army from that date.[52] He was replaced on 9 October 1790 as deputy quartermaster general by Major Thomas Garth of the 2nd Dragoon Guards. Chapman was promoted to lieutenant colonel of the Royal Irish on 28 July 1790 when Adam Williamson was promoted to colonel of the 47th Foot.[53] Chapman retired from the army when he sold his commission to David Douglas Wemyss on 12 April 1793.[54] Chapman married Maria Durant Payne after Benjamin Charnock Payne passed away in May 1793; Maria was reported to have taken a third husband, a Colonel Chapman, whom the family appears not to have liked. In fact, she continued to be known as Mrs. Payne even though she was married to Colonel Chapman. It is possible that Chapman had planned on visiting Payne upon his retirement from the army and was present at or near the time of Payne's death.[55]

Chapman left his estate at Dawlish, Devonshire, to his widow and his daughter-in-law, for their use throughout their lives. He asked for the property to be passed on to his nephew, Benjamin Chapman Browne, a major in the army at the time, who also received most of Chapman's books. Another nephew, Benjamin Chapman, a captain in the 9th Light Dragoons, received his *Encyclopedia Britannica* and *Great Atlas*. George Durant was to receive Chapman's gilt cup and large silver waiter, if that was acceptable to his wife. Durant was Maria's son from an earlier marriage. Chapman left his housekeeper, Sarah, £200. Her widowed mother received £10. Servants who had lived with him at least three full years received £15. Servants who had been with him seven or more years received £50. All his servants were to receive a "suit of mourning." He arranged for blankets to be distributed to the poor, and £100 was given to the Exter Hospital.

Chapman requested that he be buried in the parish churchyard at Dawlish and that his funeral be conducted in a "quiet unostentatious manner at a moderate expense." He wished for a horizontal gravestone and a "strong Iron railing" to protect his grave from injury.[56]

Charles Edmonstone

Charles Edmonstone (ca. 1730–?) was the third son of Archibald Edmonstone, first Baronet of Redhall, Antrim County, and Dunreath, Scotland.

The family was originally Scottish and also maintained Scottish holdings around Stirling. Charles was probably raised in an environment rich in literature, his father's library being significant enough of a bequest to be addressed in the newspapers at the time of his father's death in 1768.

Edmonstone began his military career as an ensign in the 5th Foot on 25 May 1742, when he was about twelve years old. He was promoted to second lieutenant on 29 October 1745 in the 5th Foot and was reduced to the Irish half-pay list on 21 November 1748, where he remained until 1756. He was appointed as a lieutenant from half pay in the 1st Battalion of the 1st Foot on 27 April 1756 and was promoted to captain lieutenant of the 29th Foot on 22 November 1756. The 29th Foot was stationed in Ireland at that time. Edmonstone purchased his captaincy in the Royal Irish on 27 May 1758, replacing Robert Walsh.[57]

The April 1767 inspection return for the Royal Irish listed Edmonstone as a thirty-six-year-old Irishman. Edmonstone commanded the grenadier company when the Royal Irish arrived in North America, but he turned that company over to John Stewart in April 1768, possibly because John Wilkins wanted the grenadiers to accompany him to Illinois and Edmonstone was to be left in command of two companies at Fort Pitt. It appears that Edmonstone was sent to Fort Pitt in the fall of 1767 along with a small cadre of the Royal Irish and recruits intended for the 34th Foot. Edmonstone remained at Fort Pitt and immediately had difficulties trying to remove settlers from the Indians' land around Fort Pitt. He told Gage that if the general really wanted him to remove the whites, he would have to be allowed to destroy their harvests. While at Fort Pitt, Edmonstone served on a general court-martial board that tried five deserters from the 34th Foot in July 1768.[58]

Edmonstone appears to have been involved in land speculation while at Fort Pitt, granting land to his wife, Susannah, Ensign Edmond Prideaux, and probably other officers of the Royal Irish, including Edward Hand. Edmonstone's name appears in Pennsylvania land deeds well into the mid-nineteenth century.

Edmonstone appears to have been a fairly poor administrator. He commanded Fort Pitt while the Royal Irish was stationed there from 1767 through 1772, except for brief periods when senior officers were present. He was charged with assisting in the communication between the Eastern Seaboard and the garrisons in Illinois, but on several occasions he held on to communications from the commander in chief instead of sending them on to Illinois. The commissary records at Fort Pitt appear to have been particularly badly kept. General Gage seemed to be upset with him on several occasions, at one time leveling the following nine complaints against him as part of a court of inquiry:

> Failure to deal properly with the Indians
>
> Excessive expenditures for Indian supplies
>
> Relinquishing of command to those not qualified
>
> Failure to keep the commander in chief properly advised
>
> Failure to provide proper vouchers for payment
>
> Excessive stockpiling of supplies
>
> Failure to carry out orders
>
> Excessive indulgence of the Indians
>
> Careless supervision

It also appears that the frontier inhabitants and Edmonstone did not like each other much. Edmonstone spoke of the inhabitants as being the least acceptable people he had ever met even though he had served throughout Europe. Edmonstone, appointed post major with army rank of major on 23 July 1772, considered himself a Christian and told the missionary, Reverend David McClure, that "you are engaged in a benevolent work and you have my best wished for your success. I am a Christian, and therefore please command me in any way in which I may serve." Perhaps in gratitude for the Edmonstones' hospitality, McClure gave Mrs. Edmonstone a young wildcat as a gift.

When the post at Fort Pitt was ordered abandoned, Edmonstone did not seem to do a particularly good job; he left most of the fort standing. Edward Hand, an ensign in the Royal Irish, seems to have been a silent partner in a successful scheme to purchase most of the governmental property. It is possible that Edmonstone did not properly supervise Hand, who acted as quartermaster for the post and was directly responsible for the selling off of the king's supplies.[59]

Edmonstone and his command arrived in Philadelphia in November 1772 and stayed there until 1774, leaving only a corporal's guard at Fort Pitt. Edmonstone was appointed to preside over a regimental court of inquiry ordered by Major Isaac Hamilton in April 1774 in order to inquire into the conduct of Chaplain Robert Newburgh.[60]

Edmonstone and his company then went to New Jersey. He applied to the secretary of war for a leave of absence in 1774 to go to Britain, but Gage denied the request on 14 November 1774, stating, "I told Lord Barrington that in the present circumstances I cannot permit any officer to Leave. I must currently decline his request." Edmonstone was present at New York City in April 1775. During the regiment's embarkation from New York City, Edmonstone and others stayed behind in the barracks while Captain Payne was left to evacuate the troops from New York and deal with an angry mob. Edmonstone embarked upon HMS *Asia* for Boston with the regiment on 6 June 1775. He retired from the army on 25 July 1775.[61]

However, Edmonstone did not leave America. Instead he traveled to New York, where he appears to have had substantial property in the western portion of Tyron County.

In early 1777, Edmonstone appears to have been accused of spying by a "Committee appointed by the Convention of the State of New York." He was somehow apprehended by New York authorities and accused of spying or potentially made a prisoner of war based upon his earlier status as an officer of the Royal Irish. In January 1777, he traveled to New York City to see Joshua Loring, the British commissary of prisoners, to attempt to arrange an exchange for himself with one of three congressional majors being held by the British: Williams, Brown, or Wells. General William Howe appears to have agreed with the exchange with the stipulation "provided Major Edminston [sic] who is the bearer of this is permitted to go to Canada agreeable to his own Desire."[62]

In fact, Edmonstone was not allowed to travel to Canada, because the congressional authorities in Albany believed that he had taken too long to arrive at Albany from New York and suspected that he had lodged with those known to be "greatly disaffected to the American Cause." Therefore, in their estimation, he must have been a spy and should be dealt with as such. A letter from New York to John Hancock, the president of the Continental Congress, stated that Edmonstone was being sent to Philadelphia "under the Care of Capt. Brett."[63] They also produced a letter from Edmonstone to "an unnamed noble patron" in which he mentioned "great prospect of Promotions in the American Service and requests his Patron's Interest for preferment."[64] Edmonstone was required to give his parole to a board of officers consisting of General Scott, Colonel DeWitt and Major Tappen at Kingston, New York, on or about 16 April 1777, before his departure for Philadelphia. The reason for sending Edmonstone to Philadelphia appears to be summarized in a letter from the Committee of Convention to Major Hamilton:

> He was three weeks, or thereabouts, travelling from New York to Albany; of which the Convention being informed, caused him to be made prisoner, and intend sending him to Head Quarters. He is well acquainted with the face of this country, and the disposition of its several inhabitants. He has sufficient interest with the Indians to accomplish an escape.
>
> Upon the whole (as it will not be prudent to confine him within this State), it is submitted, whether it would not be proper to secure him elsewhere until the close of the present campaign.[65]

Edmonstone is listed in Elias Boundinot's report on American prisoners being held by the British, dated 2 March 1778. The report states, "Major Edminston [sic] is sent into Philadelphia in expectation of being Exchanged for Major B. Payne of the American Army," who had been held by the British for eleven months at that time, accused of killing a Briton known only as Captain Campbell.[66]

There is no record of when Edmonstone was released from prison or when he returned to Britain. He appears to have died without children. His nephew, Archibald Edmonstone, served on the staff of Brunswick general Friedrich Adolf Riedesel during the Saratoga campaign in 1777.[67]

Edmonstone was most likely of limited means, as he was purchased over by both Henry Folliott and Isaac Hamilton when the Royal Irish's commission of major was available for purchase. As the regiment's senior captain at the time, Edmonstone should have had the right of first refusal to purchase.

John Evans

John Evans (ca. 1742–?) was Irish and approximately eighteen years old when he purchased a commission as an ensign in the Royal Irish on 7 March 1760. He was promoted to lieutenant on 3 May 1765 upon George Stainforth's promotion to captain. He was present with the regiment when it was inspected at Dublin on 11 April 1767.

Evans embarked with the regiment for America in May 1767. He was assigned as the lieutenant of Captain Stainforth's company when the regiment arrived at Philadelphia on 11 July 1767.

Evans was probably transferred to Captain John Shee's company in late spring 1768, since he was with the five companies that traveled to Fort Pitt en route to the Illinois Country.[68] While at Fort Pitt, Evans served on a general court-martial board that tried five deserters from the 34th Foot in July 1768.[69] Because of the slow nature of transatlantic communication, Evans obtained a company in the Royal Irish on 16 December 1767 but was not aware of his promotion until nearly a year later.[70]

Evans was involved in a dispute with Wilkins along with Shee and other officers that was concluded on 1 April 1770 by the officers agreeing in writing to put aside their previous differences, both public and private.

Evans remained in Illinois and commanded the detachment at Cahokia for a time. Letters between other officers of the regiment show that he sold his commission suddenly while in Illinois. It might have had something to do with the fact he allegedly took the wife of James Cairns, a private under his command, as his own and then beat Cairns "with a loaded Whip" when the private came to retrieve his wife. Cairns was tried for the incident and actually received five hundred lashes of an eight-hundred-lash sentence for his actions from a regimental court-martial. The actual charge was interfering with an officer's official acts.[71]

Evans retired on 1 June 1771. The last entry in his account with the regimental agent was 4 March 1776.[72]

Henry Fermor

Henry Fermor (1750–20 January 1780) was the eldest son of the John Fermor, the rector of Crayford, and Elizabeth Austen, a cousin of Jane Austen's father, George.[73] Henry Fermor purchased an ensigncy in the Royal Irish on 15 February 1768 at age eighteen. He was English, from Sevenoaks, Kent. He was initially assigned to Captain Stainforth's company, possibly because it was still at Philadelphia. He appears to have joined the regiment before October 1768; he was present when Stainforth's company was mustered that month, and he signed the return. At least through 1769, the regiment agent's ledgers show Fermor receiving a supplemental allowance from his father in addition to his military pay.[74]

In June 1769, Fermor was listed as being in England on General Gage's leave. Fermor, listed as Farmer, was a subscriber to Stephen Payne Adye's *A Treatise on Courts Martial*, published in 1769. It is unclear when he returned to the regiment, but he was assigned to Hugh Lord's company by April 1770. He was promoted to lieutenant on 3 June 1771 and assigned as the lieutenant of Captain Benjamin Johnson's Company at Fort Pitt. In Wilkins's letter to Gage showing officer assignments as of 7 April 1772, Fermor is listed as the lieutenant of Edmonstone's company, although he is shown as belonging to Johnson's company in the muster returns. Both companies were stationed at Fort Pitt, and since Captain Johnson was not present, the detachment effectively functioned as a single company under Edmonstone.

Fermor was removed to Captain Chapman's company upon the regiment's return to Philadelphia in the fall of 1772. Fermor was granted leave by the commander in chief and was absent at the 27 July 1773 and 29 July 1774 musters. Potentially the leave was so he could settle his family's affairs upon his father's death. He most likely returned to the regiment before October 1774, when Chapman's company embarked for Boston. He was present with the detachment in Boston during the winter of 1774–1775. In October 1775, he was put in command of Chapman's company because Chapman was removed to the grenadier company. When Major Edmonstone retired, Fermor was able to purchase his captaincy, which was backdated to 26 July 1775.

Upon the regiment's return to England, Fermor was given command of a battalion company. He was present but sick when the regiment was reviewed on 2 August 1776 at Dover Castle.[75]

Fermor was recruiting a significant portion of the time in 1777 and 1778. He was listed as being on recruiting service when the regiment was mustered on 18 August 1777, 6 March 1778, and 16 March 1779. His company was posted at Margate in March 1779. Fermor left the regiment in July or August 1779. He most likely was absent so as to begin raising men for the 89th Foot.[76]

Fermor was appointed as the senior major of the newly raised 89th Regiment of Foot on 2 November 1779.[77] His new regiment was quickly filled and embarked for the West Indies, arriving in December 1779. Fermor probably accompanied the regiment and died shortly after its arrival.[78] He died on 20 January 1780 in the West Indies, an intestate bachelor. His commission of major went to Edward Pole, the 89th's senior captain. A stained-glass window was erected in 1792 honoring Fermor, his father, and a brother in the Sevenoaks Church in Kent. The inscription for Femor incorrectly listed him as the major of the 39th instead of the 89th Regiment.[79]

Robert Hamilton

Robert Hamilton (ca. 1750–1817) purchased his colors in the Royal Irish Regiment of Foot on 3 May 1765. He was most likely from the Hamilton family seated at Ballydonell, Donegal County, Ireland. His father was most likely Andrew Hamilton. Robert had at least two sisters, Anne and Katherine. He was promoted to lieutenant in the 18th Regiment on 4 February 1769. He purchased Captain Thomas Batt's commission upon Batt's retirement from active service.

Hamilton had earlier served as the lieutenant in Captain Benjamin Johnson's company when it was posted at Fort Pitt. During his tenure at Fort Pitt, he fought a duel with Ensign Godfrey Tracy of his regiment. Tracy was killed, and Hamilton was tried for murder by a civilian court. George Buttricke mentions Tracy's death in a letter to Captain Barnsley in a letter dated 12 February 1769 from Fort Chartres. *The Minutes of the Provincial Council of Pennsylvania* show that a special commission of the three senior justices of the peace in the County of Bedford were to be formed to try Hamilton for murder on 23 November 1771. Hamilton was apparently upset that Tracey had tried to buy a vacant lieutenancy, which Hamilton, by regimental seniority, should have been allowed to purchase first. He seems to have been cleared. In all probability, he commanded Johnson's company while it was at Fort Pitt, since Johnson does not appear to have ventured to Fort Pitt.[80]

Hamilton was promoted to captain on 21 January 1773. His company was one of three ordered to Boston in October 1774. According to Lieutenant John Barker's diary, Hamilton's horse fell on him at Boston on 1 April 1775. Hamilton was seriously injured, and Barker was concerned for his recovery. According to one account, Hamilton fought gallantly in the American Revolution and was wounded. There is no record of him being wounded in the records of the 18th Regiment, however, so he might have been slightly wounded and not been hospitalized.

Hamilton served on a court-martial board in Boston from 6–14 July 1775 that considered several cases: Richard Symes, for wounding a Marine who then died; Privates James Edwards and William Moran, for assaulting Marine Lieutenant Roland Carter; Marine Thomas Bell, for robbery; and Marine Duncan McFarland, for robbing a dead Marine officer.[81]

According to the *Dictionary of National Biography,* Hamilton supposedly gave the sword and scabbard he carried up Bunker Hill to Sir Walter Scott on his deathbed. It does not seem probable that he climbed Bunker Hill with the grenadiers, however, since he was a battalion company commander at the time. He may have served as an aide de camp during the battle to one of the general officers present.

Hamilton was present on a general court-martial board at Dover, England, in November 1777 that tried William Green and Henry Knight for desertion.[82] He was promoted to major in the army on 19 March 1783. He remained at Gibraltar with the Royal Irish until he retired.

Hamilton transferred to half pay, exchanging with Captain Donald McDonald of an independent company, according to War Office orders dated 28 January 1792. When he retired, he had served nearly twenty-seven years of active service, all of that time with the Royal Irish. Hamilton later stated that "ill-health forced him to sell out and retire on half pay to North Wales."[83]

Hamilton's postmilitary career is somewhat conjectural. As early as an 1877 *Atlantic Monthly* article, he was said to be a friend of Walter Scott and a preeminent Scottish barrister. It is not certain, but that Robert Hamilton may have later taken advantage of the fact that someone by the same name had served in Boston in 1775, since he is credited with giving the sword he carried at Bunker Hill to Scott as a gesture of friendship at the end of his life.[84]

Hamilton remained at Conway, North Wales, for at least the next fifteen years.

Hamilton was jailed for debt by his deceased brother-in-law's son in December 1808. The debt was originally a loan of £100 from Katherine Babington, his widowed sister, in 1772, but it had not been properly forgiven when Katherine married Thomas Lee. When Lee passed away, his son, Robert—who, according to Katherine, "since his father's death... has behaved very badly"—apparently forged a number of letters requesting help from Hamilton's friends.

Hamilton appears to have been shocked by the action regardless of the potential well-meaning intentions of the forger. Letters had been sent to the Earl of Harrington, the Duke of York, and the Duke of Kent. Hamilton's sister tried to consider part of her inheritance from her father as repayment of the debt, but Hamilton refused and remained in debtor's prison at Caernarvon Jail from December 1808 through at least the spring of 1809. He expressed his concern that prison would kill him, since he was nearly sixty years old and he was not used to such a life, "being born and bred a gentleman."[85] It is unclear when he was released from the Caernarvon Jail. He remained on half pay until his death in 1817.

Matthew Lane

Matthew Lane (ca. 1741–1770) was first commissioned at the age of thirteen as an ensign on 4 September 1754 in the Royal Irish. The Irishman was promoted to lieutenant on 28 June 1756.[86]

Lane purchased the captain lieutenancy of the Royal Irish from John Stewart on 13 February 1765. It appears that he was unable to pay the full price on his own. According to Colonel Sebright, the captains of the Royal Irish advanced Lane the funds necessary to purchase. It would be reasonable to infer that he was held in high esteem by the captains of the Royal Irish if they were willing to help him purchase.[87]

Lane was the paymaster for the regiment when it embarked in 1767. He spent that fall stationed with the Royal Irish at Philadelphia. Gage recommended that Lane receive Hugh Antrobus's commission, but either the War Office or the king selected a half-pay officer for that commission instead.[88]

Lane accompanied the regiment to Fort Pitt in the spring of 1768. While at Fort Pitt, Lane served on a general court-martial board that tried five deserters from the 34th Foot in July 1768.[89] He then appears to have returned to Philadelphia to maintain contact with the regiment's agent and suppliers and to have remained in Philadelphia to facilitate communication with London and Levi Franks & Company, which was the contractor for many of the Royal Irish's provisions in Illinois. He was promoted to captain on 4 February 1769, in place of John Stewart, who was deceased. Lane died before February 1770 and was replaced by Benjamin Chapman as paymaster. His captain's commission was given to half-pay officer Hugh Lord. It is possible that Lane drowned in the Ohio River on his way to Illinois.[90]

Hugh Lord

Hugh Lord (ca. 1742–1829) entered military service on 2 September 1756 as an ensign in Lord Charles Hay's 33rd Regiment of Foot. Because of the large expansion of the army during the Seven Years' War, he was the 33rd's senior ensign by the end of 1757. Lord was promoted to lieutenant in the 33rd on 2 May 1758. Six days later, Charles, Duke of Richmond, was made the colonel of the 72nd Foot, which was raised by separating the 33rd's 2nd Battalion from the 1st Battalion. Lord went into the 72nd Foot, which was involved in operations along the French coast at Cherbourg in August and September 1758. The 72nd returned to England later in September.

In April 1761, the regiment was involved in the operations at Belle Isle along the French coast. The regiment was then shipped to the West Indies, where it was involved in the siege of Havana. Lord attained the rank of captain on 25 December 1762 in the 72nd Regiment of Foot. He was reduced to the half-pay list at the end of the Seven Years' War in 1763.[91]

Lord returned to active service as a captain in the Royal Irish Regiment on 5 February 1770. He was originally assigned to a battalion company in Illinois.

When the Royal Irish added a light infantry company in the spring of 1771, Lord was assigned to command it. He appears to have spent some time recruiting in Maryland. It was in command of the light company that he left Fort Pitt for Fort Chartres on 1 March 1772. When Lord's company arrived in Illinois, the majority of the regiment was preparing to return to Philadelphia. The regiment was ordered to destroy Fort Chartres and leave only a small detachment at Kaskaskia. Lord was chosen to remain with a small detachment made up of his light company, half of Lieutenant Colonel Wilkins's company, and Surgeon Thomas Thomasson.

Lord was left in Illinois with neither a wealth of experience working with Indians nor a command of the French language. His command in Illinois officially began on 12 June 1772, when Major Isaac Hamilton left for Fort Pitt with the majority of the regiment. Lord received 7 shillings and sixpence per day as an allowance for his role as commander in Illinois. The officers commanding Crown Point, Niagara, Detroit, and Pittsburgh all received similar allowances in 1772.[92]

Lord remained in Illinois for the next four years, the de facto governor of the Illinois Country in charge of America's westernmost British post at the time. His garrison included two subalterns, a surgeon, and approximately seventy-five men of the Royal Irish and three men of the Royal Artillery. The troops were stationed in what had at one time been the Jesuit compound at Kaskaskia. French documents show that the French at Kaskaskia were fond of Captain Lord, who was viewed as kind and just.

In March 1774, Lord wrote to Gage about the poor condition of the boats at his disposal and the fact that the row galley was "long since useless." Lord was also worried about the need to replace all the pickets because decay and about a large gully being cut by rainfall along the side of the post. The gully was encroaching within twelve feet of the southern redoubt. It was a similar situation to the encroachment of the Mississippi River on Fort Chartres, which had caused its abandonment two years earlier. Lord also wrote about the warfare among the Indians in the area and said that the nations along the Wabash River seldom saw the British as friends. Replacing the pickets at the post was a major project in the summer of 1774.[93]

The Crown account for 1 July through 31 December 1775 shows four major areas of expense for the garrison at Fort Gage in Illinois: garrison expenses, including soldiers' extra duty labor; the king's boats; the king's oxen; and the Indian account. The Indian account was a list of gifts ranging from a child's shirt to fusils (light muskets, as used by officers) and canoes given to tribes expressing their friendship to the Crown. The Indian gifts accounted for more than 50 percent of the total expenses incurred.[94]

Lord refined the court system at Kaskaskia based on arbitrators. He selected the justices so that half were English and the other half French. Under Lord's governance, the French inhabitants of Kaskaskia no longer petitioned to set up a civil government separate from the military.[95]

Nearly immediately, Lord was faced with managing the civilian and Indian affairs of the area. One of his first letters to Gage in April 1772 speaks to the growing unrest among the Shanawese because of the murder of Corn Cob, a Shawanese chief, by one of the Missouri nations. He anticipated conflict between the tribes and a resulting increase of expenses for the government.[96]

Lord's handling of an Indian issue with a group of Chickasaw, a tribe most friendly to the English, led Gage to reprimand him for his dealings with Indians. When Lord received a request for help from a former British officer turned trader, James Ramsey, Lord sent a platoon of men under a subaltern to forcibly drive the drunken Indians from Ramsey's store. Several Indians were killed in the skirmish and another taken prisoner. Ramsey's slave was also killed. In a letter to Major Hamilton, General Gage likened Lord's tactics to those used "to quell a Dublin mob." Lord appears to have learned his lesson and either did not use force again to deal with the Indians or at least kept the news of those activities from reaching Gage.

Gage's later letters smoothed over any ruffled feathers when he told Lord that he had a great deal of confidence and trust in the captain's abilities. The other half of the lieutenant colonel's company, which had accompanied Wilkins and Quartermaster Buttricke down the Mississippi to New Orleans, was added to the garrison later in the summer of 1772.[97]

Lord appears to have been a fairly strong administrator. Theodore Pease labeled him "upright" in comparison with Pease's negative opinions of both Wilkins and Lieutenant Colonel John Reed of the 34th Foot, who held command in Illinois before Lord. One of Lord's sergeants, Andrew Hoy, was appointed provost in Illinois and served as the area's de facto sheriff. Hoy was involved in auctioning off property for the payment of debt. In one recorded case, Hoy seized and auctioned the Kaskaskia property and chattels of John Baptist Hubardeau to pay off debts incurred to James Rumsey, a former British officer, in December 1772.[98]

In June 1773, William Murray, a representative from the Illinois and Wabash Land Company, arrived to make a treaty for land with the chiefs of the Illinois tribes. Lord told Murray that although the company might be able to purchase land, Lord's orders were clear, and his soldiers "should not suffer him to settle any of the lands as it was expressly contrary to his Majesty's Orders."[99]

Lord himself attested to the deed of sale and reported the sale immediately to his superiors along with his adverse opinion. Gage wrote to Lord that he was able to extend his approbation "for your commendable attention to the very extraordinary attempt to acquire a title to the possession of lands in a part of the Country where all new settlement has been forbidden."[100]

Lord was further ordered to convene the Illinois chiefs and inform them that the sale of their lands had been annulled by King George III. Despite Lord's determination to not allow settlement, more than twenty million acres of Illinois land were purchased from Illinois tribes during his tenure. The purchasers were a wide variety of people, including signers of the Declaration of Independence and the royal governor of Virginia.[101] Lord appears to have made a positive impression on the local Indians, and Lieutenant Governor Henry Hamilton noted in his journal that a party of the Peoria nation arrived at Vincennes on 30 January 1779 and expressed their regard for Lord.[102]

Lord wrote to Fredrick Haldimand in September 1773 about the concerns of the Illinois populace that the troops were going to be withdrawn. Because of that concern, the local inhabitants had not forwarded a new proposal for establishing a civil government in Illinois. Lord was also proud to give notice that the relationship between the Royal Irish and the Chickasaw had improved. In 1772, Gage had reprimanded Lord for being too harsh with the Indians who attacked Rumsey's store. Lord was able to share with Haldimand that a year later, the Chickasaw brought him a present in the form of a Miami slave. Lord thought that this signified that the tribe had forgiven any past injury and that it provided him with an opportunity to free the Miami slave and send him back to his tribe with an explanation that the English had saved his life.

Lord also explained that the chiefs of the Illinois applied for the help of the surgeon in order to provide medical assistance to those Indians suffering from a measles outbreak. According to Lord, they were "in the most wretched state. Humanity induced me to comply with the request." Lord informed Haldimand that the surgeon was promised the allowance of a "mate of the Hospital" for the time he was in attendance among the Illinois.[103]

Lord was ordered to reinforce Detroit in May 1776, and he left Kaskaskia with the men of his garrison sometime that month. He left his wife and children in the care of Philippe Rocheblave at Kaskaskia, whom he left as the king's representative in Illinois. Guy Carleton had ordered Lord to appoint a proper successor as he saw fit. Alternatively, Dr. John Connolly had conspired with Virginia's governor, John Murray, Fourth Earl of Dunmore, to try to get Lord's command to travel downriver to Mobile, Alabama. However, Connolly's letters were captured and sent to the Continental Congress. So Lord never received the order to go to Mobile.[104]

The men arrived at Detroit in June. Lord was the senior officer when he arrived, so he served briefly as the commander at Detroit. He was then ordered to draft the remaining men of the Royal Irish who were fit for further service into the 8th (King's) Regiment. That was accomplished on 8 July 1776, with fifty-eight men being transferred. Lord and the officers, noncommissioned officers and the few men remaining from his detachment, then traveled through Canada to embark for England. His small detachment arrived in England in December 1776.[105]

Lord still showed interest in the Illinois Country and penned a memorial to the lords of the Board of Trade dated 3 December 1776, articulating the desirability of establishing a civil government between Natchez (Mississippi) and New Orleans that would be dependent on west Florida. His reasoning was the distress of His Majesty's subjects on the Mississippi River between New Orleans and Natchez.[106]

Lord's company, designated as a battalion company upon its arrival in England, mustered only a skeleton crew of men and was commanded on 4 March 1777 by Ensign Thomas Serle. Both Lord and Lieutenant John de Birniere were absent with leave. Lord was on recruiting service when the regiment was inspected on 15 May 1777. He retired from the Royal Irish on 13 July 1777; George Bewes purchased his company.[107]

However, Lord's retirement was short-lived, and he was appointed the major of the 75th (Prince of Wales's) Regiment of Foot when it was raised on 30 May 1778.[108] The 75th was raised in Wales and mustered in Gloucester. A letter from Captain Alexander Campbell to the Earl of Denbigh, dated 15 January 1778, speaks of Captain Lord, who "is to have the direction & forming the companies" of the regiment.[109]

It also appears that Lord was to visit the Earl of Denbigh in company with Campbell and a Mr. Johns. So Lord's assignment to be major of the 75th must have been known several months before his commission was officially approved. Lord remained with the 75th Foot until he exchanged with Philip Eaggs, a major on half pay from the 109th Foot, on 13 November 1782.[110]

Even though Lord returned to England by the end of 1776, Marie Rocheblave wrote to Haldimand on 27 March 1780, stating that all of her possessions had been plundered and that her family, along with Lord's, was in dire circumstances because of the arrival in Illinois of George Rogers Clark's Illinois Regiment from Virginia. Lord's family remained in a difficult situation in Illinois for several years. In 1778, Philippe Rocheblave wrote to Carleton on behalf of Lord's family and his own, "I entreat you to have pity upon the family of Captain Hugh Lord felt with mine without resources, their effects and mine having been for the more part seized and sold."[111]

When Rocheblave arrived in New York, in July 1780, having escaped from the Americans, he wrote to Haldimand of the dire situation that his family and that of Major Lord were in. He wrote again in December 1780 asking for aid for Lord's family.[112]

Lord seems to have sold his house at the foot of the bluffs at Kaskaskia and the land surrounding it to a Catholic priest, Father Pierre Gibault. Gibault sold the house and property to George Rogers Clark on 7 May 1779.[113]

Lord remained on half pay after 1782 until he was recalled to full pay as commander of an independent company of invalids on the Isle of Jersey, according to War Office orders dated 4 April 1801. He replaced a man named Elwes, who was deceased. At the same time, Quartermaster Sergeant John Hughes was promoted to ensign in Lord's independent company, a large company with two lieutenants and an ensign.[114] Lord was transferred to be major of the 7th Royal Garrison Battalion on 25 December 1802. The battalion was raised at Fulham from men discharged from the Cavalry and Foot Guards on 24 December 1802. It was renamed the 7th Royal Veteran Battalion on 9 July 1804 and was stationed at the Tower of London upon its embodiment. One of the battalion's chief duties was to provide guards of honor for funeral processions.[115]

Lord was commanding the garrison on the Isle of Jersey in 1807, so when the 7th Royal Veteran Battalion was split to create the 11th Royal Veteran Battalion on 25 April 1807, Lord was probably assigned to the new formation. The battalion garrisoned in the Channel Islands in 1807;

in Portsmouth, England, in May 1808; and in Wincelsea, Sussex, England, in August 1808. Portions served at Anholt, Denmark, and the Hythe, Kent, in 1812 and 1813. The battalion was generally disbanded in August and November 1814. Lord most likely ended his service at that time. He was listed as retired on full pay in 1815.[116]

When Lord drafted his will in 1821, he was living in Winchester, Hampshire. The will mentioned his wife, Elizabeth, a son, John, and a stepson, Eyre Coot Lord. John was listed as a minor in 1821 and as an ensign in the 63rd Regiment of Foot in 1823. His will was proved on 6 June 1829 at London by his widow.[117]

Benjamin Charnock Payne

> As a Gentleman he knows him to possess the Strictest Integrity and Honour, and of the most Humane and Benevolent disposition, —As an Officer, the most unshaken Zeal for the Service, and the most exact attention to every point of his duty
>
> —Benjamin Chapman, on Benjamin Charnock Payne.[118]

Benjamin Charnock Payne (ca. 1736–1793) was one of the more controversial officers in the Royal Irish during its tenure in North America. According to the Royal Irish's contemporary records, Payne was made an ensign on 3 January 1757 and promoted to lieutenant on 11 February 1762. According to historian John Houlding, Payne was initially commissioned as an ensign without purchase on 3 August 1762 in the 34th Foot and then as a lieutenant in the 9th Foot on 25 September 1762, again without purchase. Since both vacancies occurred after deaths on the Cuban expedition, Houlding thought it possible that Payne accompanied that expedition as a volunteer. There is no explanation why the Royal Irish's records are so different from those of the commission books reviewed by Houlding. The War Office's 1763 army list shows his promotion to lieutenant in the 27th Foot on 30 October 1762, and his army rank of lieutenant is dated 25 September 1762. It appears most likely that he served in the West Indies as a military secretary, clerk, or volunteer before being initially commissioned.[119]

Payne became a captain in the 28th Foot on 27 January 1764. Shortly thereafter, he was in Montreal, where the relationships between the military and civilian leaders were beyond strained. The troops in Montreal were without barracks, so they were being quartered in private homes. When civil government began for Montreal in August 1764, the civilian authorities decided to make life miserable for the army, which had previously been in charge under martial law. Payne was arrested by a magistrate named Thomas Walker. Unfortunately, in the period after the French and Indian War, there are multiple examples of officers being tried by civil powers to harass the military or simply to try to establish civilian control over the military. Carleton wrote to Gage in March 1767 that Daniel Disney, an officer of the 44th Foot, was almost ruined by illogical persecution.[120]

On 6 December 1764, a group of masked men broke into Walker's home and beat him severely. Among the indignities the men committed was taking a piece of his left ear with them. Circumstantial evidence pointed to Payne along with Lieutenant Synge Tottenham and four men of the 28th Foot. None of the men were convicted, but according to John Shy, the 28th Foot was removed to Quebec, where it continued to be unruly. One the same day as the attack on Walker, Gage wrote to William Franklin that another officer accused in the civil court should be sent to New York to escape the local civil jurisdiction. The 28th Foot may have earned the nickname of the Slashers from the actions of Payne and his associates.[121]

While with the Royal Irish, Payne was accused of creating an environment that was certain to cause desertion. Although Payne was not found guilty of that charge, a soldier who deserted from his company in the 28th Foot was captured by the Royal Irish at Philadelphia in the spring of 1768.[122]

Payne obtained his captaincy in the Royal Irish on 8 August 1771 in a transfer from the 28th Foot that was most likely motivated by a desire to stay in America. Payne commanded the junior, or 5th Battalion, company of the regiment for nearly two years.

Payne received permission from General Gage to travel to the West Indies on 28 September 1772 as long as he returned to his regiment in the spring.[123] Although he was the junior captain, because of the apparent fact that Major Charles Edmonstone was not fit for daily duties and that Major Isaac Hamilton, in nominal command at New York in 1774–1775, was ill most of that winter, Payne ended up in actual day-to-day command of the regiment's five companies in New York.

Payne appears to have regularly beaten soldiers, including his sergeants. Several deserters might have left the regiment because of his ill treatment of them. Testimony at his court-martial in August 1775 shows that he gave John Dolling, a private and bandsman, a black eye and put him into iron chains for having taken his shoes off when the men had been told to sleep in their accouterments that evening. Sergeant George Smith testified that even though Payne beat him, he would not desert his colors. In 1774, a comment Payne allegedly made about the parson (Robert Newburgh) being a "buggerer" caused another set of courts-martial for some of the regiment's tailors, who were charged with falsely accusing Payne of making the comment. A regimental court found the tailors guilty, but a general court-martial overturned John Green's verdict on appeal.

The following year, Lieutenant Alexander Fowler levied charges against Payne: cowardice in the face of the enemy for giving up the spare arms and baggage of the Royal Irish to a New York mob in June 1775. The specific charges were heard by a general court-martial under Lieutenant Colonel Henry Calder,[124] beginning on 29 July 1775:

> The President and Members being met, and duly sworn, the Judge Advocate being also duly sworn, Captain Benjamin Charnock Payne of his Majesty's 18th or Royal Irish Regiment of Foot, was brought prisoner before the Court and the following charges exhibited against him by Lieut. Alexander Fowler of the same Regiment.
>
> First, That the said Captain Benjamin Charnock Payne had behaved in a scandalous, infamous, unwarrantable manner, unbecoming the character of a Gentleman and an Officer.
>
> Secondly, That he had been Guilty of tyrannical, cruel, and oppressive treatment both of the Non-Commissioned Officers and private soldiers, in consequence of which conduct [illegible] one or more of the former and several of the latter have been compelled to desert His Majesty's Service at a very important crisis.
>
> Thirdly, That he had propagated infamous, scandalous and groundless falsehoods leading not only to affect the good name and reputation of him /the said Lieut. Fowler/ as an Officer but impeaching him of High Treason against his Sovereign, as being connected with the most violent Sons of sedition and rebellion in the City of New York and thereby affecting his life and Commission.
>
> Fourthly, That he /the said Captain Payne/ had wickedly, impulsively, and of Malice aforethought, conceived and promoted a black and unnatural design against the life of his superior officer.
>
> Fifthly, That he had acted a cowardly, pusillanimous, and unsoldierly part, when at the head of five Companies of the Royal Irish Regiment of Foot, by permitting an unarmed mob not only to

entice away private Soldiers before his face but likewise forcibly to rob said Companies of their baggage, spare arms and accoutrements, without the least opposition or seemingly disapprobation, thereby entailing disgrace on the Royal Regiment of Ireland.[125]

According to testimony from Alexander Fowler and Nicholas Trist, the fourth charge was related to Surgeon's Mate John Linn's accusation that Payne had tried to bribe him into poisoning Major Isaac Hamilton, who was commanding the regiment at New York in the winter of 1774–1775.

The Court's verdict was pronounced on 18 August 1775:

> The Court being met pursuant to Adjournment and having duly Considered the Evidence for and against the Prisoner Capt. Benjamin Charnock Payne, together with what he had to offer in his defence, is of the Opinion that he is not Guilty of the first, second, fourth, and fifth Charges exhibited against him of the said Charges ~ And the Court is further of Opinion that these Charges are in General malicious, frivolous, wicked and ill grounded.
>
> With respect to the third charge, the Court is of the Opinion that Capt. Payne is Guilty of having propagated reports of Mr. Fowler's being connected with the Sons of Sedition, & etc. at New York, for which he has not made it appear to the Court, that he had sufficient Grounds, and the Court therefore direct that this their Opinion and Censure thereon, be made known to the Royal Irish Regiment of Foot, by its being read at the head of that Regiment.[126]

Regarding the charge of cowardice in the face of the enemy, most of the witnesses testified that Payne reacted to save the fifty men in his command from otherwise certain destruction. Payne had earlier removed the locks and bayonets from the spare muskets. They were destroyed in the barracks after the spare firelocks were taken by the mob.

Payne was ordered to command the land forces of a wood-gathering mission from Boston to Penobscot (Maine) in September 1775. The expedition embarked from Boston on 20 September 1775 and appears to have included a detachment of the Royal Irish under Payne and Lieutenant John Peter DeLancey as well as a detachment of the provincial Royal Fencible American Regiment under Captain John Collett. The party embarked in the transports *Diana*, *Henry*, *John and Rebecca*, and *Spy* and in the schooner *Betsy* and was escorted by the sloop HMS *Lively*. The fleet was under the command of Captain Thomas Bishop of the Royal Navy. Admiral Samuel Graves paraphrased Payne's orders from General James Robertson as follows:

> The Transports named in the inclosed List being appointed under the direction of Captain Payne of the Royal Irish to procure Wood from any of the Islands in Penobscot Bay, and BG Robertson having furnished Captain Payne with Instruction for his Guidance, I send you a Copy thereof from your information; . . . proceed with them to Long Island, or any of the Islands in the Bay where Cpt. Payne and yourself shall judge to gather the greatest quantity of wood.[127]

Payne held a conference on 28 September 1775 on the Fox Islands, but he was forced to send to Robertson for additional funds for the amount of wood required. At least one American ship was captured by Bishop's fleet and was also filled with wood for the Boston garrison.[128] The wood fleet under Payne returned to Boston on 9 November 1775, according to Lieutenant Colonel Stephen Kemble's diary.[129]

Payne's problems with lieutenants did not end with Fowler. When Payne returned to Boston from gathering wood, he leveled charges against Lieutenant Edward McGouran of the Royal Fencible Americans in November 1775 for the following: "1st Going on Shore without leave and mauroding. 2. Challenging his Commanding Officer in the execution of his duty."[130]

McGouran did not seem to like Payne, and in his defense, he portrayed Payne as a difficult officer to follow. However, the court found McGouran guilty of breaches of several articles of war and ordered him dismissed from the service.[131]

Payne was not particularly popular with the noncommissioned officers or the enlisted men of the regiment. In his own court-martial trial, Fowler presented the court with the fact that the desertion rate in Payne's company was the highest in the regiment.

Lieutenant Trist, Payne's senior subaltern at the time in question, testified that the sergeants of Payne's company, John Brogden and George Smith, frequently "declared to him that Capt. Payne treated them so cruelly that their lives were become a burthern to them; and that it was not possible that they could withstand such cruelty and oppression long, as their hearts were broke, and they were not half Soldiers, or words to that purpose."[132]

Sergeant George Smith himself testified that Payne treated him poorly but could not make him desert his colors. Smith further testified that many of the men "murmured about" Payne but were told to persevere until Wilkins returned to the regiment. Smith related the following regarding Sergeant Brogden's treatment:

> Sergeant Brogden told him that he had a heart like a Lyon to withstand Captain Payne's bad treatment, that he had began the same usage with him some months before, but that it was not in his power to put up with it; that he also told him that Captain Payne had threatened him that if he would not make a denial of what orders he (Capt. Payne) had given him concerning Mr. Newburgh not doing duty in his Company, that he would break him, which would destroy his family, and desired him to consider of it.[133]

Payne also detested the regiment's chaplain, the Robert Newburgh, and ordered his sergeants to not let the chaplain do any duty within his company.[134]

When Payne was assigned to command the wood-gathering expedition to Penobscot from Boston, the men detailed to the duty appear to have had misgivings about serving under Payne. According to McGouran, "Capt Payne was abhorred by his Soldiers, detested by the Sailors." Specifically, Payne was referred to by a sailor delivering orders on the Penobscot expedition as "that damn'd Rascal in the red Jacket." The sailors, according to McGouran, "did not hesitate to declare publickly that they would either hang or shoot him before his return to Boston." A private of the Royal Fencible Americans whose name is given only as Thompson was quoted as saying, "Patience my lads we'll soon be in hell for we are going under the devil's immediate Command" when the men were ordered to serve under Payne.[135]

Payne does appear to have had a charitable side, and testimony was given by the sergeant major that he provided milk for the regimental children and fresh meat for the men out of his own pocket while the Royal Irish was stationed in New York.[136]

Payne served as deputy assistant quartermaster general in North America when the regiment was drafted. He was ordered to Antigua by General William Howe in December 1775 to gather beef, rice, rum, and gun carriages, among other supplies, for the Boston garrison. He was also to enlist up to one hundred seaman for the transport service, if possible. He traveled south with a victualing convoy under the protection of the frigate HMS *Scarborough*, and he was particularly charged with overseeing the armed transport *Hartfield*, commanded by Lieutenant Henry Chads, and the unarmed transport *Diana*, which Payne was to outfit as a light armed transport, if practical. Payne arrived at Barbados on 29 January 1776 and took on a cargo of rum and provisions. The *Hartfield* and *Diana* then proceeded to Antigua, where Payne met up with companies of the 46th and 55th Regiments that had been blown off course en route for Boston. One of the companies of the 55th Foot was embarked on the *Diana*, now an armed transport. Payne returned to Boston sometime before April 1776, most likely in early March, about the same time the *Diana* captured an American sloop, *Unity*.[137] General orders from Howe at Halifax on 23 May 1776 officially appointed Payne as an assistant to the deputy quartermaster general.[138]

Payne is listed as having brought the news of Colonel Johann Rall's destruction at Trenton from Amboy to New York in 1776. He took part in foraging party skirmishes near Brunswick in January 1777. He was present at Millstone Creek, New Jersey, on 20 January 1777 and wrote to Stephen Kemble, the deputy adjutant general, that the British forces had killed more than four hundred rebels and taken one hundred rebel prisoners. Modern scholarship shows that Payne's numbers were greatly exaggerated.[139] He was appointed deputy barracks master general at Philadelphia in approximately February 1778 when Howe became frustrated with Colonel James Robertson's handling of the role in Philadelphia. Payne returned to England to join the Royal Irish sometime before August 1779. He is listed as being present at Warley Camp when the regiment was inspected on 23 August 1779. The inspection return still listed him as a captain, so he must have been unaware that he had been promoted to major in the army two days earlier.[140]

Payne became the major of the 99th Regiment of Foot on 2 June 1780. The 99th, also known as the Jamaica Regiment of Foot, was raised in the English Midlands for service in the West Indies in 1780. The 99th served as garrison troops in Jamaica during the later stages of the Revolutionary War and returned to England to be disbanded in 1783. The 99th was at Cumberland Fort in Jamaica in December 1780 under Payne's command. Payne's military career seems to have ended with the disbanding of the 99th Foot.[141]

Payne married Maria Beaufoy Durant, the widow of George Durant, who owned Tong Estate in Shropshire.[142] Durant had effectively owned the entire village of Tong and ruled it as a feudal king. Tong Castle was the first truly Gothic building in Shropshire and required a very large fortune to maintain. Maria was the daughter of Mark Beaufoy, a Quaker vinegar brewer or merchant from Lambeth, Surrey, whom Durant married when he decided it was timely to be married to support his parliamentary ambitions. She was his second wife, but Durant was not a particularly faithful husband, and his extramarital affairs most likely continued throughout their union.

Durant was an associate of Payne's. They most likely met while Durant was serving either as a clerk for the pay office in the West Indies or as a volunteer at the end of the French and Indian War. Durant appears to have embezzled the astonishing amount of nearly £15 million in 2008 currency. It appears those funds were raised at least in part through the slave trade.

Although Maria was raised as a Quaker, she was baptized as an Anglican in Tong Church on 17 November 1782, before her marriage to Payne.[143] Once they were married, they underwent litigation for Durant's will, which was not properly witnessed before his death. Payne was listed as one of the two executors of Durant's estate.[144] The litigation took place in 1784 and 1785.

Payne and Maria had a daughter and sometimes lived in London in Bloomsbury.

Payne was buried on 22 May 1793 at Tong Parish in Shropshire. He was buried in the Durant vault in the center of the chancel, and when his coffin was opened in 1891, it was found to bear the inscription DIED MAY 14, 1793 AGED 38. Maria died on 28 April 1832 at the age of seventy-four and was buried at Dawlish. She was supposedly a great benefactress to the people of Tong. George Durant II, her son by George Durant, moved into Tong Castle in 1797.[145]

William Richardson

> Young [William] Richardson of the Royal Irish was the first to mount the works, and was instantly shot down; the front rank which succeeded shared the same fate.
>
> —Samuel Swett[146]

William Richardson (ca. 1747–?) came to America as an ensign, having been commissioned in January 1766. He was a twenty-year-old Irishman, according to the general return of officers when the regiment was inspected at Dublin in April 1767. He was assigned as the ensign of the lieutenant colonel's company when the Royal Irish arrived in North America in July 1767. In May 1768, he went west with Captain John Evans's company.

In a letter of 6 October 1769 from General Gage to Lord Barrington, the secretary of war, Richardson was mentioned as the "eldest ensign of the [Royal Irish] Regiment, who will purchase a Lieutenancy." He was also the eldest ensign in the regiment at that time, so he was not jumping over more senior ensigns, as Godfrey Tracey had attempted to do.[147]

Richardson was promoted to lieutenant on 16 February 1770, according to the army lists. However, he was still listed as the ensign in Evans's company through April 1770, then disappeared from the extant muster rolls, indicating he was transferred to be the lieutenant of the lieutenant colonel's company.

On 20 February 1770, Richardson entered the home of a Frenchman, Paulet des Rupeau, and removed his slave. Richardson stated he was under orders to do so but gave no further justification. On 6 June 1770, Rupeau called upon the Illinois Court of Judicature to redress the wrong, since Richardson still kept the slave. Richardson was ordered to appear to explain himself at the July session of the court, but the records of that outcome have not survived.[148]

Richardson was a member of a court of inquiry established by Lieutenant Colonel Wilkins at Fort Chartres to settle a dispute between Richard Bacon and George Morgan, which began on 24 September 1770. The court found in favor of Morgan on 2 October 1770, but Wilkins ordered the court back to its task, effectively directing it to change its verdict. The five young officers, including Richardson, came to the same verdict they had earlier provided, and they also chastised their colonel as politely as possible, on 20 October 1770. Fowler referred to Richardson as a perfect negative when discussing the officers of the Royal Irish in his letters to Wilkins. Richardson was one of the officers who wrote to Wilkins in March 1774 stating that Wilkins had done nothing to intentionally disfavor them. Fowler identified Richardson at another point as a co-conspirator with John Shee to get Wilkins to retire in order to secure a company.[149]

In late 1770, Richardson was transferred to Captain Lord's company. Lord was soon removed to raise the light company, leaving Richardson in temporary command. That company changed hands frequently; after

Lord was removed, it was briefly John Cope's company before becoming Payne's company. Richardson was still listed as the lieutenant of the company, stationed at Fort Chartres, in April 1772.

Richardson returned with the majority of the regiment to the East Coast, arriving in Philadelphia by the end of October 1772. He was given leave by General Gage at some point before July 1773, when he was listed as absent by leave of the commander in chief. Richardson returned to the regiment before October 1774 and was sent with the detachment to Boston as the lieutenant of Captain Robert Hamilton's company.

Richardson was present during the march to Concord; he had been ordered to do duty with the grenadier company until further notice on 16 April 1775, even though he officially remained part of Robert Hamilton's company.[150]

Richardson was still serving with the grenadiers when he was wounded at the Battle of Bunker Hill. He was the only officer listed as wounded in official returns during the American Revolution while serving with the Royal Irish.[151] He was promoted to captain in the summer of 1775 to retroactively take his rank from 20 April 1775, the date that Benjamin Johnson sold his commission. When the Royal Irish was mustered in August 1776 at Dover Castle, Richardson was listed as on leave "for the recovery of his health," which was probably still the result of his being wounded in June 1775. He returned to the regiment sometime before March 1777, when he was listed as being on recruiting duty in England. When the regiment was inspected in August 1777, Richardson had returned and was present with his company.

In 1779, Richardson participated in the instruction at Warley Camp and was present at the July muster. In March 1780, he was present with his company at Woburn, Massachusetts. He was most likely present with the regiment when it was called to aid the civil powers in suppressing the Gordon Riots in June 1780, and he was at Finchley Camp in October 1780. In February 1781, he was present with the regiment on the outskirts of London near Highgate, and by October 1781, he had embarked to Guernsey with the majority of the regiment.

Richardson was promoted to major in the 104th Regiment of Foot on 25 June 1782.[152] The 104th was stationed on Guernsey in 1783 when the regiment mutinied. The Royal Irish under Major John Mawby Sr. led the suppression of the mutiny. It is unclear whether Richardson was present during the mutiny. From there, Richardson moved into the 14th

Regiment of Light Dragoons on 31 March 1783 by exchanging with Andrew Corbet.[153]

The 14th Light Dragoons was stationed at Clonmell, Ireland, at the time. Richardson was listed on Lieutenant Colonel Grice Blakeney's leave on 19 October 1783. The returns seem to indicate he was in Ireland during his leave. He joined the regiment sometime between February and 15 April 1784, when he was present with his company at Clouqueen, Ireland. He remained with the 14th when it moved to Loughrea, Ireland, in July 1784.

The commander in chief granted Richardson a brief leave in the winter of 1785, but he returned to his regiment by 13 April 1785, because he was listed as present at Loughrea on that date. He was also present at Athlone on 20 July 1785. Richardson was then listed on the Lord Lieutenant of Ireland's leave on 1 January 1786. He was last listed in regimental returns as absent on 11 April 1786. He formally retired on 10 April 1786.[154]

George Stainforth

FIGURE 3.1 George Stainforth's coat of arms. *Courtesy of Ryan Gale*

George Stainforth (1736–17 October 1790) was the son of William and Judith Hawksworth Stainforth of York. William was a wine merchant in York.[155] The Stainforth family was an old Yorkshire family that traced its lineage to Leuric of Stanford, who fought at the Battles of Stamford and Hastings in 1066.

George Stainforth was commissioned as an ensign in the Royal Irish on 4 October 1755 as the army was expanding to meet wartime needs. By 1757, he was the Royal Irish's senior ensign and therefore had the first chance to purchase the next vacant lieutenancy in the regiment. His opportunity came on 27 March 1758 when John Freake was promoted to the Royal Irish's captain lieutenant.[156]

Stainforth's aunt, Elizabeth Stainforth, was appointed as the royal housekeeper at Buckingham House in 1762. This position was of substantial influence, and she appeared in many social diaries of the period.

Stainforth was able to purchase his captaincy on 3 May 1765 from Robert Batt upon the latter's retirement. He was present with his battalion company at Dublin in April 1767 when it was reviewed. He embarked for America with the regiment in May and was present at the 27 October 1767 muster of the regiment at Philadelphia.[157]

Stainforth's company remained at Philadelphia, along with Major Isaac Hamilton's company, when the rest of the Royal Irish moved to postings at Fort Pitt or in the Illinois Country. His company remained at Philadelphia through the spring of 1769, when it was ordered to Fort Chartres in Illinois and almost certainly followed the Ohio River from Fort Pitt to the confluence with the Mississippi River. There the company would have turned north up the Mississippi until it arrived at Fort Chartres.

Stainforth remained with the regiment in Illinois until sometime near his retirement on 2 June 1771. His company was passed to Thomas Batt, the son of the man from whom he had purchased his captain's commission six years earlier. According to the regimental accounts, Batt paid £950 for the commission on 19 June 1771. That was the difference in price between his lieutenancy and the cost of the captaincy.[158]

Stainforth married Ann Jarratt, the daughter of Reverend Jarratt of Killaloe, Ireland, in 1765. Their first child, Sophie, was born on 28 February 1766 and died two weeks later. The Stainforths' misfortune continued: a daughter, Lucy, died at birth in 1767; Mary, who was born on 26 December 1768, most likely at Philadelphia, died in childhood; and Diana, born in 1770, also died as a child. Ann was born on 12 August 1769 and was baptized in Philadelphia on 29 August. Their son, Richard Terrick, was born on 4 March 1772.

When Stainforth left the army, he remained in America and purchased an estate near Princeton, New Jersey, on 9 March 1773. According to postwar memorials, the Stainforths lived near Ibbeston Hamer, an officer of the 7th Foot, and William and Sarah Howard. Howard was a captain in the 17th Regiment of Foot until his wartime death. George and Ann Stainforth both wrote supporting depositions for Hamer's Loyalist loss claims in 1784.

At a later time, Stainforth purchased additional property in Middlesex and Somerset Counties, New Jersey, but it was confiscated by the state of New Jersey because of his loyalty to the Crown. According to his postwar memorials, he lost 115 acres of land near Princeton (in Mercer County) and requested reimbursement for the loss of two "negroes."[159] Stainforth is also listed as purchasing the indenture of Hannah Pierce on 5 May 1772 for four years at the cost of £15.[160]

Family records indicate that the Stainforths moved from Princeton under the protection of Charles Cornwallis's forces after the Battle of Princeton, when they were evicted by the Congressional Army. The family traveled to New York, and on 2 December 1777, George and Ann swore their first affidavits for compensation for the loss of their New Jersey property.[161]

Stainforth was appointed as a captain in the 2nd Battalion of the New Jersey Volunteers on 28 January 1778, while it was in Philadelphia. The battalion was assigned to support the Royal Artillery beginning in April 1777, and in that role the battalion served at Monmouth, New Jersey, where he was most likely present.[162]

Stainforth was a member of a court-martial board from 21 December 1778 to 30 January 1779 that tried Captain William Price of the Guides and Pioneers, who was accused of scandalous behavior; Lieutenant James Ford of the 7th Foot, who wrote a letter "containing expressions very disrespectful towards His Excellency" the commander in chief; and John McTaggart and Robert Murrary, for enticing a seaman to desert to a privateer.[163] Stainforth sat on a second board from 21 June to 30 July 1779 to hear cases on smuggling, desertions, breaking and entering, and potential spying.[164] He served on a third court-martial board from 4 September to 4 October 1780 in New York that tried Captain William Barry of the Volunteers of Ireland and Lieutenant and Quartermaster Charles Colburn of the Loyal American Regiment, along with several enlisted defendants.[165] He spent more time on a court-martial board in New York, from 12 to 19 September 1781, hearing the trial of Ensign David Sutherland of the 42nd Foot for "acting in a manner unbecoming the Character of an Officer and a Gentleman."[166] That may have been one of his final duties, since the 2nd Battalion of New Jersey Volunteers was drafted into the 1st and 4th Battalions of the New Jersey Volunteers and the officers were transferred to half pay on 25 August 1781.[167]

Stainforth is listed as a subscriber to a parliamentary loan of £12 million for the sum of £10,000. The loan, which was approved by Parliament on 15 March 1781, was partly to fund the ongoing cost of the wars in America and elsewhere.[168]

Upon returning to England in 1782, Stainforth lived at Stillington, Yorkshire, his family seat. He and Ann had two more sons there: William George, born 24 November 1783; and John, born 29 May 1785.

Stainforth died of palsy on 18 October 1790; his death was announced in the *European Magazine and London Review*, where he is listed as George Stainforth, Esq.[169]

The firstborn son, Richard Terrick Stainforth, inherited the family's Hutton Estate upon his father's death. (Stainforth himself had inherited the lands upon his own father's death in 1782.) In 1790, Richard entered the army as a cornet in the 1st Dragoon Guards. He was promoted to lieutenant in 1792 and lived in Bruges, Belgium, at the end of his life because of financial difficulties. Stainforth's great-great-great-grandson, George Hedley Stainforth, served in the Royal Air Force and in 1931 became the first man to exceed four hundred miles per hour in an airplane. He was killed in action near the Gulf of Suez in 1942.[170]

John Stewart

John Stewart (ca. 1735–1768) joined the army as an ensign in the Royal Irish on 12 March 1754, at age nineteen. His surname is sometimes given as Stuart. At the time, the Royal Irish Regiment was stationed in northern Ireland, with seven companies at Derry and three at Ballyshannon. He was promoted to lieutenant in the Royal Irish on 12 May 1756 and promoted to captain lieutenant 26 May 1762. He purchased his captaincy for £1,600 from Charles Stewart on 18 September 1765, while the regiment was stationed in Dublin. This was £100 over the regulated commission price for a captaincy in the regiment of foot.[171]

Stewart was not present for the April 1767 inspection at Dublin. He was listed as "recruiting in Ireland" to raise the men necessary to complete the regiment for American service. He appears to have been alone on recruiting service, since no other officers or enlisted men were listed as recruiting.[172]

When the Royal Irish arrived at Philadelphia, Stewart was in command of a battalion company. He was transferred to command the regiment's grenadier company in April 1768. He may actually have been in command of the grenadiers, since Captain Edmonstone had left for Fort Pitt the previous fall, but the muster returns do not show such a transfer. Stewart accompanied the regiment on its journey to the Illinois Country in the spring and summer of 1768. He served on the court-martial board at Fort Pitt in July 1768 that tried several soldiers for desertion and other capital crimes.[173]

Upon arriving at Fort Chartres, Stewart purchased a farm in company with Quartermaster George Buttricke, whom he appears to have befriended when Buttricke joined the regiment. Stewart was one of the first officers to be claimed by the American wilderness; he died, probably of malaria, on 30 September 1768, less than a month after the regiment's arrival at Fort Chartres.[174] Nevertheless, his subsistence allowance continued until 3 February 1769. Cox & Meir, the regimental agents, finally settled his accounts on 25 September 1775. The agent paid Stewart's executors more than £327, based on a request dated 5 October 1773.[175]

Lewis Wynne

Lewis Wynne (ca. 1740–14 March 1771) was probably the son of Lieutenant Colonel John Wynne of the Royal Irish Dragoons and Elizabeth Knott.[176] The Wynne family was related through marriage with the Folliotts, and Sir John Folliott was the Royal Irish's colonel when Wynne received his initial commission. Wynne was an Irishman and was approximately sixteen years old when he purchased an ensigncy in the Royal Irish on 18 May 1756 from Matthew Lane, who had been promoted. He purchased his lieutenancy from Charles Stuart on 4 March 1760 and purchased the next available lieutenancy when he became the senior ensign. He was present with the regiment in Dublin in April 1767.

Upon the regiment's arrival in Philadelphia, Wynne was assigned as the lieutenant of Captain Stewart's company. When the majority of the regiment was ordered west, Wynne was transferred to Captain Stainforth's company, which remained in Philadelphia. He was listed as present with that company on its musters in Philadelphia on 25 October 1768 and 6 June 1769. Wynne was a subscriber to Stephen Payne Adye's *A Treatise on Courts Martial*, published in 1769.

In the summer of 1769, Stainforth's company was ordered to Illinois. It is unclear whether Wynne accompanied it or remained in Philadelphia. If he traveled to Illinois, he returned to Pennsylvania that fall. On 16 February 1770, Wynne purchased the captain lieutenancy of the Royal Irish for £250 when Wadman retired. Wynne was accompanied by "his lady, Mrs. Monroe," most likely his wife, who had previously been widowed.

Wynne and his wife journeyed down the Ohio River in the spring of 1770 in the company of Lieutenant Fowler and his wife, along with a group of traders bound for Illinois. Wynne does not appear to have made a positive impression on the traders. George Morgan wrote that

"Mr. Wynn [sic] appeared to be as idle and besotted as Mr. Fowler was industrious and active."[177]

Wynne was president of a court of inquiry established by Lieutenant Colonel Wilkins at Fort Chartres to settle a dispute between Richard Bacon and George Morgan, which began on 24 September 1770. The court found in favor of Morgan on 2 October 1770, but Wilkins ordered the court back to its task, effectively directing it to change its verdict. The officers, under Wynne, came to the same verdict they had earlier provided, and they also chastised their colonel as politely as possible.[178]

Wynne and his wife appear to have remained in Illinois. He died on 14 March 1771, most likely at Fort Chartres, while still the captain lieutenant of the Royal Irish. He had not yet settled his debt to Wadman for purchasing the captain lieutenancy, so Wadman's brother wrote to Wilkins through Gage in February 1771 to try to get Wilkins to assist in obtaining the £250 still owed to Wadman.[179] Wynne's wife disappears from the historical record at that point. His commission remained vacant until 19 July 1771, when it went to John Mawby Sr. without purchase.

There is an unexplained entry in the regimental ledgers showing a payment to Wynne's account for "By Cash, Lieut. Wynne's order on Mr. Garton for Havanna Prize Money" for a total of more than £5, which was paid 6 May 1773.[180] It is possible that Wynne had served as an aide-de-camp on the Havana expedition, although the Royal Irish's returns have not been located for the period, so it is not possible to check whether he was serving with the regiment in Ireland at that time.

4 Lieutenants

This chapter examines the officers who reached the rank of lieutenant during their service in North America. Many of these officers continued to a higher rank. A few retired as lieutenants, and others died in the service. Lieutenant was the most common rank in the regiment: there were nine lieutenancies before the regiment's expansion in 1770 and eleven lieutenancies after that. The role of the lieutenant was to assist the captain and command the company in his stead, should he be absent. Lieutenants regularly took on that role in the Royal Irish for both short and lengthy periods. Absentee Captain Benjamin Johnson's company, for instance, was always commanded by a lieutenant while in America. After 1772, Lieutenant Colonel John Wilkins's company was similarly commanded by a lieutenant. Several subalterns commanded detachments of nearly company size for long stretches of time at Kaskaskia, Illinois.

George Bewes

FIGURE 4.1 George Bewes's coat of arms.
Courtesy of Ryan Gale

George Bewes (ca. 1747–16 January 1782) was the son of George Warmington Bewes and Susanna Kelly of St. Stephen by Launceston in Cornwall.[1] He had two sisters, Susanna and Elizabeth.[2] His father died in late 1767, leaving him as the executor of an estate that included a wide range of properties.[3] The family seems to have been connected to the Duke of Bedford.

Bewes joined the Royal Irish on 10 April 1769 as an ensign when he was approximately twenty-two years old, so he was getting a late start in his career. He was assigned to Johnson's company, which was stationed at Fort Pitt. Bewes was still listed as an ensign at Fort Pitt in Johnson's company in April 1772 by Lieutenant Colonel Wilkins. However, he had actually purchased his lieutenancy on 27 February 1772, but news did not travel quickly from Illinois to Fort Pitt to London.[4] He had sold his ensigncy to Edward Hand.

Bewes was transferred to the grenadier company by 24 October 1772, when the Royal Irish reorganized after returning from Illinois and Fort Pitt. Bewes was a signatory of the February 1773 letter to Colonel John Sebright asking for his intervention with Wilkins (see chapter 2). Bewes appears to have left for the recruiting service in England before April 1773, because he did not sign the second letter to Sebright. He was listed as being on recruiting service on the July 1773 muster and remained on recruiting service through at least July 1774. Since he was not present in Philadelphia, he was removed from the grenadier company and assigned to one of the companies in Illinois, although he was not present in Illinois.[5]

Bewes returned to the regiment by late 1774 and was placed back in the grenadier company. He most likely was engaged with the grenadiers at Bunker Hill and survived the battle unscathed. When the grenadiers were mustered on 7 October 1775 at Charles Town Heights, he was present.

Bewes returned to England with the cadre of the regiment in December 1775 and retained his position with the grenadiers when the regiment was reorganized in England. He was listed as being on recruiting service in August 1776. In March 1777, he was present in command of the grenadier company at Dover Castle in Kent; the other officers were on recruiting duty at the time.

Bewes purchased Captain Hugh Lord's commission on 14 July 1777 and took command of one of the battalion companies at that point. He sat on the court-martial board at Coxheath Camp on 31 August 1778 to try Private Bryan Sheridan of the Royal Irish for desertion. Sheridan was found guilty and sentenced to be shot to death.[6] Bewes was present with his company at Warley Camp when it was inspected in August 1779. In March 1780, he and his company were posted as a single company garrison at Tring in western Hertfordshire. He appears to have been with the regiment when it was ordered to London to support the civil powers in putting down the Gordon Riots in June 1780.

Bewes was with the regiment at Finchley Camp when it was mustered in October 1780. In February 1781, he was with the regiment when it was posted outside London. He embarked with the regiment to the Channel Islands and was present with his company in October 1781. He appeared in returns for the last time in March 1782, but the War Office recorded his death on 16 January 1782. His commission went to Thomas Serle.[7]

George Bruere

FIGURE 4.2 George Bruere's coat of arms. *Courtesy of Ryan Gale*

George Bruere (1744–2 September 1786) was the son of George James Bruere, the governor of Bermuda from 1764 to 1780. His surname is occasionally given as Brewer.[8] His mother was Elizabeth Neale.[9] Bruere originally served in the 14th Foot with his older brother. He was commissioned as quartermaster on 4 January 1757 in the 14th Foot and as an ensign on 11 September 1759. He resigned the role of quartermaster three days later, on 14 September.

Bruere held army rank as lieutenant from 16 March 1761, the date of commission in an additional company of the 14th. He was reduced to half pay in 1763 and continued that way until joining the Royal Irish in 1769. He traveled to Bermuda with his father in 1764. His father wrote to Gage in March 1767 asking for leave for his son, who remained in the 14th Foot, to be able to visit the family in Bermuda.[10]

Bruere's lieutenancy in the Royal Irish dated from 4 February 1769. He was originally assigned to Captain Matthew Lane's company and first appeared in the October 1769 returns. He remained with that company, which became Captain Lord's through most of 1770 and early 1771. He was posted to George Stainforth's company by 24 October 1771 and remained there until transferred to the grenadier company around December 1771.

Bruere's stay with the grenadiers was short-lived, however, and he was listed as the junior lieutenant in the light company in April 1772. He does not appear to have stayed in Illinois, so in reality his movement between the companies may have simply been a paper exercise. He was listed as the senior lieutenant of the grenadier company in the July 1773 returns and was listed as on leave with the permission of the commander in chief. He remained on leave throughout 1773.[11]

Bruere was present with the regiment in Philadelphia in July 1774, still assigned to the grenadiers. When the regiment marched from Philadelphia to Perth Amboy, New Jersey, in September 1774, he was mentioned by Nicholas Trist as one of the three officers who marched the entire route with the men. The other officers apparently rode or were conveyed by carriage.[12]

Bruere went to Boston in October 1774 with the grenadiers and was with the company as part of Lieutenant Colonel Francis Smith's march to Lexington and Concord on 19 April 1775. He participated in the Battle of Bunker Hill along with the grenadier company. It is possible that he was slightly wounded, but he was not reported among the injured. His older brother, John, was killed at Bunker Hill while serving as a staff officer.[13]

Bruere petitioned both King George and General Gage for a promotion to captain in the 14th Foot, based on his older brother's death and his own earlier reduction to half pay. The petition stated the following:

> To the King's most Excellent Majesty
>
> The Petition of Lieut. George Bruere of the 18th Regiment
>
>> Most humbly sheweth, That your Majesty's Petitioner has been nineteen Years in the Service; and fifteen years a Lieutenant.
>>
>> That in the year 1763, Your Majesty's Petitioner being a Lieutenant in the 14th Regiment was reduced, and was at the time the Eldest reduced Lieutenant in that Regiment.
>>
>> That if it had not been your Majesty's Petitioner's misfortune to have been reduced in the Year 1763; He would now in Succession have been the Eldest Captain in the 14th Regiment.
>>
>> That your Majesty's Petitioner was Eldest Lieutenant of the Grenadiers of the Line, at Concord and on his Captains being wounded, commanded the Grenadier Company of the Royal Irish on the Return from Lexington.
>>
>> That by the 18th Regiments being ordered to England and there by not having additional Companies as the Regiments remaining in America have Your Majesty's Petitioner loses that preferment to which he would have been entitled in the Course of Succession.
>>
>> That your Majesty's Petitioner's Father has spent his Life in the Military Service of your Majesty, and your Royal Grandfather, and

is now Governor of your Majesty's Islands of Bermuda, but having had a Family of Ten Children to breed up, (nine of whom are still living) is unable to purchase preferment for your Majesty's Petitioner, though his Eldest Son.

That your Majesty's Petitioner's younger Brother being Eldest Lieutenant (& Adjutant) of the 14th Regiment, lost his Life attending General How, on your Majesty's Service at Bunker's Hill.

That two or three Companies being now vacant in the 14th Regiment, Your Majesty's Petitioner most humbly submits these Facts to your Majesty's Consideration, hoping to receive from your Majesty's Goodness a Company in that Regiment in which your Majesty's Petitioner and his Brother would have been both Captains at this time, but for the Reduction of your Majesty's Petitioner in 1763 and the Unfortunate Loss of His Brother at the attack of Bunker's Hill.

And your Majesty's Petitioner as in Duty Bounds [sic] will ever pray.[14]

Gage did not honor his request, and the companies of the 14th Foot went to other men. Bruere served as his father's agent during Bermuda's Stolen Gunpowder Affair in 1775 and early 1776. The Bermudian colonists sympathetic to the American revolutionaries on 14 August 1775 stole barrels of gunpowder from a cavern used as a magazine under Governor Bruere's control. The powder kegs were then transported to an American ship and sent to aid the rebellion. Bruere returned to London with the cadre of the Royal Irish in early 1776. The 1776 army list shows that Bruere resigned from the Royal Irish on 14 June 1776.

Bruere was promoted to captain in the 3rd Battalion of the 60th (Royal American) Regiment on 16 March 1776. Most likely this was at least a partial answer to his petition to the king. He was stationed at St. Augustine, East Florida, in 1776, where he met Martha Louisa Fatio, the sister of a fellow officer. The Fatio family had immigrated to Florida from Switzerland via London and established a plantation in the area called New Switzerland. Louisa was nineteen years Bruere's junior, but they were married in 1777; she was fourteen years old at the time. Bruere was already a widower by that time and apparently had three daughters whom the new wife had to raise. It is possible that Bruere's first wife was a member of the Moultrie family in South Carolina.

Bruere was on duty in New York City in mid-1777 and was ordered by General William Howe to command a detachment of the 60th Foot that was embarking on the *Springfield Transport* on 3 July 1777. It is unclear where the detachment was headed, but it may have been returning to Florida.[15] Bruere served as a staff officer in New York in 1778. He appears to have returned to his battalion by the end of the year. He was possibly wounded in February 1779 at Beauford, South Carolina, and returned to England to recover. He was promoted to the local rank of lieutenant colonel "in the island of Bermudas only" on 21 December 1779.

In 1780, in London, he was appointed as lieutenant governor of Bermuda while his father was still governor. However, he did not reach Bermuda until after his father died on 10 October 1780.

Bruere became acting governor upon his father's death and worked to keep the colonists loyal to the Crown. Bruere was not appointed as governor, so he returned to England in 1782. He was transferred to the command of a company in the 1st Battalion of the 60th Regiment on 25 April 1784, when the 3rd Battalion was reduced at the conclusion of the American Revolution.

Bruere was appointed to command one of the two independent companies of invalids at Fort George in Scotland in 1785. He arrived at Fort George before December 1785 and appears to have been the ranking officer present. Bruere died at the house of his sister, Charlotte, and brother-in-law, Alexander Todd, on 2 September 1786 in Alderston, Haddington, East Lothian. He died intestate, leaving less than £100 to Louisa. His death was noted in the *Gentleman's* magazine and the *European Magazine and London Review.* He had no children with Louisa.[16]

William Conolly

William Conolly (ca. 1747–1817) was the least experienced officer embarking from Cork Harbor, Ireland, in 1767. He had been commissioned as an ensign in the Royal Irish on 8 April 1767, less than a month before the regiment's embarkation for America. He was not listed in the 11 April 1767 inspection return, so he must have joined the regiment between 12 April and 1 May 1767, when the regiment embarked. Later returns list him as Irish. His original assignment was as the ensign of George Stainforth's company. He was stationed in command at Kaskaskia while still an ensign; some of the records of payments he made to visiting Indians and his list of repairs to the buildings at Kaskaskia still exist.

Conolly was the junior member of the court of inquiry mentioned previously that settled the dispute between Richard Bacon and George

Morgan. Conolly became sick on 28 September, causing a short delay in the proceedings. He sat on this court again on 16 October 1770.

Conolly was ordered to command at Kaskaskia on 21 December 1770. He appears to have crossed Wilkins on occasion and was placed under arrest at least twice in Illinois. The reasons for his arrest have not surfaced. According to Alexander Fowler, he was not tried but made some concessions to Wilkins in order to be reinstated to duty. The disagreements with Wilkins may in part have stemmed from Conolly's conduct of Indian affairs while stationed at Kaskaskia. Fowler also states that Corporal Saunders leveled some "very serious complaints" against Conolly while he was serving at Kaskaskia. What those complaints were has been lost to history.[17]

Conolly purchased a lieutenancy on 2 June 1771, when Benjamin Chapman was promoted to captain. The regimental agent's ledger shows Conolly paying £150 to Captain John Evans for the difference between his ensigncy and the lieutenancy. He drew on funds from London merchants Colebrooke and Nesbitt to purchase. Colebrook and Nesbitt were in partnership with Moses Franks of Franks and Company, a Philadelphia mercantile establishment with some ties to Illinois. Conolly may have used Franks to help arrange his purchase.[18] He then served as the lieutenant of Chapman's company stationed at Fort Chartres until it was sent east in May 1772. At that time, Conolly was posted to Wilkins's company, which remained in Illinois at Kaskaskia.

Conolly remained in Illinois as one of the two lieutenants under the command of Captain Lord; he was the nominal commander of Lieutenant Colonel Wilkins's company. One payment voucher from Illinois bears his signature, but the date is hard to read. It is most likely 1773.

Conolly was at the public council of chiefs and sachems held by the various tribes of Illinois Indians in early July 1773. His name appears as a witness to at least one of the land deeds obtained by William Murray from the Indians at that time.[19]

Conolly was recommended by Major Isaac Hamilton to purchase Charles Edmonstone's captaincy in July 1775, but it appears he was unable to pay, and therefore the company went to Henry Fermor.[20] Conolly remained in the Illinois Country until May 1776, when Lord's detachment was ordered to reinforce Detroit. In June 1776, the officers and men not drafted into the 8th (King's) Foot began their return to England, arriving in December 1776. Conolly was listed as the lieutenant of Robert Hamilton's company in August 1776, but as "on duty in America."[21]

As the Royal Irish was rebuilt at Dover, Conolly was listed as being on recruiting duty several times in 1777–1778. He was transferred to Benjamin Payne's company in December 1776, since Captain Payne was still absent and Conolly had been a de facto company commander since the spring of 1772.

Conolly continued with the Royal Irish, becoming a captain most likely without purchase on 26 December 1778, only shortly after his last return from recruiting duty. He was originally assigned to one of the additional companies but took command of a battalion company on 2 June 1780. On 27 June, Conolly was on picket duty in London in the aftermath of the Gordon Riots. His men appear to have taken a female prisoner that night, who exposed a plot among some rioters to burn down a house. He was at Finchley Camp with the regiment that summer.[22]

In February 1781, Conolly's company was stationed at or near Highgate on the northern outskirts of London. By October 1781, Conolly was with his company in the Channel Islands. He remained with the regiment throughout its time on the Channel Islands and was listed as present at Gibraltar in February 1784.[23] He was still with the regiment in 1787, serving at Gibraltar.[24]

Conolly became the regiment's senior captain in 1790 when John Mawby Sr. was promoted to major. He was still a captain when he was in command of the Royal Irish at the Siege of Toulon, where, on 17 December 1793, he "defended his post with great gallantry until the enemy forced the Spanish side, when he fell back fighting to another position."[25] Conolly, in command of the British quarter of the garrison, was unable to maintain his position after the Spanish quarter was breached, "notwithstanding several gallant Efforts [that] were made for that Purpose."[26]

Conolly was promoted to major of the Royal Irish on 1 September 1795, again most likely without purchase, when H. T. Montressor was promoted to lieutenant colonel upon the establishment of a second battalion of the regiment. He was promoted to lieutenant colonel in the army on 1 January 1798 and retired on 31 May 1799. His commission as major went to Sebright Mawby. When Conolly left the regiment, with him went the last of the Royal Irish's American experience. His sons, Hunt and William Jr., were both officers in the Royal Irish in 1798. Hunt had been commissioned as a lieutenant on 2 September 1795, and William Jr. was commissioned as a lieutenant on 5 June 1795.[27]

Conolly was living in Birmingham, England, in 1815 when he drafted his last will and testament. He appears to have died in 1817.[28] Conolly was not well off; he had had to borrow money to purchase his lieutenancy, and all of his further promotions had been without purchase, which slowed his career progression substantially compared to those who were able to purchase a commission as soon as it was available. Fermor, who obtained the captaincy that Conolly could not purchase in 1775 because of a lack of funds, was promoted to major in 1779. Conolly was not promoted to captain until 1778 and had to wait until 1795 to be promoted to major without purchase.

Edward Crosby

Edward Crosby (ca. 1750–26 October 1780) was originally commissioned as a second lieutenant in Gorham's North American Rangers on 14 May 1762. He is listed as English in army records (occasionally under the surname Crosbey), but he was almost certainly an American. He was commissioned at a time when several of the older officers were judged unfit for the Havana campaign because of previous hard service and wounds. It is possible that he participated in the Havana campaign, since some or all of Gorham's companies were involved.

Crosby was promoted to lieutenant on 15 September 1762. After returning to North America, the men were drafted and the officers were ordered to recruit a new body of men. Some of the Rangers were sent to Detroit to assist in putting down Pontiac's Rebellion, either in conjunction with or as draughts into the 17th Foot in 1763. Crosby's participation in either the recruiting efforts of the regiment or its deployment to Detroit is not clear. The unit was disbanded in August 1763, and Crosby was placed on half pay.[29]

He was recalled from half pay into the Royal Irish on 8 September 1774 and was assigned to Major Edmonstone's company in New York City. According to his own testimony, Crosby joined the regiment at New York City in February 1775. His appointment from half pay was posted to the Royal Irish's orderly book in Boston on 8 December 1774. He remained with the regiment while it was stationed in New York City. He appears to have either loaned money to or borrowed money from John Linn, the surgeon's mate, while in New York.

When the companies at New York marched to the wharf to embark on HMS *Asia* on 6 June 1775, Crosby would have been in command of Major Edmonstone's company. In his testimony at Payne's trial, he stated that he was posted in the center of the body of men and was unable to report on the events, but he thought that Captain Payne had handled himself in the best interests of the king's service. Crosby remained on board HMS *Asia* until 16 June when the majority of the regiment landed on Governor's Island and remained there until transported to Boston in late June.[30]

Crosby was present with the regiment in Boston in October 1775, still with Major Edmonstone's company. When the Royal Irish embarked for England in December 1775, Crosby remained in America. He was appointed captain lieutenant of the Royal Fencible Americans on 16 September 1775 and journeyed to Halifax with that regiment in March 1776. He resigned his provincial commission on 14 May 1776, when Howe ordered his regular officers to choose between their regular and provincial commissions. However, as late as 12 August 1776, Crosby was still listed as on duty in America.[31]

Crosby was present with Captain William Blackwood's company when the Royal Irish was inspected at Dover Castle in May 1777, and he was listed on recruiting service in August 1777 and March 1778. He was transferred to Captain Fermor's company in mid-1776 and remained with it until June 1779, when he was removed to the lieutenant colonel's company. He was present at Warley Camp commanding that company when it was mustered on 19 June 1779.

Crosby was promoted to captain lieutenant on 29 November 1779; however, in March 1780 he returned to the command of the lieutenant colonel's company at Dunstable. He died of an unknown cause on 26 October 1780, and his commission passed to John Joyner Ellis.[32]

John de Birniere

John de Birniere (ca. 1745– ?) began his military career on 22 November 1755 with the purchase of an ensigncy in the newly raised 55th Regiment of Foot. He came to America and fought with the 55th against the French and Indians in the North American wilderness. As a member of the 55th, he learned to fight as light infantry and use the woods to advantage, since Lord Howe, who commanded the regiment, turned the entire regiment into light infantrymen. He was present at Fort Ticonderoga on Lake Champlain in 1758, where the 55th, along with the 42nd Foot, charged the redoubts.

De Birniere was promoted to lieutenant in the 44th Foot on 9 August 1760 and served with that regiment until he was reduced to half pay in 1763.[33]

De Birniere remained in New York after the war and was involved in land speculation to some extent. He is listed as a party to several land transactions in New York between 1765 and 1769. There is also extant correspondence with Sir William Johnson regarding land sales and a letter from Thomas Gage certifying de Birniere's service as a lieutenant in the 44th Foot during the French and Indian War, possibly to support an application for a land grant.[34] Beyond purchase, de Birniere was granted two thousand acres in Albany County, New York, on 22 May 1770 for his services as a lieutenant in the 44th Foot.[35]

De Birniere returned to active service with the Royal Irish on 4 February 1769. When the regiment was authorized a company of light infantry, it was natural to choose de Birniere as one of its lieutenants. While at Fort Chartres, he also served as the deputy commissary officer and was involved in several affairs concerning the types and qualities of provisions. De Birniere served as secretary to Wilkins for a period from 9 June 1771. He was paid £100 per annum; James Rumsey had been paid a similar sum.[36]

A 1772 order for two kegs of Madeira by de Birniere from B&M Gratz arrived in bad condition at Philadelphia. However, de Birniere was able to supply himself from what was left in Illinois when the rest of the officers returned east. When the majority of the regiment returned to Philadelphia, de Birniere was left at Kaskaskia as second in command to Lord. Since Lord did not speak French, it was good that de Birniere remained with the light company. Gage allowed Lord to retain de Birniere's services as a French interpreter. Many documents within the Kaskaskia Records show de Birniere as a participant in legal dealings, although Clarence Alvord and Clarence Carter did not identify him as a British officer in their historical work.

De Birniere's signature can be found on all types of documents, from wills to bonds to extra duty payrolls. He and William Conolly witnessed Peter Murray put up a £5,000 bond to ensure that his furs were delivered to an English port in April 1773. The furs enumerated included more than 15,000 deer hides, nearly 300 beaver pelts, and 103 bear pelts. The inventory of the estate of Jean Baptiste St. Gemme Bauvais bears de Birniere's signature as official recorder of the document. According to Lord, de Birniere was paid a dollar a day for his services as an interpreter, the same price paid to the civilian French interpreter at Cahokia.[37]

At the evacuation of Kaskaskia, de Birniere marched to Detroit with Lord's detachment. De Birniere, who was acquainted with Lieutenant Governor Henry Hamilton, left a sealed copy of his will with Hamilton, which he later asked Hamilton to "commit to the flames" because it included "an instance of imprudence." He also asked Hamilton to arrange for the emancipation of Perdiac, a slave under twenty-one years old belonging to de Birniere. The emancipation was to take place at age twenty-one.[38]

De Birniere remained with the Royal Irish through 1778, by which time he was its senior lieutenant. He was made a captain of the 79th Regiment of Foot, also known as the Liverpool Regiment or Royal Liverpool Volunteers, on 11 January 1778, but he did not leave the Royal Irish until 4 June 1778. He was appointed to serve as the major of a brigade in June 1778 as well, although the exact nature of the assignment is unknown.[39]

The 79th was sent to the West Indies, so de Birniere got another chance to fight in America.[40] As a result of the same types of fevers that de Birniere had experienced in Illinois, only eighty-four men of the 79th Foot survived to return to England. He did not participate in the operations in Nicaragua that included a small detachment of the 79th Foot. De Birniere came back to England from Jamaica on account of ill health and was in Exeter in November 1779.[41]

De Birniere was reduced to half pay at the end of the American Revolution. An extant letter in Theobald Wolfe Tone's papers appears to be from de Birniere, posted from Wrexham, Wales, in August 1793, stating that he would visit Tone in November and was eager to discuss the activities of the Irish Parliament.[42]

De Birniere was appointed as the major of a "brigade to the forces" in November 1793 while still on half pay with the 79th Foot.[43] He returned to active service on 4 April 1794 with the newly raised 88th (Connaught Rangers) Regiment of Foot. However, the returns for that regiment do not show him serving with it. Although he had served as a captain with it, he had been one of many captains promoted to a major in the army on 1 March 1794.[44]

De Birniere was promoted to lieutenant colonel in the army on 17 February 1795. He was promoted to lieutenant colonel in the 60th (Royal American) Regiment on 5 March 1796, most likely because of his service as a staff officer.[45] His retirement was announced in the *London Gazette* on 7 April 1798, and his position in the 60th Foot was taken by John Hughes.[46]

De Birniere married Ann Jones, the third daughter of Mary Wray and Conway Jones, sometime before 29 April 1778. She seems to have been significantly younger than he. According to a secondary source, she was residing with a married daughter in Charleston, South Carolina, around 1820.[47]

John Peter DeLancey

John Peter DeLancey (15 July 1753–1828), was the fourth son and eighth child of Lieutenant Governor James and Anne Heathcote DeLancey.[48] His surname is sometimes given as de Lancey or Delancey. He was educated in England at Harrow and the Woolwich Military College under the care of his older brother, James, who had served as an aide de camp to General James Abercrombie at Ticonderoga.

DeLancey was commissioned on 19 July 1771 as an ensign in the Royal Irish. He joined the regiment in November 1771 as an ensign while a portion of the regiment was stationed in Philadelphia. He was listed as serving as in Philadelphia as the ensign in Captain Thomas Batt's company in April 1772.

DeLancey was present and under arms when the five companies in New York City were confronted by a mob under Captain Benjamin Payne. DeLancey seems to have been ready to fight that day, arriving on the parade with his fusil and fixed bayonet. Payne, acting under Major Isaac Hamilton's orders, directed DeLancey to unfix his bayonet for the march to the quay and embarkation aboard HMS *Asia*. Testimony from Payne's court-martial shows that DeLancey's life was threatened by the mob "merely for speaking." Most likely he was urging several of the soldiers not to desert.[49]

DeLancey was promoted to lieutenant in July 1775 and embarked on Payne's wood-cutting expedition to Penobscot that fall. From the point of view of the provincial soldiers on that expedition, he was not particularly accommodating.[50]

When the Royal Irish was drafted in late 1775, DeLancey returned to England with the remainder of the Royal Irish but quickly volunteered to return to America. He offered to Lord George Germain to return to America as a volunteer but could not obtain leave to do so. In 1777, DeLancey was finally granted the king's permission to return to America and took charge of recruits for that trip. When he arrived in America, William Howe appointed him lieutenant and adjutant to Captain Patrick Ferguson's Corps of Riflemen. He served with the riflemen throughout the Philadelphia campaign, including at Brandywine and Germantown. DeLancey distinguished himself during the campaign for his "Gallant Behaviour in that Corps," according to his agent. He remained with the riflemen until they were disbanded and the men drafted into the light infantry.[51]

At the same time that the Corps of Riflemen was being dissolved, William Allen, a former continental officer, was creating a battalion of Pennsylvania Loyalists, and in the fall of 1777 he recommended DeLancey as the unit's major.[52] DeLancey's own affidavit stated that he became major soon after the British took control of Philadelphia. It is unknown why Allen recommended DeLancey as the battalion's major, but Howe, who was the battalion's titular colonel, may have seen it as a reward for his service under Ferguson. DeLancey served with the Pennsylvanians at the Battle of Monmouth in late June 1778, where they served to escort the army's baggage. The battalion lost only two men in the battle, both captured.[53]

In the fall of 1778, DeLancey was ordered to the garrison at Pensacola, Florida, with the Pennsylvania Loyalists, the Maryland Regiment, and the Third Waldeck Regiment. By the middle of 1779, the Loyalist units at Pensacola were severely under strength, so Brigadier General James Campbell decided to reorganize the Pennsylvanians and the Maryland Loyalists into a single battalion titled the United Corps of Maryland and Pennsylvania Loyalists. He wrote to North American commander in chief General Henry Clinton for permission to do so in March 1779. Campbell had still not heard back from Clinton by December 1779, so he moved forward with the reorganization on 26 December 1779.

DeLancey was to serve as the new unit's major, and Major John McDonald of the Maryland Loyalists was left without an assignment. DeLancey remained with the Pensacola garrison and was for a time in command of the battalion because Allen was absent. DeLancey received orders to join the Royal Irish in March 1780 and was appointed its captain lieutenant at the same time. He appears to have left Florida in July 1780 to return to England to take up his captaincy in the Royal Irish. Later, Clinton returned the officers to their original positions, but by that time, DeLancey had returned to England with the Royal Irish.[54]

On his way to England, DeLancey stopped at Charleston, South Carolina, apparently in late September 1780. Because of a lack of experienced officers, Lieutenant Colonel Nesbit Balfour pressed DeLancey into an ad hoc command to retake George Town and Black Mingo in support of Colonel James Cassells, whose forces had been pushed back to George Town by Francis Marion. DeLancey's command consisted of seventy men of Brown's corps, approximately thirty convalescents from Cornwallis's army, and a dozen men of the 63rd Foot who manned a galley. Balfour wrote to Cornwallis that "I recollected a Major DeLancey who was of

Fergusons [*sic*] Corps, a Lieut. of the Royal Irish. who has seen a good deal of service and I know to be very active." DeLancey appears to have led the men to George Town about 5 October 1780. According to Balfour, he had stopped at Charleston on his way to New York to resign his provincial commission and return to his regiment, the Royal Irish.[55]

DeLancey was promoted to captain in the Royal Irish on 14 July 1780.[56] He served with the regiment while it was stationed in southern England and Jersey, and he was assigned to one of the regiment's additional companies until he took over William Richardson's Battalion company in 1782 while the regiment was posted to the Channel Islands. When Benjamin Chapman was promoted to major of the regiment, Delancey was chosen to command the Royal Irish's grenadier company. In late 1783, the Royal Irish, including DeLancey, was ordered to Gibraltar to reinforce the regiments that had weathered the Franco-Spanish siege. Throughout 1784, DeLancey was listed as present with the regiment at Gibraltar.[57]

DeLancey worked to be reimbursed for the personal loss of his New York properties while stationed at Gibraltar. He wrote to the Right Honorable Lords Commissioners of His Majesty's Treasury that when he was ordered to return to England and the Royal Irish in March 1780, he was unable to sell his New York properties because they lay partly outside British lines at the time. According to his memorial, his estate in New York City was valued at £8,000, allowing for necessary repairs and taxes, and provided a yearly income of £550.

DeLancey also mentioned an estate at Mamaroneck in Westchester County that had been willed to him by his mother. This estate was approximately six hundred acres and worth £5 per acre. DeLancey asked that the lords reimburse him the £11,000 he was losing when America was granted "absolute unconditional Independence." He also mentioned that his lack of access to his estates caused him military hardship because he was prevented from "purchasing such promotion in the Army as he otherwise had a right to expect."[58]

DeLancey used his influence to bring a number of his relatives into the Royal Irish Regiment in the 1780s. His nephew, John DeLancey, the eldest son of his brother James, was appointed an ensign in the Royal Irish on 7 February 1783. He was promoted to lieutenant on 20 December 1786. In May 1788, nephew John was transferred to the 60th (Royal America) Regiment. The will of the nephew indicated that his uncle had assisted in obtaining his commission in the 18th (Royal Irish) Regiment of Foot, so nephew John left his uncle a bequest in reciprocity.⁵⁹ Nephew John's younger brother, James, was appointed an ensign in the Royal Irish on 13 June 1781. James was also a lieutenant in the 1st Battalion of DeLancey's Loyalists from 7 March 1783.⁶⁰

On 28 September 1785, DeLancey married Elizabeth Floyd, the daughter of Colonel Richard Floyd, who had lived in Suffolk County, Long Island, before the Revolutionary War, and Arabella Jones.⁶¹

DeLancey was involved in a duel with Major Benjamin Chapman in 1788 while the regiment was stationed at Gibraltar. His conduct at the duel caused Chapman to leave the field of honor, stating that he would not fight with a murderer. The king's response to the affair of honor was to have DeLancey's name struck off of the army list forever, effectively banning him from any further military service. Here is a contemporary account of the event:

> A few weeks since a violent affray happened in the 18th regiment, stationed in Gibraltar, which unfortunately terminated in a duel between Major Benjamin Chapman, the commanding officer of the regiment at the time, and Captain de Lancey, an American gentleman belonging to the same corps.
>
> When they met at the ground, Captain de Lancey made a most extraordinary declaration, viz. "That Major Chapman might fire if he thought proper, but for his part he was resolved not to discharge his pistol, until the muzzle of it touched the Major's breast." To which the Major replied, "That he had expected, when he came there to decide their difference upon the point of honour, that it was with a gentleman, and not an assassin" at the same instant, he threw away his pistol, and left the ground with his second.
>
> His Majesty was so much offended with the conduct of Captain De Lancey, that he has commanded his name to be Struck out of the Army List for ever.⁶²

The nature of the conflict between the two officers is unclear, but it may have been related to DeLancey's money troubles.

DeLancey's commission was taken by Alexander Philip Forbes of the 60th (Royal American) Regiment on 2 June 1788.⁶³

DeLancey returned to New York in 1789 with his family, having obviously lost favor with the Crown. He fought to obtain recompense for his loss of American property, and upon his return he reestablished his claim to the property. In fact, one wonders why his property was not confiscated.⁶⁴

DeLancey built a house in Mamaroneck, known as Heathcote Hill, on the site of his grandfather's home on the north side of the Boston Post Road in Westchester County, New York. The original home had been burned down before the Revolutionary War, according to secondary sources. Another home, known as the Delancey House, was nearby, at the corner of the Boston Post Road and what was later known as Fenimore Road. A skirmish between Colonel John Haslet's 1st Delaware Regiment and the Queen's American Rangers supposedly took place in the vicinity on 21 October 1776.[65]

In 1814, DeLancey was elected warden of St. Thomas Parish in Mamaroneck. His wife died on 8 May 1820 in Mamaroneck, and he remained in Westchester County until he died on 30 January 1828.[66]

Their children were Anne Charlotte (1786–1822), who married John London MacAdam; Thomas James (1789–1822); Susan Augusta (1792–1852), who married the novelist James Fenimore Cooper on 1 January 1811 and had seven children; Maria Frances (1793–1806); Edward Floyd (1795–1820), who was killed in an accident; William Heathcote (1797–1865), who was a prominent Episcopal clergyman, provost of the University of Pennsylvania from 1827 to 1832, the first bishop of western New York from 1839 until his death, the husband of Frances Munro, and the father of five sons and three daughters; Elizabeth Caroline (1801–1860); and Marth Arabella (1803–?).

DeLancey's home was later moved to the corner of Fenimore and Boston Post Roads and later served as the Fenimore Inn.[67]

John Joyner Ellis

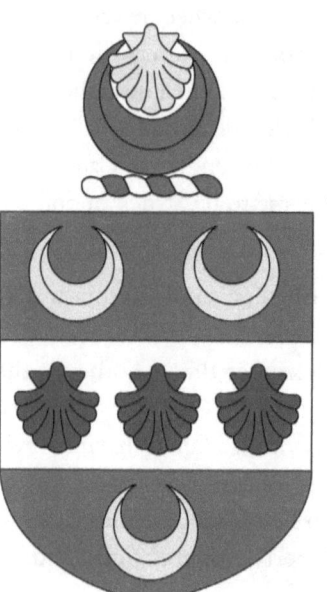

FIGURE 4.3 John Joyner Ellis's coat of arms. *Courtesy of Ryan Gale*

John Joyner (ca. 1748–1804), was the son of J. Joyner of Berkley, Gloucestershire. He took the name Ellis in honor of his adoptive father, Henry Ellis, who owned property in Lansdown Crescent, Bath, and was the resident colonial governor of Georgia from 1757 to 1760.[68]

John Joyner Ellis obtained his initial commission in the Royal Irish by purchase on 6 April 1770. He was originally posted to Captain John Evans's company at Fort

Chartres, where he remained until 27 February 1772, when he was removed to Major Isaac Hamilton's company. However, he was given permission to do duty with the major's company at Philadelphia by Gage in December 1771. It is not certain that he served in Illinois, but he most likely did not.[69]

Ellis was given leave by the commander in chief sometime between 1 January, when he was appointed lieutenant, and July 1773. He was still on leave when the regiment left Philadelphia for New York and was transferred from Major Edmonstone's company to Captain Payne's company on 9 September 1774. He was listed as being given a six-month leave on 10 November 1774. When he returned to Boston, he was posted to Captain Richardson's company. He was listed as sick on the 2 October 1775 muster at Boston but was well enough to sign the muster rolls as the company's present senior officer.[70]

Ellis remained in Boston until he embarked for England with the cadre of the regiment. He arrived in England in February 1776 and was assigned to recruiting duty. He was listed as absent from the regiment on recruiting duty on 12 August 1776, while still assigned to Captain Richardson's company. He was present with the regiment at the end of the year at Dover Castle and was transferred to the major's company in the spring of 1777. He was absent from recruiting in August 1777 and again in March 1778.

Ellis was promoted to captain lieutenant in February 1779 and to captain on 27 October 1780 upon the death of Edward Crosby. He was listed as in command of a company of the Royal Irish on its October 1780 muster but was not present with it at Finchley Camp. He had already been promoted in a newly raised corps.[71]

Ellis was commissioned as the original major of the 93rd Regiment on 10 February 1780. However, on 26 February 1780, he exchanged with Major James Susannah Patton, who had been appointed to the 89th Foot a few months earlier. He might have wished to serve with Henry Fermor, who was the regiment's other major.[72] The 89th was raised as the Worcestershire Volunteers and had already embarked for the Leeward Isles before Ellis was appointed. He appears to have been in command of the regiment at Worcester, England, on 16 March 1782. The 89th was then sent to Hereford, where it was mustered on 6 August 1782. Ellis was listed as being on recruiting service at that time. He was again present with the 89th Foot at Ludlow, Shropshire, on 7 March 1783. The regiment was disbanded on 17 March 1783. Ellis completed his final return on 12 May 1783 at Leominster, Herefordshire.[73]

To express his friendship and esteem, Ellis wrote to George Washington on 25 March 1783 from Worcester, where he was stationed with the 89th Foot. Washington responded on 10 July 1783 that he "always distinguished between a Cause and Individuals; and while the latter supported their opinions upon liberal and general ground, personally, I never could be an enemy to them."[74] Washington further stated that he wished to retain his place of friendship with Ellis. There is no record of further correspondence between them. Ellis may have met Washington when he visited Fort Pitt before the war and dined with the officers of the Royal Irish as a guest of Major Edmonstone. Ellis may also have had some contact with Washington through his adoptive father.

On 6 October 1787, Ellis, a major in the army, was appointed to a company in the 3rd Regiment of Foot. This was part of a general expansion of existing regiments.[75] When the 41st Regiment of Foot was reorganized as a marching regiment from its earlier status as an invalid regiment on 29 December 1787, Ellis was appointed major.[76]

Ellis was promoted to lieutenant colonel in the 23rd (Royal Welch Fusiliers) Regiment of Foot on 6 December 1793. He was promoted to colonel in the army on 21 August 1795 and major general in the army on 1 January 1798.[77] The 23rd was stationed at Guernsey by August 1798 at the time, having left Ramsgate earlier in the year. In 1802, the 23rd Foot was at Gibraltar.[78]

Ellis married a woman named Walton. Their eldest son, Henry Walton Ellis, was born in 1783 in Worcester. Ellis appears to have taken significant liberties in purchasing a commission for his son in his own 89th Regiment of Foot at the child's birth. He went onto half pay when the regiment was disbanded, and when he returned to active service in command of the 41st Foot, his son entered full pay as well. His father purchased a lieutenancy for him at age four, and he continued to serve in his father's regiments and received a company in the 23rd (Royal Welch Fusiliers) Regiment of Foot at age thirteen.[79]

In later life, Ellis's family was known as the Ellis of Kempsey family, because he purchased land in Kempsey, Worcestershire. Ellis adopted the arms of the Ellis of Wyham, Lincolnshire, as his own arms: on a fess three scallops between three crescents.[80]

Alexander Fowler

Alexander Fowler (?–1806) appears to have begun his military career on the island of Jamaica. He is listed as the ensign of Captain Thomas Gay's independent company in the 5th Division of Jamaican companies, and his initial commission was dated 29 October 1760.[81] His own memorial states that his military service began on 1 August 1755, but it is not clear in what capacity he was serving at that time.[82]

In 1761, the independent Jamaican companies were incorporated into the 74th Regiment of Foot. Fowler is listed as an ensign in the 74th on 29 October 1760. He participated in the 1762 expedition to Havana and stated that he served as the regiment's senior ensign on that expedition, although the army lists him second in seniority at that time. The 1763 army list shows that Fowler was promoted to lieutenant on 4 March 1763, when Anthony Whilock Gifford resigned from the 74th Foot. When the 74th was reduced at the end of 1763, Fowler was placed on half pay.

Fowler joined the Royal Irish after it arrived in America; his commission dated from 12 August 1768. He returned to America armed with a copy of Simes's *Military Medley*. It is unclear exactly when he arrived for duty at Philadelphia, but he journeyed to Illinois in 1770 along with his wife, Lieutenant Lewis Wynne and his wife, and a group of traders.

In Illinois, Fowler was a member of the court of inquiry that settled the previously mentioned dispute between Richard Bacon and George Morgan. In 1772 he was assigned as the lieutenant of the major's company in Illinois. He also served as the commander of a detachment at Kaskaskia during his stay in Illinois. He returned to Philadelphia with the majority of the Royal Irish in late 1772.

Fowler's health must have been severely injured in Illinois; he is later said to be an invalid and not have the use of his limbs. Other subalterns took on some or all of his duties at least as early as 1773. Fowler gave the impression that he was going to retire in 1773 or 1774, but he was trying to get on a sergeants' list and was not able to do so. He was originally close to Wilkins, but that association, along with his political support for the Whigs, cost him with the rest of the officers of the regiment.

On 5 July 1773, Major Isaac Hamilton wrote to General Sebright asking for his patronage of Fowler. The letter's praise of Fowler is in sharp contrast with later testimony regarding Fowler:

> I cannot omit this opportunity of recommending to your attention and favor Lieutenant Fowler of your Regiment. This Gentleman has for some time been at the Head of the Lieutenants, has long Services to plead, and has since his Joining the Royal Irish Regiment shewed a particular attention to his Duty, as well as Capacity

in the Exercise thereof. Permit me to Add that his Uniform and Honorable Deportment have engaged him in a very particular manner the General approbation of his Brother officers.[83]

In September 1774, Fowler proposed a retirement plan similar to the plan used in the 12th Regiment of Foot, in which the officers promoted throughout his retirement funded the other half of his pay out of their pay. However, he could not get anyone, except for possibly Nicholas Trist, to help him with this plan. Major Hamilton, however, forwarded Fowler's resignation to Gage as unconditional. In the end, Gage sided with Fowler, and Fowler remained with the regiment and was not forced to resign at the time.[84]

Fowler did not march from Philadelphia to Perth Amboy, New Jersey, with the regiment in September 1774. He may not have been physically up to marching that distance. However, he was with the regiment in New York in 1774, as the lieutenant of Captain Johnson's company. and he and his wife were assigned quarters adjacent to Ensign Trist and his wife.[85]

Fowler was accused of fraternizing with known rebels in New York in 1774 and 1775. His servant, Elijah Reeves, was punished by other officers several times—unfairly, according to Reeves. Fowler appears to have pleaded successfully for a remittance of Reeves's sentence at least twice.

Fowler created a serious rift with most of the other officers of the regiment. In May 1775 he wrote to Lieutenant Collins of the Royal Artillery that "B, C, and P" were out to get him. He later stated that B and C were the real masterminds behind the plotting against him and that P was just the fall guy of the plot.[86] According to his letter, Captains Chapman and Payne, along with former Captain Batt, tried to have him ordered to serve in the Illinois Country with Captain Lord. Fowler stated that such an assignment would have caused him to retire, because his constitution would not have withstood an additional tour of duty in Illinois.

"They have humanely applied to his Excellency," he wrote, "to order me to the Illinois county, to join the two companies there, under the command of Captain Lord, knowing that my infirmities would not permit me to undertake a journey of two thousand miles, and that such an order would naturally compel me to retire."[87]

Only Ensign Trist and the chaplain appear to have kept company with Fowler and his wife at that time.

Fowler then accused Captain Payne of cowardice and several other charges in the summer of 1775. When Payne was found innocent of all charges, Fowler was charged and found guilty of bearing false witness against Payne:

> Lieut. Alexander Fowler of His Majesty's 18th or Royal Irish Regiment of foot, having been put under an Arrest, by Major Hamilton Commanding the said Regiment, by desire of the Officers of the Reg.t was accused before the Court of having behaved in a manner unbecoming the Character of an Officer and a Gentleman, by Exhibiting frivolous, malicious, wicked, and ill grounded Charges against Capt. Benjamin Charnock Payne, also of the said Reg.t before a General Court Martial.[88]

Fowler was sentenced to be dismissed from the service, but Gage remitted that sentence and allowed Fowler to sell his commission instead. Gage had the proceedings of Fowler's court-martial sealed; only a brief summary appears in the returns of general courts-martial in the War Office archive. Fowler claimed that this was done to keep the actions of other officers hidden from view and further taint Fowler's reputation.

Head Quarters, Boston, Sept. 25th, 1775

> I approve of the Sentence of this General Court Martial passed upon the Prisoner Lieut. Fowler of the 18th or Royal Regiment of Foot of Ireland but in Consideration of the Recommendation of the Court in Consequences of Circumstances in the Prisoner's favour I judge proper to remit the punishment adjudged him.
>
> Thos. Gage
>
> Commander in Chief[89]

Fowler left the service on 8 October 1775. However, he had planned for this eventuality, and on 10 April 1775, he received a thousand acres in west Florida based upon his service in the French and Indian War. Fowler stated that he he had property in Pennsylvania. He then received an additional thousand acres in west Florida on 6 May 1776. After his return to America, he petitioned Virginia for two thousand acres based on his service in the 74th Foot, and as a result he received two thousand acres in Yohogania County, Virginia, on 28 February 1780.[90]

After Fowler was found guilty and sold his commission, according to him he remained a captive in Boston and survived only through the kindness of others. He ultimately was able to book passage to return to England in the early spring. Fowler and his wife, Frances Elizabeth, tried to clear his name in London. What happened during the next two years is somewhat unclear, but it appears he spent some time and effort trying to clear his name after his court-martial through the secretary of war and then through the British courts.

The *London Evening Post* of 24 June 1777 reported that Fowler brought suit against Thomas Gage in the London Court of Common Pleas, charging that Gage had acted contrary to the articles of war by forcing him to sell his commission. Justice Nares did not allow the proceedings of the court-martial to be read, but he directed the jury to find in favor of General Gage.[91]

It is unclear what other legal tactics Fowler tried, but in 1778 he took his case to the court of public opinion. Fowler went to the newspaper, printing an eight-part series of articles beginning in June 1778 in the London *General Advertiser & Intelligencer* under the title "The Case of Alexander Fowler, Esq., late of the 18th or Royal Irish Regiment of Foot."[92]

Public sentiment does not appear to have provided a groundswell of support for Fowler. So in late 1778, the Fowlers left England for Calais, France, and then traveled to Paris sometime in late 1778. Fowler articulated his situation to the American consul, Silas Deane, differently from the way the British Army recorded the end of his military career. Deane summarized Fowler's presentation as follows for the captain of any vessel bound for America:

> Mr. Alexander Fowler and his wife being bound to America where heretofore resided as a British Officer in the British Army & it being represented to us that his Friendship to America occasioned his quitting that Service, and has occasioned him some hardships & Inconveniences.
>
> We recommend him to you for a Passage to America, he paying your demands for the same, & that He & his Wife be treated with Respect.[93]

Fowler and his wife ultimately sailed from Nantes to Marblehead, Massachusetts, arriving on 20 November 1778, then traveled to Philadelphia. The *Pennsylvania Packet* of 14 January 1779 announced Fowler as "late a Captain in the 18th or royal Irish regiment" who was warm to the cause of America.[94] Of course, Fowler had never been a captain, but his delusions of grandeur were not as grandiose as those of many others; some assumed the titles of nobility, such as "Baron" von Stuben and others who inflated their European accomplishments when applying for a position in the Continental Army.

On 18 January 1779, Fowler penned a memorial to Congress that ultimately was discussed with George Washington and the Board of War. Fowler wrote that he "Humbly Submits his Case and Chearfully offers His Services, in any Station in which his experience or his Abilities may be of use, having been determined from the Commencement of this War, to stand or Fall with this Injured Country."[95]

On 20 February 1779, Fowler was appointed as an auditor for the Continental Board of War at Fort Pitt, so he moved to western Pennsylvania near Fort Pitt and purchased a tract of land that he turned into farms near the Cherties settlement, now Chartiers. This was about ten miles from Fort Pitt across the Monongahela River.

Fowler set up a store at Fort Pitt in addition to serving as an auditor for the army. He remained in the role of auditor for the western department of the Continental Army throughout the remainder of the war. His name floats through the correspondence of a number of key individuals in this period, but he is mostly related to the mundane tasks of keeping the army equipped and the soldiers and the contractors paid. According to the diary entry of Robert Morris, the American superintendent of finance, for 28 July 1784, Fowler had "supplied Goods from his store at Ft. Pitt to the Garrison and taken their orders on the Paymaster." He was inquiring how he could be paid, and he was shortly afterward paid about £962. It is doubtful that this was the entire amount he was due.[96]

Fowler also complained about the scandalous dealings of Daniel Broadhead, the commander of the western department at Fort Pitt.[97] Fowler charged that Broadhead regularly stole supplies from the commissary and used government funds to support his gambling habits in the spring of 1781. According to Fowler, Broadhead was supported by David Duncan, the quartermaster at Fort Pitt, in his endeavors. In the end, Broadhead was acquitted at a court-martial and brevetted to brigadier general, mostly through the support of General George Washington, who found Fowler's complaints "disorganized and improperly executed." Nevertheless, Broadhead was replaced and Duncan was forced to resign based on the information from Fowler and other critics. Although this issue was concluded in 1781, Fowler was still sending complaints in July

1783 to Robert Morris about "persons formerly employed in Public Service at Ft. Pitt." Morris redirected the complaints.[98]

Fowler maintained contact with Nicholas Trist after they both left the service, and in 1783 Fowler escorted Elizabeth Trist to Fort Pitt to begin her journey down the Ohio to Trist's plantation.[99] Edward Hand's election in November 1783 to Congress provided Fowler with an opportunity to attempt to improve his situation, and he wrote to Hand through Thomas Hutchins, another former British officer in American service, requesting his support for Fowler's petition to Congress to provide him with ten thousand acres of land for his military service. Hand wrote the following response:

> Dear Fowler
>
> Annapolis 27th Decr. 1783
>
> On my Arrival here Captn. Hutchins put your letter into my hands. This day on looking over the files found the report of a Committee on your Application, which is as favourable as we could wish. I believe it has not yet been Acted on but you may rest assured that I will endeavour to have it taken up as early as possible, if I see a prospect of its terminating agreably [sic] to your expectations. In the mean time I will out of doors be attentive to your interest.
>
> Farewell Dear Fowler, very Cordially yrs., Edw. Hand[100]

No action was ever taken on Fowler's petition. Fowler continued to carry on a correspondence with John Jay and other officials, primarily forwarding intelligence information about the Spanish and the state of Mississippi River travel throughout the 1780s.

Fowler is listed in the 1790 census at Pittsburgh as living in a household of two men, one under eighteen, and two women.[101] He purchased a number of lots at Port St. Vincent or Vincennes (Indiana). He also appears in the 1800 census in Pitt Township, Allegheny County, Pennsylvania, as Alexander Fowler, Esq. Fowler's household is listed as consisting of Fowler, his wife, and two younger males.[102]

Fowler is listed as a brigadier general in the Pennsylvania Militia, commanding the eight regiments of the Alleghany County Brigade in 1800. That year, as the presidential race became heated, he ordered his militia regiments to adopt the red, white, and blue cockade of the Republican

Party instead of the black and white cockade of the Federalists. Two of his regiments refused, but according to a history of Pittsburgh, Fowler claimed that he was simply listening to the voice of the people, which was the same as the voice of God. According to Charles Dahlinger, Fowler was an incessant politician and extremely fond of platitudes in later life. He appears to have left the Republican Party shortly afterward when it would not support his desire to run for office. He remained in command of the militia, however, and his brigade orders were published in the 19 February 1801 issue of the *Federal Gazette and Baltimore Daily Advertiser*. His death was announced in the 2 April 1806 issue of the *Boston Democrat* as "Gen. Fowler of Pittsburg."[103]

Francis John Kelly

Francis John Kelly (1749–ca. 1820) was the second surviving son of Arthur Kelly of Kelly, Devonshire, and Mary Tucker of Coryton, Devon.[104] He was baptized on 12 May 1749.[105] Kelly enrolled in Wadham College, Oxford, on 26 March 1768 and appears to have left in midsummer 1771 without a degree.[106] He entered the regiment as an ensign on 28 February 1772, purchasing his commission from Thomas Cumming, who removed to the 1st Dragoon Guards.[107] Kelly was initially assigned to Captain Chapman's company. He was listed as "not joined" in the 25 October 1772 muster, but he was present by the 27 July 1773 return in Philadelphia.

One of Kelly's first duties was to sit on the regimental court-martial board that judged Elijah Reeves, Joseph Sumerland, and William Moneypenny for contempt and disobedience of orders. Each man was sentenced on 3 May 1773 to receive one hundred lashes. Private Reeves was again before a court-martial board on which Kelly sat for disobedience of orders and contempt in August 1773.[108]

As a member of Chapman's company, Kelly was sent with the three company detachments to Boston in October 1774, and he remained there for the duration of his American service. Since he was assigned to a battalion company and not the grenadier company, however, he did not materially participate in the expedition to either Concord or Bunker Hill. He does not appear to have participated in any of the general court-martials involving the Royal Irish in Boston.

Kelly purchased Lieutenant Fowler's commission on 9 October 1775, when Fowler was forced to sell. Kelly embarked for England with the remainder of the regiment at Boston in December 1775. He was removed to

Major John Shee's company upon returning to England and was present with that company in August 1776 at Dover Castle. He was transferred to the Grenadier company by June 1777, where he remained for the rest of his time as a lieutenant. Kelly was present on a general court-martial board at Dover in November 1777 that tried William Green and Henry Knight for desertion.[109] He was with the grenadiers at Warley Camp in July 1779 and at Woburn in March 1780.

Kelly was promoted to captain lieutenant on 14 July 1780 in place of DeLancey. His promotion to captain in place of Crosby on 7 November 1780 was announced in the *London Gazette* on 4 November 1780. That promotion was probably without purchase. In the returns as late as February 1781, Kelly is still listed as a lieutenant with the grenadiers. He was assigned to one of the additional companies when he assumed the captaincy and remained in England when the regiment embarked for the Channel Islands.

Sometime in 1782, Kelly married Elizabeth Oakeley of Deal, Kent. He was present with the regiment by November 1782, taking command of the company previously led by Captain Bewes. Kelly remained with his company in the Channel Islands until the regiment returned to Portsmouth in mid-1783. He was listed as present at Hilsea Barracks in August 1783.

Kelly was once again assigned to an additional company in late 1783 and stayed in England when the regiment embarked for Gibraltar. He remained with the regiment when the additional companies were reduced in 1784. He was listed as "*en seconded*" to the lieutenant colonel's company in both the February and July 1784 musters at Gibraltar.[110]

Kelly appears to have remained at Gibraltar with the regiment until he sold his commission to Lieutenant George Henry Vansittart of the 38th Foot on 20 July 1790.[111] Kelly had a son, Henry, who served in the Royal African Corps as a captain, and four daughters: Elizabeth, Catharine, Mary, and Agnes.[112] Elizabeth, his wife, married Sir Charles James Napier (1782–1853) after Kelly's death.[113]

John Mawby Jr.

John Mawby Jr. (1753–1779) was the son of John Mawby Sr., the adjutant and captain lieutenant of the Royal Irish. Mawby came over to America with his father and the Royal Irish before his commissioning. He was listed as a supernumerary private in Major Henry Folliot's company, which his father was the lieutenant of at that time. For the October 1767 return, he is listed as being absent from the muster, on duty. For the April

1768 return, he is again listed as a supernumerary soldier on duty. He does not appear on any return for the October 1768 muster.[114]

Mawby was made an ensign on 28 November 1768 at the age of fifteen. Lieutenant Colonel Wilkins had actually recommended him to Gage for a commission on 25 November 1767, and Gage had responded as follows:

> I have your letter of 25 November. As I should be very glad to have it in my power to recommend the Son of Lieut Mawby. If the Young Gentleman is of Size and Abilities to serve, tho' he has not quite attainted the Age prescribed, You will be pleased therefore to give me your Opinion upon this Subject and to certify as much as you can respecting him.[115]

When appointed, Mawby remained in Philadelphia, serving as the ensign of Major Isaac Hamilton's company. His father remained the lieutenant of the same company. In July 1771, he was given his father's lieutenancy when the elder Mawby became captain lieutenant. His company came under the command of Thomas Batt in October 1771, and in April 1772 he was still assigned to Batt's company at Philadelphia, where he most likely looked after his mother and siblings. The company was once again commanded by Major Hamilton when the latter returned to Philadelphia in the fall of 1772.

Mawby was a witness in the John Green court-martial in May 1774, which involved Captain Payne calling Robert Newburgh a "buggerer." Mawby was offended by the language used by his brother officers and took his younger brother, Sebright, out of the room when he heard it; he remarked that such language was not suitable for a gentleman, both as a chastisement against Payne and an instruction for his younger brother.

In late 1774, Mawby left Philadelphia for New York City with five companies of the Royal Irish. He was present with the major's company, according to the February 1775 return. Mawby was with the regiment during the embarkation of the regiment onto HMS *Asia* on 6 June 1775 and remained on board until he was put onto Governor's Island on 20 June 1775. When he reached Boston, he was posted to Captain Payne's company, and the October 1775 muster shows him in command of that company in Boston.[116]

Mawby returned to England with the Royal Irish and was assigned to the grenadier company, which was then commanded by Captain Chapman. Mawby was in command of the skeletal company, with only two sergeants, three corporals, and four musicians present. All the other officers and men were on duty or on recruiting service. He was removed to a battalion company in late 1776.

Shee recommended Mawby to the office of the judge advocate general (JAG) as an officer capable of serving as an acting deputy adjutant general. It fact, Mawby did serve as such for the courts-martial of deserters William Green and Henry Knight in October 1777. He eceived some constructive feedback from the JAG office after it received the trial transcripts. The postscript to the JAG's letter stated, "I scarcely need recommend it to you not to make public, what I have ventured to Suggest."[117]

Mawby took his father's place as the adjutant on 14 May 1778. He remained assigned to the lieutenant colonel's company until his appointment as adjutant. He served at Coxheath Camp in 1778, where he, the "four best exercising corporals" of the Royal Irish, and similar contingents from the other regular regiments were ordered on 16 June to report to headquarters, most likely to begin learning the new 1778 manual exercise. The cause of Mawby's death on 24 February 1779 is unknown.[118]

Marcus Paterson

Marcus Paterson (ca. 1744–3 October 1768) was the son of Lord Chief Justice Marcus Paterson of Common Pleas Court in Ireland. The elder Paterson was listed as living in Kilkenny in 1771. Marcus Paterson joined the Royal Irish as an ensign on 13 February 1762. He purchased his lieutenancy in the Royal Irish on 1 October 1766 and is listed as being a twenty-three-year-old Irishman in the April 1767 inspection return.[119]

When the regiment arrived in America, Paterson was listed as the lieutenant of Captain Shee's battalion company. While traveling to Illinois, Paterson served on a general court-martial board at Fort Pitt that tried five deserters from the 34th Foot in July 1768.[120] Only two years and two days after being promoted, Paterson died of fever at Fort Chartres along the Mississippi River, which marked the western edge of British America.[121]

In December 1772, Cox & Meir paid slightly more than £19 to the agent of Lord Chief Justice Paterson, "administrator of Rec." to settle Lt. Paterson's accounts. Other entries in his ledgers are all related to his subsistence allowance.[122]

William Perkins

William Perkins (ca. 1748–29 May 1768) entered the Royal Irish as an ensign on 13 February 1762, when he was approximately fourteen years old.

He may not have immediately joined the regiment, but he purchased a lieutenancy on 1 January 1766. He was listed as English in the 1767 inspection return, and he was present with the regiment at Dublin at that time.[123]

Perkins arrived in America as the junior lieutenant of the grenadier company. He was transferred to Captain Evans's battalion company on 25 April 1768 and was listed as being under arrest on the muster return of 26 April 1768. Unfortunately, there is no record of why he was under arrest at the time. His transfer out of the grenadier company may or may not have been related to his arrest.

Regardless of the reason for Perkins's arrest, his military career quickly ended. The *Pennsylvania Gazette* announced the end of his career with the following statement: "Monday last, Lieutenant PERKINS of the Royal Irish Regiment, coming from Burlington in the Stage Boat, unfortunately fell overboard, and was drowned, before any Assistance could be given him."[124] According to the paper, he died on 30 May 1768. Captain Benjamin Chapman paid for his funeral out of regimental funds in June 1768, and Cox & Meir reimbursed the regiment out of Perkins's own funds.

According to Wilkins, at the time of Perkins's death, no purchaser from within the Royal Irish could be found for his commission. Gage told Wilkins to write to Colonel Sebright and the regimental agent at home to find a purchaser. Gage added that he thought that it might be difficult to find a purchaser for a regiment in America. Perkins's family received the balance of his account from Cox & Meir on 10 May 1769.[125]

Edmund Prideaux

Edmund Prideaux (1754–20 March 1780) was the third son of Brigadier General John Prideaux of Netherton, Devonshire, and Elizabeth Rolt.[126] He replaced his older brother, John Wilmot Prideaux, as an ensign in the Royal Irish on 12 January 1770. He was English and began his military career at approximately fifteen years of age.[127] He was originally assigned to Captain Edmonstone's Company at Fort Pitt, where he was involved in signing some of the documents related to the closure of the post as an active garrison. He remained in Edmonstone's company until the majority of the regiment returned to Philadelphia.

At that point, October 1772, Prideaux was transferred to the general's company. He remained with the regiment in Philadelphia until September 1774, when the regiment marched to Perth Amboy to replace the 47th Foot in garrisoning New Jersey. Prideaux was one of three officers who marched the entire route with the men, according to Trist.[128] In October 1774, he was sent to Boston with Captain Robert Hamilton's company while the majority of the regiment was sent to New York City. He remained with Hamilton's company in Boston until the regiment was drafted in December 1775. He was promoted to lieutenant on 21 August 1775.

During the reorganization that took place in the spring of 1776, Prideaux was transferred to Captain Fermor's company, although he was still listed as an ensign on the return dated August 1776. He was not present with the regiment during the summer of 1776 but was listed on the August 1776 return as being on recruiting duty. Upon his return from recruiting duty, he was removed to the light infantry company, where he remained until he was transferred to the grenadier company in the spring of 1777.[129]

Prideaux retired from the service on 14 July 1777, and his lieutenancy passed to Charles Hoare.[130] Prideaux apparently wanted a more active assignment than the Royal Irish was able to provide, so he traveled back to America. He and Henry Babington, previously of the 55th Foot, were appointed to "do duty as Lieuts in Morris's Corps attached to the Royl [sic] Artillery" dated 14 February 1778. This provided Prideaux with a commission as a lieutenant in the 2nd Battalion of the New Jersey Loyalists. He was commissioned as a lieutenant in the 7th (Royal Fusiliers) Regiment on 6 November 1778 and returned at that time to serve with the regular British Army. Prideaux's rank as a lieutenant in the 1780 army list was based only on his commission in the 7th Foot, so it appears that his earlier service in the Royal Irish was nullified by his "retirement" in 1777. That is possibly why he joined the 7th Foot, which had lieutenants but no ensigns: so he would not have to accept an effective demotion in order to return to regular service.[131]

While serving with the 7th Foot in New York City, Prideaux was involved in an incident that caused a minor mob to form outside the Brigade of Guards' barracks. On 15 January 1779, Prideaux was helping Captain Norman McLeod of the 2nd Battalion of the New Jersey Volunteers home along Dock Street.[132] Prideaux was being assisted by David Wilson, a soldier of the 45th Foot, and David Philips, a civilian tailor. McLeod, who was indisputably intoxicated, had some sort of fit. When Prideaux called for help from the guards' sentry, a group of thirty to forty soldiers and civilians were drawn to the scene. Lance Corporal John Lee of the 1st Foot Guards had a scuffle of some type with Prideaux, and Prideaux pressed charges against Lee with the assistance of Engineer Lieutenant Andrew Dunford. The court testimony shows that the guards seemed insolent in responding to the nonguard officers. There was also consideration of whether Prideaux was intoxicated at the time. Lee was accused of abusing, striking, and otherwise abusing Prideaux.

Lee's trial at New York City was presided over by Lieutenant Colonel Anthony George Martin of the Coldstream Guards from 23 to 26 January 1779. Lee was found guilty of the charge and sentenced to one thousand lashes.[133]

Prideaux served on a court-martial board from 22 to 28 August 1779 at Fort Knyphausen, New York. The board heard the trial of Robert Reid, a civilian charged with selling rum to the soldiers and enticing them to desert.[134]

Prideaux is listed as "retiring" on 20 September 1780, according to the history of the Royal Regiment of Fusiliers. Most likely that was actually the date of his death. His death was reported in a Carolina paper as occurring at Georgetown in the Carolinas.[135]

William Raymond

William Raymond (ca. 1749–?) was commissioned as an ensign in the Royal Irish on 11 September 1765 at the age of approximately seventeen. Military records list him as Irish. It is possible he was related to Lieutenant James Raymond, who was promoted to lieutenant in the Royal Irish in February 1765 and then left the regiment before October 1765. William Raymond was present in Dublin when the regiment was inspected on 11 April 1767. When he arrived in America, he was assigned as the ensign of Captain Shee's company.

Raymond was present in Philadelphia at the 26 April 1768 muster of Shee's company, and he resigned on 31 May 1768 while the regiment was still in Philadelphia. It is unclear why he resigned, but he may not have wished to be posted in Illinois. It seems that he tried to sell his commission as early as 25 November 1767, but his regimental accounts show him being paid through 24 June 1768. The ledger shows a 16 September 1768 bill from William Howard (Ensign Howard's father, most likely) nearly £300 being settled on 15 October 1768.

Raymond's commission went to Henry Fermor, from whom he received £400 on 8 February 1768, according to the ledgers. His accounts were settled on 17 April 1769 for about £436. He left no further record.[136]

William Smith

William Smith (ca. 1737–?) was commissioned as an ensign in the Royal Irish on 9 March 1760, at approximately age twenty-three. He was listed as Irish by nativity in the 1767 inspection return. He was promoted to lieutenant on 11 March 1765, and when the Royal Irish arrived in America in July 1767, he was assigned as the senior lieutenant in the grenadier company.

On 26 August 1767, Smith left with a body of men from the 34th Foot, along with a few men of the Royal Irish, for Fort Pitt. He returned to Philadelphia sometime before 26 April 1768, when he was the only officer present with the grenadier company when it stood muster.

While at Fort Pitt, Smith served on a general court-martial board that tried five deserters from the 34th Foot in July 1768.[137]

Smith traveled down the Ohio River to Illinois in the summer of 1768 and arrived at Fort Chartres in September 1768. He was involved in a trial at Kaskaskia in May 1769.[138] Regimental records indicate that in 1771, Smith was posted at Cahokia with the grenadiers. It is unclear when Smith left Illinois, but he probably began to travel east before his resignation.

Smith retired from the Royal Irish on 26 February 1772, having served as the senior lieutenant of the grenadier company during his entire American service. Smith's account received £150 from George Bewes, who purchased his lieutenancy. The regimental agent settled Smith's final accounts for about £265 on 8 February 1773, and the army forwarded approximately £222 for his final subsistence allowance in America in June 1774.[139]

Nicholas Trist

Nicholas Trist (24 May 1743–24 February 1784) was the fifth son of a Devonshire landowner, Browse Trist, and his wife, Agnes Hore. He was the second son named Nicholas; the first died in infancy. Trist joined the Royal Irish as an ensign without purchasing his commission, which was dated 26 December 1770. He was already at the advanced age of twenty-seven when he joined the army, making him a particularly old junior officer because many of his peers purchased their ensigncies in their midteen years.

Trist was originally posted to Captain Henry Cope's company. He served in Illinois with that company, which became Captain Payne's in 1771. Trist returned east with the majority of the regiment, leaving the Illinois Country in the late spring of 1772. He remained assigned as the ensign of Payne's company throughout his tenure as an ensign. On 27 July 1773, when Payne's company was mustered, Trist was in command as the only officer present with a sergeant, two corporals, and twenty-three privates.[140]

While in Philadelphia, Trist met Elizabeth House, the daughter of Mary House, who ran a prominent boardinghouse at the corner of Fifth and Market Streets. He married Elizabeth on 10 June 1774 in Philadelphia; he was thirty-one years old. He attempted to retire onto half pay at the time and wrote the following resignation, giving his health as the reason he needed to retire:

> Sir Having been long afflicted with Violent pains in my Breast and Rheumatic pains in my shoulders which Tender me very unfit for Active Service, and as my repeated Application for relief have hitherto been ineffectual, I now despair of ever attaining a Radical Cure, and therefore beg leave to retire on half pay with the permission to take the regulated difference. Be Assured Sire this Application particularly at this time is painfull to me, Attach'd to His Majesty's Service, From principal as well as Inclination, nothing but an inability to Service should have forced me to this Step.[141]

Although Isaac Hamilton was eager to rid the Royal Irish of Trist, who he believed was an inadequate officer, Gage denied the request, stating that there were no adequate officers on half pay in America with whom to exchange. He directed Hamilton to ask Sebright about finding a replacement in Britain. Hamilton summed up the officers' opinion of Trist in the following passage:

> I beg leave to Inform your Excellency that his Brother Officers (only one excepted) have as poor an Opinion of his Mental tendency; He is now indicating to quit the Service on his account of his Marriage with the Daughter of a Woman who keeps a Lodging house in this City, and I support intends becoming a Patriotick American, as he had Addressed to declare to a Gentleman of the City, that his Brother Officers dislike of him was occasioned by expressing his Sentiments in favor of America.[142]

Others provided an opposite impression of Trist. In September 1774, Silas Deane stayed at Mary House's boardinghouse and recorded the following impression of Trist:

> The Officer here, is much to be pitied, his Commission is his principal dependence. He loves this Country, he loves his Young Wife, who is very deserving, and who is a warm daughter of Liberty, yet is ordered this Morning, to be ready, to March in the After Noon for Boston. This is really affecting and my passions are too sensible of soft impressions to view the Struggle between duty so called, Interest & Honor military on the one hand, and Affection, & an honest Regard & Tenderness on the other. As We have all dined, & supp'd together, on a free footing at the same Table, he seems the nearer to Us, and Our repeatedly asserting that the Troops at Boston would be cut off if they attempted anything against That Town & province, gives him & his Connections the most Uneasy & Melancholy Apprehensions. Could he get rid of his Commission on any Terms, short of ruining himself he would gladly do it.[143]

Although Trist appears to have determined to leave the army, Fowler proposed selling his commission to Trist as part of a way of obtaining a half-pay retirement in September 1774. Fowler's scheme was similar to the process used by the 12th Foot in which the lieutenant remained on ensign's pay and the junior ensign's pay was given to the retired lieutenant (in this case, Fowler). However, this plan was not accepted, and it is not clear whether Trist was a willing participant in his friend's plan.[144]

Trist set off for Perth Amboy the next day with the rest of the regiment. In a letter he wrote to Elizabeth during the march, he noted that he was one of the few officers to march the entire way with the men. He shared with "His Betsy" that he was doing his best to keep his expenses on the march minimal and was preparing "for the worst" if it was to come:

> To prevent unnecessary expenses I stop in the Barracks and eat in the Tavern, whilst others stay there likewise, I do assure I don't care who knows where I am in settled matters, for the expenses in marching are too great, as I do not think less than two dollars a day will pay my expenses, yesterday we dined with Lord Stirling, Lord Drummond, Oliver DeLancey & c who drank wine like fishes, but I took care not to sup with them, they had the band of music and I make no doubt how they spent the evening very expensively & Jovial—I intend when I am as yours [?] to have a tent bedstead made and two or three other trifles to prepare for the

worst, I intent to carry nothing with me but what is of real use—Bruere, Prideaux & self marched all the way, I do assure you my feet were not in the least [?] some neither was I weary, I can with pleasure tell you I am exceedingly well, as ever in all way agrees with me.[145]

The impending conflict was too difficult for Trist, and he began planning to leave the army. On 3 November 1774, Trist purchased one thousand acres of land southwest of Manchac on the Mississippi River from Philip Brown, a former officer on half pay. This land would eventually become his Louisiana plantation.[146]

Elizabeth traveled to New York in late 1774 to be with her new husband. A son, Hore Browse, was born on 22 February 1775 in New York. Lieutenant Fowler and his wife served as Hore's godparents. Trist appears to have been the only one of Lieutenant Fowler's brother officers to take his side in the disputes that arose in the Royal Irish after their return to the Eastern Seaboard. He was still serving as Captain Payne's ensign while in New York during the winter of 1774–1775. He spoke in evidence against Captain Payne during his court-martial in 1775. Trist was allowed to purchase a lieutenancy from William Richardson on the latter's promotion to captain.

Trist served as a lieutenant; he is listed as such in the court-martial records for Payne's court-martial. The *London Gazette* of 25 November 1775 shows Trist resigning in favor of Prideaux, but Prideaux's commission in the army list dates from 20 April 1775, the date that was to have been Trist's date of rank. The date of rank is the official date from which the officer can exercise authority under the new commission; officers with an earlier date of rank are senior to those with a more recent date of rank. Trist was announced to be a lieutenant in the 2 May 1775 issue of the *London Gazette*. The exact reason Trist left the army is unclear, but the effective removal of his lieutenancy by backdating Prideaux's commission appears highly unorthodox. It could be that his commission was not formally confirmed, but his lieutenant's commission in the Royal Irish is extant in the Trist, Randolph, and Burke Family Papers, properly executed by William Legge, 2nd Earl of Dartmouth.[147]

Trist left the army in late 1775 and returned to Philadelphia. His retirement date was listed as 21 August 1775. He then went west again, this time to Louisiana and his new land. He appears to have written regularly to Elizabeth from Louisiana, but most letters did not survive. By September

1780, Trist was asking her to come to Louisiana, since his plans to return to Philadelphia to see her had become unworkable. He wrote:

> In all of You Letters you complain of the disagreeable situation You are in and in the last you say that if you imagined I was here You thought You had resolution enough to undertake the Journey, if it has not or does not fail you, and as it is both easier and safer for you to come to me I would have you endeavor to put it in practice and one the receipt of this go to Fort Pitt as soon as it is convenient and as Fowler has given you an Invitation remain with him until I can provide a safe opportunity, as genteel families are frequently coming down perhaps you might get a passage with some or other of them, or (as I would not have you to venture by Yourself) if either of Your Brothers will attend you take any opportunity he will greatly oblige me and I shall be happy to see him and well endeavour to make it as agreeable as is in my powers.[148]

Trist also mentioned the rather difficult conditions in Louisiana, including the fact that he had "nothing but a pail of water to shave by" and that he lived on cornbread because flour was too expensive.

In the same letter, Trist mentioned having borrowed money from a Mr. Pollock, who was almost certainly Oliver Pollock, the American commercial agent at New Orleans. Although the Spanish attack in September 1779 on Fort Bute, as Manchac was sometimes known, most certainly would have attracted Trist's attention, if not his support, there is no record of his involvement in the expedition, although Pollock and ten Americans guided the Spanish force under Bernardo de Galvez.

Trist's family in England appears to have tried to coax him home on at least one occasion. An extant letter from Trist's sister, Agnes Hore Campernon, of 6 April 1783, reads as follows:

> In your last letter (to my brother) you seemed in a very doubtful, unsettled State not knowing which to prefer going to Philadelphia or to remain where you are, consequently, I suppose your affairs are in as unsettled a State as your Mind and your Letters help to confirm me in that opinion, for in Truth, I cannot understand what you are about going forward I hope, or you are spending Money time and take a great deal of Trouble to very little purpose. It will give us great Pleasure if you will favour us with a particular

account of your situation, as by this Time I suppose you must be a Judge of whether you can make it do or not, if the Latter, I think you had best return to England and endevour to find out and fix on some employment that will answer your expectations.[149]

Campernon also informed Trist that his uncle had passed away and left him and his son a small share of the inheritance. Campernon appears to have kept excellent financial records for Hore Trist after Trist's death.

Elizabeth House Trist finally followed her husband's advice and left Philadelphia in December 1783 under Fowler's care to meet her husband.[150] However, Nicholas Trist died on 24 February 1784, before she arrived. She had to sell his property in order to clear debts and give up 75 percent of the proceeds to convert them into silver for the Spanish. The circumstances of his death were "deplorable. He was seiz'd with a swelling in his stomach & head & died in a few days after."[151]

Elizabeth sold his property and settled his affairs by the middle of March 1785. At that point, she was on the Acadian coast of the Mississippi River awaiting a ship to Philadelphia. She ended up taking the *Matilda* to Jamaica and then sailed on to Philadelphia. She appears to have taken up Thomas Jefferson's "friendly offer," which was some level of support in her new circumstance as a widowed mother. She continued to correspond with Jefferson, James Madison, and other luminaries of the young republic. She ultimately moved to Virginia and died in 1828 at Monticello, where she had been a guest of Jefferson's since 1823. She is buried in an unmarked grave at Monticello. Some of Trist's papers are extant at the University of Virginia.[152]

5
Ensigns and Volunteers

Ensign was the junior commissioned rank among line officers. Its title came from the fact that two of the ensigns were responsible for carrying the regiment's colours, or ensigns, in battle and on parade. The ensigns who purchased their commissions spent £400 if they purchased at the regulated price. Most ensigns were able to purchase a lieutenancy within a couple of years of service.

Volunteers were young gentlemen unable to come up with the price of a commission, so they shouldered a firelock and hoped to earn recognition on active service and thus a commission without purchase. The only volunteers identified in the muster rolls of the Royal Irish were sons of John Mawby Sr.

Most of these junior officers went on to obtain higher rank after returning to England. The careers that ended as ensigns tended to have tragic ends.

James Aldcroft

James Aldcroft (ca. 1752–27 July 1797) purchased a commission in the Royal Irish on 26 July 1775. His surname is sometimes given as Aldercroft or Alcroft. He may have served briefly in America, but he was clearly with the regiment by mid-1776. He is not mentioned, nor does he have an account listed, in the regimental agent's extant ledger. This would tend to indicate that he did not serve in America with the regiment. He was listed as the only officer present with William Blackwood's company at Dover Castle in August 1776. By the time the regiment was inspected at Dover Castle in 1777, Aldcroft was listed as a twenty-five-year-old Englishman with two years of service. He was promoted to lieutenant on 5 June 1778 and was present with the regiment at the training camps at Coxheath (in Kent) and Warley (in Essex) during the summers of 1778 and 1779. Nathaniel Cookman succeeded to his ensigncy.[1]

Aldcroft was promoted to captain on 16 November 1781 upon Benjamin Chapman's promotion to major.² In June 1783 Aldcroft was commanding one of the regiment's additional companies, and he continued to command one of the additional companies through 1783. He briefly commanded a battalion company in early 1784 but was reduced to half pay when the Royal Irish was decreased from twelve companies to ten in 1784.

Aldcroft remained on half pay until transferred into the 2nd Battalion of the 2nd (Queen's) Regiment of Foot on 6 March 1795. He was promoted to major in the army on 12 May 1795.³ The 2nd Battalion was initially raised at Portsmouth, England and remained in the country until later in 1795, when it was moved to Guernsey, an island in the English Channel. The battalion embarked from Guernsey for Martinique in November 1795, and a hurricane caused heavy casualties on the trip. Aldcroft was present at Rumsey with the 2nd Battalion on 6 October 1796. He died at Martinique on 27 July 1797.⁴

Aldcroft's will, which had been drawn up in July 1789, was validated in London on 23 November 1797. His estate was divided between his mother and his sisters. The family was living in Upper Swinton, Shropshire, at the time the will was drafted. His estate was worth several thousand pounds.⁵

Charles Hoar

FIGURE 5.1 Charles Hoar Harland's coat of arms.
Courtesy of Ryan Gale

Charles Hoar (ca. 1755–26 February 1810) was commissioned as an ensign in the Royal Irish on 10 June 1774. His surname is also given as Hoare. He was the third son of George Hoar of Middleton, St. George, Burham, and Francis Sleigh of Stockton-upon-Tees.⁶ Charles Hoar was approximately nineteen at the time of his commission and was listed as English. He was assigned to the major's company and was present with the regiment in New York

City by 8 February 1775. He was present when the regiment embarked on HMS *Asia* before the rebel mob at New York City on 6 June 1775.[7] He disembarked onto Governor's Island on 10 June 1775 with most of the regiment. Hoare was one of only a few officers present at New York City who did not testify at Captain Payne's court-martial.

Hoar traveled to Boston with the remainder of the regiment in June 1775. He is listed as present with the major's company there on 2 October 1775, but he did not sign the return. He was present with the major's company at Dover Castle on 12 August 1776. Hoare was listed as on leave on 4 March 1777 by the permission of the commanding officer. He was transferred to Benjamin Payne's company in the summer of 1777 and was promoted to lieutenant in the Royal Irish on 15 July 1777. Hoar was present on a general court-martial board in Dover in November 1777 that tried William Green and Henry Knight for desertion. He was transferred to the grenadier company by December 1777.[8]

Hoar was listed as on leave on the 19 July 1779 return of the grenadier company and was still listed as on leave on the March 1780 return. In the October 1780 return, he was listed as "Promoted to New Corps 12/22/1779."[9]

Hoar was not listed on the August 1779 general return of officers of the Royal Irish, but three lieutenancies were vacant by promotion into new corps. It is possible that the Royal Irish's summer at Coxheath Camp the previous year had made the officers of the Royal Irish particularly good choices for the new corps being raised. Hoar's promotion to captain in the 90th (Yorkshire) Regiment of Foot was official on 27 November 1779. The 90th was ordered to the West Indies in 1780 and remained there until late 1783. He remained with the 90th Foot until it was disbanded in Yorkshire in early 1784. Hoar was the senior captain listed on half pay from the 90th Foot in 1802.[10]

In late 1802, Hoar's situation improved dramatically with his impending marriage to a widow, "Ann, the only daughter and heir of Philip Harland, late of Sutton Hall, in the County of York," as she was represented in an announcement from Whitehall on 2 November 1802.[11] That announcement provided Hoar with the use the surname and arms of Harland in addition to the arms of Hoar. At the time of the Royal decree, Hoar was living in St. George Parish, Middlesex.

Hoar supposedly had a powerful ability to find water using a diving rod. According to Ann Harland's mother, Hoar discovered his gift only after Lady Milbanke discussed the issue with him, because she too was able to find water using a divining rod. He appears to have found water for several powerful individuals, including the Welsh nobleman Richard Pennant, 1st Baron Penrhyn. According to his wife, Hoar did not like either discussing or exhibiting his gift.[12]

Hoar found additional royal favor after the wedding, which was held at Easingwood. After the wedding, the Hoar Harland family moved to Ann's paternal estate at Sutton-Hall in York. Hoar was appointed captain commandant of the Yorkshire Volunteer Foresters in October 1803 and was made a baronet by the king on 24 September 1808. Since he died without children in 1810, the title expired.[13]

Hoar had a nephew, William Hoar, who upon the death of Ann in 1826 changed his name to William Harland and inherited the estate. The case ended up in the House of Lords in 1834 as *Harland v. Emerson*. However, William was successful, and his son, William-Charles, was in residence at Sutton-Hall in 1838.

Hoar's great-nephew's estates in 1838 consisted of Sutton-Hall, the family seat; Huby, also in North Riding, Yorkshire; and the Middleton estate, near Darlington in Durham.[14]

Francis Howard

Francis Howard (?–3 May 1771) obtained his commission as an ensign in the Royal Irish on 16 December 1767, after the Royal Irish was already in America. He was living with his father, William Howard in Dublin, when he obtained his commission. He seemed to be excited to remove to America, and Roger Lamb, the soldier diarist, wanted to accompany him, but "there could not be a situation procured in the regiment for a boy such as [Lamb]." So Howard arrived in America without Lamb's companionship.[15]

Howard was assigned as the ensign of General Sebright's company and served with it at Fort Chartres for his entire career with the Royal Irish. Most likely he arrived at Fort Chartres in the spring of 1769 with the annual supply shipment from Fort Pitt.

Howard drowned in Chartie Creek near Fort Chartres on 29 April 1771, according to the following newspaper account: "On Tuesday last an Express arrived here from Fort Pitt, by whom we learn, that Ensign Howard, of the 18th Regiment, was lately found drowned in Chartrie Creek; and that a Number of Indians were just come in, from their Excursions against the Southern Indians, and brought several Scalps."[16]

Howard's commission went to Thomas Cumming. His accounts with Cox & Meir appear to have been finally paid off on 8 February 1773. They indicate that he died on 3 May 1771.[17]

George Mawby

George Mawby (1761–?) joined the rolls of the general's company of the Royal Irish on 24 September 1773 as a private soldier and served through the remainder of the Royal Irish's American service. According to that return, he originally served with Captain Benjamin Johnson's company, but his name does not appear on the rolls of that company. In reality, he was serving as a volunteer. His father, John Mawby Sr., was the de facto commander of the general's company.

George Mawby is listed as "on duty" at the 21 January 1774 muster of the company in Philadelphia, but he was never present as a muster. He was listed as absent with leave on 29 July 1774 and 8 February 1775. When the regiment was mustered in Boston in October 1775, Mawby was listed as being "on command." He might have accompanied Captain Payne's woodcutting expedition, but he is not mentioned in any of its reports. He joined the regiment in Boston before its embarkation for England in late December 1775.

Mawby returned to England with the Royal Irish, arriving in February 1776. He was listed as having the lieutenant colonel's leave on 12 August 1776. He was commissioned as an ensign on 15 November 1776 and assigned to the lieutenant colonel's company. He returned to the general's company by June 1777, which was the company his father was serving in as well. In the 15 May 1777 inspection return for the Royal Irish, Mawby was listed as the regiment's junior ensign, a sixteen-year-old Englishman with one year of service. The return does not recognize his time serving as a private soldier or a volunteer.[18]

Mawby was promoted to lieutenant on 25 December 1778. He continued to serve with the general's company until he was transferred to Captain George Bewes's company in June 1779. He was transferred to his father's company by December 1779 and was present with it at Hemel Hempstead in March 1780.

Mawby was transferred to Captain Kenneth MacKenzie's Independent Company of Foot by the War Office on 7 March 1781. There were fifty-seven independent companies raised in 1781, and MacKenzie's was the first one on the printed army lists. The specifics of what caused Mawby to transfer to MacKenzie's company have been lost to history. The fact that he was not MacKenzie's first choice is clear, however.

MacKenzie wrote to Lord Townshend in February 1781 that he hoped to keep the subaltern positions vacant, since he had "not yet been able to find proper persons to recommend for my Subaltern Commissions, but I hope to be indulged to keep them open some little time." MacKenzie's recommendation for the ensigncy, Thomas Hawkshaw, was commissioned. MacKenzie had also recommended George Ross, a fellow Scot, for the lieutenancy, and Ross was offered the rank, but once it was known that the company was bound for Africa, he was uninterested. Similarly, officers interested in the lieutenancy were nonexistent, according to MacKenzie, once his company's destination was known. MacKenzie stated that he was unable to find even a single serving ensign willing to take the position without purchase.

For some reason, however, Mawby consented to the transfer. MacKenzie's company was raised for rank, with MacKenzie previously serving as a lieutenant in the 78th (Highland) Regiment of Foot. MacKenzie brought the company to Chatham Barracks in Kent to be mustered, and the original inspection return was completed on 7 February 1781. At that time the company consisted of five sergeants, five corporals, two drummers, and ninety-eight privates. Two returned deserters rounded out the company to an even one hundred private men. However, thirteen of the privates were found unfit for service and not mustered. The men were mostly English, although MacKenzie, one sergeant, two corporals, and four privates were Scottish. Later estimates observe that the company included sixteen convicts for every five volunteers.[19]

Orders were written to Captain MacKenzie, commandant of the two companies ordered to Africa at Whitehall, on 30 May 1781. The purpose of the assignment was articulated as follows: "But although the Protection of our own Trade and Settlements be the primary Objective of sending out this Force, it is hoped that a favorable Opportunity may be found, while the King's Ships remain upon the Coast, of reducing some of the Dutch Forts in the Neighbourhood of ours."[20]

The two companies embarked for Africa from Portsmouth in July 1781. MacKenzie's transports were escorted by HMS *Leander*, a fifty-two-gun, fourth-rate ship launched in 1780. It was captured by the French in 1798, recaptured by the Russians in 1799, and returned. The ship was renamed HMS *Hygeia* in 1813 while being used as a medical depot and was sold in 1817.²¹ The companies went to the Island of Goree off the coast of Senegal, West Africa, where additional forces were gathered, and then reached Cape Coast Castle at Sierra Leone on 5 February 1782.²²

HMS *Leander*'s flotilla including the sloop HMS *Alligator* and troops attacked the Dutch post at Elmina on 17 February 1782 but were repulsed after four days. The companies, supported by the Royal Navy and portions of the 75th Regiment of Foot, were then successful in the capture of the Dutch forts at Accra, Apam, Courmantyne, Fort Barracco, Kormantin, and Mouri on the west African coast. Sickness took its toll on the companies, and by March 1782, sixty-five of the men were dead and only forty-nine were left fit for duty. Another thirty-eight had deserted to the Dutch. The men were stationed near Cape Coast, Mouree, and Commendah and several smaller posts along the west African coast.

General Henry Conway, commander in chief, recommended to Lord Townshend that the remainder of the regular troops in Africa be recalled in December 1782. He wrote, "I cannot therefore help saying that in my opinion the Remainder of these Companies should be immediately withdrawn; and those Services provided by the African Company, it seeming only a Scene of certain Destruction to the Regular Troops, without any Advantage to the Service in its present situation." The company remained on the west African coast until it was recalled in 1783. Mawby was placed on half pay when the two companies from Africa were disbanded on 24 September 1783 and remained on the half-pay list through 1785. He was removed from half pay by 1786 for reasons that are not clear, but death is not the likely reason for all three subalterns to be removed at the same time.²³

MacKenzie was a difficult officer to serve under; he did not seem to have held any of the officers who served under him in any esteem. When he returned to England, he was arrested for the murder of a deserter from his company: his cousin, Kenith Murray MacKenzie, who was tried and found guilty. Captain MacKenzie was sentenced to be executed but received a pardon from the king in December 1785.²⁴

Sebright Mawby

Sebright Mawby (?–26 November 1850) was the third son of John Mawby Sr. He was named after John Saunders Sebright, the officer who was his father's patron. Sebright Mawby joined the rolls of Captain Payne's company of the Royal Irish on 25 August 1773. He was serving as a gentleman volunteer, and his brother George began serving as a volunteer at about the same time. Payne's company was stationed at Philadelphia at the time. Mawby is listed as "on duty" on the regimental returns for 21 January 1774 and as a "volunteer" on the 29 July 1774 returns. That is the only case of such a listing for the Royal Irish during its American service. Mawby remained with Payne's company throughout the rest of his service in America. He was listed as absent on 8 February 1775 in New York City and as "on command" on 2 October 1775 when his company was mustered at Boston.

When Mawby returned to England, he was transferred to the lieutenant colonel's company and remained there until he was moved to the general's company, where his father was posted by June 1777. He appears to have been given leave with his brother and was listed as absent with the lieutenant colonel's leave on 12 August 1776. He was listed as on leave from the major on 4 March 1777 through 6 March 1778, and he was listed as "on duty" on the 25 July 1778 and 16 March 1779 returns.

Mawby was probably carried on the roster of an additional company, since he is not present with the companies mustered at Warley Camp in July 1779. He was listed as present with Bewes's company at Finchley Camp near London in October 1780, which marked the first time that he was present for a muster. He was moved to his father's company by 25 December 1780. He was listed as a private at the Channel Island of Jersey in October 1781. He accompanied the Royal Irish to Gibraltar in 1783 and remained in his father's company at least through December 1784. He was listed as being discharged on 20 July 1787, at which point he had accrued slightly less than fourteen years of service as a volunteer.[25]

Mawby purchased an ensigncy in the Royal Irish on 20 July 1787 from Benjamin Chapman Jr. He remained with the regiment at Gibraltar and was promoted to lieutenant by purchase on 17 May 1791. According to at least one biographer, Mawby was present with the regiment at Gibraltar until October 1793, with the exception of a two-month leave.

In October 1793, Mawby accompanied the Royal Irish to Toulon, France, where it was to join an allied army to protect the city from the French Republicans. Mawby was detailed to serve as an assistant engineer and did outpost duty at Cape Brun until that post was evacuated on 17 December 1793. Mawby then commanded a detachment of the Royal Irish on board the French ship *Pompée* under the French royal standard. The *Pompée* was ordered to cruise to Spanish and Italian ports to gather commissary supplies for the garrison at Toulon.[26]

Mawby returned with the Royal Irish in June 1794 to participate in the assault at Calvi on the northwest coast of Corsica. According to John Philippart, Mawby was the senior lieutenant of the grenadier company when it stormed Mozelle Fort shortly before the French surrendered. Mawby remained on Corsica with the regiment until May 1795, when he was given a staff role as an assistant quartermaster general to the army in Corsica. On 1 September 1795, he was promoted to captain in the Royal Irish. In 1796, he was serving as the deputy barracks master general on Corsica. He was also put in command of a company of French artificers (craftsmen). However, Mawby was allowed to accompany the Royal Irish on its expedition to Calvi. After the surrender of Calvi, Mawby returned to his duties on Corsica. When Corsica was abandoned in 1796, Mawby was ordered to superintend the spiking of the artillery at Bastia, on the northeast coast of Corsica. He then followed the Royal Irish to Italy. The regiment remained there until it returned to Gibraltar in 1797.

Mawby purchased a commission as major in the Royal Irish on 1 June 1799 from William Conolly. When Conolly left the regiment, it no longer had any members who had actively served in America. (Mawby's own volunteer service was the exception.)

Mawby was in command of the Royal Irish in May 1800 when it was ordered to Minorca. As a result of sickness, he was forced to take leave and did not return to the Royal Irish until it was in Egypt in June 1801. He then remained with the Royal Irish until it returned to Ireland in 1802. It was originally posted at Armagh.

Mawby's service with the Royal Irish ended when he was appointed without purchase to be a lieutenant colonel in the 53rd Regiment of Foot on 5 October 1804. He joined the 1st Battalion of the 53rd Foot at Portsmouth and embarked for India on 20 April 1805.

Mawby was appointed to command a brigade in November 1809 in the Bundelcund province of India.[27] He remained in command of the brigade until the army stopped active campaigning in the area in March 1812. He commanded the unsuccessful attack on the fort at Callinger later that year. Mawby was brevetted to colonel in the army on 4 June 1813. He was promoted to major general on 12 August 1819 and to lieutenant general on 10 January 1837.

Mawby retired to London and lived at 76 Baker Street, Portman Square. In 1834, while on Fleet Street, Mawby had his pocketbook stolen. The retired general then chased the thief down and captured him. James

Berwick was found guilty and transported for fourteen years. Mawby died on 26 November 1850.[28]

John Piercy

John Piercy (ca. 1753–?) originally purchased a commission in the 45th Foot on 4 August 1774. His surname is also given as Percey, Percy, or Pearcy, and later returns for the 9th Foot list him as an Irishman born in 1753.[29] He transferred into the Royal Irish for a fee on 21 August 1775 when Nicholas Trist's promotion to lieutenant created a vacancy. When the Royal Irish was drafted and ordered to return to England, Piercy appears to have worked to stay in America. He transferred into the 47th Foot by trading commissions with Thomas Lawe, who then went into the Royal Irish.[30] His commission in the 47th dated from 12 March 1776, but he was not listed on the 47th Foot's returns for late 1776. G. K. Yates was unable to establish Piercy's company assignment in his review of the 47th Foot's records.[31]

Piercy participated in Lieutenant General John Burgoyne's Saratoga campaign. The extant company orderly book from the 47th Regiment of Foot at the Pell Library at Fort Ticonderoga shows that Piercy was an active participant in that ill-fated campaign. He was ordered out on picket duty on the evenings of 14 and 21 August 1777, after the regiment had reached Fort Ticonderoga, and took part in working parties on 22 and 27 August. Between those dates, on 25 August, Piercy sat on a regimental court of five officers under Captain Henry Marr. The young ensign was on the 47th's quarter guard on 30 August and 3 September. He sat on a regimental courtmartial board of five officers on 14 September under Captain John Dormer Alcock, was assigned to the quarter guard again on 19 September, and was out with the picket on 24 September. Piercy sat on a three-member regimental court-martial board on 25 September under Captain Marr. He surrendered at Saratoga along with the majority of the 47th Foot.

Piercy was listed among the officers who were part of the Convention Army. He signed the 13 December 1777 Cambridge, Massachusetts, parole of honor (agreement not to attempt to escape), and he was still a prisoner as late as February 1779.[32] He was able to obtain a free lieutenancy in the 9th Foot on 11 July 1778, after John Smith died.

Piercy was still listed as "Not yet Joined from America" in the return of Alexander Baillie's company of the 9th Regiment taken at Norwich,

England, on 15 March 1782. He appears to have returned to the regiment later that spring and is listed as on recruiting service on the 30 July 1782 muster. The 9th Regiment remained at Norwich through 1783, but Piercy is listed as being on leave and was most likely in Ireland. The 8 March 1784 return shows Piercy sick in Ireland. By 1 February 1785, Piercy had returned to the regiment and had been transferred to Captain John Jones's company stationed at Ayr, Ireland. He was present in June 1785 when the regiment was inspected at Newry. He was promoted to captain on 19 October 1787, but was listed on the return of Lieutenant Colonel John Campbell's company in January 1788 as an additional captain while the regiment was at Cork. Another officer was similarly commissioned to one of the additional companies to be raised as the regiment expanded. Piercy almost certainly obtained his captaincy without purchase.[33]

Piercy retired from the 9th Foot on 8 September 1791. His commission went to Richard Campbell. At that point Piercy exits the historical record. He had served approximately seventeen years in the army, including approximately five years as a prisoner of war.[34]

Thomas Serle

Thomas Serle (ca. 1753–?) purchased a commission in the Royal Irish Regiment on 20 April 1775, the day after the Battle of Lexington and Concord. He was a twenty-two-year-old Englishman.[35] Notice of his appointment was published in the 2 May 1775 issue of the *London Gazette*. It is not entirely clear when he arrived in North America, but he was present with Captain Payne's company at Boston by 2 October 1775. He may have been already present as a volunteer. He returned to England with the majority of the officers in February 1776.

Because the regiment in England designated Payne's old company as the light infantry company, Serle was officially assigned to Hugh Lord's company, which had been left in Illinois. He was probably serving with the regiment. It is also possible that he took leave upon his return or was sent out on recruiting service.

Serle was promoted to lieutenant on 25 October 1777 when William Slater was promoted to captain. At that time, he was also posted to Blackwood's light infantry company. He was appointed adjutant on 24 February 1779 upon the death of John Mawby Jr. On 28 February he was moved to Robert Hamilton's battalion company because the adjutant was needed with the main body of the regiment and not with the light infantry company. He was listed as on detached duty at Sandwich on 16 March 1779.³⁶

As the adjutant, Serle would have been busy during the summer of 1779 at Warley Camp. He was listed as serving at headquarters on 6 March 1780. He was moved to the light company again on 4 April 1780 and served with the lights during the encampment at Finchley that summer. He was removed from the light company sometime at the end of the summer and posted to one of the additional companies, then he was promoted to captainlieutenant on 27 October 1780. He returned from the additional company, most likely recruiting service, on 7 November 1780, when the regiment was stationed outside London.³⁷

For some unknown reason, possibly because of the absence of enough other officers, Serle was in command of the lieutenant colonel's company in October 1781 on the Channel Islands. He remained as both adjutant and captain lieutenant, similar to the dual roles that John Mawby Sr. held in America until his promotion to captain on 17 January 1782. He was replaced by Lieutenant Nathaniel Cookman as adjutant.³⁸

Serle appears to have been assigned to an additional company upon his promotion to captain. When a battalion company assignment opened up upon Chapman's promotion to major, Serle returned to the regiment proper and was present at the November 1782 muster of his company at Jersey, Channel Islands. The company had previously been John Peter DeLancey's company.³⁹ Serle was with his company when the regiment returned to Hilsea barracks in Portsmouth, England, in August 1783.

In February 1784, Serle was listed as the captain "en second" to Major Chapman's company after the regiment arrived at Gibraltar. He was similarly listed on the July 1784 return.⁴⁰ Serle sold his commission to Finch Mason from half pay of the 91st Foot on 11 December 1784.⁴¹ Serle is one of the few officers to have primarily served with the regiment only during wartime. However, except for some potential skirmishing around Boston, he saw no action against the Americans. Unfortunately, he fades from history upon his retirement from the army.

Henry Shaw

Henry Shaw (ca. 1742–7 November 1767) joined the 16th Foot as an ensign on 15 August 1766 at the age of twenty-three. He is listed as Irish in army records, and the 16th Foot was stationed in Ireland at the time. He appears to have transferred to the Royal Irish on 8 April 1767 in place of James Taylor

Trevor, who did not want to deploy to America. Both regiments were on their way to America, so the reason for Shaw's transfer is not clear.

Shaw was present with the regiment at the 11 April 1767 review at Phoenix Park, Dublin. Upon arrival in America, Shaw was the ensign of Captain Isaac Hamilton's company. He is listed as present at the regiment's 27 October 1767 muster. However, he did not sign the company return at that time.

Shaw died on 7 November 1767, making him the second officer casualty during the American service. His death appears to have been from a short illness, and his place of death was almost certainly Philadelphia. Cox & Meir paid his estate £18 for his subsistence from 11 July 1767 until his death four months later. His commission went to John Wilmot Prideaux. However, it appears that both Wilkins and Gage recommended Buttricke for the vacant commission without purchase.[42]

William Henry Slator

William Henry Slator (ca. 1754–?) was commissioned as an ensign on Mary 17, 1774, in the Royal Irish. His surname is sometimes given as Slater. He was listed as English and was twenty years old at the time of his commission. His original assignment was to Captain Johnson's company. He was present with the regiment by the 8 February 1775 muster at New York City and remained there with the regiment until the main body embarked on HMS *Asia* on 6 June 1775. The ship's log lists Slator as embarking with the regiment and arriving on Governor's Island on 10 June. He then sailed for Boston with the rest of the regiment. While in Boston, he testified at the court-martial of Captain Payne on Monday, 7 August 1775, about his role in embarking with the companies in New York in June 1775. His testimony was supportive of Captain Payne's actions.[43]

Slator was transferred to the general's company at some point and was present with it in Boston on 3 October 1775. He sailed for England in December 1775, and in April 1776, he was recruiting near St. Stephen's Parish in Norfolk with Sergeant Smith.[44] He was present with the skeleton of the regiment at Dover Castle in August 1776. By 4 March 1777, Slator was listed as on commander in chief's leave.[45]

When Slator returned from leave, he was assigned to Captain William Richardson's company. He was announced to be a lieutenant in the 22 July 1777 *London Gazette*, but regimental records show that he was not confirmed to the lieutenancy. He appears to have been the recipient of an unconfirmed lieutenancy. The reason the commission was not confirmed or was rescinded is unclear. Slator left the regiment at that time and does not appear to have served further. His official retirement date is given as October 1777.[46]

Godfrey Tracey

> We have an Account of one Ens: Tracy being killed in a Duell at Fort Pitt.
> —George Buttricke to Thomas Barnsley, 12 February 1769

Godfrey Tracey (ca. 1748–1768) was commissioned as an ensign in the Royal Irish on 11 September 1765 at the approximate age of 17.[47] He is listed as Irish in the regiment's 1767 inspection return. He was present with the regiment when it was reviewed on 11 April 1767 in Dublin and when it arrived in North America, where he was assigned to Major Henry Folliott's company at that time. He was listed as being on command on the October 1768 muster, most likely at Fort Pitt. When the major's company was ordered to remain at Philadelphia, Tracey was transferred to Captain Charles Edmonstone's battalion company at Fort Pitt.

The muster rolls list Tracey as having died on 24 September 1768. The regimental ledgers show him having purchased a lieutenancy on 27 July 1768, but other records of the Royal Irish do not show Tracey as a lieutenant. Most likely he was killed before the regiment obtained official word of his purchase. He seems to have been recommended for the promotion, most likely by Wilkins.[48]

Tracey appears to have been killed in a duel with Robert Hamilton. George Buttricke mentioned Tracey's death in a letter to Captain Thomas Barnsley dated 12 February 1769 from Fort Chartres.[49] The 23 November 1771 minutes of the Provincial Council of Pennsylvania show that a special commission of the three senior justices of the peace in Bedford County was formed to try Robert Hamilton for Tracey's murder.[50] Hamilton appears to have been found not guilty, but the verdict of the trial has not surfaced. At the time of the duel, Hamilton was the ensign in Johnson's company, also stationed at Fort Pitt. The nature of the argument that led to the duel is not clear, but it most likely involved Tracey's purchase of a lieutenancy over Hamilton. The regimental ledger shows that Tracey paid Wilkins more than £23 in early 1768.[51]

Tracey's father advanced him £200 in early 1768 as well. The ledgers show that Tracey advanced £200 through Allen Marlan & Company for the difference between his ensigncy and a lieutenancy on 27 July 1768. It is possible that Hamilton had wished to purchase the vacant lieutenancy. Since Hamilton was a senior ensign in the regiment when Perkins died, he should have had the right to purchase it. However, either Wilkins preferred Tracey or Hamilton did not have the funds available to advance his cause.

Tracey's accounts appear to have been finally settled in June 1773, when Captain Chapman was paid for the subsistence that Tracey's account had been advanced between 25 August 1768 and his death.[52]

Tracey's ensigncy went to John Mawby Jr. His place in Edmonstone's company was taken by John Wilmot Prideaux, who had not yet joined the regiment at the time of Tracey's death. In the end, Alexander Fowler, an officer from the half-pay list, ended up with the disputed lieutenancy.[53]

Samuel Twentyman

Samuel Twentyman (ca. 1755–1800) was the son of Childers Twentyman, the rector of Thorpe on the Hill and the vicar of Welton, and Anne Loyde.[54] Samuel had a brother, Childers Jr., and three sisters. The family appears to have been from Newark upon Trent, Nottinghamshire. A namesake, potentially his grandfather, was the mayor of Newark for three terms beginning in 1758.

Twentyman was appointed an ensign in the Royal Irish on 25 July 1775.[55] He was listed as being a volunteer when appointed and was probably serving with another regiment in Boston at that time. He is not listed in the returns of the regiment until 4 March 1777, when he was noted as the ensign of Captain Payne's company. He may have remained in America with the army for some reason. He is listed as being on recruiting duty in March 1777, and he purchased his lieutenancy in the 79th Foot on 4 June 1778 to replace John de Birniere's preferment. He was present with the regiment at Coxheath in the summer of 1778 and later testified to having mixed with the officers of the 65th Foot who were brigaded with the Royal Irish that summer.[56]

According to Twentyman, he was nominated for a company in the 90th Regiment of Foot, which the Duke of Ancaster raised in 1779.[57] Twentyman appears to have left the Royal Irish to assist in raising the 90th Foot before August 1779, since he does not appear in the general return of officers, but the army list shows him moving directly from the Royal Irish to the 90th Foot, also known as the Yorkshire Volunteers.[58] The regiment was raised in October and November 1779 and was immediately sent to the West Indies. Twentyman's commission as a captain in the 90th Foot was dated 29 November 1779. He embarked with the regiment to St. Lucia. Twentyman was in command of the 90th Foot at some point while in the West Indies, and he purchased a commission as major on 28 February 1783. The regiment remained there until it returned to Yorkshire and was disbanded on 11 May 1783.[59]

Twentyman was appointed deputy adjutant general on 26 November 1793 from half pay in the 90th Foot.[60] He embarked for Ostend, in present-day Belgium, to support the forces under the Duke of York. While serving as the deputy adjutant general to the forces under the Earl of Moira, Twentyman was brevetted to lieutenant colonel in the army as of 25 February 1794.[61] In January 1798, he was promoted to lieutenant colonel in the army while still on half pay from the 90th Foot.[62]

Sometime before November 1799, Twentyman was promoted to lieutenant colonel in the 87th (Prince of Wales Irish) Regiment of Foot, which was stationed at St. Lucia. On 6 July 1799 he was brevetted to colonel in the army, and on 2 November 1799, he was appointed as a brigadier with local rank in the West Indies only.[63] Twentyman disappears from the army list in October 1800, and he appears to have died in St. Lucia. His will was validated on 16 February 1801.

Twentyman's personal life was somewhat unorthodox: he fathered a daughter, Charlotte Harmston, out of wedlock with Susan Harmston, who according to family history was originally his servant, and recognized the child as his own, though he did not marry her mother. Charlotte was baptized on 14 April 1785 at Lincoln, St. Peter Eastgate. She lived most of her life in Darlington. Twentyman's will, dated 17 May 1788, left a £21 annuity to Susan and the rest of his estate to Charlotte. His estate at that time included a tenement at the Yard Garden in Lincoln, leased from the dean and chapter of Lincoln Cathedral.[64]

John Wilcocks

John Wilcocks (?–5 November 1772) might have been an American. Listed under the surname Wilson in the army lists for 1772 and 1773, Wilcocks (whose name is sometimes also given as Wilcox) was originally assigned to take the vacant ensigncy in Major Isaac Hamilton's company when Henry Fermor was promoted to lieutenant. Wilcocks's commission was dated 26 February 1772. He was present as the ensign of the general's company when the Royal Irish was mustered in October 1772 in Philadelphia.

According to the muster returns, Wilcocks was moved to Captain Johnson's company the next day, 25 October. He died in Philadelphia on 5 November 1772 after an extended illness, although he was not listed as sick on either of the returns on which he is included. He appears to have been given leave to sell his commission before his death, but his illness overtook him before he was able to do so.

Advertisements in the *Pennsylvania Gazette* stated that "all persons having demands against Mr. John Wilcocks, late ensign of the 18th Regiment, are requested to bring these accounts to Francis Hopkinson, executor."[65] For some reason, the regimental agent's accounts show him being paid for service only from 26 February to 24 June 1772. It is clear he was present with the regiment until his death in Philadelphia. The agents and his executor both spell his name Wilcocks, so that is most likely the correct spelling.[66]

6

Staff Officers

This chapter discusses the officers who held a staff commission in the Royal Irish during its North American service. These include the adjutant, the quartermaster, and the three professional positions of chaplain, surgeon, and surgeon's mate; the latter held a warrant from the colonel and not actually a commission from the king. Since many staff officers held a line commission as a subaltern at the same time, most of these men could have been included in the chapter on lieutenants or ensigns as well.

The adjutant was responsible for the day-to-day management of the regiment's paperwork, duty rosters, orders, and the like. He was often, but not always, also a subaltern. All the adjutants of the Royal Irish during this period held a line commission as well. The quartermaster was the officer responsible for the logistics of the regiment. He too often held a line commission. George Buttricke was the only man to fill that role while the Royal Irish was in North America. He had previously served as a soldier and an NCO in the 60th (Royal American) Regiment and ultimately served as a subaltern in the Royal Irish as well.

Adjutants and especially quartermasters were often former sergeants; this became more common after 1775. The Royal Irish followed that trend in replacing Buttricke with another former sergeant. According to historian Anthony Bruce, King George III did not consider it acceptable for captains to serve as quartermasters, so a captain lieutenant or a captain may have occasionally also served as an adjutant, but it was extremely rare for such an officer to serve as the quartermaster, too.[1]

The fact that regiments on the Irish Establishment were not authorized a quartermaster made it difficult for men holding only that rank when regiments were rotated back to Ireland from another station. On

14 April 1767, when four regiments were to be rotated back to Ireland from America, Thomas Gage, the commander in chief in North America, was ordered by Lord Barrington to inform the four quartermasters of the regiments to be rotated to Ireland that it would be the king's pleasure for them "to act in the same Station in the Regiments that go from Ireland." Barrington wrote further that since the four officers "do not appear to hold any other Commissions in their present Regiments, it is apprehended that they will think this Plan very advantageous to them as otherwise they must be reduced to Half Pay." If they did not wish to continue in North America, they were to be allowed to exchange with a quartermaster from the half-pay list. In fact, all four of the officers took advantage of the king's offer: Joseph Johnson transferred from the 27th Foot to the 10th Foot on 6 August 1767, Duncan Campbell transferred from the 42nd Foot to the 26th Foot on 13 July 1767, Peter Graham transferred from the 28th Foot to the 16th Foot on 10 July 1767, and George Buttricke transferred from the 46th Foot to the Royal Irish on 11 July 1767.[2]

The regiment's chaplain was an ordained minister in the Church of England. He was to minister to the spiritual needs of the men. Often chaplains performed their duties by hiring a younger cleric to do the actual work. These men were often referred to as deputy chaplains. It was uncommon for the chaplain of the regiment to serve with the regiment overseas. During the Saratoga campaign in 1777, the British forces had only one deputy chaplain actually present with the six British regiments on campaign.

The surgeon was the other professional officer besides the chaplain. He was responsible for the phyiscal health of the regiment. Most surgeons were trained doctors, but the poor state of medical knowledge and the lack of understanding of biology did not allow them to be as helpful as many of them would have wished to be.

The last officer, the surgeon's mate, or mate, did not hold a commission from the king but acted under a warrant granted by the colonel. The Royal Irish was lucky that most, if not all, of the mates to serve the regiment had actual university medical training. Before being appointed, a mate received a certificate from the surgeon general stating that he was qualified "for the office of Surgeons' Mate to one of his Majesty's Regiments." In part to obtain such a certificate, Edward Hand, the Royal Irish's mate when the regiment arrived in America, provided letters from two Dublin physicians stating that he had "attended lectures on the theory & practice of Physic": "I hereby certifie that Mr. Edward Hand Surgeons

Mate in the royal irish regiment of Foot did carefully and diligently attend my lectures in anatomy Physiology and Surgery last winter; and that he himself inspected the Muscle, and Blood vessels with dexterity and skill."[3]

It is unclear whether Hand purchased his warrant, but General John Sebright prohibited him from selling it when he wished to purchase an ensigncy in 1772.

George Buttricke

George Buttricke (ca. 1738–1784) originally served as a soldier in Lord Loudoun's (Royal American) Regiment of Foot. He is listed as English in military records (sometimes as Butrick or Butricke) and was almost certainly from Nottinghamshire.[4] He appears to have originally been in the 2nd Battalion of the 60th Regiment. From there he eventually made his way to sergeant major of the 1st Battalion of the 60th; there is commentary by Colonel Bouquet, the 1st Battalion's commander, about his being transferred to the 1st Battalion based on his skill as a tailor, "in which capacity he was received and employed in the Battalion." In November 1760 he was recommended by Major Walters of the 1st Battalion of the 60th to be allowed to purchase an ensigncy in the Royal Americans, but Colonel Bouquet refused his promotion because he had served as a tailor in the regiment. General Jeffery Amherst found Bouquet's objections to be well-grounded, and Buttricke had to wait four years, until 15 March 1764, to be promoted to the lesser position of quartermaster in the 46th Foot.

Buttricke appears to have had a strong mentor in Thomas Barnsley, an officer in the 60th Foot who continued to correspond with him after his promotion into the Royal Irish. Similarly, he appears to have been befriended by Captain Stewart of the Royal Irish.[5] Since the 46th Foot withdrew from America in 1767, Buttricke was offered the chance to transfer into an incoming regiment that needed a quartermaster. He was listed as the quartermaster of the Royal Irish from 11 July 1767, which is the date the Royal Irish arrived at Philadelphia. The Royal Irish came to America from the Irish Establishment, which did not allow for a quartermaster. When the regiment arrived in America, it was allowed to have a quartermaster, and Buttricke was immediately available. He was granted two thousand acres of land in Albany County, New York, on 9 January 1768 for his service as quartermaster in the 46th Foot during the French and Indian War.[6]

When Buttricke arrived in Illinois, he and Captain Stewart, purchased a farm, but with Stewart's quick demise, Buttricke had to take on additional partners, which lowered his expectations for the return on his investment. Buttricke also appears to have been severely shaken by Stewart's death, and he himself was taken with the sickness that brought the regiment to its knees. Here is his description of its effects:

> On Sunday the 18th spt. I was sitting at Dinner when a sudden Coldness struck me all over without saying any thing of it I Rose from table and walk'd into the field thinking to shake it off, But to no purpose, I then went to Bed and found myself seized with a Hott fit which did not last long and afterwards spelt pretty well till morning when I found myself quiet well, I tould the Doctor of what had happened, who said it would turn into an intermitting fever and indeed so I found it, that day Capt. Stewart, Lt. Turner and 20 men was seized in much the same manner next day as the Doctor has said mine came on again and in such a Violent manner that it laid me up for good. I had it six days with a Cold and hot fit every day But no shaking till the seventh when I had a very severe Cold fit, and shuck very much, the Doctor was pleased to see it and said he would soon put a stop to it.[7]

Buttricke survived, but he reported that he was sick for another ten days in April and nearly a week in May 1769.

In his letters, Buttricke stated that he was also doing duty as the adjutant upon Lieutenant Turner's death in the fall of 1768, but he was not to be made adjutant, because Lieutenant Colonel John Wilkins knew what was in his best interest. The regiment's new adjutant, Captain Lieutenant John Mawby Sr., remained in Philadelphia, so Buttricke served both the roles of adjutant and quartermaster while in Illinois. Wilkins was possibly taking care of Buttricke since Mawby had a clear benefactor in John Sebright; in Buttricke's taking Mawby's duty, Wilkins thought that Buttricke might earn some favor with Sebright. Sebright took an active interest in the Royal Irish, and Buttricke would have been an unknown entity to him in November 1767, since Buttricke was appointed to the Royal Irish without any input from Sebright.

However, Buttricke was still hoping for leave in Europe and was awaiting the new adjutant every day in June 1769. As early as February 1769, he believed that Wilkins was going to recommend him for a vacant ensigncy in the regiment, but Buttricke was not overconfident about his chances. In fact, it would be four more years before he would obtain his ensigncy. Wilkins had, however, recommended Buttricke for the vacant ensigncy created by Henry Shaw's death in November 1767, and Gage agreed to support the recommendation. It is not clear why Buttricke was not confirmed and why Prideaux received the commission instead.[8]

By December 1769, Buttricke was a particularly busy man at Fort Chartres. He was serving as barrack master, since Captain Campbell[9] had left for England in the spring of 1769, and he was happy to obtain the two shillings per day to which the position entitled him. He had also been serving as the regiment's temporary paymaster since the death of Matthew Lane in September 1769. He remained doing duty as the adjutant and quartermaster through 1772.[10]

Buttricke accompanied Wilkins to New Orleans and then to Pensacola, Florida. He most likely also accompanied Wilkins to England. Buttricke had been trying to get leave to England since 1768. He was finally given a line commission as an ensign on 21 January 1773. He did not sign either of the petitions to Sebright against Wilkins from the officers of the regiment.

Buttricke was listed as on the king's leave when the regiment was mustered for pay on 26 July 1773 at Philadelphia. He was assigned to Captain Thomas Batt's company, which shortly became Captain Robert Hamilton's company. He returned to the regiment before the 29 July 1774 muster and was present with his company in Philadelphia, and he testified at the court-martial of Robert Newburgh in New York in August 1774.[11]

When the regiment was split in 1774, Buttricke was ordered to accompany John Shee's command to Boston; however, his post as ensign of Robert Hamilton's company had been taken by Edmund Prideaux. Buttricke's company assignment as ensign is not clear until he was assigned to Johnson's company in June 1775. In fact, Buttricke was acting as the quartermaster for the combined detachment of the Royal Irish and the 65th Foot in Boston under Lieutenant Colonel Bruce. In November 1774, Buttricke was gathering "proper Cloth to make up Watch Coats for the Companies" and providing "immediate direction" to the regimental tailors.[12]

Buttricke returned to England in February 1776 with the majority of the regiment's officers. In England, he was initially assigned to Lieutenant Colonel Williamson's company. He finally purchased a lieutenancy on 15 July 1776 from George Bruere and was sent on recruiting duty in both 1777 and 1778 while assigned to the lieutenant colonel's company.

Buttricke also did duty with the Western Essex Regiment of Militia. He was listed as serving with its 1st Battalion while the regiment was at Coxheath Camp in 1778 and was retroactively appointed adjutant of the militia on 22 April 1778. Buttricke resigned as a lieutenant of the Royal Irish on 4 June 1778 and as its quartermaster on 18 August 1778. Buttricke still retained the position of adjutant in the Western Essex Militia when he was promoted to be its captain lieutenant on 24 February 1780.[13] When the West Essex Militia was inspected in 1780 at Danbury, Buttricke was present.[14]

It is probable that Buttricke was given the opportunity to be promoted into the West Essex Militia because it was in a fearsome state, and his significant experience as sergeant major, acting adjutant, and quartermaster would provide the necessary guidance to the militia officers. Lieutenant Colonel Richard Hunt of the West Essex appears to have been such a poor commanding officer that in October 1781 Major General Charles Rainsford, having inspected the militia, referred to "a very indifferent Corps of Officers who want great improvement. The Lieutenant Colonel is very unequal to the post and had very little weight with the Regiment, this Regiment cannot be in order until great changes are made." It is unclear whether Buttricke was part of the problem or part of the solution, but he definitely had experience working with a fractious group of officers while in America. He was present with the regiment on 10 October 1781 at Fingringhoe Camp near Colchester, England.[15] Buttricke remained with the West Essex Militia until it was disbanded in 1783 at the end of hostilities.

Buttricke was listed as being from Mansfield, Nottinghamshire, when he drafted a will in April 1784. He bequeathed his estate primarily to his Englandwife, Catherine, providing that she did not remarry; to two married sisters both living in Nottinghamshire; and to several other family members. He died later in 1784.[16]

Edward Hand

Edward Hand (31 December 1744–3 September 1802) was born on New Year's Eve outside Dublin at Clydruff, Kings County, Ireland. He was the son of John Hand. Edward Hand moved to Dublin in his early twenties to study medicine at Trinity College but does not seem to have ever formally enrolled; he probably did attend lectures, however. In early 1767, when the news of the Royal Irish's rotation to America had been received, Hand joined the Royal Irish as its surgeon's mate.

Hand kept a still-extant record of the regiment's passage from embarking on 20 May 1767 until disembarking at Philadelphia on 11 July

1767. It noted the distance traveled, the wind direction, the ship's course, the weather, and the daily sightings.[17] He was soon stationed at Fort Pitt while surgeon Thomas Thomasson accompanied part of the regiment deeper into the backwoods of America. While at Fort Pitt, Hand appears to have gotten involved in land speculation and made a significant profit from his ventures. He had made enough by 1772 that he could make the £400 investment in an ensign's commission in the Royal Irish. He asked if he was required to resign as the surgeon's mate to purchase the commission and was told by General Sebright that he was. This is interesting because Thomasson held another commission while he was the surgeon.[18]

As an ensign, Hand was assigned to Captain Johnson's company. He served as the quartermaster at Fort Pitt and was a silent partner in purchasing the post when it was auctioned off in late 1772. He remained with the regiment when it returned to Philadelphia, but his biographer, Michel Craig, states that his feelings in support of the rebellious colonists made it difficult for him to continue as a British officer. He sold his commission to Charles Hoar in 1774 and settled in Lancaster to practice medicine.

Hand married Catherine (Kitty) Ewing, the daughter of John Ewing and Sarah Yates of Lancaster, on 13 March 1775.[19] When the Revolutionary War began in the spring of 1775, Hand helped to organize the Lancaster County Associators, which became part of the Pennsylvania Rifle Regiment in late June or July 1775. He became the lieutenant colonel of the Pennsylvania Rifle Regiment with a commission dated 25 June 1775. The regiment set off for Boston shortly after being organized. He was present at Prospect Hill, outside Boston, by 20 August 1775 and participated in the later stages of the siege there.

When the Pennsylvania Rifle Regiment was reorganized as the First Continental Infantry Regiment, Hand was again appointed lieutenant colonel, on 1 January 1776. He was promoted to colonel of that regiment on 7 March 1776 when Colonel William Thompson was promoted to brigadier general in the Continental Army.

Hand's regiment was, according to Mark Boatner, George Washington's principal source of information on the British buildup before the Battle of Long Island. The regiment was one of the last to leave Long Island in August 1776, and it was further engaged in the New York campaign at Harlem Heights, Fort Washington, and White Plains. Hand's regiment was designated the First Pennsylvania Regiment on 1 January 1777, and it participated in the Continental victory at Princeton on 3 January 1777.[20]

Hand was promoted to brigadier general in the Continental Army on 1 April 1777. He was sent to Fort Pitt to organize resistance to the British and their Indian allies in the west as commander of the western frontier on 10 April 1777. He opened an expedition against the British at Detroit—which included the last remnants of the Royal Irish in America who had been drafted into the 8th (King's) Foot—but was unable to complete his march west because of swollen streams. At Salt Lick, in present-day Ohio, he attacked a small Indian village.

Hand's performance at Fort Pitt had been less than stellar, and he was sent to command the garrison at Albany, New York, in late 1778. He arrived just as the Cherry Valley Massacre unfolded. In the summer of 1779, he took part in Sullivan's punitive expedition against the Iroquois. He personally led five hundred men in the defense against the British raid on Springfield, New Jersey, in June 1780.

In August 1780, Hand was recalled to serve as a brigade commander in the Marquis de Lafayette's Light Division. He was promoted to adjutant general of the Continental Army on 8 January 1781 and remained in that post until 3 November 1783.[21] He was present at Yorktown as the adjutant general of the army. Hand was brevetted to major general for meritorious service on 30 September 1783 and resigned from the army on 3 November 1783. He was one of the original members of the Society of the Cincinnati, the organization created by former Continental Army officers.

Hand was elected as a delegate to the Continental Congress from Pennsylvania on 12 November 1783. According to congressional records, Hand took his seat on 24 December 1783 and remained in Congress through 5 February 1784. He was in session again from 27 March to 4 June and from 26 June to 19 August 1784. He did not attend the November 1784 session of Congress.[22]

In 1785, Hand was elected to the Pennsylvania legislature, and in 1789 he was elected as a delegate to Pennsylvania's first constitutional convention. In 1790, Hand was a signer of the new Pennsylvania constitution and served as a federal inspector of revenue from 1791 to 1801. On 19 July 1798, he was appointed a major general in the provisional U.S. Army, which was expanding in preparation for war with France. He retained that rank until his discharge on 15 June 1800.[23] Hand was also part of a movement at the end of the century to make Lancaster, Pennsylvania, the federal capital. Toward the end of his life, he had some difficulties with finances, and in 1802 a lawsuit was filed to force him to sell his land.

Hand and his wife had six children: Sarah Hand Bethel (1775–1850), Dorothy Hand Brien (1777–1862), Mary Hand (1786–1880), Edward Hand Jr. (1792–?), Jasper Hand (1784), and John Hand (1782–1807). He died in at Rockford Plantation, possibly of a stroke, on 3 September 1802.[24] A musical piece entitled *General Hand's March* was written in his honor, and a children's book, *Dr. Ed*, was written about him in 1978. Hand's home at Rockford Plantation near Lancaster is now a Pennsylvania State historic site.[25]

John Handamede

John Handamede (no dates available) replaced John Lynn as surgeon's mate in the Royal Irish Regiment of Foot on 25 June 1775. He may also be the man whose surname is given as Handesyde or Handyside.[26] He was most likely in Boston before joining the regiment. Handamede was not listed as embarking on HMS *Asia*, so he was most likely not in New York with the regiment.[27] He was present in Boston with the regiment in October 1775, according to the returns for that period, but he is not listed in the next set of returns after the Royal Irish went to England. Richard Babington is listed in his place as surgeon's mate in the August 1776 returns completed at Dover Castle. He may have been the brother of Ensign Talbot Blayney Handasyde of the 38th Foot.[28]

Handamede is quite possibly the same man identified as Handesyde in Howe's orderly book for 2 February 1776. He was appointed as a mate to General Hospital in Boston on that date and remained with the army in Boston until it embarked for Halifax in March 1776. At Halifax, on 24 May 1776, he was assigned to do duty with the 1st Battalion of Light Infantry.[29] This battalion was commanded by Major Thomas Musgrave of the 64th Foot.[30] It consisted of the light companies of the 4th, 5th, 10th 17th, 22nd, 23rd, 27th, 35th, and 38th Regiments of Foot.[31]

The 1st Battalion of Light Infantry landed at Long Island in August 1776 and fought at Long Island, Kip's Bay, Throg's Neck, White Plains, and Fort Washington. It was then involved in the advance through New Jersey and the forage wars during the winter of 1776–1777. When the 1st Battalion was reorganized on 23 March 1777 for the Philadelphia campaign, Handamede was not included.[32] It is possible he returned to General Hospital, but if so, he was removed before the publication of the 1779 North American army list.

A John Handasyde was commissioned as an ensign in the 93rd Foot on 8 February 1780. It is possible that this was the same man.[33]

Stanley Leathes

FIGURE 6.1 Stanley Leathes's coat of arms. *Courtesy of Ryan Gale*

Stanley Leathes (ca. 1714–21 January 1793) had a commission as chaplain dated from 1 March 1746, according to the army lists. His surname is also given as Leathea or Loath. The 1767 inspection return lists a date of 12 March 1746. Although Reverend Leathes did not serve with the regiment in America, he does warrant inclusion. He stood out as one of the worst army chaplains in a time when most were poor. According to Sylvia Frey, Leathes did not serve once with the regiment in more than twenty years of drawing pay as its chaplain. He was noted as absent on the regiment's 1767 inspection return and listed as an Englishmen of unknown age. He was also listed as having the government's license for leave until he retired on 7 October 1767.[34]

Leathes appears to have served in parishes in Lancaster, England, from 1745 and witnessed several marriages at Old Chapel and Cleator Church in Lancaster.[35] He was appointed the rector of Plumstead, Norfolk, in January 1751 and dually held that position and the chaplaincy of the Royal Irish for the better part of two decades.[36] He died on 21 January 1793 at the age of seventy-eight and was buried in Erpingham Church in Norfolk. A tablet on the wall of the south aisle marks his remains, and it includes a coat of arms. He was married to a woman named Alice and had a son, Stanley Jr., who died in 1802.[37]

John L. Lynn

John Lynn (ca. 21 March 1738–?) was most likely the son of John and Elizabeth Lynn of Philadelphia and was baptized on 3 April 1738.[38] His surname is also given as Linn or Lynne. He was a graduate of the Philadelphia College Medical School. Lynn was given the warrant as the Royal Irish's surgeon's mate when Edward Hand was commissioned as an ensign. He appears in the return for the general's company on 8 February 1775 at New York, but since that return covers the period beginning in June 1774, he almost certainly joined the regiment in Philadelphia. However, the returns that were completed in July 1774 show Hand as the mate, although he was absent through 24 June 1774.

Lynn was involved in the controversies surrounding Captain Benjamin Payne and Lieutenant Alexander Fowler. He testified with an affidavit in Payne's court-martial that Payne had offered him £100 to poison Major Isaac Hamilton while Hamilton was under Lynn's care in the winter of 1774–1775. It does not appear that the court found his testimony credible.[39]

When the five companies of the Royal Irish in New York prepared to leave for Boston, Lynn told Major Hamilton that he was not going with the regiment but was staying in New York. He resigned on 24 June 1775. Though not arrested, he was later referred to as a rebel and a deserter. He appears to have been a follower of Lieutenant Fowler and Ensign Nicholas Trist, which would have been enough to cause him discomfort among the other officers of the regiment.

Lynn did side with the rebels, as evidenced by his commission as surgeon of the 1st New York Regiment on 30 June 1775. The 1st New York, which was organized in and around New York City, was involved in the invasion of Canada, including the failed attempt to take Quebec City on 31 December 1775 under Brigadier General Richard Montgomery. He served in this capacity until Colonel John Nicholson reorganized the 1st New York on 15 April 1776.[40]

At that time, Lynn took a post with Continental Hospital in the District of Quebec, serving as the director from September 1776 through January 1777. Lynn moved to Boston by 1780, where he is listed by the town assessors as living in Ward 10 in the southwest portion of the city near Howe's Wharf.

Lynn served as the surgeon on board the thirty-six-gun frigate *Alliance*, a "continental Vessel of War," from about November 1781 until July 1782. During that time the *Alliance* carried the Marquis de Lafayette home to France from Boston, landing at L'Orient, France, on 17 January 1782. The frigate then sailed European waters looking to capture British vessels in order to force the exchange of British seamen for American seamen held by the British. However, the voyage was unsuccessful, and the *Alliance* returned to L'Orient on 26 February 1782. It remained in port until March 15, when it carried Benjamin Franklin's diplomatic observations home from France. The *Alliance* was chased by a British man of war off the Delaware coast on 10 May 1782 and finally arrived at New London, Connecticut, after severe weather and poor winds led to the deaths of eight sailors on 15 May 1782.[41]

Captain John Barry, who commanded *Alliance*, wrote to Robert Morris on 2 Augus 1782 that he had received a letter from Lynn on 22 July 1782, asking to be given leave to attend private business. Barry wrote to Morris about Lynn, "I can assure you his private business was not the Inducement which actuated me to give him leave. He is naturally of a Weak Constitution, add to that he was Very disagreeable to the Officers in the Ward Room, and as my desire is, to Keep a Quiet Ship, I thought it best on the whole to get Clear of him."[42] His voyage on the *Alliance* appears to have been his final military service.

In September 1787, Lynn was present in Philadelphia, where he was a "doctor of physic," according to his affidavit at that time on behalf of the Trist family.[43] Lynn was listed as living at 70 East Water Street in the 1790 census with a free white male under sixteen and four free white females. Two of the four women were over forty-five; the other two were between sixteen and twenty-five years old. He is listed as "Doctor John Linn," but no profession was listed on the census record. There were three vacant lots on one side of his home and a blacksmith shop on the other.[44]

Lynn was listed in the 1800 federal census for the east section of the Northern Liberties of Philadelphia. His household included two other free white males, one under ten and the other between sixteen and twenty-five years of age. Lynn appears to have passed away between 1800 and 1810, because he is not listed in the 1810 census. However, a "Widow Linn" is listed in both the 1810 and 1820 censuses in the East Northern Liberties of Philadelphia. The 1810 census shows three white males, three white females and one slave.[45]

John Mawby Sr.

John Mawby Sr. (ca. 1725–?)somehow remained out of the spotlight while the Royal Irish served in America. This was probably because he had been promoted from the ranks and did not fully associate with the rest of the regiment's officers outside the performance of his duties. He enlisted at the age of seventeen and served for fifteen years before being commissioned as a lieutenant on 13 February 1762. He does not appear to have ever been an ensign. He most likely served his enlisted time in the Royal Irish and was a sergeant before his elevation to lieutenant. The fact that his youngest son was named Sebright, after the colonel of the Royal Irish at the time of his appointment, lends support to the idea that Mawby served his enlisted time in one of Sebright's regiments, most likely the Royal Irish.

Mawby came to America as a lieutenant assigned to the major's company, and he remained in Philadelphia with that company while the majority of the regiment was sent west to Fort Pitt and Illinois. After the death of the adjutant in late 1768, Mawby was appointed adjutant on 24 April 1769; however, Buttricke wrote that it was he who was serving as the adjutant even though Mawby was receiving the pay. Of course, Mawby was in Philadelphia with only one of the nine companies, so it would have been difficult for him to perform his role. He most likely began functioning as the adjutant when the regiment gathered at Philadelphia in the fall of 1772.[46] He was a subscriber to Stephen Payne Adye's *A Treatise on Courts Martial*, published in 1769.

Mawby was promoted to captain lieutenant on 19 July 1771 and was moved to the general's company. He continued to serve as adjutant for the rest of the time the Royal Irish was on its American service and was always present with the general's company. He was given the army rank of captain on 25 May 1772, when all captain lieutenants throughout the army were made captains.

While Buttricke was in England, Mawby served as the acting quartermaster for the regiment while it was in Philadelphia. He appears to have had difficulties with Robert Newburgh, who was unhappy with the quarters Mawby assigned him and the amount of firewood and other supplies he was provided.[47] Mawby was called to testify at several general courts-martial for men from the Royal Irish while in Philadelphia and later in New York and Boston. He also testified against Newburgh at his court-martial.[48]

According to Benjamin Chapman, Mawby's wife and children remained with him in America until he sent them back to England after hostilities began. Mawby sat on a court-martial board in Boston on August 14, 1775, which determined the fate of Richard Ellingsworth of the 63rd Regiment, who was charged with attempted desertion.[49]

Mawby returned to England with the regiment, arriving in February 1776. He was at Dover Castle when the regiment was mustered in August 1776 and was listed as on recruiting service on 4 March and 18 August 1777. He was given a brief leave by the commander in chief in late 1777 or early 1778 and was listed as on leave on 6 March 1778. He rejoined the regiment that spring and resigned the adjutancy on 14 May 1778. Mawby was appointed as the major of brigade for General Jeffery Amherst's brigade at Coxheath Camp on 13 June 1778.[50]

Mawby appears to have been busy managing the affairs at Coxheath Camp in southern England throughout the summer of 1778. He was the Major of Brigade of the Day approximately twenty times between 20 June and 12 August 1778. His name appears after numerous orders given. On 27 July, Mawby issued an order for the arrest of the officers of the quarter guards of the left wing since, except for the Royal Irish, none of the other quarter guards were under arms (that is, carrying their firelocks and bayonets) when they passed by Lieutenant General William Keppel that morning during reveille. The NCOs of two posts were also to be confined.[51]

Mawby was promoted to captain on 25 December 1778 and was posted to an additional company after returning from another leave in March 1779. He returned to the battalion proper by 24 December 1780 and was present with his company on the Channel Islands in October 1781.

Mawby was promoted to the army rank of major on 19 February 1783. During the mutiny of the 104th Regiment of Foot at Guernsey (Channel Islands) in March 1783, Major Mawby led the Royal Irish in the successful conquest of that regiment. The 104th had taken a fort that Mawby invested with the Royal Irish, a company of artillery, and the local militia. The 104th was then forced to lay down its arms and surrender. The following report is by historian Jonathan Duncan:

> The authorities and inhabitants of Guernsey, duly appreciating the fidelity of the 18th regiment, and the artillery, resolved to give them a public testimony of their gratitude and approbation, and, at a convocation of the states, held on the 7th of September, 1783, the following resolutions were adopted:
>
> 1.—To return their thanks to the Hon. Paulus Æmilius Irving, lieutenant-governor of this island, for having so happily subdued, without the effusion of blood, about six hundred soldiers of the 104th regiment of infantry, who had mutinied against their officers, and driven them from the fort, by firing loaded muskets at them; and from whose violence the inhabitants had every thing to fear, if they had not been conquered into submission, and forced to lay down their arms by the present lieutenant-governor, who marched against them at midnight, on the 24th of March last, with the 18th regiment of infantry, called the Royal Irish, a company of artillery, and the town regiment of infantry and artillery of the island, whilst the other regiments of the island militia occupied different positions for the protection of the country.

The said lieutenant-governor remained all night with the troops in the country, up to the dawn of day, when the mutineers were compelled to submit, after having fired several volleys of musketry on the said troops and militia.

2.— To return similar thanks to John Mawby, esq., at that time commanding officer of the Royal Irish, and to the other officers of the said regiment, for the prudence with which they retained their soldiers in their duty, notwithstanding an example so calculated to corrupt them, and for having induced them to arm and march against the mutineers, with as much zeal, alacrity, and diligence, as good discipline.[52]

Mawby was still serving with the regiment at Gibraltar in 1790, when he was promoted to major of the Royal Irish on 28 July in place of Chapman, who was promoted to lieutenant colonel of the regiment.[53] Mawby missed the Siege of Toulon in late 1793, since he was on leave when the regiment was ordered there from Gibraltar. He sold his commission to Henry Tucker Montresor on 13 May 1794.[54] Mawby disappeared from the historical record upon his retirement after more than fifty years of service with the Royal Irish.

Mawby's family accompanied him to America. He had at least four children: John, George, Sebright, and Harriett. All the sons were originally listed as private soldiers in the ranks. It is unclear whether they were volunteers or their assignments were simply a way to generate additional funds for a family with a long history of service to the regiment. John joined the Royal Irish as an ensign in 1768, and George, who joined the Royal Irish as an ensign in late 1776. Sebright was only a child while in Philadelphia with the regiment, but he was commissioned as major of the regiment on 1 June 1799. Sebright died in late 1850, having obtained the rank of lieutenant general. Harriett married James Simpson, the Russian consul in Gibraltar, in January 1790.[55]

Robert Jocelyn Newburgh

Robert Jocelyn Newburgh (?–1826) appears to have been Irish by birth. He was ordained as a priest at the Cathedral of St. Brendan Clonfert in the Irish diocese of Clonfert and Klimacduagh on 8 October 1769. After ordination, Newburgh served in at least two parishes in the dioceses of Armagh and Kilmore. The rectors at both parishes provided positive references for him when he applied to John Sebright to become chaplain of the Royal Irish. He purchased the chaplaincy on 18 November 1772 from Daniel Thomas. One of the conditions that Sebright put on Thomas was that the purchaser would have to travel to America and serve with the regiment. Newburgh was willing to do so, and soon after his purchasing he arrived at Philadelphia from Ireland. According to Captain Payne's later testimony at a court of inquiry, Newburgh had earlier been rejected by the 47th Foot for a chaplaincy because he was a reported "buggerer."[56]

Newburgh seems to have brought some rumors with him about his sexual preferences and activities. Before leaving Ireland, he crossed paths with Thomas Batt, who was on leave in Ireland. Several other gentlemen passed information on to Batt about Newburgh's alleged inappropriate relationship with his servant boy. Specifically, there was speculation on his allowing his servant to sleep in the same room with him; according to the maids, the second bed was not always slept in.[57]

Newburgh was the cause of several legal proceedings and courts-martial. He was the cause of a court of inquiry to examine his conduct while he was with the regiment. It was ordered by Major Hamilton in April 1774, and Charles Edmonstone was the president of the court. Captains John Shee, Benjamin Chapman, and John Mawby Sr. served on the court as well as Lieutenant William Blackwood and Ensigns John Peter DeLancy and Francis John Kelly.[58]

Newburgh was also the cause of two general courts-martial. One involved a soldier, John Green, who had informed him that Captain Payne had called him a "buggerer" in front of the regimental tailors, and in the other Newburgh was charged because of his conduct while serving with the Royal Irish. He had actually requested the court-martial, in a letter to Fredrick Haldimand on 25 June 1774, in order to settle his disputes with the Royal Irish. It appears that he had been counseled by General Haldimand to try to work things out with the regiment's officers at an earlier date when he had requested a court-martial, but he had been unable to do so. This led Newburgh to make a second request for a general court-martial in the following letter:

> Philadelphia Barracks, June 25, 1774
>
> May it please your Excellency,
>
> The Officers of the Royall Irish Regiment having made some Proposals of Accommodations to me, which I declared my readiness to accede to in consequence of their assurances to me, that is

was your Excellency's wish that matters nigh be amicable settled between the Regimt and me. I agreed with them to conclude the Affair on the 24 of this Month, they have put off the matter until the 27th Inst. By which Delay I may be disappointed of the Opportunity so ardently solicited by [*not* inserted in small type] me, I mean, A Court Martial, which appears to myself and all my Friends the only proper means to set me Character in A Fair Light. I humbly beg your Excellency will pardon my giving you the trouble of so frequently addressing you, & That is absolutely necessary to this critical time to give your Excellency my reasons for repeating my Request that a General Court Martial may be ordered to take my Situation under their Consideration. I have the Honor to remain with the utmost Respect and Esteem your Excellency's most humble and most obedt Servt.

Robt. Newburgh

Chaplain, Royall Irish Regmt.[59]

Newburgh had a difficult time obtaining his desired court-martial. He finally obtained it by getting a soldier of the regiment to accuse him of an "unnatural act." He explained to Gage, "I did desire and consent to Robert Jeff, A soldier in our Regiment to give in the charge against me and as I find my Enemy's studious to convert that circumstance to my disadvantage."[60]

Newburgh's court-martial was held at New York 8–12 August 1774. He was found guilty of drinking and fraternizing with soldiers of the Royal Irish, the 47th Foot, and the Royal Artillery while stationed in Philadelphia. He was also accused of "unnatural acts" with a soldier, but that charge was dropped, since all the testimony was hearsay. The charges, as listed in the court-martial transcript, were as follows:

> Having been guilty of Vicious and immoral behaviour by committing willful perjury, Prevarication and falsehood, together with other Scandalous and Indecent Acts, unbecoming a Gentleman and Derogating from the Sacred Character which he is Invested, as also in having treated Major Hamilton his Commanding Officer in a disrespectful manner.[61]

Captain Richard England of the 47th Foot and Lieutenant Alexander Fowler and Ensign Nicholas Trist of the Royal Irish spoke in his defense at his trial. Lieutenant Colonel William Nesbit of the 47th Foot presided over the trial. According to Fowler's letter to Lieutenant Robert Collins of the Royal Artillery, Batt, who was no longer serving in the regiment at the time, spoke of the trial verdict as "that he had now made such a hole in the Parson's coat, as all the taylors in the regiment would not be able to mend."[62]

In September 1774, Newburgh appears to have been given permission to stay with a Mrs. Marsh at Perth Amboy after he had accompanied the Royal Irish at least that far on its march from Philadelphia. The exact nature of the permission is unclear. Later that fall, Newburgh brought a civil suit against Batt for his role in pressing charges against him at the court-martial in which Newburgh was found innocent.[63]

Newburgh was suspended for six months by the court-martial, but he wrote to Gage and requested a pardon, stating, "I was found innocent of the most difficult charges. Could you potentially shorten my suspension?" Gage did reduce his sentence, ending it effective 20 November 1774. He also wrote about Newburgh, "As many Circumstances have happened that will prevent his being much use to the Regiment, I shall have no Objection to his going Home, provided he finds a proper Deputy."[64]

After the court-martial, Major Isaac Hamilton tried to get Newburgh sent to Illinois to preach the Gospel at that remote post, but Newburgh never did journey west. He remained with the regiment in New York and was listed as present there in February 1775. He continued to make complaints to both Hamilton and Gage throughout his time with the regiment, particularly pressing charges against Captain Payne. Gage, now clearly sick of the drama surrounding Newburgh, wrote the following to Hamilton:

> I am to desire you to make Enquiry into the Affair and to restore Peace between the Contending Parties and prevent my being troubled with future Complaints of this Nature which are always disagreeable. If Captain Payne or the other Officers have a bad Opinion of Mr. Newburgh, it is an easy Matter to avoid him and not to enter into Altercation with him.[65]

According to Fowler, Newburgh sailed for London from New York on 13 May 1775, ending his direct service with the Royal Irish Regiment.[66]

Newburgh is listed as being on commander in chief's leave in October 1775. He was transferred to the 15th Regiment of Foot on 23 April 1776. It may have taken some time to effect that exchange, as Thomas Daliston was still listed as the chaplain of the regiment on its August 1776 muster return on Staten Island. Newburgh was present with the 15th Foot when it was mustered on 30 December 1776 in New York City.[67] He remained with the 15th Foot in America at least through the Philadelphia campaign, because he was listed in Philadelphia as part of the Earl of Cavan's company of the 15th Foot on 27 March 1778.

Most likely he remained in active service with the 15th until he exchanged to half pay, but the returns of the 15th Foot after March 1778 have been lost. He transferred from the 15th Foot to half pay, exchanging with William Chester, the chaplain for the hospital at Belle Isle during the Seven Years' War, on 9 July 1779. He does not appear to have seen any active service after 1779 but remained on the half-pay list through 1826.[68]

William Smith

William Smith (7 September 1727–14 May 1803) was born near Aberdeen in 1727 and baptized in the old Aberdeenshire Kirk on 19 October of that year. He was the son of Thomas Smith of Aberdeen and Elizabeth Duncan Smith of Camperdown, Scotland. Smith was allowed to enroll at the University of Aberdeen with support from the Society for the Education of Parochial Schoolmasters, but he does not appear to have been granted a degree. He then briefly worked in London for religious organizations before leaving for America in 1751.

Smith came to Long Island to serve as the tutor for the sons of a Colonel Martin. In 1753, Smith published a pamphlet, *A General Idea of the College of Mirania*, addressed to the New York Assembly, promoting the establishment of a college in the colony. This pamphlet attracted the attention of Benjamin Franklin, who then invited Smith to Pennsylvania as rector of the Academy of Pennsylvania. Before taking up his position in Philadelphia, Smith returned to London to be ordained a priest in the Anglican Church.

When the trustees of the academy received their royal charter for the College of Philadelphia (today the University of Pennsylvania) in 1755, Smith was appointed as the first provost. He remained in that role until the college's charter was revoked in 1779.[69]

Smith was appointed as acting chaplain to the regiments in America at the outbreak of the French and Indian War. It is unclear who appointed him, but a sermon he gave to the troops under Brigadier General Stanwix on 5 April 1757 survives. The sermon was given to the soldiers "previous to their march, after Braddock's defeat, to suppress the ravages of the French and Indians on our frontier settlements."[70]

Smith engendered the wrath of the political elite of Pennsylvania and caused a strain in his relationship with Benjamin Franklin by being a friend of the Penn family, whose money was essential for the success of the College of Philadelphia. He also wrote a tract denouncing the Quakers' pacifism and therefore the unwillingness of the colonial assembly to provide funding for the defense of the frontier. Smith was the author of an anonymous account of Henry Bouquet's expedition against the Ohio Valley Indians in 1765, which included maps by Thomas Hutchins. Smith may have accompanied Bouquet. Because of the assembly's reaction to his writings, Smith was arrested in 1758 along with William Moore, his future father-in-law, for publishing a seditious libel. He remained in prison for four months and was eventually exonerated by the King's Privy Council in London (the king's closest advisory body, which also served an appellate judicial function).[71]

Smith was appointed rector of Trinity Church in Oxford township, Philadelphia County, in 1766 and remained in that role until 1777. He was serving as the temporary rector of Christ Church in Philadelphia when the Royal Irish arrived in Philadelphia in addition to his duties at the College of Philadelphia. In the spring of 1768 he was appointed as the acting chaplain to the regiment, according to his biography. However, the regimental agent's ledgers show a deputy chaplain being paid subsistence as early as 11 July 1767; this may have been Smith. He was the deputy chaplain of the Royal Irish who was paid by Daniel Thomas in 1768 to officiate in his place.[72] The first recorded sermon Smith preached to the regiment was on 10 April 1768, on the Christian soldier's duty. Four of the sermons he gave to the Royal Irish Regiment are extant in his book *The Works of William Smith*, published in 1800, under the subjects of a Christian soldier's duty and the Christian soldier's spiritual duty.[73]

The Royal Irish's regimental band appears to have performed at the College of Philadelphia on several occasions, including the graduation ceremonies of 1767 and 1773. Most likely these performances were at least partly a result of Smith's relationship with the regiment. It is unclear how long Smith served in the capacity of deputy chaplain to the Royal Irish Regiment, but in 1774 he wrote a letter of recommendation for Edward Hand, who was at that time trying to establish himself as a physician in Lancaster. Smith presented himself in the letter as "chaplain to the 18th

Regiment of Foot," and not as the rector of either Trinity Church or the College of Philadelphia.[74]

Smith accompanied John Jay, from King's College in New York, on a fund-raising trip to Europe for their colleges in 1772. When forced out of Pennsylvania during the American Revolution, Smith founded Washington College in Maryland. He returned to Pennsylvania after the Revolutionary War and resumed his post under a conservative board of trustees in 1789. However, the merger of the college with the University of the State of Pennsylvania in 1791 denied Smith any role in the new university. He retired to land speculation and supported the development of canals. His family founded Huntingdon, Pennsylvania.

Smith was also involved in the efforts to establish the first Anglican bishop in America. He began that work as early as 1760 and was elected to that post himself in the 1780s by the Maryland convention. However, he was not confirmed to that role, and the American priests elected Samuel Seabury as the first American bishop after the Revolutionary War.

Smith was married to Rebecca Moore (1733–1793), the daughter of William Moore, his partner in publishing the anti-Quaker pamphlets. They had eight children: William Moore (1759–1821); Thomas Duncan (1760–1821); Williamina Elizabeth (1762–1790), who married Charles Goldsborough of Horn's Point, Maryland; Charles (1765–1836), who married Mary Yeates; Phineas (1767–1770); Richard (1769–1823); Rebecca (1772–1837), who married Samuel Blodget Jr.; and Elizabeth (1776–1778).[75]

Smith died at his home above the falls of the Schuylkill River near Philadelphia in 1803.

Daniel Thomas

Daniel Thomas (no dates available) was appointed to the Royal Irish as chaplain on 8 October 1767. He replaced Stanley Leathes, who had been the regiment's absentee chaplain for more than thirty years. However, Thomas does not appear to have been any more interested in serving with the regiment than Leathes was. Thomas was listed as absent by government license in the April 1768 muster. He was a subscriber to Stephen Payne Adye's *A Treatise on Courts Martial*, published in 1769, in which he was listed as "Revd. Mr. —Thomas, Chaplain of the 18th or Royal Irish Regt. of Foot."

It is possible that Thomas joined the regiment sometime after April 1768 and simply left before the regiment completed the next set of returns for the general's company in October 1772. However, he is listed as absent on all the returns until his retirement on 17 November 1772. Thomas paid eight shillings on 19 September 1771 for his last-recorded three-month leave of absence. If he did serve with the regiment, he never left Pennsylvania, since the troops in Illinois recorded more than four years of not hearing a sermon. The regimental agent's ledgers show Captain Lieutenant Matthew Lane as having paid for a deputy chaplain from 8 October 1767 to 4 June 1768 in three separate payments of £11 11s., £9 3s., and £18 6d. Additional expenses for deputies are most likely the cause of regular bills from Major Isaac Hamilton to Thomas.[76]

When Thomas articulated a desire to sell his commission in 1772, General Sebright's condition for the sale was that the new chaplain be willing to serve directly with the regiment in America. Unfortunately, the regimental agents did not record the sale price of the commission.[77]

Thomas Thomasson

Thomas Thomasson (1744–1793) was the Royal Irish's surgeon during its entire career in North America. He was commissioned as surgeon on 18 February 1767, and unlike most of the officers who joined the regiment at the time, he was English. He was approximately twenty-three years old. He may have been appointed to the regiment because of the influence of John Eardley Wilmot, a friend of General John Sebright. When the regiment was inspected on 11 April 1767, seven officers and thirteen men were sick in quarters, and a drummer was sick in the hospital. Surgeon Thomasson would soon have to face much more significant levels of sickness in Illinois.[78]

Thomasson was severely tried by the miserable conditions in the Illinois Country, and although several sources speak to his dedication, the death rate among the Royal Irish was staggering. He is not mentioned in many of the surviving records but is mentioned in the transcript of a court of inquiry because he treated a black slave who had stabbed himself twice and was injured again when recaptured and taken to Fort Chartres in June 1769.[79]

To add insult to injury, Thomasson's pay was stopped for the expense of another surgeon, who was paid to look after the company that was left in Philadelphia. This was in addition to the fact that he was unable to even look after all of the soldiers in Illinois because they were spread out. A civilian, Dr. John Conolly, and Lieutenant Smith appear to have helped him with caring for the sick in Illinois.

Possibly because of this strain on his surgeon's pay, Thomasson was allowed to purchase an ensign's commission on 14 June 1771 for £400, noted by the regimental agent on 8 August 1771. In 1772, he was assigned to the general's company, where he most likely did little outside of his medical duties.

In the summer of 1773, Thomasson was requested by the chiefs of the Illinois Indians to assist them in stemming a measles outbreak among the tribe. The effect he had is unclear, but Captain Hugh Lord promised to secure him additional pay while he attended to the Indians.[80]

When the regiment went back east, Thomasson stayed at Kaskaskia as the surgeon. He was also transferred to the lieutenant colonel's company, which remained in Illinois. This made him not only the surgeon but also the only ensign in Illinois. He was promoted to lieutenant on 26 July 1775 after William Blackwood's promotion to captain. He probably did not become aware of his promotion for some time because of his posting in Illinois. He returned to the Royal Irish at Dover in 1777 after being allowed leave and was present on a general court-martial board there in November 1777 that tried William Green and Henry Knight for desertion.[81]

An analysis of the army lists indicates that some other regular officers held both the position of surgeon and a line officer's commission, but this was uncommon. Similarly, a number of provincial officers held dual commissions as subalterns and surgeons or mates. Maybe someone finally became aware of Thomasson's double commission, because he resigned as surgeon on 8 October 1779.[82]

Thomasson remained another year as a lieutenant in the Royal Irish and was then promoted to senior captain of the newly raised 96th Foot on 8 April 1780. The 96th Foot, or the British Musketeers, were raised in England in July 1779, although the officers were not officially announced until 1780, which may explain why Thomasson resigned as a surgeon before selling his commission as a lieutenant. The 96th was sent to Ireland in 1779 and to the Channel Islands in 1780. Thomasson was listed present with his company of the 96th Foot at Castle Barreck in England on 18 November 1780. At that time, his lieutenant was Stephen Bloomfield, and his ensign was Stuart Adams. Thomasson was listed "with the convalescents in England" on the 19 September 1781 return. That month, his company was camped at Fort George in the West Indies, under the command of Lieutenant Claus Pell.[83]

While in England, Thomasson met Catherine Grierson and eloped with her to Scotland. Since he had not obtained permission from her parents, when they returned from their Scottish wedding, the honeymoon was interrupted by Thomasson's incarceration. His case was brought to trial in November 1781. The judge continued the case for a few days but released Thomasson without any additional prison time. However, the judge did order the couple to remarry because he questioned the legitimacy of the Scottish nuptials, so the two were married again on 6 November 1781 at St. Bride's Chapel, London. Thomasson had hoped to purchase a commission as major, but his legal problems over his elopement appear to have quashed his chances, and his military career was effectively over.[84]

The scant records of the 96th Foot show Thomasson selling his commission to Lieutenant Robert Webb Stone on 2 November 1782. The 96th Foot was disbanded on 31 May 1783.[85]

After retiring from the army, Thomasson returned to his original vocation of physician. He was listed as a "doctor of physic of the city of York" in 1790 when he drafted his will. He appears to have done well for himself, because his will, made out in 1790, lists household furniture, linen, liquors, a chaise and horses, and several residences. Most of his estate was to go to Catherine. They had one child, also named Catherine. Thomasson left his daughter a substantial annuity and a trust fund to be managed by her mother until the girl's twenty-first birthday or until she married, whichever came first. She married Thomas Whitmore in 1804, and they had four children. Thomasson also left small remembrances for his brothers and his sisters-in-law. His will was proved in May 1793.[86]

Samuel Turner

Samuel Turner (ca. 1742–29 September 1768) joined the Royal Irish as an ensign on 17 May 1756, when the army expanded because war with the French was escalating. He was listed as English. Turner was promoted to lieutenant in the regiment on 4 March 1760 and became the adjutant on 17 March 1761, while still retaining his lieutenancy. He was present with the regiment in Dublin in April 1767 when it was inspected, and he embarked with the regiment for America from Cork, Ireland, on 20 May 1767.

When the Royal Irish arrived at Philadelphia, Turner was the de facto commander of Hugh Antrobus's company. He remained in Philadelphia with the majority of the regiment through the spring of 1768. When the regiment was mustered for pay on 26 April 1768, Turner was still with the same company; however, it was now Johnson's company. He was transferred from that company on 15 July 1768, since it was remaining at Fort Pitt. Turner was to head to Illinois with the grenadier company, and Lieutenant Colonel Wilkins wanted him to accompany the main body of the regiment as adjutant. Turner arrived at Fort Chartres with the five companies of the Royal Irish in September 1768.

The fevers that swiftly struck the regiment turned quickly on Turner. He became the first officer of the Royal Irish to die at Fort Chartres, on 29 September 1768. With him died nearly a decade of information on the day-to-day running of the regiment, which Wilkins complained about to Gage when Gage reprimanded Wilkins for keeping improper records.[87] Although John Mawby Sr. was given the adjutancy, since Mawby was in Philadelphia, George Buttricke actually performed the adjutant's duties in Illinois.

7 Absentee Officers

Although the absentee rate among officers of the Royal Irish was the lowest of any regiment found for the period, there were still a number of officers for whom the label *absentee* is appropriate. Excluded from this group are the colonels (who are included with field officers) and the chaplains (who are included with the staff officers), since their stations in the army made absence normal in their roles.

Some of these men were young officers who appear to have been eager to purchase a commission to begin accruing seniority and were unwilling to wait to purchase directly into the regiment of their choice. Several of them purchased into the Royal Irish but then moved into mounted regiments from half pay and were unwilling or unable to travel to America to serve with the regiment. Most of these men were subalterns; only two were captains. Both of the captains were appointed from half pay, and Benjamin Johnson acted as a recruiter for the Royal Irish in England even though he did not journey to America.

Horace Churchill

Horace Churchill (ca. 1758–?) was appointed as an ensign the Royal Irish on 23 June 1773. He was listed (sometimes as Churchall) as not yet joined in both the January and July 1774 returns. He was posted to Johnson's company, which was stationed in Philadelphia at the time of his appointment. He appears to have never joined the regiment in America.

Churchill purchased a commission as cornet in the 6th (Inniskilling) Regiment of Dragoons on 11 May 1774. His commission in the Royal Irish remained vacant from then until 9 June, when it was purchased by Charles Hoar.[1]

At the time, the 6th Regiment of Dragoons was stationed at Canterbury, England, and Churchill was assigned to the colonel's troop and was listed as being on colonel's leave on 2 August 1774. Churchill was present with the 6th Regiment when it was reviewed at Blackheath on 19 May 1775. He is listed as seventeen years old, with two years of experience, on the general return of the 6th Dragoons. His nativity was listed as English. By February 1776, Churchill was assigned to Major John Robins's troop and was listed as sick at Northampton. The 8 November 1776 return shows Churchill having resigned on 1 March 1776, but he was not replaced as a cornet until 1 November by James Roper Head.[2] The difference in dates is difficult to explain. It would seem that a cornet's commission in the dragoons would not remain vacant that long.

Churchill actually left the 6th Dragoons on 17 February 1776, when he transferred to the 15th Light Dragoons as a cornet. He was promoted to lieutenant on 26 December 1778 in the 15th Light Dragoons and transferred to the newly raised 21st Light Dragoons in April 1779 when his entire troop was transferred to be part of the new regiment. When the 89th Foot was raised in 1779, he was appointed to a company on 4 October 1779. Churchill exchanged to the 40th Foot as a captain on 1 August 1780 and to the 1st Foot Guards as a lieutenant and captain on 13 November 1782. Churchill remained with 1st Foot Guards until he exchanged onto half pay on 24 September 1788 as a lieutenant and captain in the then defunct 1st Troop of Horse Grenadier Guards.

The ledgers of the Royal Irish do not have any entries for Churchill.[3]

Caesar Colclough

Caesar Colclough (?–1802) obtained his commission as an ensign in the Royal Irish on 1 October 1766 upon the promotion of Marcus Paterson to lieutenant. He is listed as the junior ensign in the regiment in the 1767 army list. He did not embark for America but instead sold his commission to William Conolly in April 1767. He is listed in the ledgers for Cox & Meir, who became the regiment agent for the Royal Irish in July 1767. Demonstrating the occasional confusion caused by great distances, the regimental agent shows Colclough being paid for subsistence from 11 July through 24 December, but it shows Conolly being paid then as well. It is not clear how the agent cleaned up the overpayment.[4]

This is possibly the same Caesar Colclough who married Anne Colclough of Tintern, a cousin, in 1767. If so, he was from New Ross,

Wexford County, and Athy, Kildare County. Colclough had one son from his first marriage who did not survive infancy and three sons and three daughters from his second marriage, to Martha Waring of Kilkenny in 1775. If this is the same man, it gives a possible reason for his not embarking with the regiment for America: he was hoping to marry shortly. He had no further military career. It is unclear why he is referred to as "Mad Caesar" in family histories.[5]

John Cope

John (or Henry) Cope (no dates available) was appointed to a captaincy in the Royal Irish Regiment on 25 December 1770 with the retirement of Captain John Evans from half pay. However the muster rolls show him taking Captain Hugh Lord's battalion company when Lord was moved to the newly formed light infantry company in the spring of 1771.[6] He served in America as a lieutenant in the 48th Foot, which he joined as an ensign on 15 March 1747. He served for twelve years as an ensign with the regiment and obtained a lieutenancy on 27 June 1755. This was only about three weeks before the 48th Foot was involved in Braddock's Defeat in western Pennsylvania, when General Edward Braddock's column was ambushed by a combined Franco-Indian force that decimated the British troops. It is unclear whether Cope was present at that event.[7]

Cope served with the 48th through the Siege at Louisburg in 1757–1758. The 48th was at the Plains of Abraham when General James Wolfe captured Quebec in 1759 and was then involved in the capture of Martinique and Havana in 1762, when Spanish possessions in the Caribbean became the focus of the British strategy. Cope was promoted to captain lieutenant in the 76th Foot on 25 March 1762, and then to captain on 11 May 1762. Since he was promoted by General Robert Monckton's orders, he was almost surely present at the fall of Martinique. He probably participated in the capture of Havana as well. He was reduced to half pay with the 76th Foot at the end of the Seven Years' War and remained there until obtaining his commission in the Royal Irish.[8]

Cope's company was posted at Fort Chartres in the Illinois Country, but he most likely never served with the regiment there. He paid eleven shillings for a three-month leave of absence on 19 September 1771. The final entry in the agent's ledgers for Cope shows him being paid for subsistence through 7 August 1771 and being paid £5 for his portion of the noneffective account on 17 January 1773.[9] According to the *London*

Gazette, Cope exchanged places with Benjamin Charnock Payne on 8 August 1771, but there is no record of Cope actually serving the 28th Foot. He retired from the 28th Foot on 28 November 1771. He is listed on the 1771 army list as Henry.[10]

Thomas Cuming

Thomas Cuming (ca. 1753–?) was appointed to an ensigncy in the Royal Irish on 23 July 1771. He was listed (sometimes as Cumming or Cummings) as being twenty-two years old in May 1775, so he would have been eighteen years old when he obtained his commission in the Royal Irish. He is listed in the returns of the 1st Dragoon Guards as English.[11] He was originally assigned to the general's company of the Royal Irish but was assigned to Captain Benjamiin Chapman's company in April 1772 because the Royal Irish did not yet know he had transferred. He is listed as John in the Royal Irish's muster rolls.[12]

Cuming transferred to the 1st Dragoon Guards as a cornet on 12 February 1772, and on 30 September 1772, he was on duty in Houston, Scotland, as the cornet of Captain Henry Whitehead's troop. He was present with the regiment at Ashby-de-la-Zouche in Leicestershire on 13 February 1774 and was at Salisbury on 8 April 1774. In the summer of 1774, he was listed as on recruiting service.

Cuming was promoted to lieutenant in the 1st Dragoon Guards on 8 March 1775 and was transferred to Captain Henry Waller's troop on 13 March. He was at Guilford on 7 April 1775 with his troop and was present with the regiment at Blackheath when it was inspected on 5 May 1775. He was present in Norwich on 3 April 1776 and was at York with the regiment on 15 July 1776. Cuming was with the regiment at Dalkieth in southern England on 30 October 1777 and 19 March 1778. He was at Salisbury Camp for the 27 July 1778 muster and is listed as being promoted to his own troop.

Cuming was promoted to captain in the 1st Dragoons Guards on 5 June 1778 in place of Henry Whitehead, his old troop commander. Jonathan Cope replaced him as lieutenant in the 1st Dragoon Guards. Cuming was absent with leave from his troop when it was mustered at Yeovil on 23 March 1779 and again at Bristol in July. Cuming was present with his troop at Warminster on 23 October 1780 and at Exeter on 2 April 1781. He was listed as retired on the 22 August 1781 return, also taken at Exeter. His troop saw no combat during his tenure, but Cuming did have a sergeant and a corporal from his troop drafted into the newly raised 19th Light Dragoons on 26 April 1780.[13]

Cuming sold out to Lieutenant The Honourable Charles Grey, who took his troop. The *London Gazette* reported Cuming's retirement as 16 May 1781.[14] This was possibly the same Thomas Cuming who was appointed on 13 May 1794 to the senior captaincy in the Ancient British Fencibles, raised by Watkin Williams-Wynn.[15] He was still with the regiment in 1797. If he did serve with the fencibles, he may have participated in putting down the 1798 Irish uprising.[16]

William Greaves

William Greaves (no dates available) was listed as an ensign in the 70th Foot on 24 May 1760. His surname is sometimes given as Graves. The 70th was raised in Glasgow in 1756 as the 2nd Battalion of the 31st Foot and designated the 70th Foot in 1758. The regiment was stationed in England while Greaves was assigned to it. He was in Guadeloupe in the West Indies when promoted to lieutenant on 4 May 1762 in the 65th Foot. He was reduced to half pay on 2 July 1763.[17]

Greaves was appointed to the Royal Irish from half pay on 25 December 1770 and was assigned to the grenadier company, which was stationed at Cahokia, Illinois. He never served in America with the regiment. He was listed as absent in returns until the October 1772 return, when he was listed as absent with leave. His account with the regimental agent shows that he paid six shillings for three- and six-month leaves of absence several times, including 19 September 1771 and 11 March 1772.[18]

Greaves went back onto the half-pay list of the 113th Foot by trading places with John Hamilton on 26 November 1772.[19] He was still listed on half pay in 1778 when he was appointed as the second senior captain of a company in the 79th Foot upon its being raised on 13 June. He was replaced, according to *London Gazette* of 16 March 1779, by Edward Jenkins of the 112th Foot.

A William Graves who served as a lieutenant in the French and Indian War was granted two thousand acres in Nova Scotia on 10 September 1781. It is most likely the same man who served in the Royal Irish.[20]

Claudius Hamilton

Claudius Hamilton (no dates available) entered the Royal Irish on 13 February 1765 as an ensign. He purchased his ensigncy from James Raymond and is listed in the 1767 army list as the second senior ensign, after Thomas Batt. He appears to have been the first officer to leave the Royal Irish when it was ordered to deploy to America. Hamilton resigned on 4 March 1767, but unlike Caesar Colclough and James Taylor Trevor, he is not listed in the regimental agent's ledgers, since he was the first to give notice that he was leaving the regiment. His commission went to William Blackwood.[21]

John Hamilton

John Hamilton (no dates available) only briefly appears in the Royal Irish. Almost certainly Scottish, he was originally commissioned as an ensign in the 70th Regiment of Foot on 28 August 1761. He joined the 113th Regiment of Foot on 26 October 1761, the same month it was embodied in Scotland. He was quickly promoted to lieutenant in the 113th Foot, perhaps because he was involved in raising men for rank, which generally entailed gathering men willing to enlist in a regiment being raised. A would-be officer would promise the regimental commander the men he had enrolled in return for a commission in the new regiment. Usually, the aspiring officer would need to raise about twenty-five men to earn a lieutenancy and fifty or more to earn a captaincy.

Hamilton was transferred to the Royal Irish from the half-pay list of the 113th Foot. His lieutenancy in the Royal Irish dated from 26 November 1772. He exchanged commissions with William Greaves, who returned to half pay. Hamilton returned to half pay by exchanging commissions with Edward Crosby on 8 September 1774.

Hamilton did not sign either of the petitions from the officers of the Royal Irish to Sebright in 1773, so he was most likely not present with the regiment in America. His actual company assignment appears to have been with either the lieutenant colonel's company or the light infantry company. He is not even listed in the regimental agent's ledgers for his period of service. It is unknown whether he was related to either of the other Hamiltons in the regiment.[22]

Benjamin Johnson

Benjamin Johnson (no dates available) is almost a ghost within the records of the Royal Irish in America. He was initially appointed as a lieutenant in the 7th (Royal Fusiliers) Foot on 30 August 1756, while that regiment was at Gibraltar. He raised an independent company in Britain on 28 October 1760, and when it was amalgamated into the 97th Foot in January and February 1761, he became its senior captain. The 97th, also known as the Foresters, remained in Britain until 1763, when the regiment was disbanded and the officers placed on half pay on 8 October of that year.

Johnson's captaincy in the Royal Irish began on 8 October 1767 when he was recalled from the half-pay list. He paid £8 2s. for his commission in the Royal Irish and paid another fee for a three-month leave of absence in February 1768. Although he is described as "not yet joined" through the October 1772 returns, he is listed as on king's leave after that until the 8 February 1775 return, where he not listed as absent but did not sign the return. He was, however, most likely still absent. The next return, completed in Boston in October 1775, shows him as retired.[23] Johnson was a subscriber to Stephen Payne Adye's *A Treatise on Courts Martial*, published in 1769.

Johnson's company was one of the two that garrisoned at Fort Pitt from 1768 until late 1772, when it was recalled to Philadelphia. However, it appears that Robert Hamilton, his lieutenant, commanded the company while at Fort Pitt. Nor was Johnson present at Philadelphia to sign the petition to Sebright in 1773. His company was stationed in New York in 1774 and early 1775, and court-martial testimony states that he was not present in New York; Lieutenant Fowler was running the company there. One might think that Johnson simply never came to America, except that he is listed as present in Boston by some sources. He resigned on 20 April 1775 and was reported killed by a rebel marksman near Boston on 9 August 1775, but the report was probably mistaken.[24]

The one activity that Johnson did appear to participate in was a short venture as a recruiting officer in England for the regiment. The changes in the American Establishment in 1770 and the establishment of a light company for the regiment in the spring of 1771 appear to have spurred Johnson to action. He employed a Sergeant Lewis from 24 December 1770 until 30 April 1771 as a recruiting agent. He is listed as "Chelsea Serjeant," so it is probable he was a retired sergeant at the Soldiers' Home, the Chelsea Hospital for disabled soldiers. Sergeant Lewis appears to have needed an assistant to drum up recruits, so Johnson engaged Styles from 23 January through 30 April 1771. Johnson's recruiting efforts netted the regiment four recruits at a cost of just over £44.[25]

Johnson obtained one recruit by the purchase of his indenture. It is not clear whether that soldier, John Lindsey, was one of the new recruits noted above. However, he was "enlisted" by Johnson at about the same time. Lindsey is noted as joining Major Isaac Hamilton's company at Philadelphia on 28 March 1771.[26] Before Lindsey "enlisted," he was a servant to Doctor Plunket of Northumberland, who sold him to Captain Johnson as a soldier. Lindsey deserted on 22 January 1773, was captured on 3 June

1773 and was detained in the Bucks County Jail. Lindsey was described in the newspaper as follows:

> [He] talks English well, and says he was born in Pennsylvania, is about 20 years of age, fair faced, wears his own hair, of a light brown, is about 5 feet 7 inches high; has on a green jacket, made in the form or shape of a coat, with large metal buttons, a coursse [sic] homespun shirt and trowsers. The owner of said servant is hereby requested to come, within a month after date, prove his property, pay charges, and take him away; otherwise he will be sold for the same.[27]

The fact that Lindsey claimed to be born in Pennsylvania is interesting, since he was almost certainly "enlisted" in England, if his story was true, because Captain Johnson never came to America. Lindsey possibly urged Plunket to sell him so he could return to America and desert at the first opportunity or might have simply wished to deny he was actually a deserter. It is also possible that Lindsey simply made up his story to obtain sympathy from his captors.

Approximately a dozen other men were enlisted during the same six-month period that Lindsey entered the regiment. It cannot be determined whether any of the other men were results of Johnson's peculiar recruiting efforts, but at least three others were enlisted by Johnson or his subordinates.[28] Johnson is also recorded as enlisting Henry Darke in 1774. So it appears Johnson was at least somewhat active as a recruiting officer for the regiment while he remained in England.[29]

John Wilmot Prideaux

FIGURE 6.1 John Wilmot Prideaux's coat of arms. *Courtesy of Ryan Gale*

Sir John Wilmot Prideaux (13 February 1747–4 March 1826) was the first son of Brigadier General John Prideaux of Netherton, Devonshire (who was the second son of Sir John Prideaux, 6th Baronet), and Elizabeth Rolt.[30] He was baptized at St. George Hanover Square, London, on 6 March 1747. The elder Prideaux was killed at Fort Niagara on 19 July 1759 while in command of the 55th Regiment of Foot.

John Wilmot Prideaux succeeded to the baronetcy in August 1766 upon the death of his grandfather, since both his father and his uncle had died in the king's service.[31] He obtained his ensigncy in the Royal Irish on 23 December 1767, when Henry Shaw died, and he was assigned to Captain Charles Edmonstone's company at Fort Pitt. He is listed in the returns as "Willmot Prideaux, not yet joined" when the muster roll was completed in May 1769. He was listed as present with the regiment on the December 1769 muster, but it was actually completed in 1772, after he had already resigned in place of his brother Edward. It is probable that John never served with the regiment. He resigned his commission on 11 January 1770, and it went to his younger brother, Edmund, who was also assigned to Edmonstone's company.[32]

Prideaux's father had removed a collection of books that had been left at the parsonage at Farway near Honiton, Devon, by Wilmot Prideau, John Wilmot's grandfather. The pastor wrote in 1779 that he had spoken to John Wilmot Prideaux about having them returned to the church but that they had not yet been returned.[33]

Prideaux married Harriet Webb on 4 June 1778, but she died childless. He married his second wife, Phebe Ann Priddle, on 28 January 1789, and they had two children: John Wilmot Jr. (1791–1833) and Edmund Sanderson (1793–1875). Prideaux married for a third time, to Sarah Smith Ellis, a widow, on 19 May 1804. Sarah's obituary in November 1851 read, "At Sidbury, aged 79, Sarah, widow of Sir John Wilmot Prideaux, Bart." Sarah's daughter, Constantia (born 1802), is suspected to have been Prideaux's daughter from before the marriage.[34]

The baronetcy became extinct with his son Edmund's death. Prideaux was interred in St. Michael's Farway, Devonshire, where there is a memorial tablet to him in the church.[35]

Prideaux's brother Edward served in the Royal Navy.[36] He also had two sisters: Elizabeth, who married Edward Chichester of Northover, Sommersetshire, and Anne.[37] The Cornwall Public Records Office of Truro, England, retains a couple of documents related to Prideaux.[38]

James Taylor Trevor

James Taylor Trevor (ca. 1755–4 November 1777) was Irish and most likely grew up in the vicinity of Dublin. An ensigncy in the Royal Irish Foot was purchased on his behalf on 13 August 1766, when he was approximately eleven years old. He received the commission of Alex

McAlister, who had died, so he may have received the commission without purchase.

The Royal Irish was ordered to America on 1 January 1767, and twelve-year-old Trevor (and his guardians) apparently did not think that he was ready for overseas service, so he exchanged commissions with Henry Shaw of the 16th Foot on 8 April 1767. However, the 16th Foot had also been ordered to America; Trevor's agent must not have been paying attention. Trevor then exchanged again to the 55th Regiment of Foot, which had recently returned from America. Patrick Moncrieff ultimately took the ensigncy in the 16th Foot, maintaining the 8 April 1767 date for his commission. Trevor is listed in the regimental agent's ledgers for America but has no entries under his name.

Trevor purchased into the 55th Foot while it was stationed in southeastern Ireland. He was promoted to lieutenant on 31 August 1770 and was assigned to Captain William Winepress's company in April 1774. Trevor was promoted to captain lieutenant on 16 July 1774 and moved to the general's company. He was present with the 55th Foot when it was inspected at Charles Fort, Ireland, on 31 May 1775.

Trevor was promoted to captain on 14 August 1775, when the 55th Foot was augmented by two additional companies in anticipation of its embarkation for American service. He was replaced by Decimus Reynolds as captain lieutenant of the 55th Foot and did not get assigned to recruiting duty but was given a battalion company.

Trevor embarked for Boston in September 1775 from Cork, Ireland. However, Atlantic storms left his vessel, the *Enterprize*, dismasted and adrift, and it arrived at English Harbor, Antigua, on 13 January 1776, and not at Boston as planned. Trevor and four companies of the 55th arrived at Halifax in April 1776.[39] He was present with his company at Fresh Kill, Staten Island, on 13 July 1776 and served throughout the New York campaign with the 55th Foot fighting at Long Island and at Kip's Bay.

Trevor commanded a detachment of the 55th Foot at Princeton on 3 January 1777, when that detachment was sent to make contact between Lieutenant Colonel Charles Mawhood's command and the 40th Foot. He reached the 40th Foot only after skirmishing with Continental troops under General John Sullivan. Trevor's conduct at Princeton came under question by some of the officers of the 17th Foot, including Dr. Andrew Wardrop, who passed the information on upon his return to Scotland.[40]

According to Wardrop, Mawhood had to continually order Trevor to bring the 55th forward, which he did not do.

> [The 55th] (who wd not advance in a line with the 17th in spite of Coll Mawhood frequently cling out to Capt [Trevor] who commanded them to mind his orders & come up) as soon as they saw such a slaughter among the first rank of the 17th, immediately run off on their commanding officer [Trevor] saying it was all over with the others.[41]

When his company of the 55th was mustered on 5 May 1777, at Perth Amboy, New Jersey, Trevor was listed as absent by leave in New York City. Lieutenant Peter Marland was in command of Trevor's company at that time.

Trevor took part in the Philadelphia campaign in the fall of 1777, including the actions at Germantown and Brandywine. While garrisoning Philadelphia, the young Irish captain got into difficulties by insulting Ensign Richard Power.[42] Trevor accused Power of behaving "unlike a Gentleman and an officer" and advised Power that if he (Trevor) were in command of the regiment, Power would be out of it. Somehow, this feud erupted on 4 November 1777, with the two officers meeting on the common before Smith's Tavern in Philadelphia.

According to Hamilton Acheson, surgeon of the 55th Foot, Trevor was struck and killed by a pistol ball to his right temple. Trevor's commission went to Captain Lieutenant Colin Lindsey. On 10 November 1777, Power was tried by a court-martial presided over by Mawhood and charged with the murder of Trevor. Power was acquitted. It is interesting that the same Charles Mawhood who had accused Trevor of cowardice on the battlefield then served as president of the court-martial of Trevor's killer.[43]

Trevor's remaining balance in the regimental accounts was given to Lady Sarah Trevor. She was almost certainly his mother.[44]

Francis Wadman

Francis Wadman (1727–1809) entered military service as an ensign in the Royal Irish on 1 October 1755 and became a lieutenant on 20 November 1756. His ethnicity was listed as Irish in the Royal Irish's 1767 inspection return.[45] He is listed as being present at a celebration honoring King George III's ascendancy to the throne held at Dublin Castle on 1 November 1760. John Foliott, the colonel of the Royal Irish at the time, was also listed as present.[46]

Sometime before 1768, Wadman was appointed as a gentleman usher to Princess Amelia Sophia, an aunt of George III.[47] A gentleman usher performed as an usher at various ceremonial functions at the royal court. His exact responsibilities were most likely fairly minimal. Princess Amelia had homes at Gunnersbury Estate, Middlesex, and in Soho. Wadman was most likely often at both.[48]

Wadman was listed as having been on leave "By License" for four months in April 1767. This coincides approximately with the period when the regiment was ordered to North America. Wadman did not embark for America with the Royal Irish. He was assigned to Isaac Hamilton's battalion company in 1767 and remained with it but was absent upon the regiment's arrival in America. His regimental account notes that he paid a fee for a six-month leave of absence on 31 December 1767. He paid a similar fee on 13 August 1768. His account's final balance was about £18 on 17 January 1772.[49]

Wadman was promoted to captain lieutenant on 4 February 1769 to replace Matthew Lane, who was deceased. The returns of the regiment prepared in America do not not show evidence of Wadman's promotion, however. He sold his captain lieutenancy to Lewis Wynne on 15 February 1770; even though Wadman had not purchased the captain lieutenancy, he was allowed by the king to sell it. He alleged that Wilkins wished him to sell to a friend of the lieutenant colonel and not to the most senior lieutenant, who would have been next in line. However, he claims to have defied Wilkins and sold to Wynne. Wadman retired, and his history splits from that of the Royal Irish.[50]

Wadman married Mary Comyns, the daughter of Elizabeth Comyns and the niece of Thomas Chiffinch, in 1775. When Mary's uncle died, also in 1775, she inherited property in Kent. Wadman lived at the Hive in Northfleet. He also owned an area known as Lower Delce. He controlled two copyhold tenements in Winterborne that had been Chiffinch's property as well.[51] He was later a major of the Northfleet Volunteer Corps, which was formed to deter a French invasion in 1794, although it is not evident if he performed any active service in that role.[52]

Wadman subscribed to the *Military Medley*, published by Simes in 1768. He is listed in Simes's 1772 *The Military Guide for Young Officers* and 1777 *A Military Course*. Wadman and his wife appear to have been book collectors, and book plates with FRANCIS AND MARY WADMAN, 1775 were extant in 1908 when William Hazlitt compiled *A Roll of Honor*.[53]

Wadman's Northfleet, Kent, property appears to have been auctioned on 21 April 1796. It is unclear why he auctioned the property. The rent of the property, which was only twenty miles from London, was £281 17s. per annum, and Wadman had a fifteen-year lease. The main dwelling house was brick with gardens and offices; four tenements adjoined the main property.[54]

Wadman was listed as present at the annual general meeting of the lieutenancy and magistrates of the County of Kent at the George Inn at Sittingbourne on 19 July 1803. He appears to have actively participated in Kentish politics and society.[55]

At some point, however, Wadman's circumstances changed, and in his old age he was a man of extremely filthy and beggarly habits. He hired a lodging in Sutfolk-Street, at half a guinea per week, where he lived without a servant and seldom or never cleaned himself. When he did indulge himself with a clean shirt, he put it on over his dirty one.

Wadman appears to have been coerced by a nephew to sign a will on 14 August 1809; at a trial after his death, both his nurse and his landlord were required to testify that he signed the will without knowing its contents. He died without issue before 1812,[56] having outlived his wife.

8

Other Officers Associated with the Royal Irish in America

Included in this chapter are those officers who, though not commissioned in the Royal Irish Regiment, spent a significant period in close association with it. The artillery officer, Robert Douglas, who was assigned to Fort Chartres in Illinois is included, along with James Rumsey, a former highland officer who served as a military secretary for the Royal Irish but was denied a commission in the regiment. Most of these officers are from the 65th Regiment of Foot who served in an ad hoc battalion with a detachment of the Royal Irish in Boston during the winter and spring of 1774–1775. Reviewing their careers provides an easy comparison to the officers of the Royal Irish.

John Bailey

John Bailey (ca. 1751–?) was appointed as an ensign in the 65th Foot on 16 August 1768. He was seventeen years old when first commissioned and was listed as Irish in the returns, sometimes as Baillie or Baylie. He was assigned to Captain John MacKay's company in Boston on 16 December 1774, at the same time that Lieutenant Jonas Watson was assigned to George Sinclair's company. These two officers were probably sent to Boston from Halifax, since the 65th Foot's companies in Boston appear to have been short of officers.

Bailey served on a regimental court-martial on 19 December 1774, as his first identified duty in the Royal Irish's orderly book. He served with Captain Sinclair and Lieutenant George Bruere and was promoted to lieutenant on 18 June 1775 in the aftermath of Bunker Hill. He became the captain lieutenant of the 65th Foot on 22 December 1779 and ended his career by transferring into half pay in the 105th Foot on 15 April 1785.[1]

Thomas Bruce

The Honourable Thomas Bruce (ca. 1740–12 December 1797) is included in this collection because of his command of the combined detachments of the Royal Irish and 65th Regiments of Foot at Boston from the fall of 1774 through June 1775. He was Scottish, the second son of William Bruce, the eighth Earl of Kincardine, and Jane Robertson. Bruce was first commissioned at the age of nineteen as a cornet in the 1st Dragoons on 19 July 1759. He was promoted to captain on 21 October 1761 in the 2nd Battalion of the 105th Regiment of Foot, which was newly raised at that time. He was promoted to major on 13 January 1763 but was put on half pay when the battalion was disbanded later that year. He returned to active service with the 60th (Royal American) Regiment on 27 May 1768 and became the lieutenant colonel of the 65th Foot on 16 March 1770.[2]

It is unclear exactly when Bruce arrived in America, since the 65th Foot had been sent there in 1768, before his appointment. He was in America by April 1773, however, because Thomas Gage wrote to Lord Barrington to ask him to send Major William Butler back to America so Bruce could take leave. Bruce was waiting for Butler to return from England. It is not clear whether Bruce ever had the opportunity for his leave. By late 1774, he was in Boston along with two companies of the 65th Foot. However, his own company was not present at Boston but remained at Halifax.[3]

Bruce pardoned Sergeant William Williams of the Royal Irish's grenadier company in November 1774 when Williams had been sentenced to be reduced by a regimental court. On 11 January 1775, Bruce ordered, "Col. Bruce pardons all Prisoners which was reported to him this morning, hoping that this lenity will be an inducement for the Men to behave well, as he is determined not to overlook any Crime they may be guilty of in future."[4] In general, however, the punishments meted out by regimental courts under Bruce were particularly harsh. He served as a member of the court-martial board that heard the case of Captain Payne in July and August 1775.[5]

Bruce served as the field officer of the lines in Boston on 16 October 1775. On 25 October, he was the field officer of the day. He served in both roles multiple times while in Boston. He was ordered to take command of the detachment at Charleston, South Carolina, on 8 February 1776, to be composed of the 47th and 63rd Regiments of Foot, Clerk's light infantry battalion, and the 1st Battalion of Marines. His detachment was relieved on 22 February 1776.[6]

A portion of the 65th Foot remained in Boston until March 1776, when the army embarked for Halifax. The regiment was drafted there in May 1776, and the officers and NCOs returned to England. Bruce was in command of the 65th Foot when it was next inspected at Doncaster, England, in June 1777. On 4 June 1778, he was the field officer of the day at Coxheath Camp. On 13 June 1778, the 65th Foot under Bruce was again joined with the Royal Irish at Coxheath Camp as part of the 2nd Brigade of the Left Division under Major General Robert Sloper.[7] Bruce was appointed as an aide-de-camp to the king on 27 February 1779, in place of Edward Mathew. Five other officers were so appointed at the same time. Bruce was present with the 65th Foot when it was inspected at Coxheath Camp in November 1779.[8]

Bruce was promoted to lieutenant colonel commandant of the 100th Foot in February 1782 and was replaced as an aide-de-camp to the king upon his promotion. The 100th Foot was originally raised in Ireland for service, along with the 98th Foot, on the western coast of present-day Mexico, but circumstances changed its eventual destination to India. The 100th Foot surrendered at Bednore in May 1783 and was interned until 1784. The regiment then returned to Ireland and was disbanded in 1785. Bruce was promoted to major general on 23 September 1782 and was made a resident major general on the staff of Ireland on 3 June 1786. He was given the command of the 16th Regiment of Foot on 25 March 1788.[9]

Bruce became a member of Parliament from Marlborough in July 1790 and from Great Bedwin in June 1796. He was promoted to lieutenant general on 14 May 1796 and remained in command of the 16th Foot until his death on 12 December 1797.[10]

Bruce died in Exeter, Devon, with no record of any marriage or children.

Robert Douglas

Robert Douglas (ca. 1744–4 April 1827) began his military career with his admission to the Royal Military Academy at Woolwich as a gentleman cadet on 2 August 1760. He was commissioned as a lieutenant and fireworker on 26 August 1762, just as the French and Indian War was winding down. He was placed on half pay at the end of the war and returned to active service by 1769. He was a subscriber to Stephen Payne Adye's *Treatise on Courts Martial*, published in 1769.[11]

Douglas was assigned to the 1st Battalion of the Royal Artillery and arrived in North America sometime before 1771. He was promoted to second lieutenant on 1 January 1771 with the reorganization of the Royal Artillery into four battalions. He served in Illinois at Fort Chartres in command of the small Royal Artillery detachment at that post, and he returned to the East Coast with the majority of the Royal Irish Regiment in the fall of 1772, leaving only a handful of Royal Artillerists with Captain Hugh Lord's detachment.

Douglas was married, and his wife lived on Hester Street in New York City in 1776 while Douglas was on a campaign.[12] Douglas was in command of the artillery at Verplank's Point on the Hudson River in 1776, where his guns forced an American sloop to be hulled and scuttled. General William Howe thanked Douglas's detachment for its good behavior during the action.[13]

Douglas was promoted to first lieutenant in the Royal Artillery on 25 March 1777. Douglas married Mary Kearsley, the daughter of loyalists John Kearsley and Mary Magdalene Valleau, on 22 October 1777 at Old St. Paul's Episcopal Church, Philadelphia. He was promoted to captain lieutenant & captain on 21 July 1779, promoted to captain on 20 November 1783, and given command of the No. 5. Company of the 3rd Battalion of the Royal Artillery.

Douglas was promoted to major in the army on 1 March 1794 and was given local rank as a colonel in America on 17 November 1790. He became a major in the Royal Artillery on 14 August 1794, as hostilities erupted with France, and he became a lieutenant colonel in the Royal Artillery on 6 March 1795, as the Royal Artillery was further expanding in response to the French Revolution. He was made commandant of the Corps of Royal Artillery Drivers on 20 April 1795 and remained in command until it was disbanded in 1817.

Douglas was promoted to the army rank of colonel on 29 April 1802 and promoted to colonel in the Royal Artillery on 12 September 1803. He was promoted to colonel commandant of the Royal Invalid Artillery Battalion on 4 September 1809, became a major general on 25 October 1809, and was promoted to lieutenant general on 4 June 1814.[14]

At its height in 1814, the Royal Corps of Drivers included 88 officers and 7,352 other men under Douglas's command. Douglas was appointed as superintendent of the Royal Arsenal at Woolwich on 3 November 1823 and remained there until his death at age eighty-three on 4 April 1827. In the *Naval and Military* magazine, which reported his death, he was listed as the senior colonel commandant of the Royal Regiment of Artillery and director general of the field train (the collection of wagons, animals, and so on that carry the army's reserve supplies).[15]

George Gordon

George Gordon (ca. 1756–?) was appointed as an ensign in the 65th Foot on 12 January 1770. He was English and approximately fourteen years old when first commissioned. He was first listed for duty with the Royal Irish on 18 November 1774, serving on a guard detail with Captain John Shee and Lieutenant William Richardson. He was present throughout the winter of 1774–1775 with the Royal Irish and was officially assigned to Captain John MacKay's company from Major William Butler's company on 24 June 1775, but he had actually been serving with MacKay's company since November 1774. Gordon succeeded to a lieutenant on 2 August 1775 upon the death of John Smith and was promoted to captain lieutenant on 22 July 1778 and to captain on 16 December 1778.[16]

Francis Seymour Hearst

Francis Seymour Hearst (1752–1809) was an English officer assigned as the lieutenant of Captain MacKay's company of the 65th Foot when it was brigaded with Captain Shee's detachment of the Royal Irish in Boston from the fall of 1774 through the late spring of 1775. Hearst was appointed as an ensign in the 65th Foot on 20 January 1766 and purchased a lieutenancy for 26 December 1770. He was most likely absent from Boston during the time the Royal Irish and the 65th Foot served together; he is never mentioned for duty in the extant orderly book covering the period. He was listed as absent by the king's leave on the 4 October 1775 return for MacKay's company.

It is not clear whether Hearst returned to the regiment before it was drafted in May 1776, but he was present with the regiment when it was inspected in June 1777 at Doncaster. He was promoted to captain lieutenant of the 65th Foot on 27 December 1778 and to captain on 22 December 1779. He was present with the regiment at Coxheath Camp in 1779.

Hearst exchanged into the 99th Regiment of Foot on 29 October 1782 with James Wemyss, formerly of the 65th Foot. It is possible that with the war winding down, Hearst was hoping the regiment would be disbanded and he could retire on half pay. He was placed on half pay in 1784 with the disbanding of the 99th Foot and remained there until his death in 1809.[17]

Thomas Hutchins (1730–28 April 1789) was born in Monmouth County, New Jersey, in 1730. His parents died while he was young. Hutchins (occasionally listed as Hutchinson) received a commission as a lieutenant on 18 December 1757 in the Pennsylvania Regiment, which had been raised that year to fight the French. On 7 June 1758, he was appointed quartermaster in Colonel Hugh Mercer's battalion, and he was present at the siege of Fort Duquesne and remained at the site through at least August 1759. He does not appear in the list of Pennsylvania officers printed in 1760. It is unclear whether this is an error or he found some employment with the regulars. He completed the march from Fort Pitt to Venango and then Presqu'Isle, both in Pennsylvania, with Colonel Henry Bouquet in July 1760, because he printed his journal from that march.[18]

Hutchins was appointed as an ensign on 2 March 1762 in the 60th (Royal American) Regiment of Foot. He was part of the garrison at Fort Pitt when it was besieged by Pontiac's forces in 1763. He was ordered to leave the fort on 19 March, but he returned on 29 May 1763 with six additional recruits. He was present with the garrison from that time through 17 October. Returns show him serving on guard duty, sitting on courts-martial, and doing the other regular tasks of garrison work. Captain Simeon Ecuyer wrote to Colonel Bouquet in June 1763 that Hutchins "has taken no rest. He oversaw the works and did his duty, at the same time, that is praiseworthy and he merits recompense."[19]

Hutchins was appointed adjutant to the detachment under Captain John Stewart marching from Fort Pitt to Fort Ligonier on 17 October 1763. His maps of the 1764 Indian campaigns under Bouquet were published in 1765 in Philadelphia as part of an account of the expedition against the Ohio Valley Indians.

Hutchins made his first trip to Illinois in the company of Captain Harry Gordon, the chief engineer of the western department in North America, and George Groghan, the deputy Indian agent, in the spring of 1766 to survey the territory acquired from France east of the Mississippi. They were also accompanied by merchants from the Philadelphia trading firm of Baynton, Wharton, and Morgan. Hutchins was Gordon's acting assistant engineer. They reached the mouth of the Ohio River on 7 August and were met by troops from Fort Chartres, which they reached on 18

August 1766. The expedition then set out down the Mississippi River to New Orleans and traveled to Pensacola, Florida, before sailing to Havana on 12 November 1766. Hutchins returned to his role as a troop officer and was at the 26 April 1768 conference with Indian chiefs from several nations at Fort Pitt. He was stationed at Fort Chartres as an acting engineer by 15 November 1768.[20]

Hutchins was the only officer from outside the Royal Irish to serve on the court of inquiry that settled the dispute between Richard Bacon and George Morgan in 1770.[21]

Hutchins was promoted to lieutenant in the 2nd Battalion of the 60th Regiment of Foot on 7 August 1771. He was transferred to Florida in early 1772 and left Fort Chartres, spending the next five years primarily in West Florida engaged in many engineering projects. He presented the American Philosophical Society at Philadelphia, of which he was a member, with his *Account of the Country of Illinois*, according to the *Pennsylvania Gazette*. He was granted one thousand acres on 12 May 1773 and two thousand acres on 15 July 1775 in west Florida for his service as a field officer and as an assistant commissary in the French and Indian War. He received a third grant for service as paymaster on 18 April 1776.[22]

Hutchins was promoted to captain lieutenant of the 2nd Battalion of the 60th Foot on 24 September 1775. He was transferred to the 4th Battalion of that regiment on 18 November 1776 and promoted to captain. He was in London on 8 May 1777, when he submitted his estimate for the expenses to improve the fortifications at Pensacola. In November 1778, he published a number of maps and accompanying descriptions in London. He appears to have been offered a commission as major in one of the regiments being raised during the war, but he refused it because he did not want to bear arms against his countrymen.

Similarly, Hutchins was not allowed to sell his commission in the 4th Battalion, although according to his own account, he frequently tried. At some point, he began a correspondence with Benjamin Franklin, a congressional minister in France. Hutchins was taken into custody by the British government and placed in London's Clerkenwell Prison in irons. He remained there for seven weeks before being released. Hutchins was ultimately allowed to resign from the British service on 11 February 1780. He seems to have been bitter at the loss of nearly £3,000 that the government owed him. He embarked for France and met with Franklin, who wrote him a letter of introduction to Congress.

Hutchins reached Charleston, South Carolina, in early December 1780 and was appointed geographer to the southern army on 4 May 1781 under General Nathanael Green. Hutchins became the geographer of the United States on 11 July 1781. However, he was not the only person in that role. He did not become the sole geographer until 10 June 1785, according to a congressional resolution.

Hutchins was asked to extend the boundary between Virginia and Pennsylvania in September 1783. On 3 November 1783, with the end of hostilities with Great Britain, his role became a civil one. He presented Congress with materials on 16 April 1784 while in Philadelphia, possibly working on getting his book, *An Historical, Narrative and Topographical Description of Louisiana and West-Florida*, published.

The desire to settle the current state of Ohio by former Continental Army officers led to Hutchins being asked to survey the area for settlement. Ultimately, the Land Ordinance of 1785, which established the precedent for nearly all future states settled by the United States, was significantly influenced by Hutchins. By September 1785, Hutchins was again at Fort Pitt, now Pittsburgh, to begin surveying the new lands. Indians inhibited his ability to conduct the survey after about a month of work. Between July and December 1786, he conducted surveys dividing the ranges into townships. He was reappointed as geographer to the United States for a two-year term on 26 May 1788.

Hutchins died in Pittsburgh on 28 April 1789 and was buried in the graveyard of the First Presbyterian Church.[23] Shortly after his death, Hutchins was described by Ebenezer Hazard in a letter to Jeremy Belknap, one of America's first historians, as "a man of good character, of polite manners, of great integrity, who made a regular profession of religion."[24]

John MacKay

John MacKay (ca. 1739–?) was the commander of one of the companies of the 65th Foot that was joined with the detachment of the Royal Irish in Boston from October 1774 to June 1775. He was a Scot, and his surname is sometimes spelled McKay. MacKay was originally commissioned as an ensign in the 2nd Battalion of the 1st Regiment of Foot on 14 March 1760. He was promoted to lieutenant in the 103rd Foot on 29 April 1762, and when that regiment was disbanded on 10 June 1763, he was reduced to half pay.

OTHER OFFICERS ASSOCIATED WITH THE ROYAL IRISH IN AMERICA

MacKay joined the 65th Foot as a lieutenant from half pay on 27 February 1764 and was commissioned as a captain on 26 August 1767. His company was mustered at Castle Island near Boston on 24 April 1769. Although he was the junior captain of the 65th Foot present in Boston, he was still senior to Shee, the most senior member of the Royal Irish's detachment. MacKay was first listed in the Royal Irish's orderly book for picket duty on 17 November 1774, along with Ensign Edmund Prideaux. MacKay retired by selling his commission to Alexander Macgregor on 2 November 1787. MacKay had remained with the 65th Foot for twenty-three years.[25]

Henry Miller

Henry Miller (ca. 1752–?) purchased his ensigncy in the 65th Foot on 16 April 1771. He is listed as English on the returns. He arrived in Boston sometime before his assignment as the ensign of Captain MacKay's Company in the fall of 1774. He served in that company while it was part of an ad hoc battalion with three companies of the Royal Irish.

Miller was able to purchase a lieutenancy in the 65th Foot on 16 August 1775. He was appointed as the adjutant on 24 May 1776, about the time the regiment was drafted. He would have been busy on his return to England in overseeing the training of the new recruits.

Miller was present with the regiment when it was inspected at Doncaster in June 1777. He remained the adjutant until 1 June 1779. He was also present at Coxheath Camp when the regiment was inspected in November 1779.

Miller remained as a lieutenant in the 65th Foot until May 1789, when he exchanged into the 50th Foot. If he served with the 50th at Gibraltar, he would have again been serving with the Royal Irish, which was also posted to Gibraltar at that time. He remained with the 50th Foot until he was promoted to captain without purchase and appointed to raise an independent company on 27 January 1791. It is unclear how long he remained in command of an independent company.[26]

John Pexton

John Pexton (ca. 1752–ca. 1810) purchased his ensigncy in the 65th Foot on 28 February 1766, when he was approximately fourteen years old. He is listed as Irish on the returns. He purchased a lieutenancy on 3 May 1771 and was assigned to Captain George Sinclair's light infantry company when it was stationed at Boston in 1774 to 1775. during that time, Pexton served alongside the companies of the Royal Irish. He participated in the march to Concord and to Bunker Hill and was wounded in one of these battles. He is listed as sick on the 14 October 1775 return of the light company and appears to have remained with the regiment until it was drafted at Halifax in 1776.

Pexton obtained a captaincy in the 65th Foot on 26 December 1778 in an additional company. He was recruiting when the regiment was inspected at Coxheath Camp in 1779. He retired to half pay in May 1785 by exchanging commissions with William Ashe of the 104th Foot. He probably died in 1810.[27]

James Rumsey

James Rumsey (ca. 1740–ca. 1800) was of Scottish ancestry. Sometimes listed as Ramsey or Remsey, he was commissioned on 4 February 1762 as the lieutenant of an independent company of Free Negroes. It was a common practice to provide white officers for black troops. He was removed to the 77th Regiment of Foot (Montgomery's Highlanders) on 28 July 1762 and was placed on half pay with the reduction of that regiment on 24 December 1763. On 17 March 1764, he returned to active service with the 42nd (Royal Highland) Foot as a lieutenant on ensign's pay but with seniority as a lieutenant.

Rumsey arrived from New York in time to participate on the 1764 Muskingum expedition against the Ohio Indians. The following year he served as the commissary officer for Captain Thomas Stirling's expedition down the Ohio and Mississippi Rivers to take possession of Fort Chartres. Rumsey is mentioned as the first officer of the expedition to reach Fort Chartres; he was sent ahead from Fort Massiac, Illinois, to announce the arrival of Stirling's detachment to the French and to arrange for guides to assist Stirling's command in reaching the French post. He was later identified as getting lost in the cane breaks near Fort Chartres for three days in December 1765.

After the expedition finally straggled into New York the summer of 1766, Rumsey retired on 27 August, "drowned in debt" and "obliged to sell out," according to Stirling.[28] Rumsey was granted two thousand acres in Albany County, New York, for his service as a lieutenant in the 77th Regiment of Foot in the French and Indian War on 19 October 1765.[29]

His Illinois experience soon landed him a job with the trading firm of Baynton, Wharton, and Morgan of Philadelphia, and he returned to the Illinois Country in 1766 as an assistant to George Morgan. However, difficulties with the military, growing competition from other traders, and charges of unscrupulous business practices brought about a decline in the company's fortunes by 1767, and the partners went into voluntary receivership, with their creditors administering the business. By 1768, Rumsey was putting down his own roots as a merchant.

Captain Gordon Forbes, 34th Foot, the commanding officer at Fort Chartres, reported to General Gage in June 1768 that he had "given leave to one Mr. Rumsey, Late a Lieutenant in the 42nd Regiment (who has the honour of being known to your Excellency) to settle upon a Spot of Ground near Kasakaskies; it has been forfeited to the King ever Since we have been in possession of this Country."[30]

Even though Rumsey had been some time in Illinois, it appears that he also suffered from the illness that swept through Fort Chartres in late September 1768. According to Morgan, Rumsey was "frequently & Most Violently attacked." In November 1768, Rumsey was one of the seven civil magistrates appointed by Wilkins to manage Illinois's first civil court. On 25 June 1769, Morgan and Rumsey agreed to give Wilkins a sixth share in their land dealings in the Illinois Country to obtain his support of the Baynton, Wharton, and Morgan enterprise.[31]

On several occasions, Rumsey was involved in bringing West Indian slaves to Illinois on behalf of his backers. The first such instance may have been as early as 1766. Another shipment arrived in 1768 from Jamaica. Rumsey managed affairs for the Illinois branch of Baynton, Wharton, and Morgan during Morgan's leave of absence in 1770, and, although he was a friend of Morgan's, Rumsey soon left the company to become the fort's commissary and the secretary to Lieutenant Colonel John Wilkins at Fort Chartres. Rumsey continued as Wilkins's secretary through 8 June 1771. Wilkins recommended him for a vacancy in the Royal Irish, but Gage would not confirm the appointment. When Matthew Lane died in 1769, Rumsey was one of two candidates for the position of regimental paymaster. Rumsey's appointment to that position was dependent on his obtaining the ensigncy in the Royal Irish for which Wilkins had recommended him. However, in the end, Rumsey secured neither position.[32]

In January 1771 Rumsey appears to have entered business for himself in partnership with William Murray. Rumsey and Murray were backed by Bernard and Michael Gratz, a Philadelphia merchant firm. Rumsey's movement away from Baynton, Wharton, and Morgan was a result of his personal falling-out with Morgan. In late 1771, Wilkins sent Rumsey to New York to meet with Gage and "crush all complaints against me."[33]

Rumsey returned to Kaskaskia in early 1772. It seems reasonable that Rumsey traveled with the Gratz children—Rachel, Solomon, and Frances—who were being sent to Illinois on "an adventure" under Rumsey's watchful eye. He appears to have also taken a new clerk, a distiller, and a smith for his store at Kaskaskia that spring.[34]

In May 1772, a raid of his store by Chickasaw Indians caused Rumsey to turn to Captain Hugh Lord's garrison for assistance. The Royal Irish killed several warriors and took another prisoner in its defense of Rumsey's store. In December 1772, Sergeant Andrew Hoy seized and auctioned the Kaskaskia property and chattels of John Baptist Hubardeau to pay off the debts he had incurred to Rumsey. In July 1773, Rumsey is mentioned in a large land deal with the Kaskaskia Indians. Murray was the key partner in the land deals and the organization of the various Illinois Land Company deals, and Rumsey managed the retail operations.[35]

In 1773, sometime after the Illinois Land Company deals, which Captain Lord tried to block, Rumsey relocated to New Orleans and was there by 1775 with Murray. One source mentions that Rumsey moved to west Florida along with his wife in 1773. At that point, his story no longer connects with that of the Royal Irish.[36]

George Sinclair

George Sinclair (1739 or 1748 to 9 November 1790) was the captain of one of the two companies serving with the Royal Irish's detachment in Boston from October 1774 to June 1775. The information about him recorded by the 65th Foot during the inspection returns shows great disparities. He was a Scot and entered the army at age twenty-two, according to the 65th Foot's returns in 1777 and 1779. These are more likely the accurate dates. However, in the 1767 return, Sinclair was listed as twenty years old with fourteen years of service, having been first commissioned at age six.

Most likely the clerk made an error on the 1767 return, and he was originally commissioned at age sixteen, not six. A separate note on the 1767 return states that Sinclair did not know the dates of his commission as ensign or lieutenant. The 1767 return lists his ensigncy as being dated 1754, but later returns do not include a date for this. In fact, according to the War Office succession books, Sinclair entered service as a lieutenant in the 2nd Battalion of the 42nd Regiment of Foot on 30 December 1758. He was promoted to first lieutenant in the 85th Foot on 6 August 1759 and was made the captain lieutenant of the 85th Foot on 12 February 1762 and captain on 2 June 1762. When the 85th Foot was disbanded on 24 May 1762, Sinclair went on half pay. According to historian John Houlding, the 85th Foot was a "high tone" corps, so Sinclair most likely was financially well-off.[37]

Sinclair was appointed to the 65th Foot from half pay on 28 February 1766. He appears to have been in Boston with his light infantry company during the entire time the Royal Irish and the 65th Foot were formed into an ad hoc battalion. He was first listed for duty as the officer of the guard for 15 November 1774. He was the first officer of the 65th Foot listed in the Royal Irish's orderly book. Sinclair returned wounded from Bunker Hill and was promoted to major in the army on 29 August 1777. He was appointed as a lieutenant colonel in the army in February 1783 in the same orders in which John Mawby Sr. was promoted to major in the army.[38]

Sinclair remained with the 65th Foot until he retired in May 1789. He had served nearly thirty years in the army and twenty-three in command of a company in the 65th Foot. He sold his company to Thomas Earl of Elgin, who purchased his ensigncy in the 3rd Regiment of Foot Guards. Sinclair died in Kensington on 9 November 1790.[39]

John Smith

John Smith (ca. 1752–2 August 1775) was appointed as an ensign on 16 May 1766 in the 65th Foot. He was approximately twelve when first commissioned and is listed as English in the returns. He was present in Boston, although his company assignment is not clear. He was first listed as sitting on a regimental court-martial board on 27 November 1774, along with Captain MacKay of the 65th Foot and Lieutenant Henry Fermor, Lieutenant William Richardson, and Ensign Francis John Kelly of the Royal Irish. It appears he was promoted to lieutenant by purchase on 11 January 1774, but he was first referred to as Lieutenant Smith on 6 December 1774 in the orderly book. He was wounded at Bunker Hill on 17 June 1775 and succumbed to his wounds on 2 August 1775.[40]

Jonas Watson

FIGURE 8.1 Jonas Watson's coat of arms. *Courtesy of Ryan Gale*

Jonas Watson (12 June 1748–30 May 1798) was English by birth, the son of Lovegood Watson and Anne Pipe. He was appointed as an ensign in the 65th Foot on 29 April 1762 at age thirteen and was promoted to lieutenant on 28 February 1766. He was present with the 65th Foot when it was inspected in May 1768 in Limerick, Ireland. He was assigned to Captain MacKay's battalion company in Boston while it was joined with companies of the Royal Irish in an ad hoc battalion. He first served with the Royal Irish when he was appointed to Captain Sinclair's company on 16 December 1774. He was ordered on piquet on 21 December 1774, along with Captain Shee, as the first duty recorded in the Royal Irish's orderly book.[41]

Watson was promoted to captain on 18 June 1775 because of the 65th Foot's loss of Captain William Hudson at Bunker Hill. Watson served on a court-martial board in Boston beginning on 16 November 1775 to hear three cases. He remained with the 65th Foot at Boston and then at Halifax until the 65th Foot was drafted in May 1776.

Watson returned to England after the regiment was drafted and was on recruiting duty in June 1777. He was appointed as the major of a brigade on 20 July 1779. He was on duty but was not present when the 65th Foot was inspected at Coxheath Camp in 1779.[42]

Watson was promoted to major in the army on 25 October 1782. He married Harriet Colclough on 7 February 1785 at Fermanagh, Ireland, and they had seven children.

Watson returned to Canada with the 65th Foot in the summer of 1785 when the regiment replaced the 8th (King's) Regiment of Foot. He was in command at Fort Niagara from July 1787 to May 1788. In 1793 he was stationed with the 65th Foot in Barbados.

Watson was promoted to lieutenant colonel in the army on 1 March 1794. Later that year he was advanced to the 65th Foot's major without purchase. His family tradition was that his greatest desire was to become the lieutenant colonel of the 65th Foot, but that was not to be. He was promoted to the lieutenant colonelcy of the 13th Regiment of Foot on 20 May 1795 without purchase as the army expanded. He retired from the army in 1796, having never served with the 13th Foot.

Watson retired to Ireland and in 1798 took up arms to suppress another rebellion. He was killed near Wexford on 30 May 1798 while leading some of the county's yeomen against the rebels. He is buried in Castlebridge Church, County Wexford.[43]

Epilogue

> A few days ago the shattered remains of the 18th Regiment of Foot, which was engaged in the action at Bunker's Hill and reduced to only twenty-five men, arrived at Maidstone.
>
> —Unidentified British newspaper, 5 March 1776[1]

The Royal Irish arrived at Maidstone, England, at the end of February 1776. The Royal Irish had left Cork Harbor, Ireland, in 1767 approximately 450 strong, but only 94 officers and men returned to England. Many of them would be discharged shortly, having been worn out in America.

The remains of the Royal Irish were ordered from Portsmouth, England, on 20 January 1776 and were marched about 45 miles to Basingstoke. The 59th Regiment of Foot, which had arrived with the Royal Irish from America, was ordered to nearby Petersfield at the same time. The officers and remaining core of men were sent out on recruiting parties to raise a new body of soldiers around the standards of the Royal Irish. After two months at Maidstone, on 7 May 1776, the Royal Irish was ordered to march to Dover Castle, in southern England, where it remained for the next two years. On 15 May 1777, the regiment was inspected at Dover Castle, and Captain Hugh Lord, four subalterns, six sergeants, three corporals, four drummers, and two privates were listed as recruiting. Captain Lord's detachment arrived from America at the Downs near Deal and was ordered on 21 November 1776 to march the fifteen miles from Deal to

Dover Castle to join the rest of the Royal Irish for the first time in more than four years.[2]

In March 1777, a detachment of a subaltern, a sergeant, four corporals, two drummers and thirty-five private men were sent to Hampton Court to serve with a detachment of the 69th Regiment of Foot. The detachment remained there until ordered to return to Dover Castle on 13 May 1778.[3]

On 28 May 1778, the Royal Irish was ordered to march to Canterbury by 1 June and was then to march to Sittingbourne, Milton, and Lenham. The Royal Irish was ordered to arrive at the training camp at Coxheath on Wednesday 3 June. According to British historian Alfred Temple Patterson, the regiments gathered at Coxheath were to be the main defending army against a Franco-Spanish Invasion in August 1778.[4] The Royal Irish appears to have been on the left flank of the camp, with the Royal Dragoons, five other infantry regiments, fifteen regiments of militia, and three companies of artillery.[5]

In apparent preparation for the camp at Coxheath, the king appointed five new majors of brigade on 2 April 1778. John Mawby Sr. was one of those officers, and John de Birniere another. Mawby would play a significant role in the day-to-day operation of Coxheath. He was formally appointed as the major of brigade for Major General Jeffery Amherst's brigade on 13 June. The Royal Irish was assigned to the left brigade of the left wing of the camp on 16 June. The left brigade of the left wing consisted of the Royal Irish, the 65th Foot, the 2nd (Queen's Royal), and the West Yorkshire Militia. The 1st and 2nd Battalions of the 1st (Royal) Foot, the 59th Foot, and the South Hampshire Militia completed the left wing.[6]

Two primary reasons for the camp, as part of preparing for the invasion threat, were to instruct the regiments in working as part of formations above the battalion level and to learn the new 1778 manual of arms that was being introduced. Orders for the adjutants and the four best exercising corporals of each regiment to report to headquarters on 16 June identify the beginning of instruction in the new manual exercise. John Mawby Jr. was the Royal Irish's adjutant at the time. George Buttricke's experience as the acting adjutant in Illinois and his previous experience as the sergeant major of the 2nd Battalion of the 60th (Royal American) Foot appears to be the reason he was assigned to work with the Essex Militia at Coxheath.

In addition to instruction on the new manual of arms and brigade maneuvers, the Royal Irish was also taught to work with battalion guns, smaller artillery pieces designed to work directly with the infantry battalion to which they were assigned. The battalions at Coxheath all appear to have been issued such guns, and this would have been the Royal Irish's first experience with artillery work since it left Illinois. Since most of the men of the Royal Irish had enlisted since 1776, it would have been the first artillery instruction for them.

The camps of instruction were intended to prepare England to deal with any possible invasion threat from France and its allies that had recently entered the American Revolution on the side of the Americans. However, according to Patterson, there were so many wives, children, and friends at Coxheath and Warley in 1778 that these camps rivaled the social scenes at Bath and Tunbridge. However, 1779 brought a more serious invasion threat, so the socializing seems to have been reduced.[7]

In July 1778 the Royal Irish's brigade command was given to Major General Robert Sloper, the colonel of the 1st (King's) Dragoon Guards. The Royal Irish remained at Coxheath Camp through the summer of 1778. Additional camps of instruction were set up at Warley, Winchester, Salisbury, Bury, Pendennis, and Portsmouth during the summer of 1778, but Coxheath was the largest. Warley Camp was the second largest and had four marching regiments and four militia regiments encamped. Winchester Camp had only six militia regiments encamped. Salisbury had four regiments of Dragoons or Dragoon Guards.[8]

While still at Coxheath on 29 October 1778, the Royal Irish was expanded in size to seventy privates per company. This augmentation made the Royal Irish one of the nine largest battalions in the British Army, at least on paper. This augmentation of the army in Britain created a total of thirteen thousand more soldiers in England itself as a direct response to the French invasion threat. Each company consisted of three officers, three sergeants, four corporals, two drummers, and seventy privates. At the same time, the Royal Irish was authorized two additional companies to be used for recruiting purposes. The other regiments that were authorized the same strength as the Royal Irish were the 1st, 2nd, 13th, 25th, 50th, 59th, and 69th Regiments of Foot. The 12th, 39th, 51st, 56th, 58th, 61st, 65th, and 70th Regiments of Foot included fifty-six private men per company, as did the regiments serving in America.[9]

The Coxheath encampment was broken up in early November 1778. The Royal Irish was marched to Canterbury by 9 November and then to winter quarters at Sandwich, Deal, Margate, and Ramsgate along the southeastern coast of England. Three companies were posted at Sandwich and Dean, and two at Margate and Ramsgate. The companies at Ramsgate were further scattered to quarters at St. Peter's, St. Lawrence, and Broadstairs in December 1778. In March 1779, the Royal Irish was still posted in the same places they were mustered for pay.[10]

On 9 March 1779, the Royal Irish was ordered to guard the French prisoners of war at Deal. The next day, the Royal Irish was ordered to provide a guard at the Naval Hospital at Deal as well. These assignments continued for the rest of the spring.[11]

The two additional companies of the Royal Irish were ordered to Sandwich in March 1779 and ordered to Worcester and Kidderminster to recruit in the English Midlands on 21 May 1779. On 31 May, the Royal Irish was ordered from its quarters to march to Warley Commons by 11 June. The route to Warley Camp from Sandwich was directed through Canterbury, Wilton, Sittingbourne, Rochester, and Brentwood, among other towns, for the first division of five companies. The second five companies followed a slightly different route.[12]

The Royal Irish was at Warley Camp as part of the 1st Brigade along with the 2nd Battalion of the 1st Foot. The 2nd Brigade was made up of the 2nd and the 59th Regiments of Foot. The 3rd and 4th Brigades were each made up of four militia regiments.[13] The camps in 1779 were the largest since 1758, during the last significant French invasion threat. This was partly a result of the Spanish officially entering the war in June 1779. Besides brigade drill and other maneuvers, the Royal Irish and other encamped regiments took the time and resources for target practice, something generally not done in peacetime.

According to historian John Houlding, the ten battalions (approximately forty-two hundred men) at Tiptree Heath in 1780 went through nearly a quarter of a million cartridges. Mock battles were also part of the training, and Lieutenant General George Lane Parker introduced additional realism by marching the troops through rough country and training them to fire in more realistic combat conditions. The training camps seem to have improved the Royal Irish, and when the regiment was inspected at Warley Camp in August 1779, Lieutenant General Parker, the reviewing officer, wrote, "The Regiment is fit for immediate Service, makes a very Good appearance and does its business regularly in handling Arms and is remarkably steady when halted."[14]

When last reviewed in May 1777, the Royal Irish had not yet been "fit for service." According to Houlding, this was common, and of the twenty-nine marching regiments to encamp, sixteen had been listed as unfit for service before being encamped. That consisted of nine of the regiments drafted in America, including the Royal Irish. Houlding's finding was that regiments that were lucky enough to be encamped tended to be fit for service at least a year before those regiments not encamped.[15]

The Royal Irish remained encamped at Warley Camp until November 1779. Orders were issued for the camp to begin to break up on 22 November. The Royal Irish was the last of the regular regiments to decamp, on 27 November. The regiment was ordered to be quartered at Dunstable, Woburn, Hemel Hempsted, and other unnamed places. Specifically, three companies were to be posted at Dunstable and Market Street; one at Luton; another at Hemel Hempsted and Kings Langley; one between Berkhamstead and Tring; three at Woburn, Brickhills, and Hockliffe; and one at Leighton Buzzard. On 11 December, the company at Berkhamstead was spread out farther to North Church. So the members of the Royal Irish went from several months of being encamped together to a winter of being extremely spread out—not a good way to maintain efficiency and discipline.[16]

In March 1780, the regiment's quarters were modified, and the companies at Woburn were marched to Luton. Further changes were made that spring, and the companies at Hemel Hempstead were ordered on 23 May 1780 to retire to Redburn and King's Langley during a fair at Hemel Hempstead and then to return at the end of the fair.[17]

The Royal Irish was ordered back to a camp of instruction at Tiptree Heath on 27 May 1780. It was to march in two divisions of five companies each, the first to reach St. Albans by 9 June and the second on 10 June. The entire regiment was to arrive at Tiptree Camp on 15 June. However, the Gordon Riots intervened, and the Royal Irish never arrived at Tiptree. The camp of instruction at Tiptree Heath in the summer of 1780 included the 45th Foot and nine battalions of militia. It is not clear whether the 45th Foot originally intended on being encamped at Tiptree or replaced the Royal Irish.[18]

The riots began with demonstrations for the repeal of the Catholic Relief Act of 1778 orchestrated by the Protestant Association under Lord George Gordon. A mass meeting of about fifty thousand was held at St. George's Field on 2 June 1780. Nearly twenty thousand marched to Parliament to formally demand the repeal of the Catholic Relief Act. Over the next two days, mobs ravaged the Moorfields Area, which was filled with Irish immigrants and was ripe for attack by the anti-Catholic mobs. Catholic chapels attached to foreign embassies were destroyed as well.

On 6 June, the rioters assembled at Newgate Prison and demanded the release of rioters previously arrested. That evening, the statutory hour between the reading of the Riot Act and the ability of troops to fire on mobs was waived by the London authorities. Officers were now effectively permitted to shoot on sight. The London officials who had been slow to address the rioters were not scared into action and firmly supported the king. The early hours of 7 June saw the first deaths caused by troops, and by the afternoon, thousands of regulars and militia were posted throughout the city.

The Royal Irish was ordered to march immediately for Hyde Park without halting. Dispositions of troops for 8 June 1780 show five regiments of cavalry, the foot guards, two battalions of regulars, and six battalions of militia in London and its environs. The cavalry regiments included the 3rd Dragoon Guards; the 3rd, 4th, and 11th Dragoons; and the 16th Light Dragoons. The 2nd Battalion of the 1st Foot and the 2nd (Queen's Royal) Foot were the two marching battalions present. The Royal Irish was expected to arrive on 10 June along with two more battalions of militia.[19]

On 10 June, when the Royal Irish arrived, the riots had subsided and the lifeless bodies of rioters were hanging from lampposts. Shops reopened for the first time on that day. Estimates usually show about 285 rioters who were either killed by troops or died of wounds shortly afterward. About another 170 were wounded, and about 450 were arrested. Estimates indentify between 18 and 25 rioters hanged and another 50 sentenced to death but ultimately transported instead of executed.[20]

The Royal Irish and the other troops, including much of the militia, remained in London for most of the summer. The Royal Irish was encamped at Hyde Park through June and July. A return for 24 June 1780 shows the Royal Irish as part of the three-thousand-man brigade consisting of the 2nd Battalion of the 1st Foot, the 2nd (Queen's Royal) Foot, and three regiments of militia.[21]

Only two incidents from the Royal Irish's riot duty survive: (1) a detachment under Captain William Conolly being involved in the disruption of a plot by rioters to burn a house on 28 June, and (2) a man knocking down a Royal Irish soldier on sentry at Hyde Park on 23 July and seizing his firelock. The man was secured and delivered to the London Civil Powers for punishment.[22]

The Royal Irish, along with the 2nd (Queens) Foot and the South Hampshire militia regiment, was ordered to decamp from Hyde Park and march to Finchley Common via Whetston, arriving on 9 August 1780. Unlike the other camps, Finchley was designed more to provide ready access to troops to support the London Civil Powers than to provide further training. However, with three regiments encamped, the opportunity for training could not be passed up. The order allowing troops to act without the reading of the Riot Act or the one-hour waiting period and without direction from the civil authorities was officially revoked on 27 September 1780. Effectively, this ended the military occupation of London.[23]

The Royal Irish remained at Finchley until 20 October, when it was ordered to Tottenham, Edmonton, Endfield Wash, Woltham Abbey, and Woltham Cross. After two weeks, they were to spread out farther. Winter quarters for the regiment were in the same area, with five companies being spread out through Hemstead, Highgate, Ramsey, and Edgeware and their environs. The regiment remained in the same area until ordered to Petersfield on 2 April 1781.

While there, the Royal Irish learned it was to be sent to Jersey and Guernsey. It was ordered to march to Plymouth on 9 April 1781 and then embark for Jersey. The additional companies were in Birmingham by late 1780, then they were ordered to Liverpool on 2 November to continue to recruit in that area. The additional companies were ordered to send their recruits "from time to time and in such Divisions as you shall judge most convenient to Hilsea Barracks" on 19 April 1781. The recruits would then be sent to the Channel Islands to reinforce the regiment.[24]

The Royal Irish arrived in Jersey in late April. It appears that the 6th Foot was posted to Jersey at the same time. The Royal Irish was moved to Guernsey in February 1782.[25]

In March 1783, the 104th Foot was stationed at Fort George, an unfinished coastal fort in Guernsey. According to Jonathan Duncan, the 104th had been quartered in the fort during the previous winter and had generally been troublesome to the local inhabitants. Duncan stated that the men remained in "tolerable order" until a few discharged men from the 83rd Foot arrived and boasted that they had been able to defy the articles of war shortly before. That seems to have incited the men of the 104th to act up as well.

As the war with America was ending, the men of the 104th, who had been enlisted in Ireland about eighteen months earlier for three years or the duration of the war, believed that they should be discharged. They demanded that the officers leave the fort's gates open at night so they could come and go into town as they pleased and that they should no longer have any duties. For some reason, the governor granted their demands on 18 March. On 21 March, the officers of the 104th were sent scurrying out of the fort when their evening meal was interrupted by the "whistling of musket balls among them."

That evening, the officers of the local militia regiments were to call up their men while the Royal Irish, quartered in the town, and an artillery company formed to deal with the mutineers. There was some concern that the men of the Royal Irish might side with the mutineers or at least be unwilling to actively participate in putting down the mutiny, but all contemporary sources state that the Royal Irish formed to a man under the command of Major John Mawby Sr. At about eleven o'clock at night, the Royal Irish, the town regiment of militia, and the artillery marched out to Fort George. The Royal Irish and the town militia's flank companies, along with four cannons and two howitzers, formed a line about one hundred yards in front of the citadel behind a low ridge. A sergeant and the drum major of the Royal Irish were sent forward for a parley. The mutineers refused to lay down their arms, and a few "straggling shots" were taken at the Royal Irish.

At four o'clock in the morning, the mutineers began to open fire on the lieutenant governor, who was admonishing the mutineers. That set in motion a final push by the Royal Irish under Mawby's command and now four militia regiments. The men of the 104th quickly realized their situation was untenable and plied their arms. Later that morning, the lieutenant governor gave the following order: "The Lieutenant-Governor takes this publick Manner of thanking the 18th or Royal Irish Regiment for their good and spirited Behaviour last Night, and will take the earliest Opportunity to have their Merit represented to the King."[26]

As a result of the mutiny, the 104th Foot was disbanded on 24 April 1783, after the ringleaders of the mutiny were court-martialed.

On 7 April 1783, the Assembly of the States of the Island showed their thanks for the excellent conduct of the Royal Irish by voting the men of the regiment one hundred guineas to be divided among the NCOs and soldiers. Along with the following resolutions were the following:

> To return similar thanks to John Mawby, esq., at that time commanding officer of the Royal Irish, and to the other officers of the

said regiment, for the prudence with which they retained their soldiers in their duty, notwithstanding and example so calculated to corrupt them, and for having induced them to arm and march against the mutineers, with as much zeal, alacrity and diligence, as good discipline.

To recognize the good service of the privates of the said regiment of Royal Irish, and of the artillery, for the attachment and submission that these said privates and artillerymen shows to their officers,—for the good order and discipline they observed,—and for the courage with which they marched against the mutineers,—and to vote, to the said soldiers, one hundred guineas, which some shall be paid to their officers to distribute among them.[27]

Thirty-six of the mutineers were picked out of the 104th to be tried by general court-martial. The rest of the regiment—except for the grenadier company, which had been posted separately and did not participate in the mutiny—was to be immediately disbanded. However, the ability to court-martial the soldiers if the regiment was disbanded created a legal issue for the lieutenant governor, so the regiment was intact until late April 1783. The lieutenant governor also mentioned that the Royal Irish was required to take up most of the duties of the 104th Foot and that this was causing hardships for the men of the Royal Irish, who were effectively doing double duty.[28]

On 14 June 1783, because of the reduction of hostilities with the new United States, the Royal Irish was reduced from twelve to ten companies, and each company was reduced to forty-eight privates. The additional company officers were not immediately put on half pay but were to remain in the regiment en second, or as supernumerary to the authorized strength. On 7 July 1783, the regiment was ordered to proceed to Hilsea, Portsmouth, and from there to Gibraltar as soon as transports were ready to take it to its new post. The Royal Irish was part of the relief that allowed the regiments that had survived the Siege of Gibraltar to return to Britain. This rotation saw the effective end of hostilities at Gibraltar, and peace with the new United States came formally at the end of 1783.

The Royal Irish and the other regiments affected were to be reduced to six battalion companies and two flank companies. In fact, it appears that the regiments actually lost two companies and not the four companies that the War Office's letter would indicate. By the time the 1784 army list was published, the affected regiments all show ten companies, and so do the muster rolls. The Royal Irish was effectively reduced to 20 sergeants, 30 corporals, 20 drummers, 2 fifers, and 480 privates.[29]

The Royal Irish remained at Gibraltar for a decade before it embarked for France. The regiment saw combat again at the Siege of Toulon in 1793 under the command of Captain William Conolly, one of the last men to have served in North America. The men of the regiment later served as shipboard marines in the Mediterranean and then in Egypt in 1801. The regiment returned to the Americas in 1805, serving in the West Indies, where the 1st Battalion remained until 1814.

When recruiting districts were assigned to each regiment, the 18th (Royal Irish) Regiment was assigned to the counties of Kilkenny, Tipperary, Waterford, and Wexford. The recruiting depot was at Clonmel, Ireland. The Royal Irish saw further service in Burma, the Crimea, and Afghanistan before 1880. In 1881, the regiment was officially retitled as the Royal Irish Regiment as part of the Cardwell Reforms.[30] It was posted to South Africa in 1899.[31]

The regiment earned the following battle honors during its 230 years of service before World War I: Namur, (1695); Blenheim, (1704); Ramillies, (1705); Oudenarde, (1708); Malplaquet, (1709); Egypt (1801); China (1840–1842); Pegu (1852–1853); Sevastopol (1854–1855); New Zealand (1863–1866); Afghanistan (1879–1880); Tel-el-Kebir, Egypt (1882); the Nile (1884–1885); and South Africa (1900–1902).

World War I saw the regiment expand to ten battalions, and it fought in France, Flanders, Macedonia, and Palestine. The regiment's final service to Britain came as part of the army of occupation in Germany through 1920. It earned battle honors for the Marne, Ypres, Somme, Messines, Hindenburg Line, Struma, Suvla, and Gaza, among others. In addition to fighting the Germans and their allies in World War I, a portion of the Royal Irish was involved in putting down the Easter Rising of 1916 in Ireland. This was one of the final events leading to the creation of the present Republic of Ireland.[32]

The Royal Irish Regiment of Foot concluded its service to Britain in 1922, when several Irish regiments were disbanded because of the independence of the Republic of Ireland. The regimental colors were presented to King George V for safekeeping at Windsor Castle.

The title the Royal Irish Regiment was reused when Britain merged the Royal Irish Rangers and the Ulster Defense Regiment as part of the "options for change" proposal from the Ministry of Defense in 1992. The

262   Royal Irish Rangers was an amalgamated regiment formed from the old 27th (Inniskilling), 83rd (County of Dublin), 86th (Royal County Down), 87th (Royal Irish Fusiliers), 89th (Princess Victoria's), and 108th (Madras Infantry) Regiments of Foot.

Notes on Sources

The manuscript records kept by the British War Office form the core of materials that support this volume. The majority of those records are extant in the United Kingdom's Public Record Office at Kew. The best starting point for easily determining an officer's commission history is the War Office 65 Series, which are copies of the printed army lists, with the handwritten notations of the War Office clerks showing changes between printings and often additional annotations on why officers transferred or left service.

Supplementing the army lists are Thomas Desbrisay's *The Quarters of the Army in Ireland* for the years 1733–1754, when the first regular army list was printed. James Rivington's *North American Army List*, printed in contemporary New York City, was helpful for some of the officers who remained or returned to America.

Of course, in the British Army of the Georges, simply having a commission didn't necessarily mean actual service with a regiment. To determine the officer's actual service, the first two official resources are the muster rolls of the War Office 12 Series and the War Office 27 Series. The WO 12 Series are the muster or pay rolls completed approximately every six months in order to show the strength of each company of the regiment. Included were casualties of all types, including desertions and discharges as well as promotions, demotions, leave, and detached duty. Company officers signed each of the rolls. Officers serving with the regiment are easily identified, as are the absentee officers. The WO 12 series is the single best source for determining an officer's specific company assignment.

Only the earliest army lists identify company assignments, leaving the WO 12 Series as the only consistent resource for determining such assignments. The Royal Irish's muster rolls are remarkably complete for the period from 1767 through 1780. Relatively few of the returns for the Royal Irish are missing. Those lost are for two companies stationed in Illinois after 1772.

War Office 27 Series, Office of the Commander-in-Chief and War Office: Adjutant General and Army Council, holds the inspection returns from the annual inspection visits by general officers in Britain and Ireland. These inspections include a general return of officers showing the name, age, nativity, and dates of commissions for each officer and the reason for any absences. The ages of officers in these returns do fluctuate at times, which appear to make officers older in the earlier years of their service, possibly to have legitimized purchasing initial commissions at a younger age than they should have been allowed to do.

The returns are bound in volumes by year and establishment; those from Ireland are in a separate volume from those inspected in Britain (England, Scotland, and Wales). Unfortunately, these returns are not all extant. The inspection returns completed in America do not appear to have made it into the War Office files. Not every regiment has an extant return for each year, even when stationed in Britain or Ireland. Some inspection returns exist before 1766, but the period from 1767 through the rest of the years of the American Revolution appears to be generally complete.

Supplementing those records are the War Office Series 25 Commission and Succession Books that record each officer's commission. Some entries also include information on whether the commission was purchased or otherwise obtained, and sometimes initial commissions give some insight into whether the officer was being promoted from the ranks or was entering from civil life. Other entries are frustratingly meager. For determining the end of life for officers, the Records of the Prerogative Court of Canterbury, PROB (i.e., Probate) Series 11, Will Registers, were often helpful in determining an officer's family members and something about their personal wealth.

Additional manuscript sources include the variety of letters that were transmitted between the officers and their commanders in official capacities as well as unofficial letters between these officers and their superiors or their patrons. The Thomas Gage Papers in the William Clements Library at the University of Michigan is by far the richest resource of official letters, particularly regarding the Royal Irish officers' actual service in America. The Fredrick Haldimand Papers from the British Museum, the Amherst Papers—both those from the Center for Kentish Studies and those from the War Office 34 Series—helped round out the personalities of the officers and identify their problems, concerns, and ideas.

James Sullivan's *The Papers of Sir William Johnson* provided context for some of the officers, particularly those who remained in America after the French and Indian War. *The Journals of Lieut. Col. Stephen Kemble, 1773–1789* shed some additional light on the careers of those officers who remained in America as provincial officers, particularly Benjamin Charnock Payne and John Peter DeLancy.

Quartermaster George Buttricke's letters, published as "Affairs at Ft. Chartres" in the *Historical* magazine, help readers see service in Illinois through the eyes of the officers themselves. The Edward Hand Papers at Rockford Plantation in Lancaster, Pennsylvania, include some materials about Hand's British service and the accounts and operations of Captain Benjamin Johnson's Company, to which Hand was assigned as an ensign. The George Washington Papers at the Library of Congress, 1741–1799, and both the *Journals of the Continental Congress* and the *Papers of the Continental Congress* provided additional information about the officers of the Royal Irish, particularly about Alexander Fowler, Edward Hand, and Nicholas Trist and who remained in or returned to America after 1775. The Papers of the Trist, Randolph, and Burke Families, University of Virginia Archives, provided additional details about Alexander Fowler, John Lynn, and Nicholas Trist.

Stranded in Illinois, like the regiment that left the documents 225 years earlier, the Walter Elliott Papers are a few sets of extra-duty payrolls and similar mundane military documents that somehow found their way into the Illinois State Historical Society Collection in Springfield, Illinois. They are named for the man who served as a company paymaster sergeant. The Randolph County Papers in the Illinois Historical Society contain some spotty records from Colonel John Wilkins's court. Most likely the military records were left when the Royal Irish departed for Detroit in 1776, since it was planning to return. When it didn't, the pastor or an inventive parishioner repurposed the books to serve for the Catholic parishes in Illinois.

For those officers who crossed swords with military justice, the War Office 71 Series, Court Martial Proceedings and Board of General Officers'

Notes on Sources

Minutes, is a wonderful repository of trial transcripts often along with supporting documents and letters that help paint a more complete picture of each officer. In addition to being defendants in such a trial, many officers testified at one or more such proceedings. Each volume of the WO 71 Series has a table of contents at the front of the volume indentifying the defendant, his regiment, and his location. Don Hagist went further and created an index for the WO 71 Series from 1775 through 1783 for those courts-martial that took place in America, including the defendant, the court members, and the witnesses.

The War Office 72 Series, Records Relating to the Judge Advocate General's Office, which is less well organized and less often consulted than the WO 71 Series, provides a range of transcripts and pretrial documentation. The real limitation of the WO 71 Series is that records of the courts-martial in Ireland were kept separately in Dublin and were lost in a fire at the Dublin general post office near the turn of the twentieth century. Courts-martial conducted in America are included, but those conducted in Canada appear to have been lost.

Another manuscript source helpful in rounding out the records of the individual officers are the regimental agent's ledgers. Those of the Royal Irish are currently in the possession of Lloyd's of London, which is the successor organization to Cox & Meir, the regimental agent during the Royal Irish's American service. The ledgers consist of a single bound volume covering the period from July 1767 through 1775. The ledgers for a number of other regiments from the same period are also extant in the Lloyd's archive, including those of the 10th, 12th, and 55th Regiments of Foot.

A wide range of primary and secondary sources provided context for the information gleaned from the manuscripts. For a general overview of the Georgian army, see Alan Guy's "The Army of the Georges, 1714–1783" and Tony Hayter's "The Army and the First British Empire, 1714–1783" in David Chandler and Ian Beckett's *The Oxford History of the British Army*. John Houlding's *Fit for Service: The Training of the British Army, 1715–1795* covers the training of the Georgian army for the majority of the century. Houlding also addresses the issues of rotation of regiments and the effect of both overseas postings and the officer corps on the training of the regiments. These provide a basic overview of the army of King George III during the early portion of his reign and that of his namesake predecessors. Hew Strachan's work *The Politics of the British Army* puts the army in context with the political culture of Georgian England. Charles Messenger's *For Love of Regiment: A History of British Infantry, 1660–1914* helps put the Georgian army in context with the post-Napoleonic army that succeeded it.

Interpreting the regimental agent's ledgers requires an understanding of the British Army's administrative practices in the period. Both Alan Guy's *Oeconomy and Discipline: Officership and Administration in the British Army, 1714–1763* and Edward Curtis's *The Organization of the British Army in the American Revolution* provide excellent overviews of the administrative organization of the British Army during the period in question. Guy's text provides a more detailed overview than Curtis's. A subsection of the administration of the army was the system of commission purchasing that is the scope of Anthony Bruce's *The Purchase System of the British Army, 1660–1871*. Charles Clode's work *The Military Forces of the Crown: Their Administration and Government* was written in 1869 just as the purchase system was finally being dismantled, which makes for an interesting perspective on the system.

Stephen Brumwell's *Redcoats: The British Soldier and the War in America, 1755–1763* paints a fairly complete picture of the British Army's officers and other men during the French and Indian War. Using this text along with Stephan Conway's "British Army Officers and the American War for Independence" and M. F. Odnitz's dissertation from the University of Michigan, *The British Officer Corps, 1754-1783*, the reader can develop a fairly well-grounded understanding of the officers of the British Army from 1767 to 1780. Sylvia Frey's *The British Soldier in America: A Social History of Military Life* provides some additional context on the officers and other men of the British Army in North America during the Revolutionary War.

Further contextual information about the British Army in America directly before and during the American Revolution can be gathered by John Shy's *Toward Lexington: The Role of the British Army in the Coming of the American Revolution*, which explores the army and its relationship to the colonies in great detail. John Barker's diary, *The British in Boston: Being the Diary of Lieutenant John Barker of the King's Own Regiment from November 15, 1774, to May 31, 1776*, provides a window into the day-to-day happenings of the British troops in Boston. Using this source along with the extant orderly book of the 18th (Royal Irish) Regiment of Foot's Detachment at Boston from the National Army Museum in London and *General Sir*

Notes on Sources

William Howe's Orderly Book at Charlestown, Boston, and Halifax, a researcher can put together a remarkably detailed account of the troops at Boston in 1775. The Society of the Cincinnati Library in Washington, D.C., holds a bound manuscript volume called *Orders from Coxheath Camp* that provides a day-by-day account of the troops at Coxheath Camp in 1778.

Richard Frothingham's *History of the Siege of Boston and Bunker Hill* is dated but provides a great deal of detail about the army in Boston in 1775. The expansive collection of documents published by the U.S. Naval Historical Center as *Naval Documents of the American Revolution* provides a number of windows into the world of the officers of the Royal Irish. Its title is misleading, because the collection contains much about the army in Philadelphia, Boston, and New York as the war was beginning.

Specifically addressing the British Army's role on the pre–Revolutionary War frontier is Michael McConnell's *Army and Empire: British Soldiers on the American Frontier, 1758–1775*. McConnell tries to address the similarities and differences of military life on a frontier that stretched from the Great Lakes posts at Michlimackinac through Detroit and the Illinois posts down to Mobile and Pensacola in what was then called the Floridas. William Nester's Haughty *Conquerors: Amherst and the Great Indian Uprising of 1763* also addresses the frontier army, but more directly in the context of Pontiac's Uprising.

Jeffrey Spanbauer's unpublished master's thesis from Illinois State University, *Indian Affairs at Fort De Chartres during the British Occupation, 1765–1772*, provides an exhaustive look at one facet of the frontier military experience in Illinois. Matt Spring's book, *With Zeal and with Bayonets Only: The British Army on Campaign in North America, 1775–1783*, provides a deeper understanding of the tactics used by the army in battle and to some extent a deeper look into the mind of the British officers commanding the troops in the field on active campaign. John Jackson's *With the British Army in Philadelphia, 1777–1778* provides information about the barracks in Philadelphia where the Royal Irish were posted before the war. James Wilkinson's *Memoirs of My Own Times* provides an interesting perspective on the officers and the parade ground of the Royal Irish in prewar Philadelphia.

The Royal Irish's service upon its return to Britain must be viewed within the environment of the Franco-Spanish invasion threat and the concerns of a second world war in the space of slightly more than a decade. Alfred Temple Patterson's *The Other Armada: The Franco-Spanish Attempt to Invade Britain in 1779* is still the definitive book on the British preparation to thwart the invasion. Backing up to the invasion threat was the most violent British civil protest of the eighteenth century, the Gordon Riots. John Nicholson's *The Great Liberty Riot of 1780* provides a background for the Gordon Riots along with Nicholas Rogers's *Crowds, Culture, and Politics in Georgian Britain* and John Archer's *Social Unrest and Popular Protest in England, 1780 to 1840*.

The Amherst Papers, the War Office 34 Series, and Marching and Militia Orders (English), the War Office 5 Series, allow a researcher to track a regiment's postings throughout England. These allowed for a careful tracking of the Royal Irish from 1776 through 1781. Unfortunately, the Irish marching orders have been lost.

The two complete histories of the Royal Irish Regiment itself, Richard Cannon's 1844 *Historical Record of the 18th (Royal Irish) Regiment of Foot* and George Gretton's 1911 *The Campaigns and History of the Royal Irish Regiment*, cover the regiment's North American service only in broad strokes. Both contain errors about the specifics of the regiment's American service. Other regimental histories were often helpful in the development of this text, including Lewis Butler's *The Annals of the King's Royal Rifle Corps*, Francis Duncan's *The History of the Royal Regiment of Artillery*, and John Percy Groves's *Historical Records of the 7th or Royal Regiment of Fusiliers*. George Raikers's *Roll of Officers of the York and Lancaster Regiment, Formerly 65th (2nd Yorkshire, North Riding)* was particularly helpful in filling out the information about the officers of the 65th Foot that served with the Royal Irish in Boston.

A large number of county, family, and regional histories were helpful in providing information or context for individual officers. Theodore Calvin Pease's *The Story of Illinois* and Clarence Alvord's multiple volumes about colonial Illinois were helpful in developing the story of the Royal Irish in Illinois. Similarly, Charles Dahlinger's *Pittsburgh: A Sketch of its Early Social Life* was helpful in rounding out information about Alexander Fowler's career after he separated from the British military.

Supporting information could be gathered from a wide range of electronic databases as well. The *Assessors' "Taking Books" of the Town of Boston 1780* is available online and helped pinpoint John Lynn's postmilitary career. *Episcopal Visitation Returns, 1779* are online and helped define Stanley Leathes's clerical career. *The Proceedings of the Old Bailey, London's Central Criminal Court* from 1674 through 1913 is also online. Todd Braisted's Online Institute for Advanced Loyalist Studies has a wealth of primary materials on the British provincial troops and was extremely helpful in tracking the service histories of the officers who served in provincial units.

Rounding out the primary sources were several orderly books that illuminated the specific assignments of individual officers. A few other manuscript sources were utilized from the UK National Archives, including the Log of HMS *Asia* (Admiralty Records Series 36/8080), the American Loyalist Claims, Series 2 (Audit Office, AO Series 13) and the Colonial Office Papers of the Secretary of State for America and the West Indies (Series 5).

Many contemporary newspapers were used. The *London Gazette* provided regular updates on promotions in the British Army and is available online. The *Pennsylvania Gazette* provided many articles on the Royal Irish and its officers. The *Gentleman's Magazine*, the *Royal Military Calendar*, and the *Scots Magazine* were other contemporary periodicals that provided regular updates on the officers of the British Army and proved useful in the development of this text.

Notes

Abbreviations Used in the Notes

DNB	*Dictionary of National Biography*
Gage Papers	Thomas Gage Papers, William Clements Library, University of Michigan, Ann Arbor
Haldimand Papers	Fredrick Haldimand Papers, British Museum Additional Manuscripts, London
Hand Papers	Edward Hand Papers, Rockford Plantation Manuscripts, Lancaster, Pennsylvania
JCC	*Journals of the Continental Congress*
NDAR	*Naval Documents of the Revolution,* U.S. Department of the Navy
PCC	Papers of the Continental Congress
Trist Papers	Papers of the Trist, Randolph and Burke Families, University of Virginia, Charlottesville
Wilmot Papers	Wilmot-Horton of Osmaston and Catton Correspondence, Derbyshire Record Office, Matlock, Derbyshire, UK

NATIONAL ARCHIVES (UK) COLLECTIONS

ADM	Admiralty Office Series
AO	Audit Office Series
Army Lists	List of all the General Officers of the Army; The Officers of the Several Troops, Regiments, Independent Companies and Garrisons; also WO 65 Series
CO	Colonial Office Series
PROB	Records of the Prerogative Court of Canterbury Series
T	Treasury Office Series
WO	War Office Series

Introduction

1. Kohn, 564–67.

THE EARLY HISTORY OF THE REGIMENT

2. Messenger, 1:16.
3. Richards, 264.
4. Cannon, 2–17.
5. Messenger, 1:25.
6. Ibid., 28.
7. Cannon, 32–35, 42–43.
8. Sir William Cosby (1690–10 March 1736) served as the colonel of the Royal Irish from 1717 until his death. From 1732 until his death, he also served as the governor of New York.
9. Houlding, 400.
10. Cannon, 43–46; Gretton, 76–78; and War Office Series (hereafter WO) 27/4, Inspection Return of the 18th (Royal Irish) Regiment of Foot, October 1755.
11. Cannon, 46–47; Gretton, 77; Houlding, 418, 421; and Desbrisay, 1750–1754.
12. Robert Walsh was promoted from lieutenant to captain in the Royal Irish on 4 September 1754. He remained with the Royal Irish until he was promoted to major of the 54th Regiment of Foot on 10 May 1758. Walsh was promoted to lieutenant colonel in the army on 9 January 1762 and was promoted to that rank in the 54th Foot on 16 January 1765. Walsh sold his commission on 26 October 1775. Charles Edmonstone replaced him in the Royal Irish. WO 65.
13. WO 27/4, Inspection Return of the Royal Irish Regiment, October 1755. Of the 232 men enlisted since June 1754, 217 were present with the regiment. One had died, three had been discharged, and nine had deserted. WO 65.
14. The regiment was renumbered as the 54th Foot in 1757. That regiment embarked as marines in May 1756 and sailed to Gibraltar under Admiral John Byng. After service as marines, these men remained at Gibraltar as part of the garrison until 1765. Chichester and Burgess-Short, 516–17; and Houlding, 402.
15. Desbrisay, 1757.
16. Houlding, 98.

NORTH AMERICAN SERVICE

17. Cannon, 46.
18. WO 4/988, Lord Barrington to Thomas Gage, 14 February 1767.
19. Guy, "The Army of the Georges," 97; Hayter, 112; and Houlding, 20–22.
20. Houlding, 20–22, 412–13; and Shy, 274–77.
21. For a complete explanation of drafting in the eighteenth-century British Army, see Guy, *Oeconomy and Discipline*, 126–27; and Houlding, 120–25. As it relates to the rotation of troops, see Houlding, 48–50.
22. WO 12/4649, Muster Rolls of the 31st Regiment of Foot; and WO 12/2666, Muster Rolls of the 8th (King's) Regiment of Foot. Similarly, when the 55th Foot was ordered home in January 1765 at the end of the French and Indian War, the king ordered the soldiers drafted "into the Other Corps serving in North

America." Only the officers, NCOs, and drummers embarked for Ireland. Thomas Waite to Thomas Gage, 29 January 1765, Gage Papers.

23. WO 27/14, Return of the 50th Regiment of Foot, 1768; WO 8/5/121, Return of Drafts to Regiments Embarked for America, 21 October 1767. In total, 794 men were drafted into the four regiments bound from Ireland to America, according to Houlding, 123. For an explanation of the issues related to a separate Irish Establishment and the difficulties it caused in troop rotation, see Shy, 275–78.

24. *Dublin Journal*, 23 May 1767; and *Pennsylvania Gazette*, 16 July 1767. Edward Hand's log, Hand Papers, shows 20 May as its first entry.

25. Edward Hand, unpublished journal, 1767, Hand Papers.

26. Watson, 361–62; and Jackson, 20–22.

27. Cresson, 187.

28. Buttricke, 4; see also *Pennsylvania Gazette*, 29 October 1767.

29. Thomas Gage to John Wilkins, 5 May 1768, Gage Papers.

30. Hazard, 10:17.

31. WO 71/77, Court martial of Patrick Brannon.

32. WO 71/77, Court martial of Pvt. Bluett, 34th Foot.

33. Leake to Thomas Gage, 18 January 1772, Gage Papers.

34. WO 71/77, 73–82.

35. Alvord, *Mississippi Valley*, 1:86–132.

36. Buttricke, 5–6. The Royal Irish appears to have been transferred to the British Establishment upon arrival at Philadelphia on 11 July 1767. However, Boyle, 66, gives the date as 25 June.

37. Buttricke, 7–9.

38. Thomas Gage to Earl of Hillsborough, 6 January 1770, Gage Papers.

39. Gage to Hillsborough, 18 August 1770, Gage Papers.

40. Gage to Hillsborough, 1 October 1771, Gage Papers.

41. Wilkins to Gage, 7 April 1772, Gage Papers.

42. Gage to Hillsborough, 6 January 1770, Gage Papers.

43. Dunn, 100; and Thomas Gage to Lord Dalrymple, 21 April 1771, Gage Papers. For an overview of the Falkland Island crisis of 1770–1771, see Rice, 273–305.

44. Report of ordnance stores issued at Fort Chartres from 26 May 1771 to 31 March 1772, in Wilkins to Gage, 7 April 1772, Gage Papers.

45. Gage to Hillsborough, 6 January 1770, Gage Papers.

46. Boyle, 67; and Hayter, 119. Boyle gives 3 September 1771 as the date when the regiment was authorized to raise a company of light infantry.

47. Sumner, 146.

48. Benjamin Chapman to Thomas Gage, 15 December 1771, Gage Papers.

CAPTAIN HUGH LORD'S DETACHMENT IN ILLINOIS

49. Huston, 317–29.

50. Charles Edmonstone to Thomas Gage, 1 March 1772, Gage Papers.

51. Gage to Wilkins, 9 March 1772, Gage Papers; see also Gage to Hillsborough, 4 March 1772, Gage Papers.

52. Isaac Hamilton to Thomas Gage, 8 August 1772, Gage Papers.

53. Hugh Lord to Thomas Gage, 10 June 1772, Gage Papers.
54. Ibid.
55. "Extra Duty Payroll for the Lieut. Colonel's Company, 18th Foot, June 24 to Dec. 25, 1774," Walter Elliot Papers.
56. Gage to Barrington, 21 July 1775, Gage Papers.
57. Russell, 292.
58. Pease, 38–42.

ATLANTIC SEABOARD SERVICE

59. Hamilton to Gage, 5 August 1772, Gage Papers.
60. Gage to Edmonstone, 10 May 1772, Gage Papers.
61. Hamilton to Gage, 12 December 1772, Gage Papers.
62. *Pennsylvania Gazette*, 28 July and 10 November 1773.
63. Wilkinson, I: 12–13.
64. Boyle, 63–68.
65. Barker, 43.
66. WO 36/3, "Lost and Broken Equipment for April 19, 1775."
67. Dann, 6–8; Sewell, 363–64; and Shattuck, 117.
68. Cannon, 48.
69. WO 71/81, 2–165, Court martial of Benjamin Charnock Payne; and WO 71/81, 401–4, Court martial of A. Fowler.
70. Boyle, 63–68.
71. Lord Dartmouth to Thomas Gage, 2 August 1775, Gage Papers.
72. Howe, 159.
73. Houlding, 124–25.

Chapter 1: The Officer Corps of the 18th (Royal Irish) Regiment

1. Houlding, 104.
2. Guy, "The Army of the Georges," 105.
3. Curtis, 37–38. Guy, *Oeconomy and Discipline*, 59–62, provides an excellent overview of the work of the regimental agent.
4. The firm Cox & Drummond became Cox & Meir by 1776.
5. Clode, 62–64.
6. Hamilton to Gage, 20 July 1775, Gage Papers.
7. Wilkins to Gage, 4 May 1774, Gage Papers. Houlding, 107, cites a similar situation in which the colonel of the 39th Foot in 1747 went out of his way to ensure that neither of the two senior captains in the regiment succeeded to a vacant majority because "the first was a rogue and the second incapable."
8. Guy, "The Army of the Georges," 105; see also Guy, *Oeconomy and Discipline*, 90; and Houlding, 102–3.
9. Strachan, 22.
10. John Ellis to Thomas Gage, 9 October 1764, Gage Papers.
11. Bruce, 25; Guy, *Oeconomy and Discipline*, 137–38; Guy, "The Army of the Georges," 104; Strachan, 199; and Arthur Wadman to John Wilkins, 21 February 1771, included in Gage to Wilkins, 20 February 1771, Gage Papers.

THE MAKEUP OF THE OFFICER CORPS

12. WO 27/35, Returns of the 42nd (Royal Highland) Regiment of Foot; WO 27/39, Return of the 18th (Royal Irish) Regiment of Foot, 1787; and WO 27/52, Return of the 42nd (Royal Highland) Regiment of Foot.

13. Brumwell, 319.

14. WO 27/33 and 27/34, English Inspection Returns for 1775; and *1772 Review of Troops in Ireland*.

15. Odnitz, 212; Guy, *Oeconomy and Discipline*, 89; and Strachan 23.

16. WO 72/7, Court of Inquiry Records Relating to Rev. Mr. Robert Newburgh; *1772 Review of Troops in Ireland;* and Curtis, 12–13. Brudenell was immortalized in George Bernard Shaw's play *The Devil's Disciple: A Melodrama* in 1897, set during the Saratoga campaign.

17. WO 65.

18. Guy, *Oeconomy and Discipline*, 13–14; Conway, 265–76; and Duke of Northumberland to Lord Barrington, in Barrington to Gage, 14 May 1768, Gage Papers. According to WO 65, Henry Pulleine was commissioned as the major of the 16th Foot on 15 June 1764 and retired on 19 May 1771. He was replaced as major by Alexander Dickson, the 16th Foot's senior captain.

19. Brumwell, 86.

20. WO 34/188/111, [November 1779?]. John Sebright is shown on the list of field officers at Warley Camp along with Lieutenant Colonel Adam Williamson and Major John Shee, but it is not clear whether he was actually present or simply listed. All the regiments listed show their colonels present, so the listing might not have been meant to show actual attendance.

21. Conway, 265–76; WO 12/3501, Returns of the 18th (Royal Irish) Regiment of Foot; and WO 27/11, 27/36, and 27/42, Inspection Returns of the 18th (Royal Irish) Regiment of Foot.

22. Bruce, 74, 161; Houlding, 105; Patterson, 118; Odnitz, 180–84; and Baule and Gilbert.

23. Brumwell, 94–95.

24. WO 65; and Thomas Gilfillan to James Grant, 5 April 1776, James Grant Papers.

25. Brumwell, 92–93.

26. WO 34/231, Jeffery Amherst to Lord North, 30 July 1779.

27. Even though Thomas Dixon served as the 75th's initial quartermaster, his name was not included among those whose appointments were announced in the 20 June 1778 issue of the *London Gazette*. Dixon was promoted to ensign in 1780 and later to lieutenant in the 75th Foot. WO 25/211, 75th Foot.

28. In the mounted services, a quartermaster was the senior enlisted soldier in a troop of horse or dragoons. Although the title is the same as a regimental quartermaster in a regiment of foot, the quartermaster in a regiment of foot is a commissioned officer. Quartermasters in mounted regiments were warrant officers.

29. *London Gazette*, 13 and 20 June 1778.

30. Kehoe, 10; and WO 65.

31. Maurice, 1:184, 295. It is possible, but not probable, that Sergeant Major William Campbell, who was killed in action while serving as the adjutant for the brigade of guards in America, was promoted posthumously to ensign in the Scots guards, but no official record of his promotion exists.

32. *London Gazette*, 5 May 1778, 25 July 1778, 5 October 1779, 4 December 1779, and 25 April 1780.

33. Pace, n.p.

OFFICER CAREERS

34. WO 65.

35. Baule and Gilbert, 21, 77; *1772 Review of Troops in Ireland*, 9; and Brown and Russell, 227.

36. Chambers, 580; see also Colonel Sir Henry Walton Ellis, available at http://british-cemetery-elvas.org/ellis.html, which lists his age as nine when he received the lieutenancy.

37. Odnitz, 258.

38. WO 27/34, Inspection Returns, British Establishment, 1775.

39. WO 27/12, Inspection Return of the 8th (King's) Regiment, 1768; and WO 27/14, Inspection Returns, Irish Establishment.

40. WO 27/11 and WO 27/36, Inspection Returns for the 18th (Royal Irish) Regiment of Foot, 1767 and 1777.

41. WO 27/52, Inspection Return of the 1/42nd Regiment of Foot, 1784.

42. Houlding, 108–13.

43. Strachan, 26.

COURTS-MARTIAL AND DISCIPLINE

44. WO 71/81, 401–4, Court martial of Lt. Alexander Fowler.

45. WO 71/81, 401, Court martial of Lt. Alexander Fowler.

46. WO 71/80, 1–175, Court martial of Robert Newburgh.

47. Gage to Hamilton, 14 November 1774, Gage Papers.

48. Alexander Fowler to John Wilkins, 16 May 1774, enclosed in Wilkins to Gage, 6 July 1774, Gage Papers.

49. Wilkins to Gage, 3 August 1774, Gage Papers.

50. WO 71/79, 234–57, Court martial of John Green; and House of Lords, Journal Office 10/7/544, regimental court-martial data from Ireland enclosed in correspondence of William Tatum, 17 November 2009.

WIVES AND CHILDREN

51. Barrington to Gage, 22 June 1775, Gage Papers.

52. Baule and Gilbert, 22, 37.

53. WO 25, Commission Registers.

54. WO 12/3501, Returns of the 18th (Royal Irish) Regiment of Foot; *London Gazette*, 19 June 1787; and Philippart, 2:3–5.

55. Odnitz, 256–58; and Brumwell, 85.

56. Odnitz, 254.

THE OFFICERS' BIOGRAPHIES

57. For an overview of the reading habits of British officers in this period, see Gruber.

Chapter 2: The Field Officers

1. WO 65.
2. Houlding, 107–9; and Guy, "The Army of the Georges," 101.
3. For a detailed explanation of the fiscal advantages of commanding a company, see Guy, *Oeconomy and Discipline*, 88–115.

HENRY FOLLIOTT

4. John Folliot was also the governor of Ross Castle and a member of the Irish Parliament for Sligo. He was appointed to the colonelcy of the Royal Irish on 22 December 1747, after serving as the colonel of the 61st Regiment of Foot from 1743. Cannon, 80, states that John Folliot was colonel of the 62nd Foot (disbanded) and died in January 1762.
5. WO 25; and WO 27/4, Return of the 18th (Royal Irish) Regiment of Foot, October 1755.
6. WO 65; and J & J Limited Company.
7. Wilkins to Gage, 27 July 1767, Gage Papers. The Cox & Meir ledgers begin in July 1767, when the regiment arrived in America. Before that date, William Montgomery of Dublin was the regimental agent.
8. WO 12/3501, Muster rolls of the 18th (Royal Irish) Regiment of Foot; WO 27/11, Irish Establishment; Returns for 1767; WO 65; and Knox, 4.
9. Vicars, 105.
10. Cox & Meir, Ledgers of the 18th (Royal Irish) Regiment of Foot, 5–5c.

ISAAC HAMILTON

11. WO 65. The 1755 army list shows his ensigncy as dating from 9 October 1749. Millan shows Hamilton as the senior ensign from 9 November 1749; and Desbrisay, 13.
12. Gage to Hamilton, 8 December 1771, Gage Papers.
13. Wilkinson, 1:13.
14. Nicholas Trist to Elizabeth House Trist, 1 September 1774, Trist Papers.
15. Isaac Hamilton to James Moncrief, 11 July 1774, and Hamilton to Gage, 2 August 1774, Gage Papers.
16. WO 71/81, 2–165, Court martial of Captain Benjamin Charnock Payne.
17. Memorial of Isaac Hamilton to Gage, 20 July 1775, Gage Papers.
18. Barrington to Gage, 22 June 1775, Gage Papers; see also Conway, 265–76.
19. Fowler to Wilkins, 4 October 1774, in Wilkins to Gage, 4 April 1775, Gage Papers.
20. Hamilton to Gage, 20 July 1775, Gage Papers; WO 12/3501, Muster rolls of the 18th (Royal Irish) Regiment of Foot; WO 27/11, Irish Establishment Returns for 1767; WO 65; and WO 71/81.

21. WO 25/20, Commission Books.

22. The date for raising the regiment in Ireland is given as 16 October 1757 on http://www.regiments.org.

23. WO 65; Bigoe Armstrong, a lieutenant colonel of the Royal Irish, was promoted to colonel of the 83rd in Sebright's place. For more information on the Portuguese campaign, see Francis.

24. Namier and Brooke, 2:342.

25. Ibid., 2:306, 2:366–376, and 2:419.

26. The *London Gazette*, 23 November 1782, reported his promotion to general as 26 November 1782.

27. Schnitzer, n.p.

28. Cannon, 89, gives the date as 1765, but Valentine, 2:778, gives the date as 1761. Valentine lists Sebright as joining the guards in 1744 and being promoted to captain in the same year.

29. *Gentleman's Magazine*, May 1766. Secondary sources locate the wedding at St. George's, Hannover Square, London, with the same date.

30. WO 4/122/395, War Office to John Saunders Sebright, 1 August 1783; and WO 27/39, 1787 Inspection Return of the 18th (Royal Irish) Regiment of Foot. See also *Edinburgh Advertiser*, 14 May 1790, 4 June 1790, and 6 May 1794.

31. *Edinburgh Advertiser*, 29 July, 5 August, 14 October, and 31 October 1794. See also *London Gazette*, 24 January 1794.

32. *The Book of Leinster* dates from about 1150 and is the earliest book entirely in Irish. It is an anthology of Irish prose, verse, and genealogy that takes its name from an ecclesiastical foundation in Laois County. *The Yellow Book of Lecan* is dated no later than the early fifteenth century. It is a composite manuscript, containing medical tracts; grammatical and aphoristic material; the famous glossary "Sanas Chormaic," attributed to Cormac Mac Cuileannáin; and miscellaneous prose tales, including almost the whole of the Ulster Cycle. Koch, 1126.

33. *Daily Universal Register*, 8 April 1786. See also *Times*, 6 November 1789; 28 February 1788; and 19 January 1792.

34. Cannon, 80; Valentine, 778.

JOHN SHEE

35. Also known as Ballreddin or Ballyreddin.

36. Shee is listed as being Irish in the 1777 Inspection Return of the Royal Irish, although no nationality is given for him in the 1767 return. He is also listed as Shea in some records, but his own signature was always Shee. Carrigan, 3:61–62; and WO 27/11, Inspection Return of the 18th (Royal Irish) Regiment of Foot.

37. WO 71/77, 73, Court martial of James Robertson, private soldier in the 34th Foot.

38. WO 12/3501, Returns of the 18th (Royal Irish) Regiment of Foot; and WO 71/79, Court martial of Nicholas Gaffney, 345–53.

39. Fowler to Wilkins, 24 October 1774, and Robert Newburgh to John Wilkins, 17 December 1774, Gage Papers.

40. Captain Charles Edmonstone was senior to Shee but does not ever appear in command except at Fort Pitt.

41. *Boston Gazette*, 13 February 1775.

42. WO 71/80, 207–65, Court martial of Ensign Somerville Murray, 43rd Foot.

43. Petition of George Bruere to King George III, n.d., Gage Papers.

44. WO 71/80, 375–80, Court martial of William Beck, 43rd Foot; WO 71/82, 90–102, Court martial of William Shields, 10th Foot; and WO 71/82, 102–15, Court martial of Lt. Edward McGouran, Royal Fensible [*sic*] American Regt.

45. WO 72/8, Shee to Judge Advocate General (JAG), 22 October 1777, and JAG to Mawby, 16 November 1777.

46. *Orders at Coxheath Camp*; WO 71/54, Court martial of Bryan Sheridan, 18th Foot, 31 August 1778.

47. Randolph County Records, 4–2 Court of Judicatory, 1768–1770; WO 12/3501, Muster rolls of the 18th (Royal Irish) Regiment of Foot; WO 27/11, Irish Establishment Returns for 1767; WO 27/36, British Establishment Returns for 1777; WO 65; and WO 71/79.

48. WO 27/47, Inspection Return of the 75th Foot, 18 August 1781.

49. An Edward Shee is listed as a prisoner taken at Vincennes on a list of 9 March 1779. It is possible (but not probable) that this was another son who for some reason remained in Illinois when Shee returned to Philadelphia with his company. Fowler to Wilkins, 16 May 1774, included in Wilkins to Gage, 6 July 1774, Gage Papers.

50. The stone, now in the ruins of the church, reads as follows: "Near this place lie interred the remains of Col. Shee who died Novr. 1822, aged 19 years. And underneath this stone are interred the remains of John Shee Esq. his eldest son who died in September 1839 aged x years. And of Richard Shee his third son who died 29th Dec. 1845 aged x years." Most likely, the 1822 date is an error in either transcription or engraving. Breen, n.p.

51. The gravestone of his father, Marcus Shee, reads as follows: "Underneath this stone lies interred the body of Marcus Shee Esq. Doctor of Physick who departed this life the 23rd of December 1762 at the age of 55. On the right of this stone lies also interred the body of James Shee Esq., son of the above Marcus who died on the 3rd of August 1783 aged 37 years." Ibid.

JOHN WILKINS

52. England and Wales Christening Records, 1530–1906.

53. W. Smith, *Works*, 1:411.

54. WO 65, The 1767 inspection return for the 18th (Royal Irish) Regiment of Foot lists his captaincy as dating from 30 December 1755. See also *Scots Magazine*, August 1764.

55. Swiney, 299; and WO 25/21. The rank titles of the 32nd Foot were changed from second lieutenant to ensign in 1752.

56. Wilkins to Gage, 25 December 1771, Gage Papers.

57. Nester, 145–70.

58. Wallace, 85; and Butler, 128 and 199. The 4th Battalion of the 60th Regiment had returned to England in 1762 to be disbanded. However, Wilkins exchanged

with Munster, according to General Gage. Thomas Gage to Henry Bouquet, 11 November 1764, Gage Papers.

59. WO 71/77, 73, Court martial of James Robertson, Private Soldier in the 34th Foot.

60. Gage to Barrington, 15 May 1768, Gage Papers.

61. Brown, *History of Illinois*, 13–215; Alvord and Carter, xiv–xv; and Buttricke, 12.

62. Alvord, 267; Alvord and Carter, 473; and Pease, 27–28.

63. Pease, 28–29. Storm, 12, relates that the conditions were so grim at Fort Chartres that one officer took his own life. However, there does not appear to be any primary-source confirmation of that allegation.

64. Brown, *History of Illinois*, 215; see also Smith, *America State Papers*, 2:180. Wilkins appears to have signed his name to land deeds as "John Wilkins, Esquire, Lieutenant-Colonel of His Majesty's Eighteenth Royal Regiment of Ireland and Governor and Commandant through the Illinois County." Dillon, 102.

65. Buttricke, 10; Wilkins journal, 16 May 1769, Gage Papers; Spanbauer, 56–58.

66. Carter, 1, 73–74; "Journal of Transactions and Presents Given the Indians," enclosed in Wilkins to Gage, 1 June 1772, Gage Papers; Johnson, 7:132–40; Spanbauer, 302–3.

67. Spanbauer, 129–30.

68. Spanbauer, 61; WO 71/79, 231–344, Court martial of Nicholas Gaffney.

69. Wilkins to Gage, 25 December 1771, Gage Papers.

70. Officers of the 18th Foot to Gage, in Isaac Hamilton to Gage, 29 April 1773, Gage Papers; see also Wilkins to Gage, 3 August 1774, Gage Papers.

71. Lord Barrington to John Wilkins, 1 February 1775, and Barrington to Gage, 22 June 1775, Gage Papers.

72. Wilkins to Gage, 4 May 1774, Gage Papers.

73. Wilkins to Gage, 10 January 1772, Wilkins to Gage, 7 October 1772, and Wilkins to Gage, March 1773, Gage Papers; WO 65; and Storm, 9–22.

74. Treasury Board Papers and In-Letters, T 1/525/127–28, Petition of Lt. Colonel John Wilkins to the Right Honourable Lords of the Treasury, 28 February 1776.

75. PROB (Records of the Prerogative Court of Canterbury and Related Probate Jurisdictions; subsequent numbers refer to register and quire numbers) 11/1178/11, the Will of John Wilkins; and Churchill, 2:li.

ADAM WILLIAMSON

76. Williamson is listed as being born in 1735 in Valentine, 2:934.

77. *Orders at Coxheath Camp*, n.p.

78. *Times* (London), 27 April and 22 July 1790.

79. "The Life of Sir Brent Spencer," 235–42; and *DNB*, 42:2–3.

80. Society of Arts, 9:329–72.

81. U.K. and U.S. Directories, 1680–1830; and *Biography Database, 1680–1830*.

82. Farrar, 192.

83. WO 65; WO 12/3501; and Valentine, 2:934–35. Some secondary sources list his place of death as Jamaica.

Chapter 3: *The Captains and Captain Lieutenants*

HUGH ANTROBUS

1. Antrobus, 33–34, 104. Antrobus lists his baptismal year as 1729.

2. Hugh's siblings were Reverend George Antrobus, who married Jane Carpenter (also Cullen); Sarah, who died in 1776; Charles; and Elizabeth, who married Michael Sweeny of Dublin. Antrobus, 104–5.

3. WO 25/23, Commission Book, gives this date for Antrobus's ensigncy, but WO 27/11, Inspection Return of the 18th (Royal Irish) Regiment of Foot, lists it as 27 March 1754, which is an error.

4. WO 65. The 1755 army list shows a handwritten date of 3 October 1755 and a notation that Antrobus was from the 14th Foot.

5. *Pennsylvania Gazette*, 16 July 1767.

6. WO 12/3501, Muster rolls of the 18th (Royal Irish) Regiment of Foot; WO 27/11, Irish Establishment Returns for 1767; WO 65; and Antrobus, 104. Lieutenant Colonel Hugh Antrobus Jr. married Eliza Naughton of Thornhill in 1805. He was listed in his own will as being from Ballinlass, County Galway.

7. Cox & Meir, Ledgers of the 18th Regiment, 8.

THOMAS BATT

8. WO 65; Robert Batt was listed as a volunteer when first commissioned as an ensign in the Royal Irish on 26 August 1747. He was commissioned as lieutenant on 25 November 1752, and became a captain in the Royal Irish Regiment on 28 June 1756, where he remained until selling his commission to George Stainforth on 3 May 1765. The elder Batt also served as the Royal Irish's quartermaster from 24 April 1755 until 9 August 1756.

9. Sutton's testimony is part of WO 71/77, 80, Court martial of Robert Clay.

10. Samuel Wharton to William Johnson, 23 March 1768, Johnson, 6:171.

11. WO 27/11, Inspection Return of the 18th (Royal Irish) Regiment of Foot, April 11, 1767; and WO 71/77, 73.

12. West. Batt's wife is also listed as Catharine. She was born in Philadelphia on 20 November 1747.

13. WO 71/79; Ford, 13, 51; WO 65, 1775 Army List; and Wilkins to Gage, 7 April 1772, Gage Papers.

14. Hood, 61, 99, 100.

15. WO 71/80, 1–175, Court martial of Alexander Fowler; and "Case of Alexander Fowler," *General Advertiser & Intelligencer*, 29 July 1778.

16. Audit Office (hereafter AO) 13/70B, 124–25, Memorial of Catherine Batt of Pennsylvania to the Right Honourable the Lords Commissioners of his Majesty's Treasury, n.d.

17. Barker, 54.

18. "Case of Alexander Fowler," *General Advertiser & Intelligencer*, 29 July 1778.

19. Gorham's Proposal to Raise a Battalion of Light Infantry, 15 April 1775; Thomas Gage to Thomas Batt, 7 June 1775; and Gage to Batt, 11 August 1775, Gage Papers.

20. WO 1/681/57, Return of Officers of the Royal Fencible Americans, http://www.royalprovincial.com/Military/rhist/rfa/rfaretn.htm.

21. WO 30/55/676, American Headquarters Papers, Howe to Gorham, 27 November 1777; Kemble, 1:368; and General Orders, Head Quarters, Halifax, 23 May 1776. Other sources give the date as 26 May 1776.

22. Howe, 290; and Donkin, n.p.

23. Harvey, 8–9. Goreham listed the reinforcement as 209 men. Eddy estimated 400 men in Batt's reinforcement.

24. Eddy's version of the events has Batt's sortie occurring on 30 November 1777. Harvey, 8–9.

25. Coldham, 450.

26. John Bayard to Henry Clinton, June 22, 1780, Sir Henry Clinton Papers, vol. 105, item 47.

27. WO 30/55/2829, Lieut. Colonel Commandant Goreham of the Royal Fencible American Regiment, Complaint or Crime Exhibited against Major Thomas Batt of the Same Regiment, n.d.

28. Rivington, 1779 (n.p.); Katcher, 99, who lists the Royal Fencible Americans as being disbanded in 1783; and Flint, 477. The Royal Fencible Americans served the entire war in Nova Scotia. It was one of the provincial regiments voted for half pay by the House of Commons on 17 June 1783.

29. M. Clark, *Loyalists,* 3:384.

30. Burial Records, Christ Church, Philadelphia.

31. Baptismal Records, Christ Church, Philadelphia, 1769 to 1794; M. Clark, *Loyalists in the Southern Campaign,* 3:356; and Sabine, 2:477. It is possible that Thomas Batt Jr. returned to active British military service in the 26th (Cameronians) Regiment of Foot. If that is the case, his ensigncy in the 26th dated from 13 July 1791, and he was promoted to lieutenant on 16 October 1793. There is no direct evidence that the man in the 26th Foot is the son of Batt, but it is possible, and the Cameronians were stationed in Canada at the time. Kitzmiller, 544.

WILLIAM BLACKWOOD

32. Although Blackwood was listed as eighteen years old in the April 1767 return, in the May 1777 return, he was listed as twenty-seven, not twenty-eight.

33. WO 12/3501, Returns of the 18th (Royal Irish) Regiment; and WO 27/11, Inspection Return of the 18th (Royal Irish) Regiment of Foot.

34. Fowler to Wilkins, 16 May 1774, and Wilkins to Gage, 3 August 1774, Gage Papers.

35. Orderly Book of the 18th Regiment of Foot, 16 April 1775.

36. WO 12/3501, Returns of the 18th (Royal Irish) Regiment of Foot; WO 71/82: Court martial of Thomas Bailey, Marine, 137–52; Court martial of Richard James, 10th Foot, 152–58; and Court martial of Lt. Wm. Hamilton, 158–88.

37. WO 27/42, Inspection Return of the 18th (Royal Irish) Regiment of Foot; WO 12/3501, Returns of the 18th (Royal Irish) Regiment of Foot; and WO 71/148, Courts martial of William Green and Henry Knight, privates in the 18th Regiment of Foot.

38. WO 27/39, Inspection Return of the 18th (Royal Irish) Regiment of Foot, 29 March 1787 (misfiled with earlier returns); and WO 12/3501, Returns of the 18th (Royal Irish) Regiment of Foot.

39. *Edinburgh Advertiser*, 4 June 1790.

40. WO 65; and *London Gazette*, 6 July 1790.

41. PROB 11/1242/269, Will of William Blackwood.

BENJAMIN CHAPMAN

42. WO 12/3501; and WO 27/11.

43. WO 71/77, 73, Court martial of James Robertson, private soldier in the 34th Foot.

44. Benjamin Chapman to John Wilkins, 20 January 1770, Gage Papers.

45. Gage to Chapman, 4 December 1771, and Gage to Wilkins, 5 February 1773, Gage Papers; WO 12/3501, Muster rolls of the 18th (Royal Irish) Regiment of Foot; WO 27/11, Irish Establishment Returns for 1767; WO 27/36, British Establishment Returns for 1777; and *Pennsylvania Gazette*, 7 November 1771.

46. Chapman to Gage, 28 May 1774, and Robert Newburgh to Thomas Gage, 7 August 1774, Gage Papers.

47. Barker, 26.

48. WO 71/80, 266–327, Court martial of Lt. Colonel Walcott and Ensign Patrick.

49. WO 71/148, Courts martial of William Green and Henry Knight, privates in the 18th Regiment of Foot.

50. WO 71/54, Court martial of Bryan Sheridan, 31 August 1778.

51. WO 27/39, Inspection Return of the 18th (Royal Irish) Regiment, 1787; WO 27/39, British Establishment Returns for 1779; WO 65; and *Salisbury & Winchester Journal*, 2 June 1788.

52. *London Gazette*, 22 May 1790.

53. *Scots Magazine*, 9 October 1790.

54. WO 65.

55. "The Infamous George Durant," BBC, 2008, http://www.bbc.co.uk/shropshire/content/articles/2007/03/02/slavery__george_durant_feature.shtml.

56. PROB 11/1760/195, Will of Benjamin Chapman.

CHARLES EDMONSTONE

57. WO 25; WO 65; WO 27/11, Inspection Return of the 18th (Royal Irish) Regiment of Foot, 11 April 1767; and WO 12/3501, Muster rolls of the 18th (Royal Irish) Regiment of Foot.

58. WO 71/77, 73, Court martial of James Robertson, private soldier in the 34th Foot; Edmonstone to Gage, 24 November 1767, Gage Papers.

59. Gage to Hamilton, 8 December 1771, and Leake to Thomas Gage, 9 December 1771, Gage Papers.

60. WO 72/7, JAG Inquiry In The Conduct of Chaplain Robert Newburgh; McConnell, 68.

61. Gage to Hamilton, 14 November 1774, Gage Papers; Huston, 317–29; and WO 71/81.

62. General William Howe to Major General Philip Schuyler, 10 February 1777, quoted in Robert Benson to John Hancock, 23 April 1777, PCC, no. 136, 3:193.

63. Most likely this was Stephen Brett of Connecticut, who was commissioned a first lieutenant on July 6, 1775, and promoted to captain of the 2nd Connecticut Regiment on 1 January 1777. He was transferred to the 3rd Connecticut Regiment on 1 January 1781, and was wounded at Yorktown on 14 October 1781. Heitman, 102.

64. Benson to Hancock, 23 April 1777.

65. The Committee of Convention to Alexander Hamilton, 8 April 1777, in Hamilton, *Works of Alexander Hamilton*, 1:19–20.

66. Sterling, 388.

67. Edmonstone, 54–55.

JOHN EVANS

68. WO 12/3501. The returns are not clear on which company he was in after April 1768 and until he obtained his own company in October 1768.

69. WO 71/77, 73, Court martial of James Robertson, private soldier in the 34th Foot.

70. WO 65.

71. Wilkins to Gage, April 1772, and Wilkins to Gage, 3 August 1774, Gage Papers; WO 12/3501, Muster rolls of the 18th (Royal Irish) Regiment of Foot; WO 27/11, Irish Establishment Returns for 1767; WO 65; and WO 71/83, Court martial of James Cairns.

72. Cox & Meir, Ledgers of the 18th Regiment of Foot, 93.

HENRY FERMOR

73. Reverend John Fermor (1719–1773) and Elizabeth Austen (1724–1800) had a second son, John Shirley Fermor (1754–1791), who married Catherine Burton. Reverend Fermor was the rector at Crayford Church from 1744–1758 and the incumbent at Crowborough from 1759–1773. He was the illegitimate son of Colonel John Fermor and Ann Johnson. Hackworth, 24.

74. Cox & Meir, Ledgers of the 18th Regiment, 72, 77.

75. WO 12/3501, Returns of the 18th (Royal Irish) Regiment of Foot.

76. WO 12/3501; and WO 27/42, Inspection Return of the 18th (Royal Irish) Regiment of Foot, August 1779.

77. *Scots Magazine*, November 1779. Lieutenant John Sayer of the Royal Irish was appointed to one of the new captaincies in the 89th Foot.

78. A family history written in 1994, however, seems to indicate his death was at Sevenoaks, England. Hackworth, 23–24.

79. Parson, 469.

ROBERT HAMILTON

80. Wilkins to Gage, 7 April 1772, Gage Papers.

81. WO 71/80, 336–50, Court martial of Cpt. Richard Symes, 52nd Foot; 351–55, Court martial of James Edwards and William Moran, 35th Foot; 360–67, Court martial of Thomas Bell, Marines; and 360–67, Court martial of Duncan McFarland, Marine.

82. WO 71/148, Courts martial of William Green and Henry Knight, privates in the 18th Regiment of Foot.

83. *London Gazette*, 24 January 1792; Robert Hamilton to the Earl of Harrington, Dublin, 13 December 1808, letter 486, Poole Papers.

84. "A British Officer in Boston in 1775," *Atlantic Monthly* 39, no. 234 (April 1877): 389–401.

85. Poole Papers, items 486–96.

MATTHEW LANE

86. WO 65.

87. Extract of memorial of Colonel John Sebright to the Earl of Northumberland, in John Sebright to Robert Wilmot, 2 June 1763, Wilmot Papers.

88. Gage to Barrington, 23 August 1767, Gage Papers. Francis Wadman was similarly recommended for Lane's commission, and Batt would have received Wadman's ensigncy.

89. WO 71/77, 73, Court martial of James Robertson, private soldier in the 34th Foot.

90. Benjamin Chapman to Thomas Gage, 15 December 1771, and Gage to Chapman, 23 December 1771, Gage Papers; WO 27/11, Inspection Return of the Royal Irish; WO 12/3051, Muster Rolls of the 18th (Royal Irish) Regiment of Foot; and WO 65.

HUGH LORD

91. Mills, "72nd Regiment of Foot"; and WO 65.

92. "List of Officers Who Have Commanded at the Out Posts from 25 December 1771 to 24 December 1772 Included Who Are Intitled to an Allowance for the Same," n.d., Haldimand Papers.

93. Hugh Lord to Thomas Gage, 23 March 1774, Gage Papers.

94. Treasury Board Papers and In-Letters, T 1/517/108, "The Crown Account at Ft. Gage, Illinois, from 1 January to 1 July 1775."

95. Monforton to Cerre, 22 September 1778, in Alvord, 121.

96. Lord to Gage, 20 April 1772, Haldimand Papers.

97. Gage to Lord, 29 July 1772, Gage Papers.

98. Pease, 30.

99. William Murray's journal, n.d., quoted in McCormick, 3.

100. Gage to Lord, n.d., quoted in McCormick, 16.

101. Hammes, 101–14.

102. Henry Hamilton's journal, 1778–1779, http://www.in.gov/history/2812.htm.

103. Hugh Lord to Fredrick Haldimand, 3 September 1773, Haldimand Papers.

104. Guy Carleton to Hugh Lord, 19 July 1776; H. Hamilton, *Unpublished Journal*. Lord appointed Rocheblave as commandant and judge in Illinois. Edward

Gay Mason, *Philippe de Rocheblave*, 365–67; and Lord Dunmore to John Connolly, Colonial Office Papers 5/90, 312.

105. WO 4/98, 457–58, Barrington to Cox & Meir, 23 December 1776.
106. Alvord, Carter, and Croghan, 199 and 478; and Ledward, 83:56–60.
107. *London Gazette*, 22 July 1777.
108. *London Gazette*, 20 June 1778.
109. Alexander Campbell to the Earl of Denbigh, 15 January 1778, in Balderston and Syrett, 158.
110. *London Gazette*, 19 September 1782; and WO 65.
111. Philippe de Rocheblave to Guy Carleton, 3 April [August?] 1778, quoted in Mason, *Philippe de Rocheblave*, 419.
112. Mason, *Philippe de Rocheblave*, 375, 382–83.
113. Alvord, *Kaskaskia Records*; Alvord, *Illinois Country*, 317, 383.
114. *London Gazette*, 31 March 1801.
115. Mills, "7th Royal Garrison Battalion" and "11th Royal Garrison Battalion."
116. WO 65; Mills, "11th Royal Veteran Battalion."
117. PROB 11/1757/126/112, Will of Hugh Lord.

BENJAMIN CHARNOCK PAYNE

118. WO 71/81, 162.
119. Houlding, 103; WO 25, Commission books; WO 65; and WO 27, Inspection Return of the 18th (Royal Irish) Regiment of Foot.
120. Shy, 155–67; Guy Carleton to Thomas Gage, 23 March 1767, Gage Papers.
121. Shy, 162; Daniell, 47–52; Thomas Gage to William Franklin, 6 December 1766, Gage Papers.
122. Gage to Wilkins, 5 May 1768, Gage Papers. The soldier was William Williamson. Gage ordered him sent to New York as a deserter.
123. Thomas Gage to Benjamin Charnock Payne, 28 September 1772. Gage Papers.
124. WO 71/81, 2–165, Court martial of Captain Benjamin Charnock Payne; serving as members of the court-martial board besides Lieutenant Colonel Calder were Lieutenant Colonel Thomas Bruce, 65th Foot; Major Harry Blunt, 23rd Foot; Captain George Barker, 22nd Foot; Captain Nicholas Wade, 49th Foot; Captain Richard Grieve, 17th Light Dragoons; Captain Edward Evans, 22nd Foot; Captain Kurt Fitzgerald, 35th Foot; James Figge, 59th Foot; Julius Kirk, 10th Foot; Andrew Browne, 44th Foot; Captain James Wilson, 49th Foot; and Captain Edward Hubbard, 45th Foot. Captain Stephen Payne Adye of the Royal Artillery served as the deputy judge advocate.
125. Ibid., 94–96.
126. Ibid., 164–65.
127. Samuel Graves to Thomas Bishop, Boston, 21 September 1775, in W. Clark, *NDAR*, 2:170–71.
128. WO 71/82, "Remarks on Capt. Payne's Expedition from Boston to Penebscot Sept 20th, 1775 by Lieut. Edward McGouran of the Royal Fencible Americans," 102, 116–27; Samuel Graves to Thomas Bishop, 21 September

1775, and Bishop to Graves, 7 October 1775, in W. Clark, *NDAR*, 2:169–71, 2:331–32.

129. Kemble, 1:62.

130. WO 71/82, Court martial of Lt. Edward McGouran, Royal Fencible American Regiment, November 1775, 102–3. McGouran also had the following charges exhibited against him by Captain John Collett of the Royal Fencible American Regiment: "1st Being drunk on duty and behaving unlike a Gentleman to an Officer on duty. 2. Disobedience of Orders, & quitting his Post and taking his party to a Tavern, when the Enemy were within four or five miles."

131. Ibid., 115.

132. WO 71/81, 27–28, Testimony of Lt. Nicholas Triste; WO 12/3501, Returns of Cpt. Payne's Company of the 18th (Royal Irish) Regiment of Foot.

133. WO 71/82, 43–45.

134. Ibid.

135. WO 71/82, 118–21. The Thompson named was most likely Private James Thompson of Captain Gilfred Studholme's company. No date of enlistment is known. He served the whole war and settled with the corps at Passamaquoddy, Nova Scotia.

136. WO 71/81, 2–165, Court martial of Captain Benjamin Charnock Payne.

137. B. C. Payne to James Young, 30 January 1776, in W. Clark, *NDAR*, 3:1056–57; James Young to William Howe, 10 February 1776, in W. Clark, *NDAR*, 3:1209–10; Henry Chads to Philip Stevens, 3 June 1776 (estimated date), Audit Office AO 13, 1/1611; and Captain Enoch Linnel's affidavit, in W. Clark, *NDAR*, 4:123.

138. Kemble, 1:368.

139. Kemble, 1:108; Rees, 24–35.

140. WO 27/42, Inspection Return of the 18th (Royal Irish) Regiment of Foot, 23 August 1779; Jackson, 170.

141. WO 65; WO 17/221, Returns of the 99th Foot at Cumberland Fort under Major B C Payne, Dec. 1780.

142. George Durant (1734–1780) had two children with his second wife, Maria: George, born 25 April 1776; and Maria, 2 July 1779–24 April 1783. "Tong Parish Register," August 1756.

143. Maria was supposedly twenty-five years younger than Durant, so she was approximately twenty-four years old when she married Payne in 1783. Ibid.

144. "The Infamous George Durant," BBC, 3 February 2007.

145. Ibid.; Court of Chancery: Six Clerks Office, Pleadings 1758 to 1800, C 12/1553/64, Payne v. Durant, 1784; and "Tong Parish Register." Payne's age on his coffin appears to be off by about thirty years. His age was more likely sixty-seven or so at the time of his death. "Tong Timeline"; and Auden, 1, 33.

WILLIAM RICHARDSON

146. Swett, 43.

147. Gage to Barrington, 6 October 1769, in Gage, 2:524.

148. Randolph County Records.

149. Mason, *Early Chicago*, 446–84; and Fowler to Wilkins, 26 September and 24 October 1774, Gage Papers.

150. If Richardson had not been present in October 1774 with the regiment, he would not have been assigned to the companies embarked for Boston, because those companies were to be filled to full strength including officers. Orderly Book of the 18th Regiment of Foot, 16 April 1774.

151. Richardson was listed as a captain in the casualty list in the *Pennsylvania Gazette*, 19 July 1775. A Captain Otter Baver from the Royal Irish was also erroneously listed as wounded. No such officer served with the Royal Irish.

152. The 104th Foot was raised by Stuart Douglas in Ireland beginning on 24 February 1782. It was disbanded after the mutiny.

153. *London Gazette*, 1 April and 12 August 1783.

154. WO 12/1142, Returns of the 14th Regiment of Light Dragoons.

GEORGE STAINFORTH

155. William Stainforth (1704–1782) was the Esquire of Stillington, 1728–1782. Stainforth, n.p.

156. WO 65.

157. Ibid.

158. WO 12/3501, Returns of the 18th (Royal Irish) Regiment of Foot; and Cox & Meir, Ledgers of the 18th Regiment, 10.

159. "New Jersey Volunteers, List of Officers, 1776–1783"; M. Clark, *Loyalists*, 3:349 and 378; Coldham, 401 and 432. The Stainforth family records list 155 acres.

160. *Records of Indentures of Individuals Bound Out as Apprentices*, 82.

161. Stainforth, n.p.

162. Cole and Braisted, n.p.

163. WO 71/88, 104–35.

164. WO 71/89, 194–34.

165. WO 71/92, 295–318 and 343–56.

166. WO 71/95, 129–85.

167. Cole and Braisted, n.p.

168. *The Parliamentary Register*, 266.

169. *European Magazine and London Review*, Cotober 1790, 320.

170. *Stainforth*, n.p.

JOHN STEWART

171. WO 65; WO 27/11, Inspection Return of the 18th (Royal Irish) Regiment of Foot, 11 April 1767; and Sebright to the Earl of Northumberland, in Sebright to Wilmot, 2 June 1763, Wilmot Papers.

172. WO 27/11, Inspection Return of the 18th (Royal Irish) Regiment of Foot.

173. WO 71/77, 73, Court martial of James Robertson, private soldier in the 34th Foot.

174. WO 71/77; WO 12/3501; and Buttricke, 6–7.

175. Cox & Meir, Ledgers of the 18th Regiment, 9.

LEWIS WYNNE

176. Lieutenant Colonel Wynne (?–1747) was the member of Parliament for Castlebar, Aglish County Mayo, from 1727 to 1747.

177. Oaks, 185.
178. Mason, *Early Chicago*, 446–84.
179. Arthur Wadman dated 21 February 1771 [*sic*] in Gage to Wilkins, 20 February 1771, Gage Papers.
180. Cox & Meir, Ledgers of the 18th Regiment of Foot, 102.

Chapter 4: Lieutenants

GEORGE BEWES

1. George Warmington Bewes lived from 1723 to 15 November 1767. Susanna Kelly was from Kelly, Devon, and is listed as a spinster in an extant prenuptial agreement. She died on 27 June 1796, at age eighty-seven. Cornwall Public Records Office, Records of the William family of Werrington Park, Werrington, 1433–1909, WW 62, 23 May 1740; Polsue, 165–67; and Cornwall Public Records Office, WW 69, 24 August 1769.
2. Susanna died on 1 January 1774 and was buried with her parents and sister in the chancel of St. Stephens by Launceston. Elizabeth married Edmund Herring, the rector of Newton St. Petrock in Devon, and died on 18 June 1811 at age sixty-five. Polsue, 165–67.
3. Cornwall Public Records Office, WW 65, 24 August 1769.
4. Bewes's lieutenancy is listed as 27 July 1772 on the general return of officers in the inspection returns for 1777 and 1779.
5. WO 12/3501.
6. WO 71/54, Court martial of Bryan Sheridan, 31 August 1778.
7. WO 12/3501 and 12/3502; and WO 65.

GEORGE BRUERE

8. He is listed as Brewer only in some early returns, when he had most likely not yet joined the regiment. WO 12/3501.
9. Elizabeth Neale Bruere (1722–August 8, 1788) was unsuccessful in obtaining compensation for her losses in the American Revolution from the Crown. *Gentleman's Magazine* 58 (August 1788): 757, and Dobson, 42.
10. George Bruere Sr. to Thomas Gage, 23 March 1767, Gage Papers.
11. WO 12/3501, Returns of the 18th (Royal Irish) Regiment.
12. Nicholas Trist to Elizabeth House Trist, 15 September 1774, Trist Papers.
13. WO 65; WO 12/3501; "Hallowes Genealogy"; and Gage Papers.
14. Petition of George Bruere to King George III, n.d., Gage Papers.
15. Kemble, 1:460. The detachment may have included draughts from the 14th Foot, which was drafted in New York City at the same time.
16. WO 65; *European Magazine and London Review*, October 1786, 306; "Hallowes Genealogy"; and *Scots Magazine*, December 1779.

WILLIAM CONOLLY

17. Memorial of William Conolly, in Wilkins to Gage, 10 January 1772, Gage Papers; and Fowler to Wilkins, 16 May 1774, in Wilkins to Gage, 6 July 1774, Gage Papers.

18. Cox & Meir, Ledgers of the 18th Regiment, 37 and 37a; and Reiss, 131.
19. Hurlbut, 276.
20. Hamilton to Gage, 20 July 1775, Gage Papers.
21. WO 12/3501, Returns of the 18th (Royal Irish) Regiment of Foot.
22. WO 65; *London Gazette*, 30 January 1779; WO 34/104, Report of the Detachment in the City, 28 June 1780.
23. WO 12/3501.
24. WO 65; WO 12/3501, Muster Rolls of the Royal Irish Regiment; and WO 27/39, Inspection Returns of the Royal Irish Regiment.
25. Cannon, 52.
26. *London Gazette*, 17 January 1794.
27. WO 65. Hunt appears to have purchased his ensigncy in October 1794 and transferred into the 2nd Battalion of the Irish Brigade in August 1799. William Jr. was given a captaincy without purchase in the Royal Irish in September 1804. He had received his ensigncy without purchase in the regiment. *London Gazette*, 28 October 1794, 20 October 1795, 17 August 1799, and 8 September 1804.
28. PROB 11/1594/100/76, Will of William Conolly. His will was proved (verified) on 24 July 1817.

EDWARD CROSBY

29. WO 27/39, Inspection Returns of the 18th (Royal Irish) Regiment of Foot; and Jasper.
30. WO 71/81, Court martial of Benjamin Charnock Payne; ADM 36/8080; Orderly Book of the 18th Regiment of Foot.
31. WO 12/3501; Howe, 276.
32. WO 65; WO 12/3501, Returns of the 18th (Royal Irish) Regiment of Foot.

JOHN DE BIRNIERE

33. Ford, 15.
34. New York Public Library, 64.
35. Bockstruck, 98.
36. Invoice number 4, enclosed in Wilkins to Gage, 25 December 1771, Gage Papers.
37. Inventory of the estate of Jean Baptiste St. Gemme Bauvais of Kaskaskia, Illinois, 4 May 1773, Ruggles Manuscript Collection; list of furs to be delivered from Illinois, 6 April 1773, and Lord to Haldimand, 9 April 1773, Haldimand Papers, reel 27; and Byars, 126.
38. Historical Manuscripts Commission, 241.
39. *Edinburgh Magazine, and Literary Miscellany*, 1778.
40. Kemble, 2:197.
41. WO 34/157/385; and "Regarding Jamaica," Amherst Papers, November 1779.
42. Tone, 1:498.
43. *Gentleman's Magazine*, November 1793; and *Scots Magazine*, November 1793, which gives the date of his appointment as major of brigade as 2 November 1793.

44. *London Gazette*, 6 September 1794; WO 12/9023, Returns of the 88th Regiment of Foot, 1795–1796.
45. WO 65.
46. *London Gazette*, 7 April 1798; and WO 65.
47. Historical Manuscripts Commission, 241–42; Heber, 360–61.

JOHN PETER DELANCEY

48. Story, 17–18, 35–36. James DeLancy (1703–1760) was born in New York and educated in England at Cambridge and the Inner Temple. He was a member of the New York Council from 1729 to 1731 and a member of the New York Supreme Court from 1731 to 1760, serving as chief justice from 1744. He served as lieutenant governor of New York from 1747 until his death in 1760. Anne Heathcote was the daughter of Caleb Heathcote, the lord of the manor of Scarsdale and the mayor of New York.
49. WO 71/81, Court martial of Captain Benjamin Charnock Payne, 116.
50. WO 71/82, Court martial of Lt. Edward McGouran; and "A History of the Provincial Corps of Pennsylvania Loyalists."
51. Audit Office, American Loyalist Claims, AO 13/113/ part I/309, "Memorial of Captain John Peter DeLancey of the 18th Regt. of Foot to the Commissioners Appointed by Act of Parliament to Enquire into the Losses and Services of American Loyalists," n.d.; AO 13/94/33, "Memorial of Captain John DeLancey of the 18th Regt. of Foot to the Rt. Honble the Lords Commissioners of His Majesty's Treasury, James DeLancey," 17 March [1783?]; and "A History of the Provincial Corps of Pennsylvania Loyalists."
52. Allen was commissioned as a captain in the 1st Pennsylvania Battalion on 27 October 1775 and became lieutenant colonel of the 2nd Pennsylvania Battalion on 4 January 1776. Heitman, 69.
53. Officially, the battalion was titled the 1st Battalion, Pennsylvania Loyalists; AO 13/113/ part I/309, "Memorial of Captain John Peter DeLancey of the 18th Regt. of Foot to the Commissioners Appointed by Act of Parliament to Enquire into the Losses and Services of American Loyalists, n.d.; Story, 36; and "A History of the Provincial Corps of Pennsylvania Loyalists."
54. "History of the Pennsylvania Loyalists," 26 December 1779; and AO 13/113/ part I/309, "Memorial of Captain John Peter DeLancey of the 18th Regt. of Foot to the Commissioners Appointed by Act of Parliament to Enquire into the Losses and Services of American Loyalists," n.d.
55. Nesbit Balfour to Charles Cornwallis, 1 and 5 October 1780, Charles Cornwallis Papers, 3:158–59, 3:193–94.
56. Sabine, 371. DeLancey was listed as "doing service in America" in the 18th Foot's October 1780 return. WO 27/39, Inspection Return of the Royal Irish Regiment, 29 March 1787.
57. WO 12/3501 and 12/3502, Returns of the 18th (Royal Irish) Regiment of Foot.
58. AO 13/113/ part I/309, "Memorial of Captain John Peter DeLancey of the 18th Regt. of Foot to the Commissioners Appointed by Act of Parliament to Enquire into the Losses and Services of American Loyalists," n.d.; AO 13/94/33,

292   "Memorial of Captain John DeLancey of the 18th Regt. of Foot to the Rt. Honble the Lords Commissioners of His Majesty's Treasury, James DeLancey," 17 March [1783?].

59. John DeLancey (1765–1809) served in the 60th Foot and was promoted captain on 5 July 1793. He was promoted to paymaster of the 5th Royal Veteran Battalion on 8 April 1802, a position he held until his death. He may have been appointed captain in the 20th Jamaica Regiment in 1803. Story, 24–25.

60. James DeLancey (1767–1808) moved to Annapolis, Nova Scotia, after the American Revolution. He then emigrated to the Bahamas and began a career as a sugar planter. In 1805 he was appointed collector of customs at South Crooked Island in the Bahamas. Story, 31–32.

61. Richard Floyd removed to Nova Scotia after the Revolutionary War according to Story, 36. Elizabeth was at Bloomingdale, New York, with the DeLancey family in November 1777 when that residence was burned by Continental forces. Floyd added his wife's surname, Jones, on 14 March 1778 and was thereafter known as Richard Floyd-Jones. Woodhull and Stevens, 264.

62. *Salisbury & Winchester Journal*, Monday, 2 June 1788.

63. WO 65.

64. Jenkins, 141–42.

65. Cushman, 107.

66. "History of St. Thomas Parish"; and *New York, Death Newspaper Extracts, 1801–1890*. Elizabeth DeLancey's age was listed in her obituary as sixty-two, making her birth year around 1758.

67. "James Fenimore Cooper Biography"; McAdam is also given MacAdam's surname. He was the inventor of the Macadamized road; S. Jenkins, 142. Story, 36–37.

JOHN JOYNER ELLIS

68. Henry Ellis (1721–1806) was later governor of Nova Scotia and the primary architect of the British capture of Cuba in 1762. He died in Naples. According to Ellis, 68–69, he died in 1803. No first name is given for John Joyner Ellis's biological father. John Joyner Ellis's brother, William Joyner, served as the coroner of Gloucestershire and also assumed the surname of Ellis upon Ellis's death. *DNB*. The *DNB* entry for Ellis lists this man as Ellis's nephew.

69. Gage to Chapman, 4 December 1771, Gage Papers.

70. WO 12/3501, Returns of the 18th (Royal Irish) Regiment of Foot; and Orderly Book of the 18th Regiment of Foot, February 1775.

71. WO 12/3501; and WO 65.

72. *Scots Magazine*, February 1780. Unlike the Royal Irish, the 89th Foot had two majors as part of the establishment. WO 65.

73. WO 12/9091, Returns of the 89th Regiment of Foot.

74. George Washington to John Joyner Ellis, 10 July 1783, George Washington Papers.

75. *London Gazette*, 2 October 1787.

76. *London Gazette*, 25 December 1787.

77. The June and October 1802 army lists show Ellis's date of promotion to major general as 18 June 1798 in the listing of major generals and as 3 December 1793 under the regimental listing for the 23rd Foot. Both appear to be inaccurate. His name is spelled Joinour in the 1802 army list. WO 65.
78. WO 65, June and August 1798.
79. Brown and Russell, 227.
80. Ellis, 68–69.

ALEXANDER FOWLER

81. WO 65. Some secondary sources list him as in Henry Peyton's company.
82. Letter and testimonial from Alexander Fowler to the Continental Congress, 18 January 1779, PCC, no. 78, 9:237–42.
83. Isaac Hamilton to John Sebright, 5 July 1773, PCC, no. 78, 9:242.
84. Fowler to Gage, 22 September 1774, Gage Papers.
85. Affidavit of Alexander Fowler, 15 September 1787, Trist Papers.
86. Fowler to Collins, 15 May 1775, in "Case of Alexander Fowler," *General Advertiser & Intelligencer*, 29 July 1778.
87. Ibid.
88. WO 71/81, Court martial of Lt. Alexander Fowler, 401–4.
89. Ibid., 404.
90. Bockstruck, 132.
91. *London Evening Post*, 24 and 26 June 1777.
92. *General Advertiser & Intelligencer*, 18 June 1778.
93. Silas Deane to Joseph Reed, 22 August 1778, PCC, no. 78, 9:237–42.
94. *Pennsylvania Packet*, 14 January 1779.
95. PCC, no. 78, 9:237.
96. Morris, 6:303, 9:451 9:453, 9:470.
97. Daniel Broadhead (1736–1809) served as surveyor general of Pennsylvania before the Revolutionary War and again from 1798 to 1809. He served at Long Island in 1776 and was put in command at Fort Pitt in 1779. He was promoted to brigadier general in 1781.
98. Mann, 130, 142–43; and Morris, 9:8.
99. *The Travel Diary of Elizabeth House Trist*, n.d., 29, Trist Papers.
100. *JCC*, 27:403, 33:745, 34:621; and Edward Hand to Alexander Fowler, 27 December 1783, in *Letters of Delegates to Congress*, 25:760.
101. U.S. Federal Census, 1790; and Alexander Fowler to John Jay, 1 October 1785 and 24 May 1786, PCC, no. 80, 2:49, and no. 78, 9:547; *JCC*, 1:336 and 2:284.
102. U.S. Federal Census, 1800; and Smith, *America State Papers*, 23–26, 36. Fowler's sons may have been John and George. Both appear in the 1810 census in Allegheny County.
103. Dahlinger, 74–75, 127–30; *Federal Gazette and Baltimore Daily Advertiser*, 19 February 1801; and *Boston Democrat*, 2 April 1806.

FRANCIS JOHN KELLY

104. Kelly's eldest brother, Arthur, commanded the South Devon Regiment of Militia for a long time until he died in 1823. Worthy, 410. A second brother,

294 William, appears to have died as an infant in 1745, and another brother, William Hancock, became an admiral of the blue. *Burke's Extinct and Dormant Baronetcies* (1844), 96.

105. His age in the general return of officers as part of the annual regimental inspections is consistent with a birth year of 1752. It is possible that he was trying to present himself as younger than his actual age, since he had a relatively late start in his military career.

106. Gardiner, 126.

107. WO 65; *London Gazette*, 28 March 1772.

108. WO 71/79, Court-martial of Elijah Reeves, 157–77.

109. WO 71/148, Courts-martial of William Green and Henry Knight, privates in the 18th Regiment of Foot.

110. WO 12/3501 and WO 12/3502, Returns of the 18th (Royal Irish) Regiment of Foot.

111. *London Gazette*, 20 July 1790. Gardiner, 126, lists his retirement as 23 June 1791.

112. *Burke's Genealogical and Heraldic Dictionary*, 1:667. Agnes is listed as married to Samuel Laing of Orkney, New Brunswick.

113. Loge, 421. Elizabeth married Napier in 1827 and died on 31 July 1833. She was born circa 1767. The *DNB* gives Elizabeth's surname as Oakeley.

JOHN MAWBY JR.

114. WO 12/3501, Returns of the 18th (Royal Irish) Regiment of Foot.

115. Gage to Wilkins, 1 December 1767, Gage Papers.

116. WO 12/3501; and ADM 36/8080, Log of *HMS Asia*.

117. WO 72/8, JAG to John Mawby Jr., 16 November 1777.

118. WO 65; WO 12/3501, Muster Rolls of the Royal Irish Regiment; WO 71/79, Court martial of John Green; and *Orders at Coxheath Camp*.

MARCUS PATERSON

119. WO 27/11; and J & J Limited Company.

120. WO 71/77, 73, Court martial of James Robertson, private soldier in the 34th Foot.

121. WO 12/3501; and WO 65. The return of Captain Shee's company incorrectly lists Paterson's death as 3 October 1769 instead of 1768.

122. Cox & Meir, Ledgers of the 18th Regiment of Foot, 21.

WILLIAM PERKINS

123. WO 27/11, Inspection Return of the 18th (Royal Irish) Regiment of Foot.

124. *Pennsylvania Gazette*, 2 June 1768. Most likely this refers to the stage boat from Burlington, New Jersey. McConnell, 130, quotes Wilkins stating to Gage that Perkins died "on a Jaunt of Pleasure on the Water" but misidentifies the body of water as the Ohio River.

125. Gage to Wilkins, 5 May 1768, Gage Papers; and Cox & Meir, Ledgers of the 18th Regiment, 20, which lists Perkins's date of death as 28 May 1768.

EDMUND PRIDEAUX

126. Elizabeth was the daughter of Thomas Rolt of Saycombe, Hertfordshire, and the sister of Edward Baynton Rolt of Wiltshire. Miller, 258–59.
127. WO 27/36, Inspection Return of the 18th (Royal Irish) Regiment, 1777.
128. Nicholas Trist to Elizabeth House Trist, 15 September 1774, Trist Papers.
129. WO 12/3501, Returns of the 18th (Royal Irish) Regiment of Foot.
130. WO 65.
131. *London Gazette*, 20 March 1779, lists Prideaux's date of rank in the 7th Foot as 16 March 1779. This is clearly incorrect. "New Jersey Volunteers List of Officers, 1776–1783."
132. Norman McLeod was commissioned as a captain in the 2nd Battalion of the New Jersey Volunteers on 23 November 1776. He was transferred to the 4th Battalion on 24 July 1781. "New Jersey Volunteers List of Officers, 1776–1783."
133. WO 71/88, 144–66, Court martial of Lance Corporal John Lee.
134. WO 71/90, Court martial of Robert Reid, inhabitant of Phillipsburgh.
135. Groves, 446; *South Carolina & American General Gazette*, 27 September 1780. The death notice erroneously listed Prideaux as a captain at the time of his death.

WILLIAM RAYMOND

136. WO 27/11, Inspection Return of the 18th (Royal Irish) Regiment of Foot; WO 12/3501; Cox & Meir, Ledgers of the 18th Regiment, 25; and Gage to Wilkins, 1 December 1767, Gage Papers.

WILLIAM SMITH

137. WO 71/77, 73, Court martial of James Robertson, private soldier in the 34th Foot.
138. Alvord, *Kaskaskia Records*, 461.
139. WO 12/3501, Returns of the 18th (Royal Irish) Regiment of Foot; Cox & Meir, Ledgers of the 18th Regiment, 19.

NICHOLAS TRIST

140. WO 12/3501, Returns of the 18th (Royal Irish) Regiment of Foot.
141. Nicholas Trist to Isaac Hamilton, 26 July 1774, in Hamilton to Gage, 30 July 1774, Gage Papers.
142. Hamilton to Gage, 30 July 1774, and Gage to Hamilton, 22 August 1774, Gage Papers.
143. *Letters of Delegates to Congress, 1774–1789*. Deane wrote the following about the 18th Foot itself, stationed in Philadelphia at the time:

> The Troops here which are to assist in reducing New England, & all America amount to One Hundred & Eighty of which [Sixty?] are old worn out, invalids, unable to March [as far] as Boston in Six Weeks were they to have the [plunder] of the Town for their asking ·and the rest disaffected to the unnatural employ. It is a doubt with me, whether the People here will

let them March. Had Blood been shed by the Soldiery at Boston, there would have been No doubt at all for these Soldiers in that Case would before this have been disarmed, & dispersed, but it is dangerous to begin hostility, but on the most urgent occasion & indeed absolute Necessity. I design to view them when on their March.

144. Fowler to Gage, 22 September 1774, Gage Papers.
145. Nicholas Trist to Elizabeth House Trist, 15 September 1774, Trist Papers.
146. Indenture of Nicholas Trist to Philip Brown, 3 November 1774, Trist Papers.
147. WO 65; WO 12/3501; WO 71/82, Court martial of Captain Benjamin Charnock Payne; *London Gazette*, 2 May 1775; and "Commission of Lt. Nicholas Trist," n.d., Trist Papers.
148. Nicholas Trist to Elizabeth House Trist, 15 September 1780, Trist Papers.
149. Agnes Hore Campernon to Nicholas Trist, 6 April 1783, Trist Papers.
150. Trist Papers; *DNB*. Elizabeth left a diary of her travels; see Andrews, 183–232.
151. Susanna Taylor to My Dear Nieces, 15 June 1784, Trist Papers.
152. Elizabeth House Trist to Thomas Jefferson, 12 March and 4 May 1785, Trist Papers.

Chapter 5: Ensigns and Volunteers

JAMES ALDCROFT

1. *London Gazette*, 16 January 1779.
2. *London Gazette*, 22 January 1782.
3. *London Gazette*, 7 March and 9 May 1795. The latter lists the date of his majority in the army as 12 May 1795.
4. WO 27/42, Inspection Return of the 18th (Royal Irish) Regiment, August 1777; WO 12/3501, Returns of the 18th (Royal Irish) Regiment of Foot; WO 12/2021, Returns of the 2/2nd (Queen's) Regiment of Foot; and WO 65.
5. PROB 11/1297/255/486, Will of James Aldcroft.

CHARLES HOAR

6. George Hoar married Francis Sleigh on 1 January 1750. They had six other children: William, whose own son William would later inherit Sutton-Hall from Charles; George; Thomas, the fourth son, who was an admiral in the Royal Navy; Ralph; Mary; and Frances.
7. Hoar is listed as Philip in the ADM 6/8080, Log of HMS *Asia*.
8. WO 12/3501; WO 27/36, Inspection Return of the 18th (Royal Irish) Regiment of Foot; and WO 71/148, Courts martial of William Green and Henry Knight, privates in the 18th Regiment of Foot.
9. WO 12/3501.
10. WO 65; and Mills, "90th Regiment of Foot (1779–1784)."

11. *London Gazette*, 2 November 1802. Ann Harland had previously been married to the Henry Goodricke, the rector of Hunfinder and the vicar of Aldborough. Burke lists the date of the wedding as 26 May 1802.

12. Stead, 3:427.

13. *London Gazette*, 20 October 1803 and 24 September 1808. *Burke's Extinct and Dormant Baronetcies,* 245, give the creation date of the baronetcy as October 3, 1808.

14. Bligh, 8:62–87; and *Burke's Genealogical and Heraldic Dictionary* 3:195.

FRANCIS HOWARD

15. Lamb, 5.

16. *Pennsylvania Gazette*, 30 May 1771.

17. WO 12/3501, Returns of the 18th (Royal Irish) Regiment of Foot; WO 65; and Cox & Meir, Ledgers of the 18th Regiment, 33.

GEORGE MAWBY

18. WO 12/3501, Returns of the 18th (Royal Irish) Regiment of Foot; and WO 27/36, Inspection Return of the 18th (Royal Irish) Regiment of Foot, 1777.

19. WO 34/172, Inspection Return of Cpt. MacKenzie's Independent Co, 7 February 1781. The complete return showed seventy-three Englishmen, eight Scots (including MacKenzie), twelve Irishmen, and two foreigners. Crooks presented the companies as having been raised from among the convicts at Savoy, London, and the hulks (old navy ships used as "temporary" prisons). Letters between MacKenzie and Townshend mention only two deserters being included in the company.

20. Crosby, 48.

21. National Maritime Museum, Vessel ID 369980.

22. WO 65 gives 7 February 1781 as Mawby's date of commission, but 7 March 1781 is listed in the succession book in WO 25/212. The embarkation date is from WO 379/1. The other company sent to Africa was commanded by Captain George Katenkamp, previously of the 1st Regiment of Foot. Crooks, 47. The area of operations was in modern Ghana.

23. Crooks, 47–69; *London Gazette,* 13 March 1781; and WO 65.

24. "The Proceedings of the Old Bailey," trial of Kenith Mackenzie for killing, 10 December 1784.

SEBRIGHT MAWBY

25. WO 12/3501 & 12/3502, Returns of the 18th (Royal Irish) Regiment of Foot.

26. Gretton, 93–95. The *Pompée* was a seventy-four-gun ship of the line commissioned in 1793. It was then commissioned in the British Royal Navy at the end of 1793 as HMS *Pompee*. It ended its career as a prison hulk at Portsmouth in 1816. Winfield, 62.

27. This is the modern area of Bundelhkand in north-central India. It is divided between the states of Uttar Pradesh and Madhya Pradesh.

28. *London Gazette*, 22 April 1851; "The Proceedings of the Old Bailey," James Berwick theft; and Philippart, 2:2–4.

JOHN PIERCY

29. D. Hagist to J. A. Houlding, 2 May 2009; WO 12/55/2, Returns of the 9th Regiment of Foot, 1785.
30. Orderly Book of an Unidentified Company of the 47th Foot.
31. Yates, n.p.; *London Gazette*, 25 November 1775; and *Scots Magazine*, 26 March 1776. Lawe is crossed out on the army list for the Royal Irish and replaced with John White, whose commission dated from 26 April 1776.
32. "Parole of Honour," Boston Public Library, 25:1147; George Washington Papers, January 1779; and Burgoyne, 179.
33. WO 12/2654, Returns of the 9th Regiment of Foot; and *London Gazette*, 3 November 1787.
34. WO 12/2654, Returns of the 9th Regiment of Foot, 24 December 1791.

THOMAS SERLE

35. WO 27/42, Inspection Returns of the 18th (Royal Irish) Regiment of Foot. It is possible that this is the same Thomas Serle who was born on 22 November 1753 at Bolam, Northumberland, son of Joseph Serle. Or he might have been born at Tiverton, Devon.
36. WO 27/42; and *London Gazette*, 16 March 1779.
37. WO 12/3501 and 3502.
38. WO 12/3502; *London Gazette*, 22–26 January 1782; and WO 65.
39. WO 12/3502.
40. Ibid.
41. *London Gazette*, 11 December 1784.

HENRY SHAW

42. WO 12/3501, Returns of the 18th (Royal Irish) Regiment of Foot; WO 27/11, Inspection Returns of the 18th (Royal Irish) Regiment of Foot, 11 April 1767; Cox & Meir, Ledgers of the 18th Regiment, 71; and Gage to Wilkins, 1 December 1767, Gage Papers.

WILLIAM HENRY SLATOR

43. WO 71/81, Court martial of Captain Benjamin Charnock Payne.
44. *Norfolk Chronicle*, 6 April 1776.
45. WO 12/3501.
46. Ibid.; and *London Gazette*, 22 July 1777.

GODFREY TRACEY

47. The last name was also occasionally spelled as Tracy, but all formal military records record it as Tracey.
48. WO 27/11, Inspection Return of the 18th (Royal Irish) Regiment of Foot, 11 April 1767; Cox & Meir, Ledgers of the 18th Regiment, 26.

49. Alvord and Carter, 496.
50. *Minutes of the Provincial Council of Pennsylvania*, 10:7. John Frazer, Bernard Dockerty and Arthur St. Clair were to hold the court.
51. One could speculate that this payment was a bribe to allow Tracey to purchase over Hamilton. Wilkins was known to try to enrich his own purse when the opportunity arose.
52. Cox & Meir, Ledgers of the 18th Regiment, 26.
53. WO 12/3501, Inspection Return of the 18th (Royal Irish) Regiment of Foot.

SAMUEL TWENTYMAN

54. Mungo Paumier lists Samuel Twentyman's baptism as 6 October 1758 at St. Margaret in the Close, Lincoln. Childers Twentyman was appointed the rector of Thorpe on the Hill on 7 June 1759, and the vicar of Welton on 20 November 1764. Scott, *Admissions to the College of St. John*, 488. Childers died in 1781, leaving Samuel as the executor of his estate. Bailey, 920.
55. Scott, *Admissions to the College of St. John*, 488, lists Samuel Twentyman as being in the 100th Foot, but that appears to be incorrect.
56. Howell, 25:944–46.
57. Loftus Anthony Tottenham was the colonel of the 90th Foot. Robert Bertie, the fourth Duke of Ancaster and Kesteven (1756–1779), died before the regiment was embodied.
58. WO 27/42, Inspection Return of the 18th (Royal Irish) Regiment of Foot, 1779.
59. Howell, 25:944–46.
60. *Scots Magazine*, December 1793, 623.
61. *Scots Magazine*, March 1794, 179.
62. *Annual Register of World Events*, 1800, 108; and *London Gazette*, 6 January 1798.
63. *Annual Register of World Events*, 1799, 54; and WO 65.
64. PROB 11/1354, Will of Samuel Twentyman.

JOHN WILCOCKS

65. *Pennsylvania Gazette*, 18 November 1772 and 9 December 1772. Most likely this was Francis Hopkinson (1737–1791), an attorney and customs collector and later a U.S. District Court judge for eastern Pennsylvania.
66. Cox & Meir, Ledgers of the 18th Regiment of Foot, 119.

Chapter 6: Staff Officers

1. Bruce, 29.
2. WO 4, Barrington to Gage, 14 April 1767, 988:142–44; and WO 65. Johnson had originally been commissioned as quartermaster on 30 July 1761 in the 27th Foot. He died on 27 January 1775, while still serving with the 10th Foot. Peter Graham was commissioned on 6 November 1762 in the 28th Foot, and he retired from the 16th Foot on 30 January 1768. Duncan Campbell was commissioned as quartermaster on 3 September 1766 in the 42nd Foot. He was promoted to ensign

in the 26th Foot on 19 October 1778 and to lieutenant on 25 September 1781. He appears to have retired in 1784. Campbell served as quartermaster during his entire service with the 26th Foot.

3. Affidavit of George Gleghorn, 13 April 1767, and affidavit of David McBridem n.d., Hand Papers.

GEORGE BUTTRICKE

4. WO 27/46, Inspection Returns of the West Essex Militia, 1780.

5. Barnsley had also come from the ranks and served with Buttricke in the Royal American Regiment. He was originally commissioned as an ensign in the 1st Battalion of the 60th Foot (the 62nd Foot, at the time) while serving as sergeant major of the 30th Foot on 26 December 1755. Barnsley was promoted to lieutenant on 2 December 1756 and to captain on 30 May 1759. He was transferred to the 2nd Battalion of the 60th in 1763 when the regiment was reorganized. He retired on 8 May 1767, purchased an estate in Pennsylvania, and remained in the area of Bristol, Pennsylvania until his death in 1771.

6. Bockstruck, 56.

7. Buttricke, 6–7.

8. Ibid., 7–8; and Gage to Wilkins, 1 December 1767, Gage Papers.

9. It is unclear who Captain Campbell was. There was no such officer in the 34th or 18ty Foot at the time.

10. Buttricke, 9–11.

11. WO71/80, Court martial of Robert Newburgh; and WO 12/3501, Inspection Returns of the 18th (Royal Irish) Regiment of Foot.

12. Orderly Book of the 18th Regiment of Foot.

13. WO12/3501, Inspection Returns of the 18th (Royal Irish) Regiment of Foot; WO 65; and Brumwell, 93. The muster rolls of the 18th report Buttricke's resignation from the regiment as 2 September 1778.

14. WO 27/46, Inspection Return of the West Essex Militia, 1780. Buttricke was shown as having only two years of service (equivalent to the time he had served in the militia), not the nearly twenty years he had actually served. Similarly, the date given for his lieutenancy is 25 March 1778, which does not match any of his actual dates of commission.

15. WO 27/48, Inspection Return of the West Essex Militia, 1781.

16. PROB 11/1122/150/178, Will of George Butricke.

EDWARD HAND

17. Edward Hand, list of weather observations from leaving Cork, 20 May 1767, Hand Papers.

18. Gage to Hamilton, 8 December 1771, Gage Papers.

19. The year of Hand's marriage was given by his granddaughter as 1852. An alternative spelling of his wife's name is given as Katharine. Hand Papers.

20. Boatner, 484–85.

21. Ibid., 485, gives the date as 23 January 1781.

22. *Letters of Delegates to Congress, 1774–1789.*

23. United States Congress; and Heitman, 497.
24. Ellis and Evans, 44–45.
25. Shelley; and Craig, 3–7.

JOHN HANDAMEDE

26. He is listed as "John Handyside" in Kemble, 1:368–69.
27. Admiralty Office, ADM 36/8080, Log of HMS *Asia*.
28. Talbot Handasyde was promoted to lieutenant in an additional company on 25 August 1775 and retired in 1776.
29. Howe, 207, 291.
30. Musgrave was promoted to lieutenant colonel of the 40th Foot while in command of the battalion.
31. The light company of the 42nd Foot was added on 6 August 1776.
32. Peebles, 56–61; and Morrissey, 72. For an explanation of the role of the light infantry and grenadier battalions, see Spring, 57–62.
33. WO 65.

STANLEY LEATHES

34. WO 12/3501; WO 27/11, Inspection Return of the 18th (Royal Irish) Regiment of Foot, 1767; and WO 65.
35. "Lancashire and Westmoreland Marriage Bonds."
36. *Gentleman's Magazine*, January 1751; WO 12/3501; WO 27/11; WO 65; and Frey, 116–17.
37. Farrer, 2:32.

JOHN L. LYNN

38. Baptismal and Burial Records, Christ Church, Philadelphia. Lynn is listed in other sources as being born in 1740 in New York.
39. WO 71/81, Court martial of Captain Benjamin Charnock Payne, 94–95.
40. Roster of Officers of the 1st New York, 15 April 1776, PCC, no. 19, 1:315.
41. Morris, 7:681; and "*Alliance*." According to the U.S. Navy, the USS *Alliance* was a 900-ton frigate; length 151 feet; beam 36 feet; depth of hull 12 feet 6 inches; speed 13 knots; complement 300; armament 28 12-pounder smooth bores, 8 9-pounder smooth bores.
42. Morris, 6:132–33.
43. *Assessors' "Taking Books" of the Town of Boston 1780*; affidavit of John Lynn, 15 September 1787, Trist Papers.
44. U.S. Federal Census, 1790.
45. U.S. Federal Census, 1800; and U.S. Federal Census, 1810; Morris, 5:308, lists Lynn's death as 1793, but that does not appear accurate, according to the census records.

JOHN MAWBY SR.

46. WO 12/3051; WO 25 shows his appointment as adjutant as 4 February 1769, but WO 12/3501 gives the April date.

47. WO 72/2, Court of Inquiry of Rev. Mr. Newburgh.
48. WO 71/77, 71/78, and 71/79.
49. WO 71/80, 368–74, Court martial of Richard Ellingsworth, 63rd Foot; Benjamin Payne to John Sebright, 3 May 1775, Amherst Papers.
50. WO 12/3501; and *Orders at Coxheath Camp*.
51. *Orders at Coxheath Camp*.
52. Duncan, *History of Guernsey*, 163–64. Additional resolutions were passed for the local militia and the Royal Artillery.
53. Cannon, 50; WO 27/42; and WO 71/79 and 71/82.
54. WO 65.
55. *Edinburgh Advertiser*, 12 January 1790.

ROBERT JOCELYN NEWBURGH

56. WO 72/7, Court of Inquiry materials related to the Rev. Mr. Robert Newburgh; *London Gazette*, 21 November 1772; and court of inquiry materials included in Hamilton to Gage, 26 June 1774, Gage Papers. In the April 1774 court of inquiry, Ensign Henry Hamilton of the 64th Foot testified that he had heard Newburgh was suspected of "buggery" in County Sligo and elsewhere in Ireland.
57. WO 72/7, Court of Inquiry Materials Related to the Rev. Mr. Robert Newburgh.
58. WO 71/7, JAG inquiry into the conduct of Chaplain Robert Newburgh.
59. Robert Newburgh to Fredrick Haldimand, 25 June 1774, Haldimand Papers, BM Add. MS 21,371, reel 27.
60. Newburgh to Gage, 4 June 1774, Gage Papers.
61. WO 71/80, 1–175, Court martial of Rev. Mr. Robert Newburgh.
62. Alexander Fowler to Robert Collins, 15 May 1775, quoted in "Case of Alexander Fowler," *General Advertiser & Intelligencer* [London], 29 July 1778. Robert Collins was a lieutenant in the 4th Battalion of the Royal Artillery stationed at Castle William in Boston Harbor at the time Fowler wrote to him.
63. Nicholas Trist to Elizabeth House Trist, 15 September 1774, Trist Papers; "Case of Alexander Fowler," *General Advertiser & Intelligencer*, 29 July 1778; and Newburgh to Gage, 19 December 1774, Gage Papers.
64. Gage to Hamilton, 14 November 1774, Gage Papers.
65. Gage to Hamilton, 2 April 1775, Gage Papers. Gage wrote to Newburgh the same day directing him to apply for redress to his commanding officer rather than to Gage. Gage to Newburgh, 2 April 1775, Gage Papers.
66. Fowler to Collins, 15 May 1775, quoted in "Case of Alexander Fowler," *General Advertiser & Intelligencer*, 29 July 1778; and Newburgh to Gage, 16 October 1774, Gage Papers.
67. WO 12/3501 lists 15 May 1776 as his date of transfer and the date of commission for the man with whom he exchanged. WO 12/3229, Returns of the 15th Regiment of Foot, first shows Newburgh present in New York on 30 December 1776.
68. WO 12/3229, Returns of the 15th Regiment of Foot; and WO 65.

WILLIAM SMITH

69. Smith, *Life and Correspondence,* 1:350; Duffin, Lloyd, and Snyder; and Smith, *A General Idea,* 1–92.
70. Smith, *Works of William Smith,* 2:155.
71. Hutchins, 15; and Duffin et al.
72. Cox & Meir, Ledgers of the 18th Regiment, 30, 39.
73. Smith, *Works of William Smith,* 2:155–251.
74. Smith recommendation, Hand Papers.
75. Smith, *Life and Correspondence,* 514; and Duffin et al.

DANIEL THOMAS

76. WO 12/3501; Cox & Meir, Ledgers of the 18th Regiment, 30, 92.
77. WO 72/7, Court of Inquiry records relating to Rev. Mr. Robert Newburgh.

THOMAS THOMASSON

78. WO 27/11, Inspection Return of the 18th (Royal Irish) Regiment of Foot.
79. Mason, *Philippe de Rocheblave,* 437.
80. Lord to Haldimand, 3 September 1773, Haldimand Papers.
81. Cox & Meir, Ledgers of the 18th Regiment, 28; and WO 71/148, Courts martial of William Green and Henry Knight, privates in the 18th Regiment of Foot.
82. WO 65.
83. Stephen Bloomfield was commissioned as a lieutenant in the 96th Foot on 20 September 1780 and held army rank from 8 March 1780; Stuart Adams was commissioned as an ensign on 13 April 1780 and promoted to lieutenant in 1782; and Claus Pell was commissioned as a lieutenant in the 96th Foot on 8 June 1782. WO 65.
84. *Hibernian,* December 1781, 558, 622.
85. WO 65; and WO 12/9591, Returns of the 96th (British Musqueters) Regiment of Foot.
86. PROB 11/1233/16–22, Will of Thomas Thomasson.

SAMUEL TURNER

87. WO 27/11; WO 12/3501; and WO 65.

Chapter 7: Absentee Officers

HORACE CHURCHILL

1. WO 12/3051.
2. WO 27/34, Inspection Return of the 6th (Inniskilling) Regiment of Dragoons; and WO 12/704, Returns of the 6th (Inniskilling) Regiment of Dragoons.
3. WO 65.

CAESAR COLCLOUGH

4. WO 65; Cox & Meir, Ledgers of the 18th Regiment, 9, 37.
5. Conroy, 57.

JOHN COPE

6. WO 12/3501.

7. WO 25/22 and WO 25/23.

8. WO 65; WO 25/28, Commission Books, 1762, Promotions given out in Public Orders by General Monckton. The entry for Cope does not identify his former corps. That item is left blank.

9. Cox & Meir, Ledgers of the 18th Regiment, 105–105c.

10. WO 65; Ford, 20; and *London Gazette*, 20 August 1771; Cope is listed as exchanging with Payne on 25 July 1771, in WO 65.

THOMAS CUMING

11. It is possible he was the son of John and Jemima Cumming of Bishopsteignton, Devon.

12. WO 12/3501, Returns of the 18th (Royal Irish) Regiment of Foot; and WO 27/34 Inspection Return of the 1st Dragoon Guards, 5 May 1775. The 1st Dragoon Guards did not include his time with the Royal Irish when listing his years of service in the army.

13. WO 12/82 and 12/83, Returns of the 1st Regiment of Dragoon Guards; and WO 65.

14. *London Gazette*, 2 July 1781; and WO 12/83, Returns of the 1st Regiment of Dragoon Guards.

15. Watkin Williams-Wynn (1772–1840), 5th Baronet, was known as the Lord-Lieutenant of Merionethshire and Denbighshire. He also carried the unofficial title of Prince of Wales. Wynnstay manuscripts, Denbighshire Records Office, Wales.

16. *London Gazette*, 20 May 1794.

WILLIAM GREAVES

17. WO 25; and WO 65.

18. Cox & Meir, Ledgers of the 18th Regiment, 107.

19. WO 12/3501, Returns of the 18th (Royal Irish) Regiment of Foot.

20. Bockstruck, 155.

CLAUDIUS HAMILTON

21. WO 25; Sebright to the Earl of Northumberland, in Sebright to Wilmot, 2 June 1763, Wilmot Papers; and WO 27/11, Inspection Returns of the 18th (Royal Irish) Regiment of Foot, 1767.

JOHN HAMILTON

22. WO 65; *London Gazette*, 16 January 1773 and 24 September 1774; Mills, "113th Regiment of Foot (Royal Highlanders)."

BENJAMIN JOHNSON

23. WO 12, Inspection Return of the 18th (Royal Irish) Regiment of Foot, 350.

24. WO 65; *Pennsylvania Journal*, 16 August 1776; and WO 71/82. He is also listed as retiring on 19 April 1775.

25. Cox & Meir, Ledgers of the 18th Regiment, 90–91.
26. It is not clear whether this was his date of enlistment or his actual date of joining the regiment in America.
27. *Pennsylvania Gazette*, 7 July 1773.
28. WO 12/3501.
29. WO 71/82, 76, Court martial of Henry Darke.

JOHN WILMOT PRIDEAUX

30. The birth and death dates are from Leigh Rayment's Peerage Page, http://www.leighrayment.com/baronetage/baronetsP3.htm. Elizabeth was the daughter of Thomas Rolt of Saycombe, Hertfordshire, and the sister of Sir Edward Baynton Rolt of Wiltshire. Miller, 258–59.
31. His uncle, Sanderson Prideaux, first son of the sixth baronet, was killed at Cartagena, Spain, in April 1741.
32. WO 12/3501; and WO 25/210. The succession books show Prideaux's commission as dated 2 December 1767. Regimental returns show his resignation as 12 January 1770, but the Cox & Meir Ledgers and the date of his brother's commission support the date of 11 January 1770.
33. Episcopal Visitation Returns, 1779, Friends of Devon's Archives, http://www.foda.org.uk/visitations/1779/Chanter232A/Farway.htm.
34. Dates for Prideaux's first and third marriages are from Ancestry, http://www.ancestry.com; *Gentleman's Magazine*, November 1851.
35. Cherry & Pevsner, 447.
36. Edward Baynton Prideaux (ca. 1747–1797) married Lucretia Gilbert in 1788.
37. Anne is also listed as Georgina Frances Anne. Another sister is listed on Ancestry, http://www.ancestry.com, as Maria Constantia Prideaux (1746–1793), but she is not listed in the *Barontage of England*, which might indicate that she was born out of wedlock.
38. Cornwall Record Office, PB/1/934 Deed of Assignment, and PB/1/958 Quit Claim, 11 November 1796.

JAMES TAYLOR TREVOR

39. WO 25/210; and William Howe to Lord Dartmouth, 16 January 1776, CO 5/5/61/265.
40. Andrew Wardrop, surgeon to the 17th Foot from 15 July 1772 until he retired on 31 January 1777. He purchased his commission. Baule and Gilbert, 186.
41. WO 12/6471, Returns of the 55th Regiment of Foot; Wardrop is the source of the information in a letter from John Wishart Belsches to David Melville, 6th Earl of Leven, 21 May 1777, William Leslie Papers, Scottish Record Office, GD 26/9/513/8.
42. Power was commissioned as an ensign on 16 March 1775. His first name is given as William in the army lists but as Richard in a court-martial. He was twenty-one when first commissioned. The Return of Officers taken at Halifax, April 1776, lists his commission as date of rank from 16 May 1775. James Grant Papers. Power resigned from the army on 2 December 1777. WO 65.

43. WO 71/84, Court martial of Ensign Richard Power, 55th Regiment of Foot.
44. Cox & Meir, Ledgers of the 55th Regiment of Foot, n.p.

FRANCIS WADMAN

45. WO 27/11, Inspection Return of the 18th (Royal Irish) Regiment of Foot.
46. *Belfast News*, 4 November 1760.
47. Princess Amelia Sophia Eleanor (1711–1786) was the second daughter of George II. She was born in Hannover, Germany, and moved to England in 1714 when George I was appointed king of Britain.
48. For more on the historic role of the gentleman usher, see Jones.
49. Cox & Meir, Ledgers of the 18th Regiment, 13, 28. The fee for a six-month leave appears to have been sixty shillings, but it may have been six shillings; the ledger is not clear.
50. WO 12/3501; WO 65; Cox & Meir, Ledgers of the 18th Regiment, 28; Gage to Wilkins, 20 February 1771, Gage Papers.
51. Hasted, 3:302–18, 4:153–82; and "Tithe Apportionments: Winterborne Monkton, 1841." The total was approximately sixteen acres of arable land in the east section of Winterborne and four acres of western pasture.
52. *Times*, 1 July 1812.
53. Hazlitt, 249.
54. *Times*, 12 and 16 April 1796.
55. *Times*, 22 July 1803.
56. *Times*, 1 July 1812.

Chapter 8: Other Officers Associated with the Royal Irish in America

JOHN BAILEY

1. Raikers, 42; and Orderly Book of the 18th Regiment of Foot. It is possible he was confused with Ensign Zachary Bayly of the same regiment, but Bayly did not arrive in Boston until May 1775.

THOMAS BRUCE

2. WO 27/42, Return of the 65th Regiment of Foot, 1 November 1779. The returns of the 65th Foot show him listed as obtaining his majority in March 1763. The 1769 Army List shows his majority as 13 January 1763.
3. Gage to Barrington, 3 March 1773, Gage Papers.
4. Orderly Book of the 18th Regiment of Foot, 11 January 1775.
5. Orderly Book of the 18th Regiment of Foot, 1774–1775; WO 71/81, Court martial of Captain Benjamin Charnock Payne.
6. Howe, 160, 209, 217.
7. Robert Sloper (1729–1804?) was named a knight companion of the Order of the Bath in 1788. He served as commander in chief in India from 1785 to 1786.
8. *Orders at Coxheath Camp*, 4 June and 13 June 1778; WO 27/42, Returns of the 65th Foot. The 2nd (Queens) Regiment and the West Yorkshire Militia were the other regiments assigned to the 2nd Brigade. *London Gazette*, 23 February 1779.

9. *London Gazette*, 12 and 16 February 1782, 19 March 1782, 23 September 1782, 10 June 1786, and 29 March 1788. The date of his appointment to the colonelcy of the 16th Foot is also given as 6 March 1788.

10. *London Gazette*, 14 May 1796, 3 July 1790, and 25 June 1796.

ROBERT DOUGLAS

11. WO 65.

12. Duncan, *The History of the Royal Regiment of Artillery*, 1:338; Philippart, 2:330, lists Douglas's initial commission as 26 June 1762.

13. Duncan, 1:354.

14. *List of Officers of the Royal Regiment of Artillery*, 9; WO 65; and Philippart, 247–48. See also *London Gazette*, 13 September 1803, 28 October 1809, and June 1814. The *Gazette* lists his date of commission as 1 September 1803 and ties it to the expansion of the army.

15. Hime, 50; *Naval and Military*, December 1827, 668.

GEORGE GORDON

16. Raikers, 72; WO 12/7277, Returns of the 65th Regiment of Foot; and Orderly Book of the 18th Regiment of Foot.

FRANCIS SEYMOUR HEARST

17. WO 27/36, Return of the 65th Regiment of Foot. An alternate date of 28 February 1766 is given for his ensigncy in Raikers, 9, 79.

THOMAS HUTCHINS

18. Ibid., 7–12.

29. Hutchins, 18.

20. Alvord, Carter, and Croghan, 67, 79; Hutchins, 15–19; and *Pennsylvania Gazette*, 5 February 1767.

21. Mason, *Early Chicago*, 446–84.

22. Bockstruck, 198; Hutchins, 19–21; and *Pennsylvania Gazette*, 16 September 1772.

23. Hutchins, 21–40.

24. Hutchins, 7.

JOHN MACKAY

25. Raikers, 4; WO 12/7377, Muster rolls of the 65th Regiment of Foot; and Orderly Book of the 18th Regiment of Foot.

HENRY MILLER

26. Raikers, 54, 94; WO 27/36 and WO 27/42, Returns of the 65th Regiment of Foot; and *London Gazette*, 26 May 1789 and 29 January 1791.

JOHN PEXTON

27. Raikers, 103; WO 27/42, Returns of the 65th Regiment of Foot; and *London Gazette*, 10 May 1785. Raikers mistakenly gave his year of retirement as 1786.

JAMES RUMSEY

28. Gordon Forbes to Thomas Gage, 23 June 1768, Gage Papers.
29. Bockstruck, 325.
30. Forbes to Gage, 23 June 1768, Gage Papers.
31. Alvord and Carter, 440; and Davidson and Stuve, 167.
32. Wilkins to Gage, 25 December 1771, Gage Papers; Buttricke, 11; and Byars, 120, 342.
33. Wilkins to Gage, 16 May 1772, Gage Papers; and Byars, 347.
34. Byars, 124–125.
35. Flagg, 27:273; and Hurlburt, 273.
36. Pease, 28; and James, 250.

GEORGE SINCLAIR

37. WO 27/14, Returns of the 65th Regiment of Foot, 1768. The returns of the 65th Foot show Sinclair being commissioned as an ensign in 1754 and a lieutenant in March 1759. Both dates appear to be incorrect.

38. WO 27/36, Returns of the 65th Regiment of Foot, 1777; and *London Gazette*, 2 September 1777 and 18 February 1783. He was the probably the fourth son of John and Elizabeth Sinclair of Durran. If so, he died without children.

39. *London Gazette*, 9 May 1789; *Scots Magazine*, November 1790; and Orderly Book of the 18th Regiment of Foot.

JOHN SMITH

40. Raikers, 110; WO 27/14, Inspection Returns of the 65th Regiment of Foot; WO 12/7277, Returns of the 65th Regiment of Foot; and Orderly Book of the 18th Regiment of Foot.

JONAS WATSON

41. Orderly Book of the 18th Regiment of Foot.
42. WO 71/82, 137, Court martial of Thomas Bailey; WO 27/14 and WO 27/36, Inspection Returns of the 65th Regiment of Foot; and *London Gazette*, 20 July 1779.
43. Raikers, 126; and *London Gazette*, 2 December 1794 and 19 May 1795.

Epilogue

1. Frothingham, 197; and WO 5/59/283.
2. WO 27/36, Inspection Return of the 18th (Royal Irish) Regiment of Foot, May 1777; WO 5/59/231, 255, 283, and 398; and WO 5/60/48, Marching and Militia Orders.
3. WO 5/60/114 and 60/406. The Royal Irish was ordered to send thirty-four privates, but the inspection returns show that it sent thirty-five.
4. Patterson, 109; WO 5/60/441 and 443. The quartermaster and camp colormen were ordered to Maidstone at the same time. The camp colormen were assigned to assist the quartermaster with organizing the regimental and company camp layout.

5. WO 5/60/453; and Houlding, 325. For more information about the operations of Coxheath Camp, see *Orders at Coxheath Camp*, 129–48, and Houlding, 322–41. For a novel that features the camp and allegedly some of the officers of the Royal Irish see "A Lady."

6. *Orders at Coxheath Camp*, 16 June 1778.

7. Patterson, 127.

8. *Orders at Coxheath Camp*, 13 July 1778; WO 34/188/180, Disposition of Battalion Guns from Cock's Heath; and WO 34/188/67, Monthly Return of the Forces Encamped in S. Britain, 1st Sept. 1778. For a more complete analysis of the Franco-Spanish invasion threat of 1778 and 1779, see Patterson.

9. Patterson, 107–9; WO 34/188/101, Present State of the Establishment of the Infantry, 29 Oct. 1778.

10. WO 5/61/91 and 128; and WO 12/3501.

11. WO 5/61/191 and 194.

12. WO 5/61/197, 287, 302, and 303.

13. WO 12/3501, Muster rolls of the 18th (Royal Irish) Regiment of Foot; and WO 34/188/303, Monthly Return of His Majesty's Forces Encamped in South Britain, 1 November 1779.

14. Houlding, 334–43; Patterson, 123–24; and WO 27/42, Inspection Return of the 18th (Royal Irish) Regiment of Foot, 23 August 1779. The 6th, 10th, 14th, 26th, 45th, 50th, 52nd, 59th, and 65th were all drafted and experienced the same opportunity as the Royal Irish to rebuild and train in the wartime camps. According to Houlding, only the 16th and 26th Regiments were drafted in America but were not encamped in England afterward.

15. WO 27/36, Inspection Return of the 18th (Royal Irish) Regiment of Foot, 15 May 1777; and Houlding, 334–43.

16. WO 34/187/110, Dates of Regiments Marching from Warley Camp; WO 34/188/269, Proposed Winter Quarters for the Troops at present encamped in Lieut. Genl. Parker's District, Oct. 1779; and WO 5/62/95.

17. WO 5/62/183.

18. WO 5/62/279; and Houlding, 334–35. WO 34/194/29 shows marching orders to encamp four marching regiments and nine militia regiments at camps at Danforth, Dartford, Dorking, Portsmouth, Tiptree, and Waterdown.

19. WO 34/234/28–29; and WO 5/62/321–22.

20. Archer, 58–59; and Nicholson, 78–79.

21. WO 34/104, State of Regiments at Hyde Park, 24 June 1780.

22. WO 34/104, Report of the Detachment in the City, 28 June 1780 and Report of the Camp in Hyde Park, 24 July 1780.

23. WO 5/62/409 and 410; WO 34/234/119; and WO 34/194/71. The quartermasters and camp colormen of the entire brigade were ordered to Whetston the day before the brigade was to march from Hyde Park. The orders from Whitehall came on 27 September 1780, and were reinstated briefly on 5 February 1781, for "suppressing the Illegal and tumultuous Assemblies of the People." WO 34/104/377, Adjutant General's Office, 5 February 1781.

24. WO 5/62/459; WO 5/63/27, 29, 165, and 171. Four companies were quartered at Bonnet, Hadley, Kitt's End, Merns Ridge, Potter's Bar, and Northhaw. One company was quartered at Whetstone, two between Endfield and Endfield Marsh, two at Woltham Abbey and Woltham Cross, and one between Edmonston and Tottenham.

25. Cannon, 49–50; WO 34/132/102, Richard Baily to Lord Amherst, 13 April 1781; and WO 34/187/104, untitled document showing postings for thirty-one regiments, including twelve marching regiments of foot.

26. *Daily Advertiser*, 23 March 1783.

27. Duncan, *History of Guernsey*, 163–64; see also Cannon, 52–54; Duncan, *History of Guernsey*, 162–64; and *Daily Advertiser*, 23 March 1783.

28. *Daily Advertiser*, 23 March 1783; *London Courant and Daily Advertiser*, March 31, 1783; *Morning Chronicle and London Advertiser*, 3 May 1783; and WO 1/1019/656, Irving to War Office, 18 April 1783.

29. WO 4/122/98, R Fitzpatrick to John Sebright, 14 June 1783; and WO 4/122/190, Fitzpatrick to Sebright, 7 July 1783.

30. Cardwell Reforms refer to the policies of Edward Cardwell, secretary of state for war between 1868 and 1874. The reforms addressed a perceived poor logistical response to the Crimean War and a need to overhaul practices in place for nearly a century. Most regiments were combined with another regiment to provide a two-battalion model in which one battalion served at home and another was overseas. Among other changes, the reforms abolished the purchase of commissions, and enlisted men saw the term of enlistment drop from twelve years to six.

31. Cannon, 54–63.

32. Richards, 1:264; and Gretton, 2:102–4.

Bibliography

Primary Sources

MANUSCRIPTS

National Archives (UK)
Admiralty Office, ADM 36/8080, Log of HMS *Asia*
Amherst Papers, Center for Kentish Studies, Maidstone, UK
Audit Office, AO 13, American Loyalist Claims, Series 2
Colonial Office Papers Series 5, Secretary of State, America and West Indies
Charles Cornwallis Papers, Public Record Office, Domestic Records, PRO 30/11
Court of Chancery: Six Clerks Office; Pleadings 1758 to 1800, C 12/1553
House of Lords Papers, LO/PO/JO/10/7/544, Regimental Court-Martial Data from Ireland
Prerogative Court of Canterbury Records (PROB), Series 11, Will Registers
Treasury Board Papers and In-Letters
War Office Series 1, In-Letters
War Office Series 4, Secretary-at-War, Out-Letters
War Office Series 5, Marching and Militia Orders (English)
War Office Series 8, Muster Master General of Ireland, Out-Letters
War Office Series 12, General Muster Books and Pay Lists
War Office Series 17, Monthly Returns to the Adjutant General
War Office Series 25, Commission and Succession Books
War Office Series 27, Regimental Inspection Returns
War Office Series 30, Miscellaneous Papers, 1684–1951
War Office Series 34, Papers of Baron Jeffrey Amherst, Commander in Chief
War Office Series 36, Military Headquarters, North America: Entry Books, American Revolution
War Office Series 65, Army Lists with Notations
War Office Series 71, General Courts Martial

Bibliography

War Office Series 72, Records Relating to the Judge Advocate General's Office
War Office Series 379, Disposition and Movement of Regiments, Returns and Papers

Other Archival Sources

Baptismal and Burial Records, Christ Church, Philadelphia, PA
Sir Henry Clinton Papers, William L. Clements Library, University of Michigan, Ann Arbor
Cornwall Public Records Office, Truro, UK
Cox & Meir, Ledgers of the 18th (Royal Irish) Regiment of Foot, Lloyd's Archive, London
Cox & Meir, Ledgers of the 55th Regiment of Foot, Lloyd's Archive, London
Edinburgh Commissariat Court Testaments, 1830–1833, Scottish Record Office, Edinburgh
Walter Elliot Papers, Illinois State Historical Society, Springfield
Thomas Gage Papers, William Clements Library, University of Michigan, Ann Arbor.
James Grant Papers, Ballindalloch Castle, Scotland; copies in Library of Congress
Fredrick Haldimand Papers, British Museum Additional Manuscripts, London
Edward Hand Papers, Rockford Plantation Manuscripts, Lancaster, PA
William Leslie Papers, National Archives of Scotland, SRO GD26/9/513
"New Jersey Volunteers List of Officers, 1776–1783." Royal Provincial, http://www.royalprovincial.com/military/rhist/njv/njvofficers.htm
Orderly Book of an Unidentified Company of the 47th Foot, August to September 1777, Pell Library, Fort Ticonderoga, NY
Orderly Book of the 18th Regiment of Foot at Boston, 1774–1775, Item 7609-3, National Army Museum (UK)
Orders at Coxheath Camp, Society of the Cincinnati Library, Washington, DC
Poole Papers, Gwynedd Archives, Caernarfon Record Office, UK
Randolph County Records, Illinois State Historical Society, Springfield
Ruggles Manuscript Collection, Newberry Library, Chicago
Trist, Randolph, and Burke Family Papers, University of Virginia, Charlottesville
U.S. Federal Censuses, 1790, 1800, and 1810, Ancestry, http://www.ancestry.com
George Washington Papers, Library of Congress
Wilmot-Horton of Osmaston and Catton Correspondence, Derbyshire Record Office, Matlock, Derbyshire, UK
Wynnstay Manuscripts, Denbighshire Record Office

PERIODICALS

Annual Register of World Events (London)
News (Belfast)
Boston Democrat
Boston Gazette
Daily Advertiser (London)
Dublin Journal
Edinburgh Advertiser

Edinburgh Magazine, and Literary Miscellany
European Magazine and London Review
Federal Gazette and Baltimore Daily Advertiser
General Advertiser & Intelligencer (London)
Gentleman's Magazine
Hiberian magazine (Dublin)
London Courant and Daily Advertiser
London Evening Post
London Gazette
Morning Chronicle and London Advertiser
Naval and Military Magazine
Norfolk Chronicle (Virginia)
Pennsylvania Gazette
Pennsylvania Packet
Salisbury & Winchester Journal
Scots Magazine
South Carolina & American General Gazette
Times (London)

BOOKS, JOURNALS, AND REPORTS

Adye, Stephen Payne. *A Treatise on Courts Martial*. London: H. Gaine, 1769.

Assessors' "Taking Books" of the Town of Boston, 1780. Boston: Bostonian Society, 1912. http://www.ancestry.com.

Balderston, Marion, and David Syrett. *The Lost War: Letters from the British Officers during the American Revolution*. New York, Horizon Press, 1975.

Barker, John. *The British in Boston: Being the Diary of Lieutenant John Barker of the King's Own Regiment from November 15, 1774, to May 31, 1776*. Cambridge, MA: Harvard University Press, 1924.

Bligh, Richard. *New Reports of Cases Heard in the House of Lords: On Appeals and Writs of Error, and Decided during the Session*. 10 vols.. London: Saunders and Benning, 1827–1837.

Burgoyne, John. *Orderly Book of Lieut. Gen. John Burgoyne*, ed. E. B. O'Callaghan. Albany, NY: J. Munsell, 1860.

Buttricke, George. *Affairs at Fort Chartres, 1768–1781*. Albany, NY: J. Munsell, 1864. Reprinted from "Affairs at Ft. Chartres." *Historical Magazine* 8, no. 8 (n.d.): 257–65.

Byars, William V., ed. *B. & M. Gratz Merchants in Philadelphia 1754–1798: Papers of Interest to Their Posterity and the Posterity of Their Associates*. Jefferson City, MO: Hugh Stephens, 1916.

Chambers, John. *Biographical Illustrations of Worcestershire: Including Live of Persons Eminent Either for Piety or Talent*. Worcester, UK: William Walcott, 1820.

Clark, William B., ed. *Naval Documents of the American Revolution*. 11 vols. Washington, DC: U.S. Naval Historical Center, 1964–2005.

Desbrisay, Thomas. *The Quarters of the Army in Ireland*. Dublin: George Faulkner, 1733–1755.

Bibliography

Donkin, Robert. *Military Collections and Remarks.* New York: H. Gaine, 1777.

Episcopal Visitation Returns, 1779. Friends of Devon's Archives. http://www.foda.org.uk/visitations/parishes.htm.

Gage, Thomas. *The Correspondence of General Thomas Gage, with the Secretaries of State, and with the War Office and Treasury, 1763–1775,* ed. C. E. Carter. 2 vols. New Haven, CT: Yale University Press, 1932.

Hamilton, Alexander. *The Works of Alexander Hamilton; Containing His Correspondence, and His Political and Official Writings, Exclusive of the Federalist, Civil and Military.* Edited by John C. Hamilton. 6 vols. New York: J. F. Trow, 1850. http://www.archive.org/details/worksofalexander07hamirich.

Hamilton, Henry. *The Unpublished Journal of Lieut. Gov. Henry Hamilton.* Edited by J. D. Barnhart. Indiana Historical Bureau. http://www.in.gov/history/2812.htm.

Hasted, Edward. *The History and Topographical Survey of the County of Kent.* Vols. 3 and 4. London, 1797–1798. http://www.british-history.ac.uk/report.aspx?compid=53801.

Hazard, S., ed. *Colonial Records of Pennsylvania.* 16 vols. Philadelphia: Joseph Severns, 1860.

Howe, William. *General Sir William Howe's Orderly Book at Charlestown, Boston, and Halifax, June 17, 1775, to 1776, 26 May.* Port Washington, NY: Kennikat Press, 1970.

Howell, Thomas B. *A Complete Collection of State Trials for High Treason and Other Crimes to the Year 1783.* 33 vols. London: Longman, 1826.

Hutchins, Thomas. *A Topographical Description of Virginia, Pennsylvania, Maryland, and North Carolina.* Rev. ed. Cleveland, OH: Burrows Brothers, 1904.

J & J Limited Company. *Irish Records Index, 1500–1920.* Provo, UT: Ancestry.com Operations, 1999. http://www.ancestry.com.

Johnson, William. *The Papers of Sir William Johnson.* 14 vols. Albany: State University of New York, 1921.

Journals of the Continental Congress, 1774–1789. 38 vols. Washington, DC: Government Printing Office, 1904–37.

Kemble, Stephen. *The Journals of Lieut.-Col. Stephen Kemble, 1773–1789.* 2 vols. New York: New York Historical Society, 1885.

Knox, John. *Historical Journal of the Campaigns in North America, for the Years 1757, 1758, 1759, and 1760.* London: W. Johnston and J. Dodsley, 1769.

"A Lady." *Coxheath Camp: A Novel in a Series of Letters.* 2 vols. London: Fielding and Walker, 1779.

Lamb, Roger. *A British Soldier's Story: Roger Lamb's Narrative of the American Revolution,* ed. D. N. Hagist. Baraboo, WI: Ballindalloch Press, 2004.

Ledward, K. H., ed. *Journals of the Board of Trade and Plantations.* 83 vols. [London]: Institute of Historical Research, 1938.

Letters of Delegates to Congress, 1774–1789. 25 vols. Summerfield, FL: Historical Database, 1998.

"The Life of Sir Brent Spencer." *The Royal Military Chronicle or British Officers' Monthly Mentor,* November 1811.

List of Officers of the Royal Regiment of Artillery, As They Stood in the Year 1763 with a Continuation to the Present Time: Greenwich, UK: Elizabeth Delahoy, 1815.

London and County Directory, 1811. Provo, UT: Ancestry.com Operations, 2004. http://www.ancestry.com.

Mason, Edward G. *Early Chicago and Illinois.* Chicago: Fergus, 1890.

Millan, John. *Millan's List of All the Officers in the Horse, Dragoons, and Foot on the Irish Establishment for 1755.* Dublin: John Millan, 1755.

Minutes of the Provincial Council of Pennsylvania. Harrisburg: State of Pennsylvania, 1852.

Morris, Robert. *The Papers of Robert Morris.* 9 vols. Pittsburgh: University of Pittsburgh Press, 1984.

Oaks, Robert F. "George Morgan's "Memorandums": A Journey to the Illinois Country, 1770." *Journal of the Illinois State Historical Society* 69, no. 3 (August 1976): 185–200.

Papers of the Continental Congress, 1774–1789. National Archives Microfilm Publication M247. 204 rolls. Washington, DC: National Archives and Records Administration. Cited as PCC.

The Parliamentary Register or History of the Proceedings and Debates of the House of Commons. London: J. Debrett, 1781.

Parson, Philip. *Monuments and Painted Glass of Upwards of One Hundred Churches Chiefly in the Eastern Part of Kent.* Canterbury, UK: Simions, Kirkby & Jones, 1794.

Paumier, Mungo. *Family History and Autobiography of Mungo Paumier.* Unpublished manuscript in the Kemp family papers.

Peebles, John. *John Peebles' American War: The Diary of a Scottish Grenadier, 1776–1782,* ed. Ira D. Gruber. Mechanicsburg, PA: Stackpole Books, 1998.

Philippart, John. *The Royal Military Calendar.* 2 vols. London: Valpy, 1820.

"The Proceedings of the Old Bailey, London's Central Criminal Court, 1674 to 1913." Old Bailey Online, n.d. http://www.oldbaileyonline.org/browse.jsp?id=t17841210-1.

Records of Indentures of Individuals Bound Out as Apprentices, Servants, Etc. Philadelphia: Pennsylvania German Society, 1907.

Rivington, James. *North American Army List.* New York: Rivington, 1779–1781.

Scott, Walter. *The Journal of Sir Walter Scott from the Original Manuscript.* New York: Franklin, 1970.

———. *The Poetical Works of Sir Walter Scott.* Edinburgh: Robert Cadell, 1833.

1772 Review of Troops in Ireland. Vol. 2. Royal Gloucestershire, Berkshire, and Wiltshire (Salisbury) Museum, 2005.

Smith, Clifford N. *America State Papers, French and British Land Grants in the Post Vincennes (Indiana) District, 1750–1784.* McNeal, AZ: Genealogical Publishing, 1996.

Smith, William. *A General Idea of the College of Mirania.* New York: J. Parker and W. Weyman, 1753.

———. *The Works of William Smith, D.D., Late Provost of the College and Academy of Philadelphia.* 2 vols. Philadelphia: Maxwell, 1802.

Society of Arts. *Transactions of the Society Instituted at London for the Encouragement of Arts, Manufactures, and Commerce; with the Premiums Offered in the Year 1791.* London: Society of Arts, 1791.

Tone, Theobald W. *The Writings of Theobald Wolfe Tone, 1763–98*, edited by T. W. Moody. 2 vols. New York: Clarendon Press, 1998.

"Tong Parish Register." *Shropshire, England, Extracted Parish Records.* Provo, UT: Ancestry.com Operations, 2001. http://www.ancestry.com.

U.K. and U.S. Directories, 1680–1830. Provo, UT: Generations Network, 2003. http://www.ancestry.com.

Vicars, Arthur E., ed. *Index to Prerogative Wills of Ireland, 1536—1810.* Boston: Genealogical Publishing, 1987. http://www.ancestry.com.

War Office. *List of All the General Officers of the Army; The Officers of the Several Troops, Regiments, Independent Companies, and Garrisons.* London: War Office, 1755–1820.

Wilkinson, James. *Memoirs of My Own Times.* 2 vols. Philadelphia: Abraham Small, 1816.

Secondary Sources

"Alliance." *Dictionary of American Naval Fighting Ships,* n.d. http://www.history.navy.mil/danfs/a7/alliance-i.htm.

Alvord, Clarence W. *The Illinois Country, 1673–1818.* Chicago: University of Illinois Press, 1922.

———, ed. *Kaskaskia Records, 1778–1790. Collections of the Illinois State Historical Society,* vol. 5; Virginia Series, vol. 2. Springfield: Illinois State Historical Society, 1909.

———. *The Mississippi Valley in British Politics.* 2 vols. Cleveland, OH: A. H. Clarke, 1917.

Alvord, Clarence W., and Clarence E. Carter, eds. *Trade and Politics, 1767—1769. Collections of the Illinois State Historical Society,* vol. 16; British Series, vol. 3. Springfield: Illinois State Historical Society, 1921.

Alvord, Clarence W., Clarence E. Carter, and George Croghan, eds. *The New Regime, 1765–1767. Collections of the Illinois State Historical Society,* vol. 11; British Series, vol. 2. Springfield: Illinois State Historical Society, 1916.

Andrews, William L. *Journeys in New Worlds: Early American Women's Narratives.* Madison: University of Wisconsin Press, 1990.

Antrobus, Reginald L. *Antrobus Pedigrees: The Story of a Cheshire Family.* London: Mitchell, Hughes and Clarke, 1929.

Archer, John E. *Social Unrest and Popular Protest in England, 1780 to 1840.* Cambridge, UK: Cambridge University Press, 2000.

Auden, J. E. *Auden's History of Tong,* ed. Joyce Frost. London: Arima, 2005.

Bailey, Thomas. *Annuals of Nottinghamshire.* London: Simpkin, Marshall & Co., 1852.

Baule Steven M., and Stephen Gilbert. *British Army Officers Who Served in the American Revolution, 1775–1783.* Westminster, MD: Heritage Books, 2004.

Biography Database, 1680–1830. Newcastle-upon-Tyne, UK: Avero, 1998.

Boatner, Mark M. *Encyclopedia of the American Revolution*. Harrisburg, PA: Stackpole Books, 1994.
Bockstruck, L. D. *Bounty and Donation Land Grants in British Colonial America*. Baltimore: Genealogical Publishing, 2007.
Boyle, G. E. "The Royal Irish in America." *Journal of the Society for Army Historical Research* 2, no. 2 (1922): 63–68.
Braisted, Todd. *The Online Institute for Loyalist Studies*. Royal Provincial, n.d. http://www.royalprovincial.com.
Breen, Mary. "The Civil Parish of Treadingstown." *In the Shadow of the Steeple*, no. 1 (1989). http://homepage.eircom.net/~duchas/steeples/SteepleVol1/treadingstown.htm.
"British Officer in Boston in 1775, A." *Atlantic Monthly* 39, no. 234 (April 1877): 389–401.
Brown, Henry. *The History of Illinois, from Its First Discovery and Settlement to the Present Time*. New York: New World Press, 1844.
Brown, James. *The Epitaphs and Monumental Inscriptions in Greyfriars Churchyard, Edinburgh*. Edinburgh: J. Moodie Miller, 1848.
Brown, Philip L., and George Russell. *Clyde Company Papers: Prologue, 1821–35*. London: Oxford Press, 1941.
Bruce, Anthony. *The Purchase System in the British Army, 1660–1871*. London: Royal Historian Society, 1980.
Brumwell, Stephen. *Redcoats: The British Soldier and War in the Americas, 1755–1763*. Cambridge, UK: Cambridge University Press, 2002.
Burke, John, and John Bernard Burke. *A Genealogical and Heraldic Dictionary of the Landed Gentry of Great Britain and Ireland*. 3 vols. London: H. Colburn, 1847. (Cited as *Burke's Genealogical and Heraldic Dictionary*)
———. *A Genealogical and Heraldic History of the Extinct and Dormant Baronetcies of England, Ireland, and Scotland*. London: John Russell Smith, 1844. (Cited as *Burke's Extinct and Dormant Baronetcies*)
Butler, Lewis. *The Annals of the King's Royal Rifle Corps*. London: Smith Elder, 1913.
Cannon, Richard. *Historical Record of the Eighteenth, or the Royal Irish Regiment of Foot*. London: Parker, Furnivall, and Parker, 1848.
Carrigan, William. *The History and Antiquities of the Diocese of Ossory*. 4 vols. Dublin: Sealy, Bryers & Walker, 1905.
Carter, Clarence. *Great Britain and the Illinois Country, 1763–1774*. 2 vols. Washington, DC: American Historical Association, 1910.
Chalmers, George. *Caledonia, or A Historical and Topographical Account of North Britain*. Paisley, UK: A. Gardner, 1890.
Cherry, Bridget, and Nikolaus Pevsner. *Devon: The Buildings of England*. 2nd ed. New Haven, CT: Yale University Press, 1991.
Chichester, Henry, and George Burgess-Short. *The Records and Budgets of Every Regiment and Corps in the British Army*. Aldershot: Gale and Polden, 1900.
Churchill, Charles. *Poems by C. Churchill*. 2 vols. London: John Churchill, 1768.
Clark, Murtie J. *Loyalists in the Southern Campaign of the Revolutionary War*. 3 vols. Boston: Genealogical Publishing, 1981.

Bibliography

Clode, Charles M. *The Military Forces of the Crown: Their Administration and Government.* 2 vols. London: John Murray, 1869.

Coldham, Peter W. *American Migrations, 1765–1799.* Baltimore: Genealogical Publishing, 2000.

Cole, Nan, and Todd Braisted. *A History of the 2nd Battalion, New Jersey Volunteers.* Royal Provincial, n.d. http://www.royalprovincial.com/military/rhist/njv/2njvhist.htm.

Conroy, Gay. "Pedigree and History of the Colclough Family of Staffordshire and Wexford." *Journal of the Wexford Historical Society* 22 (2009): 50–60.

Conway, Stephen. "British Army Officers and the American War for Independence." *The William and Mary Quarterly* 41, no. 2 (April 1984): 265–76.

Craig, Michel W. *General Edward Hand: Winter's Doctor.* Lancaster, PA: Rockford Plantation Foundation, 1984.

Cresson, Anne H. "Biographical Sketch of Joseph Fox." *Pennsylvania Magazine of History and Biography* 32, no. 2 (1908): 175–99.

Crooks, John Joseph. *Records Relating to the Gold Coast Settlements for 1750–1874.* London: Frank Cass, 1973.

Curtis, Edward E. *The Organization of the British Army in the American Revolution.* New Haven, CT: Yale University Press, 1926.

Cushman, Elizabeth. *Historic Westchester, 1683–1933: Glimpses of County History.* [Tarrytown, NY]: Westchester County, 1933.

Dahlinger, Charles W. *Pittsburgh: A Sketch of Its Early Social Life.* New York: G. P. Putnam's Sons, 1916.

Daniell, David S. *Cap of Honour: The 300 Years of the Gloucestershire Regiment.* London: White Lion, 2005.

Dann, John C. *The Revolution Remembered: Eyewitness Accounts of the War of Independence.* Chicago: University of Chicago Press, 1980.

Davidson, Alexander, and Bernard Stuve. *A Complete History of Illinois from 1673 to 1873.* Springfield: Illinois Journal, 1874.

Dictionary of National Biography. London: Smith, Elder, 1903.

Dillon, John B. *A History of Indiana, from Its Earliest Exploration by Europeans to the Close of the Territorial Government in 1816.* Indianapolis: Binghand & Doughty, 1859.

Dobson, David. *American Vital Records from the Gentleman's Magazine, 1731–1868.* Baltimore: Genealogical Publishing, 1987.

Duffin, J. M., Mark Lloyd, and Theresa R. Snyder. "William Smith: Biographical Sketch." University of Pennsylvania University Archives and Records Center, 2001. http://www.archives.upenn.edu/faids/upt/upt50/smithwm.html#3.

Duncan, Francis. *The History of the Royal Regiment of Artillery.* London: John Murray, 1872.

Duncan, Jonathan. *History of Guernsey with Occasional Notices of Jersey, Alderney, and Sark and Biographical Sketches.* London: Longman, 1841.

Dunn, Walter S. *Choosing Sides on the Frontier in the American Revolution.* Westport, CT: Praeger, 2007.

Edmonstone, Archibald. *Genealogical Account of the Family of Edmonstone of Duntreath.* Edinburgh: Constable, 1875.

Ellis, Franklin, and Samuel Evans. *History of Lancaster County, Pennsylvania, with Biographical Sketches of Many of Its Pioneers and Prominent Men.* Philadelphia: Everts & Peck, 1883.

Ellis, William Smith. *Notices of the Ellises of England, Scotland, and Ireland, from the Conquest to the Present Time.* London: n.p., 1857.

Farrar, Henry. *Irish Marriages Being an Index to the Marriages in Walker's Hibernian Magazine, 1771 to 1812.* 2 vols. London: Phillimore and Co., 1897. http://www.ancestry.com.

Farrer, Edmund. *The Church Heraldry of Norfolk.* Norwich, CT: A. H Goose, 1889.

Flagg, Edmund. *The Far West; or, A Tour beyond the Mountains.* Edited by Reuben Gold Thwaites. 2 vols. Cleveland, OH: Arthur Clark, 1906.

Flint, Martha B. *Early Long Island: A Colonial Study*, New York: G. P. Putnam's Sons, 1896.

Ford, Worthington C. *British Officers Serving in America, 1754–1774.* Brooklyn, NY: Historical Printing Society, 1897.

Francis, A. D. "The Campaign in Portugal, 1762." *Journal of the Society for Army Historical Research* 45, no. 237 (Spring 1981): 25–43.

Frey, Sylvia R. *The British Soldier in America: A Social History of Military Life in the Revolutionary Period.* Austin: University of Texas Press, 1981.

Frothingham, Richard. *History of the Siege of Boston and Bunker Hill.* 6th ed. Boston: Little, Brown, 1903.

Gardiner, Robert B. *Registers of Wadham College, Oxford, from 1613 to [1871].* London: Bell and Sons, 1895.

Gretton, George L. M. *The Campaigns and History of the Royal Irish Regiment.* 2 vols. Edinburgh: William Blackwood & Sons, 1927.

Groves, John P. *Historical Records of the 7th or Royal Regiment of Fusiliers.* Guernsey, UK: Frederick Guerin, 1903.

Gruber, Ira D. *Books and the British Army in the Age of the American Revolution.* Chapel Hill: University of North Carolina Press, 2010.

Guy, Alan. "The Army of the Georges, 1714–1783." In *The Oxford History of the British Army*, edited by David Chandler and Ian Beckett, 92–111. New York: Oxford University Press, 1994.

———. *Oeconomy and Discipline: Officership and Administration in the British Army, 1714–63.* Dover, NH: Manchester University Press, 1985.

Hackworth, John. *Sir Henry Fermor School, 1744–1994: A History.* Crowborogh, UK: Ashdown Press, 1994.

Hallowes Genealogy. 2007. http://www.hallowesgenealogy.co.uk.

Hammes, Raymond H. "Land Transactions in Illinois Prior to the Sale of Public Domain." *Journal of the Illinois State Historical Society* 77, no. 2 (Summer 1984): 101–14.

Harvey, D. C. "Settlement, Revolution, and War." Blupete, n.d. http://www.blupete.com/Hist/NovaScotiaBk2/Part2/Ch12.htm.

Hayter, Tony. "The Army and the First British Empire, 1714–1783." In *The Oxford History of the British Army*, ed. David Chandler and Ian Beckett, 112–31. New York: Oxford University Press, 1994.

Hazlitt, William C. *A Roll of Honor: A Collection of the Names of over 17,000 Men and Woman throughout the British Isles and in Our Early Colonies Who Collected Manuscripts.* New York: B. Franklin, 1971.

Heber, Reginald. *The Life of the Right Rev. Jeremy Taylor, D.D., F.D.* 1st American ed. Hartford, CT: F. J. Huntington, 1832.

Heitman, Francis B. *Historical Register of Officers of the Continental Army.* Rev. ed. Washington, DC: Rare Book Shop, 1914.

Hime, Henry W. L. *History of the Royal Regiment of Artillery, 1815–1853.* London: Longman, Green, 1908.

Historical Manuscripts Commission. *Report on American Manuscripts in the Royal Institution of Great Britain.* Hereford, UK: Historical Manuscripts Commission, 1904.

"History of St. Thomas Parish." Saint Thomas Episcopal Church. 2008. http://www.saintthomasmmrk.org/index.php/history.

"History of the Pennsylvania Loyalists." Institute for Loyalist Studies. 2010. http://www.royalprovincial.com/military/rhist/paloyal/pal1hist.htm.

"A History of the Provincial Corps of Pennsylvania Loyalists." Institute for Loyalist Studies. 2010. http://www.royalprovincial.com.

Hood, Samuel. *A Brief Account of the Society of the Friendly Sons of St. Patrick: With Biographical Notices of Some of the Members, and Extracts from the Minutes.* Philadelphia: Hibernian Society, 1844.

Houlding, John. *Fit for Service: The Training of the British Army, 1715–1795.* London: Oxford University Press, 1981.

Hurlbut, Henry H. *Chicago Antiquities.* Chicago: privately printed, 1881.

Huston, John W. "The British Evacuation of Fort Pitt, 1772." *Western Pennsylvania Historical Review* 48, no. 4 (October 1965): 317–29.

"The Infamous George Durant." British Broadcasting Corporation, February 3, 2007. http://www.bbc.co.uk/shropshire/content/articles/2007/03/02/slavery__george_durant_feature.shtml.

Jackson, John W. *With the British Army in Philadelphia, 1777–1778.* San Rafael, CA: Presidio Press, 1979.

James, James A. *Oliver Pollock: The Life and Times af an Unknown Patriot.* Freeport, NY: Books for Libraries Press, 1970.

"James Fenimore Cooper Biography." Literature Network, n.d. http://www.online-literature.com/cooperj/.

Jasper, C. "Gorham's Rangers." Land Forces of Britain, the Empire, and Commonwealth, 2007. http://www.regiments.org.

Jenkins, Stephen. *The Old Boston Post Road.* New York: G. P. Putnam's Sons, 1913.

Jones, Paul V. B. *The Household of a Tudor Nobleman.* Cedar Rapids, IA: Torch Press, 1918.

Katcher, Philip R. N. *Encyclopedia of British, Provincial, and German Army Units, 1775–1783.* Harrisburg, PA: Stackpole Books 1973.

Kehoe, Vincent J. R. *An Officers' Guide for Re-Created British Regiments of Foot.* Somis, CA: RCMA, 1996.

Kitzmiller, John M. *In Search of the Forlorn Hope: A Comprehensive Guide to Locating British Regiments and Their Records (1650–World War I)*. Salt Lake City, UT: Manuscript Publishing, 1988.

Koch, John T. *Celtic Culture: A Historical Encyclopedia*. Santa Barbara, CA: ABC-CLIO, 2006.

Kohn, Richard H. "The Social History of the American Soldier: A Review and Prospectus for Research." *American Historical Review* 86 (1981): 553–67.

"Lancashire and Westmoreland Marriage Bonds." Ancestry, n.d. http://www.ancestry.com.

"The List of Jamaican Governors." In *Jamaican Directory, 1878*. Jamaican Family Search Genealogy Research Library. http://www.jamaicanfamilysearch.com/Samples/dgovern.htm.

Loge, Edmund. *The Peerage and Baronetage of the British Empire*. 28th ed. London: Hurst & Blackett, 1859.

Mann, Barbara A. *George Washington's War on Native America*. Westport, CT: Praeger, 2005.

Mason, Edward G. *Early Chicago and Illinois*. Chicago: Fergus, 1890.

Mason, Edward G. *Philippe de Rocheblave and Rocheblave Papers*. Chicago: Fergus, 1890.

Maurice, Frederick. *The History of the Scots Guards, from the Creation of the Regiment to the Eve of the Great War*. 2 vols. London: Chatto & Windus, 1934.

McConnell, Michael N. *Army and Empire: British Soldiers on the American Frontier, 1758–1775*. Lincoln: University of Nebraska Press, 2004.

McCormick, Cyrus H. *The Illinois-Wabash Land Company Manuscript*. Chicago: privately printed, 1915.

Messenger, Charles. *For Love of Regiment: A History of British Infantry, 1660–1914*. 2 vols. London: Pen & Sword Books, 1994.

Miller, William. *The Baronetage of England, or the History of the English Baronets*. Ipswitch, UK: Burrell and Bansby, 1801.

Mills, T. F. *Landforces of Britain, the Empire and Commonwealth*. Regiments. 2005. http://www.regiments.org.

Morrissey, Brendan. *Boston 1775: The Shot Heard around the World*. Oxford, UK: Osprey, 1995.

Namier, Lewis B., and John Brooke. *The House of Commons, 1754–1790*. 2 vols. London: Secker & Warburg, 1964.

National Maritime Museum. *Warship Histories*. 2 vols. Royal Museums Greenwich, 2010. http://www.rmg.co.uk/upload/pdf/Warship_Histories_Vessels_ii.pdf.

Nester, William R. *Haughty Conquerors: Amherst and the Great Indian Uprising of 1763*. Westport, CT: Greenwood, 2000.

New York, Death Newspaper Extracts, 1801–1890 (Barber Collection). Provo, UT: Generations Network, 2005. http://www.ancestry.com.

New York Public Library. *Bulletin of the New York Public Library, Astor, Lenox, and Tilden Foundations*. New York: Public Library, 1898.

Nicholson, John. *The Great Liberty Riot of 1780*. London: BM Bozo, 1985.

Odnitz, Mark F. "The British Officer Corps, 1754–1783." PhD diss., University of Michigan, Ann Arbor, 1988.

Pace, Paul. "Kilts and Courage: The Story of the 42nd or Royal Highland Regiment in the American War for Independence, 1776–1783." Unpublished manuscript.

Patterson, Alfred Temple. *The Other Armada: The Franco-Spanish Attempt to Invade Britain in 1779*. Manchester, UK: Manchester University Press, 1960.

Pease, Theodore C. *The Story of Illinois*. 3rd ed. Chicago: University of Chicago Press, 1965.

Polsue, Joseph. *A Complete Parochial History of the County of Cornwall*. London: William Lake, 1870.

Raikers, George A. *Roll of Officers of the York and Lancaster Regiment, Formerly 65th (2nd Yorkshire, North Riding) Regiment, 1756–1884*. London: Richard Bentley, 1885.

Rees, John. "The Road Appeared Filled with Red Coats: An Episode in the Forage War—the Battle of Millstone, 20 January 1777." *Military Collector & Historian* 62, no. 1 (Winter 2010): 24–35.

Reiss, Oscar. *The Jews in Colonial America*. Jefferson, NC: McFarland, 2004.

Rice, Geoffrey W. "British Foreign Policy and the Falkland Islands Crisis of 1770–1771." *International History Review* 32, no. 2 (June 2010): 273–305.

Richards, Walter. *Her Majesty's Army: A Descriptive Account*. 3 vols. London: Virtue, n.d.

Rogers, Nicholas. *Crowds, Culture, and Politics in Georgian Britain*. New York: Oxford University Press, 1988.

Russell, Nelson V. *The British Regime in Michigan and the Old Northwest*. Philadelphia: Porcupine Press, 1939.

Sabine, Lorenzo. *Biographical Sketches of Loyalists in the American Revolution*. 2 vols. Boston: Little, Brown, 1864.

Schnitzer, Eric. "Transcription of the Court Martial of Lt. General William Strode from the Original Transcript Housed in the British National Archives." Unpublished manuscript.

Scott, Robert F. *Admissions to the College of St. John the Evangelist in the University of Cambridge*. Vol. 3, *July 1715 to November 1767*. Cambridge, UK: Deighton Bell, 1903.

Sewell, Samuel. *The History of Woburn, 1640 to 1860*. Boston: Wiggin & Lunt, 1868.

Shattuck, Lemuel. *The History of the Town of Concord*. Boston: Russell Osborne, 1835.

Shelley, Mary V. *Dr. Ed: The Story of General Edward Hand*. Lititz, PA: Sutter House, 1978.

Shy, John W. *Toward Lexington: The Role of the British Army in the Coming of the American Revolution*. 2 vols. Princeton, NJ: Princeton University Press, 1965.

Smith, Horace W. *Life and Correspondence of the Rev. William Smith, D. D.* Philadelphia: Ferguson Brothers, 1880.

Spanbauer, Jeffrey A. "Gift Giving and the Role of 'Father' in the Illinois Country: John Wilkins's Journal of Transactions with the Indians, 1768–1772." *Journal of Illinois History* 8, no. 2 (Winter 2005): 295–320.

———. "Indian Affairs at Fort De Chartres during the British Occupation, 1765–1772." Master's thesis, Illinois State University, Carbondale, 1993.
Spring, Matthew H. *With Zeal and with Bayonets Only: The British Army on Campaign in North America, 1775–1783.* Norman: University of Oklahoma Press, 2008.
Stainforth, Peter. *Not Found Wanting: A History of the Stainforths, an Anglo-Saxon Family.* Manhattan, KS: Able Books, 2003.
Stead, William T., ed. *Borderland: A Quarterly Review and Index.* London, 1896.
Sterling, David L. "American Prisoners of War in New York: A Report by Elias Boudinot." *William and Mary Quarterly* 13, no. 3 (July 1956): 376–93.
"Stevenson's Bell Rock Lighthouse." Bellrock. 2010. http://www.bellrock.org.uk/.
Storm, Colton. "The Notorious Colonel Wilkins." *Journal of the Illinois State Historical Society* 40, no. 1 (March 1947): 7–22.
Story, D. A. *The DeLanceys: Romance of a Great Family.* Toronto, Canada: Nelson & Sons, 1931.
Strachan, Hew. *The Politics of the British Army.* Oxford, UK: University Press, 1997.
Summer, Percy. "Cox & Co, Army Agents: Uniform Items from their Ledgers." *Journal of the Society for Army Historical Research* 12, no. 2 (1938): 135–46.
Swett, Samuel. *History of Bunker Hill Battle, with a Plan.* 2nd ed. Boston: Munroe & Francis, 1826.
Swiney, G. C. *Historical Records of the 32nd (Cornwall) Light Infantry, Not the 1st Battalion Duke of Cornwall's L. I.: From the Formation of the Regiment in 1702 Down to 1892.* London: Simpkin, 1893.
Ten-Pounder: An Exposure of the Spy System Pursued in Glasgow, during the years 1816–17–18–19 and 20. Glasgow: Muir, Gowans, 1833.
"Tithe Apportionments: Winterborne Monkton, 1841." Dorset Coast Digital Archives, n.d. http://www.dcda.org.uk/TitheApps/TITHEwmn.htm.
"Tong Timeline." Discovering Tong. 2007. http://www.discoveringtong.org/timechart.htm.
United States Congress. "Edward Hand." In *Biographical Directory of the United States Congress.* Washington, DC: U.S. Government Printing Office, 2005. http://bioguide.congress.gov.
University of Edinburgh School of Law. "History of the Faculty of Law." University of Edinburgh, 2010. http://www.law.ed.ac.uk/history/chpt2.aspx.
Valentine, Alan C. *The British Establishment, 1760—1784: An Eighteenth-Century Biographical Dictionary.* 2 vols. Norman: University of Oklahoma Press, 2010.
Wallace, Nesbit W. *A Regimental Chronicle and List of Officers of the 60th or the King's Royal Rifle Corps, formerly the 62nd or Royal American Regiment of Foot.* London: Harrison, 1879.
Watson, John F. *Philadelphia: Being a Collection of Memoirs, Anecdotes, and Incidents of the City and Its Inhabitants.* Philadelphia: E. L. Carey and A. Hart, 1830.
West, Edmund. *Family Data Collection—Marriages.* Provo, UT: Generations Network, 2001. Available online at ancestry.com.
Winfield, Rif. *British Warships in the Age of Sail, 1793–1817: Design, Construction, Careers, and Fate.* London: Seaforth, 2007.

Bibliography

Woodhull, Mary G., and Francis B. Stevens. *The Woodhull Family in England and America*. Philadelphia, Henry T. Coates, 2007.

Worthy, Charles. *Devonshire Wills*. London: Bemrose & Sons, 1896.

Yates, G. K. *Officers, Staff and Other Ranks of His Majesty's 47th Regiment of Foot*. Unpublished manuscript.

Index

Abercrombie, James, 156
Acheson, Hamilton, 234
adjutant, 29–32, 44, 48–49, 51–52, 59, 65, 92, 106, 148, 156, 172, 192–93, 199–204, 211, 222–23, 242, 245, 253. *See also* Mawby, John, Jr.; Mawby, John, Sr.; Serle, Thomas; Turner, Samuel
adjutant general (British): deputy, 65, 100, 134, 197; records, 264
adjutant general (Continental), 206
Adye, Stephen Payne, 81, 104, 118, 142, 211, 219, 230, 239
Africa, 54, 187–88, 261; Royal African Corps, 170
agents (Indian). *See* Indian agents
agents (regimental), 18, 33–34, 81, 86, 118, 122, 150, 173, 218, 266–67. *See also* Cox and Meir
age of officers, 53–58
aide de camp, 120, 143, 156; to the King, 239
Aldcroft, James, 182–83
Amherst, Lord Jeffrey, 45, 49–50, 86, 93, 201, 211, 253
Antrobus, Hugh, 29, 39, 46, 62, 103, 122, 222
Armstrong, Bigoe, 75, 80

Bailey, John, 237
barracks, 13, 22, 24, 71, 80, 89, 107, 116, 131, 170, 187, 193, 214, 258; Brigade of Guards, 174; officers staying in, 178; troops without, 128; women ordered out of, 111
Barrington, Lord, 25, 45, 68, 73, 78, 84, 94, 98, 136, 200, 238

Bath, 66, 78, 85–86, 112, 160, 254
Bath, Order of the. *See* Order of the Bath
Batt, Robert, 74, 104, 139
Batt, Thomas, 15, 19, 63, 67–68, 71, 74, 104–8, 120, 139, 156, 164, 171, 203, 214–16, 228
battalion companies, 17, 21, 79, 81, 88–89, 102, 103, 145, 260; organization of, 29–32
battalion guns, 253
battles and sieges: Blenheim, 5; Bunker Hill, 23–24, 73, 100, 109, 121, 137, 145, 147, 246; Cherry Valley Massacre, 206; Germantown, 158, 234; Lexington and Concord, 90, 109, 192, 246; Long Island, 205; Malplaquet, 5; Monmouth, 140, 157; Namur, 4–5; Princeton, 45, 139–40, 205, 233–34; Saratoga, 117, 191, 200; Toulon, 12, 151, 189, 213, 261; Vincennes, 25; Yorktown, 1, 206
Baynton, Wharton, and Morgan, 94–95, 136, 142–43, 242–43, 247–48
Bell, Martin, 76
Bewes, George, 32, 71, 113 126, 144–46, 170, 176, 186
Blackwood, William, 32, 34, 57, 65, 68–69, 98, 108–10, 214, 221, 229
books owned or subscribed to, 81, 99, 101, 104, 118, 142, 163, 211, 219, 230, 235, 239
Breed's Hill and Charleston Heights, 73, 90, 145. *See also* battles and sieges: Bunker Hill
brigade major. *See* major of brigade
British Establishment, 7, 8, 11–12, 32–33

Index

British navy. *See* Royal Navy
British Parliament, 33, 35, 86, 135; 1781 Loan to, 140; members of, 66, 78, 85, 239
British regiments
Artillery: Royal Artillery, 9, 21, 28, 38, 43, 75, 123, 140, 164, 215, 239–41; Royal Corps of Drivers, 240; Royal Invalid Artillery, 240
Dragoon Guards and Dragoons: 1st Dragoon Guards, 51; 3rd Dragoon Guards, 257; 3rd Dragoons, 257; 4th Dragoons, 257; 5th Dragoons, 33; 6th (Inniskilling) Dragoons, 41, 64, 224–25; 7th (Light) Dragoons, 87, 110; 8th Dragoons, 33; 9th Dragoons, 33, 113; 10th Dragoons, 41; 11th Dragoons, 257; 13th Dragoons, 33; 15th Light Dragoons, 225; 16th Light Dragoons, 26, 257; 24th Light Dragoons, 87
Foot: 1/1st Foot, 114, 253, 254; 2/1st Foot, 79, 253–57; 2nd (Queen's Royal) Foot, 253–57; 3rd (Buffs) Foot, 70, 162; 4th (King's Own) Foot, 207; 5th Foot, 99, 102, 114, 207; 6th Foot, 25, 99, 258; 7th (Royal Fusiliers) Foot, 139–40, 174, 229; 8th (King's) Foot, 10–11, 25, 52, 56, 75, 102, 126, 150, 206, 250; 9th Foot, 11, 64, 128, 191–92; 10th Foot, 10, 23, 26, 52, 110, 200, 207; 12th Foot, 6, 51, 52, 74, 254; 13th Foot, 251, 254; 14th Foot, 6, 10, 103, 146–48; 15th Foot, 216–17; 16th Foot, 6, 8, 10, 26, 45, 99, 193–94, 200, 233, 239; 17th Foot, 52, 74, 140, 152, 207, 233–34; 21st (Royal N. British Fusiliers) Foot, 6; 22nd Foot, 15, 52, 49, 207; 23rd (Royal Welch Fusiliers) Foot, 41, 50, 54–55, 162, 207; 24th Foot, 6; 25th Foot, 8, 254; 26th Foot, 9–10, 18, 26, 103; 27th (Inniskilling) Foot, 10, 45, 128, 200, 207, 262; 28th Foot, 6, 8, 10, 64, 128–29, 200, 227; 29th Foot, 10, 18, 114; 31st Foot, 10, 11, 18, 23, 228; 32nd Foot, 41, 92; 34th Foot, 15, 17, 20, 88, 94, 111, 114, 118, 122, 124, 128, 172, 176, 247; 35th Foot, 52, 74, 91, 207; 36th Foot, 6, 8, 41, 70; 38th Foot, 10, 170, 207; 39th Foot, 254; 40th Foot, 99, 225, 233; 41st Foot, 54; 42nd (Royal Highland) Foot, 10, 41, 52–54, 57, 153, 200, 246–47, 249; 43rd Foot, 73, 90; 44th Foot, 45, 49, 53, 129, 153–54; 45th Foot, 26, 64–65, 87, 110, 174, 191, 256; 46th Foot, 10, 49, 83–84, 134, 200–201; 47th Foot, 64, 100, 113, 173, 191, 214–17, 238; 48th Foot, 226; 49th Foot, 100; 50th Foot, 12, 25, 91, 245, 254; 51st Foot, 50, 254; 52nd Foot, 10, 26, 51, 73; 53rd Foot, 190; 55th Foot, 41, 44–46, 50, 52–54, 61, 63, 92–93, 134, 153, 174, 231, 233–34; 56th Foot, 8, 254; 58th Foot, 254; 59th Foot, 10, 25, 28, 51, 73, 252–55; 60th (Royal American) Foot; 18, 39, 48–49, 148, 155, 158–59, 199, 201 238, 242; 1st Bn, 93, 149, 201; 2nd Bn, 69, 97, 201, 243, 253; 3rd Bn, 148; 61st Foot, 35, 79, 100, 254; 62nd Foot, 52, 56; 63rd Foot, 110, 157, 238; 64th Foot, 10, 50, 207; 65th Foot, 10, 22–25, 75, 109, 196, 203, 228, 236–39, 241, 244–46, 248–51, 253–54; 68th Foot, 50; 69th Foot, 253–54; 70th Foot, 228, 254; 72nd (Highland) Foot, 100; 83rd (County of Dublin) Foot, 262; 86th (Royal County Down) Foot, 262; 87th (Royal Irish Fusiliers) Foot, 197, 262; 88th (Connaught Rangers) Foot, 87, 155; 89th (Princess Victoria's) Foot, 262; 108th (Madras Infantry) Foot, 262
Horse: 1st Horse, 7, 33; 2nd Horse, 33, 41
Household Troops: 1st Foot Guards, 85, 174–75, 225; 3rd Foot Guards, 249
British regiments, disbanded ca. 1763 *(note: numbers were reused, so the 74th Foot disbanded in 1763 has no actual relationship to the one disbanded in 1784):* 70th Foot, 228–29; 72nd (originally 2/33rd Foot), 122; 74th Foot, 163, 165; 76th Foot, 226; 77th (Montgomery's Highlanders) Foot, 246; 80th (Gage's Light Armed) Foot, 93, 106; 83rd (Sebright's Invalids) Foot, 85; 85th Foot, 249; 90th Foot, 88; 93rd Foot, 12; 97th (Foresters) Foot, 229; 103rd Foot, 35, 244; 104th Foot, 246; 105th, 238; 109th Foot, 127; 112th Foot, 228; 113th Foot, 228; 122nd Foot, 51; Gorham's North American Rangers, 36, 40, 65, 152
British regiments, disbanded ca. 1783: 19th Light Dragoons, 228; 21st Light Dragoons, 225; 71st (Frazer's Highland) Foot, 72; 75th (Prince of Wales) Foot, 51, 91, 126–27, 188; 78th (Highland) Foot, 187; 79th Foot, 51–52, 155, 196, 228; 83rd Foot, 259; 86th (Rutland) Foot, 51; 89th Foot, 54, 119, 161–62, 225; 90th (Yorkshire Vol.) Foot, 51, 184, 196–97; 91st Foot, 51, 193; 93rd Foot,

Index

161, 207; 95th Foot, 51; 96th Foot, 51; 97th Foot, 51, 221–22; 98th Foot, 239; 99th (Jamaica) Foot, 64, 134, 241; 100th Foot, 239; 104th Foot, 258–60; 105th Foot, 237; Ferguson's Rifle Corps, 47, 65, 156–58
British regiments, disbanded ca. 1814: 7th Royal Garrison Bn, *later* 7th Royal Veteran Bn, 127–28; Royal African Corps, 170
British regiments, Loyalist: King's Orange Rangers, 107; Maryland Loyalists, 157; New Jersey Volunteers, 140, 174; Pennsylvania Loyalists, 157; Royal Fencible Americans, 25, 106–8, 132–33, 153; United Corps of Maryland and Pennsylvania Loyalists, 157
Bruce, Thomas, 22, 203, 238–39
Bruere, George, 23, 59, 61, 66, 90, 146–49, 179, 203, 237
Burgoyne, John, 43, 191
Buttricke, George, 14, 17, 20, 39–40, 48–50, 57, 94–97, 124, 142, 194–95, 199–204, 211, 223, 253, 265

Cahokia, 16–17, 21, 88–89, 96, 118, 154, 176, 228
Carleton, Guy, 77, 127–29
cashiered, 24, 62, 66
Catholic Relief Act, 256
Catholics. *See* Roman Catholics
Channel Islands, 42, 110, 127, 146, 151, 158, 179, 193, 212–13, 221, 258. *See also* Guernsey (island of); Jersey (island of)
chaplain, 24, 29–32, 43–44, 49, 56–59, 63, 165, 199–200, 208, 213–20, 224; deputy, 31, 43, 93, 200, 216, 218, 220; court martial involving, 67, 105, 112, 118, 203, 211, 214–16. *See also* Leathes, Stanley; Newburgh, Robert Jocelyn; Smith, William (deputy chaplain); Thomas, Daniel
Chapman, Benjamin, 18, 25, 32, 65, 68–71, 74, 89, 98, 100, 104, 109, 111–13, 119, 122, 128, 150, 158–59, 164, 169, 173, 183, 193, 196, 211, 214, 227
children, 12, 70–72, 87–89, 105, 108, 126, 133, 148, 160, 207, 213, 219, 222, 232, 248, 250; died, 17; sent to England, 211
Christ Church (Philadelphia), 104, 108, 218
Churchill, Horace, 64, 224–25
Church of England, 3, 31, 200, 217
civil litigation and courts, 66–67, 82, 120, 129, 166; in Illinois, 68, 88, 94, 124, 136, 247

Clinton, Henry, 107, 157
Colclough, Caesar, 44, 63, 225–26, 229
Collins, Robert, 164, 216
Colonial Assembly: New York, 217; Pennsylvania, 13–14, 218
commissary, 96–97, 154, 243, 246–47; records, 115; supplies, 69, 89, 93, 122, 134, 167, 189
commissions, 33–37; colonelcies, 37–38; pre-approved sale, 80; prices of, 30, 36–37, 52; recommended but not confirmed, 36, 49, 122, 150, 195; refused, 35; sold, 44, 54, 61–62, 98, 105, 113, 118, 137, 166, 205, 213, 225, 235; without purchase, 35, 37, 54, 56, 72–73, 128, 143, 151–52, 170, 182, 187, 190, 192, 194, 233, 245, 250–51
conflict among officers, 68–69, 164–65, 210, 216; litigation, 106, 129; petitions regarding, 94, 97–99, 203, 229–30
Conolly, William, 34–35, 70, 74, 94, 96, 98, 149–52, 154, 190, 225, 257, 261
Continental Congress, 116, 126, 167–68, 206, 243–44
Continental Navy, 65, 209–10
Continental regiments: 1st New York, 24, 209; Lancaster Associators, 205; Pennsylvania Rifle Regiment, 205; 1st Pennsylvania Regiment, 205–6
Cope, John, 31, 137, 176, 226–27
Cornwallis, Charles, 140, 157
corporals, 7–8, 15, 17–21, 29–32, 150, 177, 187, 254, 261; best exercising, 172, 254; drafted, 228; former, 68, 89; corporal's guard, 115; lance, 174; recruiting, 252
court-martials, 24, 66–70, 82, 90, 105, 131, 140, 156, 175, 179, 209, 215, 230, 234, 259–60; charges brought by Payne, 90, 165; Continental Army, 167; for desertion, 14, 91, 94, 104, 110–12, 141, 145, 170, 184, 211, 221; regimental courts, 130, 169 , 191, 237–38, 249; for having withheld clothing, 86–87
court of inquiry, 115, 136, 143, 149, 163, 214, 220, 243
Cox and Drummond. *See* Cox and Meir
Cox and Meir, 33, 103, 142, 172, 176, 182, 186, 194, 198, 218, 220–21, 225–26, 229, 233, 266
Coxheath Camp, 65, 91, 100, 112, 145, 172, 182, 184, 196, 211–12, 239, 241, 245–46, 250, 253–54
Crosby, Edward, 36, 40, 65, 152–53, 161, 170, 229

327

Index

Cumberland Fort (Jamaica), 134
Cumming, Thomas, 169, 186, 227–28

De Birniere, John, 39, 53, 72, 153–55, 196, 253
debtors' prison, 121
De Lancey, John, 40
De Lancey, John Peter, 25, 34, 40, 47, 64–65, 71, 75, 112, 131, 156–60, 170, 193
De Lancey, Oliver, 178
deputy chaplain. *See under* chaplain
deputy quartermaster general, 65, 113, 133–34, 190
desertion, 23–24, 129–30, 132, 156, 231; court-martials for, 14, 91, 94, 104, 110–12, 141, 145, 170, 184, 211, 221; enticing men to desert, 24, 140, 175
Detroit, 11, 16, 20–21, 25, 47, 66, 72, 93, 103, 123, 126, 150, 152, 154, 206, 265
Disney, Daniel, 129
Douglas, Robert, 75, 235, 239–41
Dover Castle, 25, 47, 65, 110, 119, 137, 145, 153, 161, 170, 183–84, 194, 207, 211, 252
drafting, 11, 12, 25–26, 63, 78, 133, 140, 150, 152, 156, 174, 191, 228, 239, 245, 250, 256
drummers, 2, 7–8, 11, 18, 25, 29–32, 187, 220, 253–54, 261
Dublin, 7, 9, 12, 33, 39, 58, 80, 87, 91, 103, 124, 141, 185, 204; physicians from, 200; Prerogative Court at, 103; Royal Irish inspected at, 47, 88, 93, 109, 117, 136, 139, 142, 173, 175, 194, 195, 222
Dublin Castle, 39, 234
duels, 36, 61–62, 67, 112, 120, 159, 195
Dutch forts (Africa), 188

Edinburgh, 6, 8, 56
Edmonstone, Charles, 15, 19, 21, 29–31, 34, 59, 63, 68, 69, 77, 84, 94, 102, 104, 113–17, 119, 129, 141, 150, 162, 214
Elliot, Walter, 76, 265
Ellis, Henry Walton, 54–55, 152
Ellis, John, 36
Ellis, John Joyner, 46, 54, 59, 153, 160–62
Ellis, Welborne, 10
engineer officers, 99–100, 175, 242; acting engineers, 75, 98, 189, 242–43
Evans, John, 31, 70, 81, 98, 117–18, 150, 226

Fermor, Henry, 32, 34–35, 57, 118–19, 150, 152, 161, 175, 197, 249
Finchley Camp, 110, 137, 145, 151, 189, 193, 258
flank companies, 100, 109, 259, 260. *See also* grenadiers; light infantry

Folliott, Henry, 29, 30, 40, 55, 60, 63, 71, 75, 79–81, 117
Folliott, John, 75, 142
Forbes, Lord Arthur, 3
Forbes, Gordon, 247
foreign officers, 34, 38, 41–43. *See also* nationality
Fort Augustus (Scotland), 6
Fort Bute (Louisiana), 180
Fort Cavendish. *See* Fort Chartres
Fort Chartres, 14–21, 75, 81–82, 92–97, 109, 120, 123, 136–39, 142–43, 150, 154, 160–61, 172, 176, 185, 195, 203, 220–21, 223, 226, 237, 240, 242–43, 247, 265; Royal Irish ordered to, 14; sickness at, 17
Fort Cumberland (Nova Scotia), 107–8
Fort Du Quesne. *See* Fort Pitt
Fort Gage. *See* Kaskaskia
Fort George (Guernsey), 258–59
Fort George (Scotland), 149
Fort George (West Indies), 221
Fort Knyphausen, 175
Fort Ligonier, 242
Fort Loudon, 104
Fort Marvoa (Portugal), 85
Fort Massiac, 246
Fort Michilimackinac, 21, 25
Fort Niagara, 21, 25, 93, 231, 250
Fort Pitt, 14–21, 61, 81–82, 88, 89, 93–94, 102, 104, 111, 114–15, 118–20, 122, 139, 141, 145, 162, 167–69, 172, 176, 180, 185, 205; Continental Army at, 167–69, 206, 244; duel at, 67, 195; Indians at, 66, 243; Royal Irish ordered to, 14; settlement at, 168–69, 244; supplies at, 67, 167–68
Fort Schlosser, 93
Fort Ticonderoga, 71, 93, 99, 153, 156, 191
Fort Washington, 205, 206
Fort William (Scotland), 9
Fowler, Alexander, 24, 40, 46, 63, 65–69, 71, 82, 84, 89, 95, 97–98, 105–6, 109–11, 130–32, 136, 142–43, 150, 162–69, 178–81, 196, 209, 215–16, 230
French, 5, 6, 9, 15, 27, 93, 99, 187, 222; abolished purchase system, 34; in Illinois, 16, 94–96, 123–24, 246; invasion threat, 235, 254–55; language, 123, 154; prisoners of war, 255; Republicans, 189–90

Gage, Thomas, 9, 14–19, 22, 24–25, 34, 36, 44–46, 66, 68–69, 72–75, 78, 80, 82–84,

328

Index

92, 94–99, 106, 111–12, 115, 116, 118, 122–25, 129–30, 136, 143, 146–48, 154, 161, 164–66, 171, 173, 177, 194, 200, 215–16, 223, 238, 247–48
German auxiliaries, 59, 76; Third Waldeck Regiment, 157
Gibraltar, 10–12, 42, 71, 74, 110, 112, 121, 151, 162, 170, 189–90, 193, 213, 229, 250, 260–61; 1727 siege, 5; duel at, 158–59
Gilfillan, Thomas, 50
Gilfillan, William, 40
Gordon, George, 241
Gordon, Harry, 242
Gordon Riots, 100, 137, 145, 151, 256
Greaves, William, 40, 228–29
grenadiers, 15, 21, 23, 25, 61, 68, 88–90, 96, 103, 109, 112, 114, 137, 146–47, 158, 176, 190, 228, 238; equipment lost, 23; killed, 17, 23; organization of, 29–32; of 104th Foot, 260
Guernsey (island of), 137, 162, 183, 212–13, 258

Haldimand, Fredrick, 67, 125–27, 214, 265
half pay, 35–40, 58, 63–64, 98, 111, 114, 121–22, 127, 140, 146–47, 152–53, 155, 162–63, 177–79, 183–84, 188, 193, 196–97, 200, 217, 224, 225–26, 228–30, 238–39, 340, 244–46, 249, 260
Hamilton, Claudius, 44, 228–29
Hamilton, Henry, 72, 125, 154
Hamilton, Isaac, 24, 34, 57, 60, 63, 66–68, 78–84, 89–90, 94, 98, 102, 115, 117, 123–24, 129, 131, 163–65, 171, 177, 195, 204, 214–15, 220
Hamilton, John, 40, 228–29
Hamilton, Robert, 57, 62, 103, 105, 119–21, 230; tried for murder, 195–96
Hamilton, William, 110
Hand, Edward, 40, 61–63, 65, 71, 114–15, 145, 168, 200–201, 204–9, 218
Handamede, John, 207
Hearst, Francis Seymour, 241
Hoar, Charles, 57, 71–72, 174, 183–85, 205, 224
Holland, Thomas, 50, 76
House of Lords, 185
Howard, Francis, 175, 185–86
Howe, William, 1, 77, 116, 133–34, 148, 153, 156–57, 240
Hutchins, Thomas, 69–70, 75, 97–99, 168, 218, 242–44

Illinois Country, 11, 14–21, 24–25, 46, 50, 61, 68, 72, 75, 88–89, 97–98, 104, 109, 111, 114, 118, 122–27, 139, 142, 150, 154, 163–64, 172, 175–76, 201–2, 211, 216, 237, 240, 242, 247–48, 253–54; courts in, 94, 136; governor of, 82, 92, 102; Indian relations at, 96, 125, 221
Illinois Land Company, 248
indentured servants, 140, 230
independent companies, 9, 50, 53, 56, 127, 186, 229, 245; of Free Negroes, 246; of Invalids, 127, 149; Irish, 3; Jamaican, 40, 163
influence at court, 35, 56, 78, 87, 234–35
Indian agents, 15, 66, 96, 104, 242
Indians, 20, 96, 124; land deals, 124–25; premium on scalps, 95; raids, 124, 248; relations with, 15, 20, 90, 93, 96, 124, 150, 206, 242; supplies and gifts, 115, 123–24
Irish Establishment, 7, 11–12, 27, 29, 33, 199, 201
Irish Parliament, 39, 155
Irish Rebellion of 1798, 251

Jacobites, 6, 88
Jersey (island of), 127, 158, 189, 193, 258
Johnson, Benjamin, 19, 30–31, 39, 46, 63, 69, 103–4, 119, 137, 144, 222, 224, 229–31
Johnson, Sir William, 96, 104, 154

Kaskaskia, 16, 19–22, 82, 94–96, 111, 123–27, 144, 149–50, 154, 163, 176, 221, 248
Kelly, Francis John, 169–70, 214, 249
Knight, John, 17

Lamb, Roger, 185
land grants, 95, 154, 167–86, 179, 201
Land Ordinance of 1785, 244, 247
land speculation, 150, 153, 205, 219; with Indians, 114, 125, 150, 248
Lane, Matthew, 55, 121–22, 142, 146, 203, 220, 235, 247
Leathes, Stanley, 43, 56–57, 63, 208, 219
Lee, Samuel, 23
Levi Franks and Company, 122, 150
light infantry, 18–19, 22, 28, 29, 31–32, 36, 109–10, 123, 153–54, 156, 174, 192, 226, 229, 245, 249; battalions, 72, 106, 207, 238; establishment of, 18; raising of, 136, 230
London, 3, 7, 15, 33, 47, 68, 87, 91–92, 97–99, 101, 110–11, 122, 128, 135, 137, 145, 148–51, 155, 166, 183, 189, 190, 193, 216–18, 222, 231, 236, 243, 257–58

Index

Lord, Hugh, 19–22, 25, 31–32, 40, 47, 51, 66, 69, 71, 82, 91, 102, 112, 118, 122–28, 136, 145–46, 150, 154, 164, 192, 221, 226, 240, 248, 252
Louisiana, 15, 179–80, 244
Loyalist claims, 106, 139–40, 158–59
Loyalist regiments. *See* British regiments, Loyalist
Lynn, John L. 40, 56, 207–10

MacKay, John, 22, 237, 241, 244–45, 249–50
major of brigade, 65, 92, 211, 253; of the day, 212
manual of arms (1778), 253
marines, 38, 107, 109–10, 120, 238; Royal Irish serving as, 3, 261
marriage. *See* wives
mate. *See* surgeon's mate
Mawby, George, 73–74, 186–88
Mawby, John, Jr., 65, 73, 91, 170–72, 192, 196, 253
Mawby, John, Sr., 47, 49–50, 53, 56–57, 65, 70, 80, 102–3, 137, 143, 151, 171, 182, 193, 202, 210–14, 223, 249, 253, 259
Mawby, Sebright, 71, 73–74, 151, 188–91
medicine, 31, 204, 218, 222; care of Indians, 221; fever, 17, 108, 172, 202; preparation, 200–201, 208; officers resigning to practice, 40, 62, 205
merchants, 94–95, 122, 136, 142–43, 150, 242–43, 247–48
militia (British), 51, 53, 97, 253–57, 259; Essex, 204, 253; Jersey, 212–13; Kaskaskia, 47; South Hampshire, 253, 258; West Yorkshire, 253
militia (Continental), 168, 205
Miller, Henry, 245
Minorca, 5, 10–11, 190
Musgrave, Thomas, 207
Musgrave, William, 50, 76
mutiny, 108; Indian, 38; of the 104th Foot, 137, 212, 258–60

nationality, 38–43
nepotism, 73–75
Newburgh, Robert Jocelyn, 24, 67–68, 89, 105–6, 112, 114, 130, 133, 171, 203, 211, 213–17
New York City, 9–10, 19, 22, 24–26, 67, 71, 80, 83, 95, 97, 105, 107, 111, 116, 129, 133, 149, 152, 153, 159, 161, 164, 171, 174, 179, 183, 194, 208, 230, 234, 240, 246, 248; barracks at, 71; court-martials at, 140, 203, 211, 215–16; French at, 127; mobs at, 129–31, 152–53, 156, 174, 209; officer commanding at, 102, 129; refugees at, 108, 140
noncommissioned officers, 2, 126, 132. *See also* corporals; sergeants
No Popery Riots. *See* Gordon Riots
North, Lord, 50, 86

officers from the ranks, 47–48, 50–53, 56. *See also* Buttricke, George; Mawby, John, Sr.
Order of the Bath, 55, 100

parole. *See under* prisoners of war
Paterson, Marcus, 172, 225
paymaster, 69, 92, 111, 122, 167, 203, 243, 247. *See also* Chapman, Benjamin; Lane, Matthew
Payne, Benjamin Charnock, 24–25, 32, 47, 64–68, 70–74, 83, 90, 102, 113, 116, 128–34, 151–53, 156, 164–65, 171, 179, 184, 186, 194, 209, 214, 216, 227, 238, 265
Perkins, William, 70, 171–72, 190
petitions: to the king, 90, 147–48; to Lords of Treasury, 98–99; against Wilkins, 94, 97–98, 124, 203, 229–30
Pexton, John, 245–46
Philadelphia, 10–22, 26–27, 71, 81, 89, 93–94, 97, 103–8, 116, 118, 122–23, 145, 150, 156–57, 161, 164, 167, 171, 177, 179–81, 194, 198, 201–7, 217–19, 230, 234, 240, 242; barracks at, 12, 22, 80, 111, 214; barracks master general at, 134; Christ Church at, 104, 108, 200; merchants, 248–49; Royal Irish mustered at, 46, 139, 176
Piercy, John, 64, 191–92
Pontiac, 96–97
Pontiac's Rebellion, 10, 93, 145, 242, 268
Prideaux, Edmund, 57, 114, 173–75, 179, 203, 245
Prideaux, John Wilmot, 45–46, 61, 71, 194, 196, 203, 231–32
prisoners (criminal), 130–31, 151, 165, 222, 238
prisoners of war, 3, 6, 21, 64, 116–17, 134, 191–92, 255; parole, 116, 191
provincial commissions, 153, 157–59, 174

quartermaster, 14, 17, 20, 27–32, 39, 49–52, 54, 59, 92, 97, 115, 142, 146, 167, 199–204, 205, 242. *See also* Buttricke, George; Holland, Thomas

Index

Raymond, William, 61, 175
recruiting, 8, 10, 12, 15, 17–19, 25, 35, 90, 104, 114, 242, 254–55, 258, 261; officers assigned to recruiting service, 80, 106, 120, 123, 126, 138, 139, 145, 151–53, 156, 161, 172, 174, 192–94, 196, 203, 211, 224, 227, 230–31, 233, 246, 250; parties, 39, 46–47, 54, 156, 252; for rank, 35–36
Reed, John, 124
regimental agent. *See* agent (regimental)
Richardson, William, 23, 32, 47, 61, 74, 135–38, 158, 161, 179, 241, 249
Rocheblave, Philippe de, 20–21, 126–27
Roman Catholics, 3, 92, 257; Jesuit land sold to British, 127; prohibited from service, 34
British navy (Royal Navy), 34, 71, 132, 188, 232; HMS *Alligator*, 188; HMS *Asia*, 24, 116, 152–53, 156, 171, 184, 194; HMS *Hygeia*, 187; HMS *Leander*, 187–88; HMS *Lively*, 132; HMS *Scarborough*, 134; HMS *Vulture*, 107; transports, 24, 103, 134, 149
Rumsey, James, 20, 75, 124–25, 154, 238, 246–48
Russell, John, 23

Sebright, John Saunders, 15, 29–32, 35, 42–44, 47–48, 57–59, 63, 65, 74, 77–81, 85–88, 97–98, 110, 122, 145, 163, 173, 177, 188, 201–3, 205, 210, 213, 220, 230
sergeant majors, 48, 50–52, 133, 201, 204, 253
sergeants, 7–8, 18, 20, 25, 29–32, 48–53, 73, 76, 104, 125, 127, 171, 177, 187, 194, 199, 210, 238, 254, 259, 261; beaten, 129, 132–33; drafted, 228; recruiting, 230, 252; serving as sheriff, 124, 248
Serle, Thomas, 126, 146, 192–93
Shaw, Henry, 46, 193–94, 203, 232–33
Shee, John, 22–23, 25, 29–34, 40, 51, 57, 60–61, 68–71, 79, 84, 88–92, 96, 98, 102, 109, 111–12, 118, 136, 172, 203, 214, 241, 245, 250
sieges. *See* battles and sieges
Simes, Thomas: *Military Guide for Young Officers*, 235; *Military Medley*, 163, 235
Sinclair, George, 22, 109, 237, 245, 248–50
Slator, William Henry, 194–95
slaves and slavery, 20, 68, 72, 124–25, 135–36, 155, 210, 220, 247
Smith, John, 241, 249
Smith, William (deputy chaplain), 92–93, 217–19
Smith, William (line officer), 61, 104, 176, 220

soldiers, 2, 19, 24, 38, 89–90, 174–75, 212–13, 220, 252, 254; commissioned, 47–53, 56; from convicts, 187; extra duty, 123, 167; families of, 24, 72, 107; fraternizing with, 215; poor treatment of, 129–30, 133; punished, 14–15, 94, 104, 129–33, 141; rewarded, 259–60; Roman Catholic, 3; servants, 72; urged to desert, 156, 175
Spanish, 6, 9, 15, 96, 100, 158, 189, 226; in Illinois, 16, 96, 151, 168, 181; invasion threat, 100, 253, 255; threat in Illinois, 17–18, 180
Stainforth, George, 29–31, 71, 117, 138–41
Stewart, John, 29–30, 88, 109, 114, 121–22, 141–42, 201–2
St. Louis, 17–19, 96
surgeon, 6, 19–20, 24, 28–32, 44, 49, 123, 125–26, 199–200, 205, 209, 220–21, 234
surgeon's mate, 19, 24, 27–32, 39–40, 56, 58–59, 61, 126, 131, 152, 199–201, 204–9

Thomas, Daniel, 43–44, 214, 218–20
Thomasson, Thomas, 20, 34, 40, 62, 123, 205, 220–22
Tracey, Godfrey, 62, 120, 136, 195–96
traders. *See* merchants; *individual firms*
Trevor, James Taylor, 44, 53–55, 63, 194, 229, 232–34
Trist, Elizabeth House, 177–81
Trist, Nicolas, 35, 40, 56, 63, 71, 82–83, 131–32, 147, 164, 168, 174, 176–81, 191, 209–10, 215
troop rotation, 10–12, 204, 260
Turner, Samuel, 202, 222–23
Twentyman, Samuel, 73, 196–97

United States Congress, 169, 206, 265
USS *Alliance*, 209–10

Vincennes, 21, 125, 168

Wabash Land Company, 125
Wadman, Francis, 37, 44, 56, 60, 66, 142–43, 234–36
Warley Camp, 47, 91, 110, 113, 134, 138, 145, 153, 170, 182, 189, 193, 254–56
War of Spanish Succession, 5
Washington, George, 65, 162, 167, 205, 207, 219
Waterloo, 55
Watson, Jonas, 237, 250–51
Wilcocks, John, 197–98

331

Wilkins, John, 14–20, 22, 29–31, 35–37, 49, 58, 60–61, 66–70, 75, 78–82, 88–89, 92–100, 109, 111–14, 118, 119, 123–24, 133, 136, 143–45, 150, 154, 163, 171, 173, 194–96, 203, 223, 235, 247–48, 265

Williamson, Adam, 32, 35, 45, 59, 61, 65–66, 98–101, 113, 203

Winepress, William, 44, 233

wives, 68–72, 82, 87, 91, 95, 99, 103, 106, 110, 113–14, 118, 126, 128, 135, 142–43, 148, 160, 163–64, 166, 168, 170, 176, 178–79, 185, 207, 211, 232, 235, 240, 248, 245

Wynne, Lewis, 71, 142–43, 163, 235

years of service, 41, 56–58, 78

York (England), 40, 138, 184–85, 222, 227

www.ingramcontent.com/pod-product-compliance
Lightning Source LLC
Chambersburg PA
CBHW031232290426
44109CB00012B/262